MEDICINE AN

Medicine and Victory

British Military Medicine in the Second World War

MARK HARRISON

OXFORD
UNIVERSITY PRESS

OXFORD
UNIVERSITY PRESS

Great Clarendon Street, Oxford OX2 6DP

Oxford University Press is a department of the University of Oxford.
It furthers the University's objective of excellence in research, scholarship,
and education by publishing worldwide in

Oxford New York

Auckland Bangkok Buenos Aires Cape Town Chennai
Dar es Salaam Delhi Hong Kong Istanbul Karachi Kolkata
Kuala Lumpur Madrid Melbourne Mexico City Mumbai Nairobi
São Paulo Shanghai Taipei Tokyo Toronto

Oxford is a registered trade mark of Oxford University Press
in the UK and in certain other countries

Published in the United States
by Oxford University Press Inc., New York

© Mark Harrison 2004

The moral rights of the author have been asserted
Database right Oxford University Press (maker)

First published 2004

First published in paperback 2008

British Library Cataloguing in Publication Data
Data available

Library of Congress Cataloging in Publication Data
Data available

ISBN 978-0-19-926859-7(Hbk.)   978-0-19-954121-8 (Pbk.)

1 3 5 7 9 10 8 6 4 2

Typeset by Laserwords Private Limited, Chennai, India.
Printed in Great Britain
on acid-free paper by
Biddles Ltd,
King's Lynn, Norfolk

Acknowledgements

While researching and writing this book I have received valuable assistance from many people, among whom I should particularly like to thank Professor Roger Cooter and Professor David French, who read the entire manuscript as referees, and offered many valuable suggestions. Dr R. S. Morton, MBE, who served with the RAMC during the Second World War, also read an early version of the manuscript and later made important contributions to it. I would like to express my gratitude to him and to the following people for sharing their knowledge of the Second World War and the history of medicine: Mr Tarak Barkawi, Dr Sanjoy Bhattacharya, Professor Bill Bynum, Mrs Shirley Dixon, Sir Richard Doll, Dr Lesley Hall, Dr Trevor Hughes, Professor Bob Joy, Mr David Kenyon, Dr Mervyn Lewis, the late Dr Stephen MacKeith, OBE, Mr Phil Mills, Dr Tim Moreman, Professor Douglas Peers, Professor Kim Pelis, Dr Lutz Sauerteig, Mr Ben Shephard, Dr Julia Sheppard, Captain Peter Starling, Dr Steve Sturdy, Lord Walton, Dr Ian Whitehead, and Professor Michael Worboys. Staff and students at the Wellcome Unit for the History of Medicine and Green College, Oxford, have also provided much inspiration and support. I would also like to thank Mrs Belinda Whitty, the Unit's secretary for, helping me with word processing and photocopying, Loreen Salleh who checked parts of the manuscript for clarity, and Mr Jeff New for his excellent copyediting.

Writing this book involved countless visits to libraries and archives, during which I incurred many debts to the staff at the Army Medical Services Museum, the Gloucestershire County Record Office, the Imperial War Museum, the Liddell Hart Centre for Military Archives, the Public Record Office, the Oriental and India Office Collection at the British Library, and the Wellcome Library for the History and Understanding of Medicine. I should like to thank them all for their helpful assistance and also, in the case of the Army Medical Services Museum and the Wellcome Library for the History and Understanding of Medicine, for giving permission to reproduce photographs as illustrations for this book. I also owe a huge debt to the Wellcome Trust for awarding me a three-year research grant that funded the research for this book. Last but not least, I should like to thank my family and friends for their love and support.

Contents

List of Tables

List of Illustrations

List of Abbreviations and Acronyms

AAMS	Australian Army Medical Service
ABDS	Army Blood Supply Depot
ADH	Assistant Director of Hygiene
ADMS	Assistant Director of Medical Services
ADS	Advanced Dressing Station
AEF	American Expeditionary Force
AFHQ	Allied Forces Headquarters
AFV	Armoured Fighting Vehicle
AMD	Army Medical Department
AMS	Army Medical Service
AMU	Anti-Malaria Unit
AMSM	Army Medical Services Museum
BDA	British Dental Association
BEF	British Expeditionary Force
BMA	British Medical Association
BMU	Brigade Medical Unit
BNAF	British North African Force
BPC	Base Psychiatric Centre
Bn. (Btn.)	Battalion
BOR	British Other Ranks
BRCS	British Red Cross Society
Brig.	Brigadier
BSHC	British Social Hygiene Council
BTS	Blood Transfusion Service
CAB	Cabinet
Capt.	Captain
CCHE	Central Council for Health Education
CCS	Casualty Clearing Station
CD	Contagious Diseases (as in CD Acts)
CEC	Corps Exhaustion Centre
CEP	Casualty Evacuation Point
CMAC	Contemporary Medical Archives Collection
Cmdr.	Commander
Cmdt.	Commandant
CMF	Central Mediterranean Force
CMWC	Central Medical War Committee
Co.	Company
Col.	Colonel
Coll.	Collection

Crpl.	Corporal
DADMS	Deputy Assistant Director of Medical Services
DDH	Deputy Director of Hygiene
DDMS	Deputy Director of Medical Services
DDT	Dichlorodiphenyltrichloroethane
DGAMS	Director-General of the Army Medical Service
DGIMS	Director-General of the Indian Medical Service
DGMS	Director-General of Medical Services
DMO	Director of Military Operations
DMS	Director of Medical Services
DUKW	Amphibious landing craft
EMS	Emergency Medical Service
ENT	Ear, nose, and throat
FA	Field Ambulance
FAU	Friends Ambulance Unit
FDS	Field Dressing Station
FSU	Field Surgical Unit
FTU	Field Transfusion Unit
Gen.	General
GH	General Hospital
GHQ	General Headquarters
GOC	General Officer Commanding
GORs	Gurkha Other Ranks
HMHS	Her/His Majesty's Hospital Ship
HMSO	Her/His Majesty's Stationary Office
IMS	Indian Medical Service
IORs	Indian Other Ranks
IWM	Imperial War Museum
JRAMC	Journal of the Royal Army Medical Corps
LC	Liddle Collection
Lce.-Crpl.	Lance Corporal
LHCMA	Liddell Hart Centre for Military Archives
LMF	Lack of Moral Fibre
L of C	Line(s) of Communication
LST	Landing Ship Tank
Lt.	Lieutenant
MAC	Motor Ambulance Convoy
Maj.	Major
MCU	Malaria Control Unit
MDS	Main Dressing Station
MEF	Mediterranean Expeditionary Force
MF	Maxillo-Facial
MFTU	Malaria Forward Treatment Unit
MFU	Maxillo-Facial Unit

misc.	Miscellaneous
MNSU	Mobile Neuro-Surgical Unit
MO	Medical Officer
MRC	Medical Research Committee (Council)
NAM	National Army Museum
NCCVD	National Council for Combating Venereal Diseases
NCO	Non-Commissioned Officer
NMA	National Medical Association
NMS	Naval Medical Service
NSPVD	National Society for the Prevention of Venereal Disease
NYD	Not Yet Diagnosed
OC	Officer Commanding
OIOC	Oriental and India Office Collection
P & N	Psychiatric and Neurological
Parl.	Parliamentary
PMO	Principal Medical Officer
POW	Prisoner of War
PRO	Public Record Office
Procs.	Proceedings
Pte.	Private
QAIMNS	Queen Alexandra Imperial Military Nursing Service
QMG	Quartermaster-General
RADC	Royal Army Dental Corps
RAF	Royal Air Force
RAMC	Royal Army Medical Corps
RAMC(T)	Royal Army Medical Corps (Territorial)
RAP	Regimental Aid Post
RASC	Royal Army Service Corps
RCAMC	Royal Canadian Army Medical Corps
RCSEng.	Royal College of Surgeons of England
RCSWSA	Royal Commission on the Sick and Wounded in South Africa
RMO	Regimental Medical Officer
RPC	Royal Pioneer Corps
SEAC	South-East Asian Command
Sgt.	Sergeant
SMO	Senior Medical Officer
Surg.	Surgeon
TAB	Inoculation against typhoid and paratyphoid A and B
TA	Territorial Army
TF	Territorial Force
UNRRA	United Nations Relief and Rehabilitation Association
US	United States
USAAF	United States Army Air Force
VAD	Voluntary Aid Detachment

VD	Venereal Disease
WAORs	West African Other Ranks
WIHM	Wellcome Institute for the History of the Medicine
WO	War Office
YMCA	Young Men's Christian Association

Introduction

In 1945 Field-Marshal Bernard Montgomery declared that the contribution of the military medical services to Allied victory had been 'beyond all calculation'.[1] In an age of total war, with manpower at a premium, all resources had to be used to their fullest extent and good medical services were essential if the maximum benefit was to be derived from Britain's forces. But though the importance of medicine was generally acknowledged in wartime, it has been strangely ignored ever since. With the sole exception of the official histories,[2] there have been no books on medicine in any of the British armed services.[3] It is hard to think of any other aspect of military life that has been so poorly served. But the invisibility of medicine in the historical record belies its true significance and masks some of the Army's greatest achievements. Although medical provisions during the early campaigns in Europe and the Far East were far from perfect, the medical services rose to the difficult challenge of caring for the sick and wounded of a retreating army. There was to be no repeat of the medical disasters that had dogged the British Army in earlier campaigns. There were no embarrassing revelations such as those during the Crimean and South African wars and no commissions of inquiry, like those that followed the Mesopotamian and Gallipoli

[1] Montgomery, quoted in Sir Neil Cantlie, 'Health Discipline', *US Armed Forces Medical Journal*, 1 (1950), 232.

[2] It would be tedious to cite the many volumes of the official histories at this juncture; however, they are to be found in the Bibliography at the end of this book and in the notes to the following chapters. Although there are no other book-length studies that examine the armed forces medical services during the war, certain aspects have recently been examined in detail. Psychiatry, for example, is discussed in Ben Shephard's *War of Nerves: Soldiers and Psychiatrists 1914–1994* (London: Jonathan Cape, 2000). Attempts to control sexually transmitted diseases in the British Army are considered in Lesley A. Hall, '"War always brings it on": War, STDs, the Military, and the Civilian Population in Britain, 1850–1950', and Mark Harrison, 'Sex and the Citizen Soldier: Health, Morals and Discipline in the British Army During the Second World War', both in Roger Cooter, Mark Harrison, and Steve Sturdy (eds.), *Medicine and Modern Warfare* (Amsterdam and Atlanta: Rodopi Press, 1999), 205–24 and 225–50. Both of these aspects are developed further in the present volume.

[3] There is very little historical literature on medicine during the Second World War, but basic overviews are provided in Richard A. Gabriel and Karen S. Metz, *A History of Military Medicine, Volume II: From the Renaissance Through Modern Times* (Westport, Conn.: Greenwood Press, 1992), 252–7, and Mark Harrison, 'Medicine', in I. C. B. Dear and M. R. D. Foot (eds.), *The Oxford Companion to the Second World War* (Oxford: Oxford University Press, 1995), 723–31.

campaigns of the First World War. But the Army did not only manage to avoid disaster—its medical services were vital in nursing its men back to health and in preparing the ground for the military successes that were to follow. The medical services played an important role in the Western Desert, Burma, and North West Europe, for example, where the efficiency of sanitary and medical arrangements provided the British with a crucial edge.

The key factor in the success of medical arrangements in all theatres was the relationship between medical and combatant officers. If the latter were not medically minded, they and their men invariably suffered the consequences; on the other hand, if hygienic regulations were strictly enforced, the resulting savings in manpower could confer great advantages. This proved to be the case in the Western Desert, where the Afrika Korps was debilitated by sickness at a crucial stage in the campaign. The 8th Army, by contrast, was able to field the vast majority of its men. British commanders also did their utmost to provide excellent curative facilities and operational plans were always drawn up in close co-operation with medical officers. Headquarters also kept in close touch with medical officers while the battle was in progress, and this was essential to the effectiveness of medical arrangements in mobile warfare. Close co-operation between combatant and medical branches of the Army had not always existed in the past. As late as the First World War, medical officers in theatres such as Gallipoli and Mesopotamia were routinely excluded from meetings of the headquarters staff, and their advice was frequently ignored. In both these campaigns, the sick and wounded were slow to receive treatment because the General Staff had not made adequate arrangements for medical transport and hospital facilities.

The close relationship that existed between doctors and combatant officers during the Second World War reflected a common desire to avoid the humiliating losses of previous campaigns. But this is not a sufficient explanation of why the Army became more medically conscious. In Britain, like other advanced industrial nations, the public and private sectors were beginning to harness medical science in order to improve their efficiency.[4] Medical expertise was valued because it helped to define and regulate the requirements of the human body; thus, physiologists were called upon to calculate

---

[4] On scientific medicine and administrative efficiency see: Roger Cooter, *Surgery and Society in Peace and War: Orthopaedics and the Organisation of Modern Medicine, 1880–1948* (London: Macmillan, 1993); Steve Sturdy, 'The Political Economy of Scientific Medicine: Science, Education and the Transformation of Medical Practice in Sheffield, 1890–1922', *Medical History*, 36 (1992), 125–59; Susan Reverby, 'Stealing the Golden Eggs: Ernest Amory Codman and the Science and Management of Medicine', *Bulletin of the History of Medicine*, 4 (1981), 156–71; George Rosen, 'The Efficiency Criterion in Medical Care, 1900–1920: An Early Approach to the Evaluation of Health Service', *Bulletin of the History of Medicine*, 1 (1976), 28–44. For wartime, in particular, see the introductions to Roger Cooter, Mark Harrison, and Steve Sturdy (eds.), *War, Medicine and Modernity* (Stroud: Sutton, 1998), and id., *Medicine and Modern Warfare*.

military rations in relation to energy expenditure, while psychologists and psychiatrists aimed to determine the circumstances under which human beings performed most effectively. After the First World War medical experts thus became increasingly involved in many aspects of private and public life, from big business to the military, commenting on everything from the selection of personnel to managerial practices.[5]

The employment of medical experts in the Army and on the staff of service ministries exemplifies the high priority that was given to the development and use of medical knowledge. Indeed, the British armed forces were more scientifically and technologically oriented than their detractors have claimed. For some time it was accepted wisdom among historians that the Army's officer corps lacked technical expertise and that it saw the service as a refuge from a strange and hostile industrial world. The inter-war Army—and the high command during 1939–45—was portrayed as rigidly hierarchical, backward looking, and parochial. Its victories in the Second World War were said to be the result of 'brute force' and of reversion to the manpower-intensive tactics of the Western Front.[6] But some recent histories of the Army between 1919 and 1945 have painted a rather different picture, showing that the British enthusiastically embraced new technologies in order to enhance or compensate for inferiority in manpower.[7] After the enormous losses of the First World War, the General Staff developed a new doctrine that aimed to

[5] Nikolas Rose, *The Psychological Complex: Psychology, Politics and Society in England 1869–1939* (London: Routledge, 1989). For physiology in the army see: Joel D. Howell, ' "Soldier's Heart": The Redefinition of Heart Disease and Specialty Formation in Early Twentieth-Century Great Britain', *Medical History*, suppl. no. 5 (1985), 34–52; Steve Sturdy, 'From the Trenches to the Hospitals at Home: Physiologists, Clinicians and Oxygen Therapy, 1914–30', in J. V. Pickstone (ed.), *Medical Innovations in Historical Perspective* (London: Macmillan, 1992), 104–23; id., 'War as Experiment. Physiology, Innovation and Administration in Britain, 1914–1918: The Case of Chemical Warfare', in Cooter, Harrison, and Sturdy (eds.), *War, Medicine and Modernity*, 65–84. The influence of physiologists can be seen outside the armed forces too, as several were appointed as advisers to the Ministry of Food established by Lloyd George towards the end of 1916. See M. Teich, 'Science and Food During the Great War: Britain and Germany', in H. Kamminga and A. Cunningham (eds.), *The Science and Culture of Nutrition, 1840–1940* (Amsterdam & Atlanta: Rodopi Press, 1995), 213–34; John Pickstone, 'Production, Community and Consumption: The Political Economy of Twentieth Century Medicine', in R. Cooter and J. V. Pickstone (eds.), *Medicine in the Twentieth Century* (London: Harwood, 2000), 1–19.

[6] See Corelli Barnett, *The Collapse of British Power* (London: Eyre Methuen, 1972); id., *Britain and Her Army: A Military, Political and Social History of the British Army 1509–1970* (London: Cassell, 1970); Carlo d'Este, 'The Army and the Challenge of War, 1939–45', in D. Chandler and I. Beckett (eds.), *The Oxford Illustrated History of the British Army* (Oxford: Oxford University Press, 1994), 298–99; John Ellis, *Brute Force: Allied Strategy and Tactics During the Second World War* (London: Andre Deutsch, 1990); Max Hastings, *Overlord: D-Day and the Battle for Normandy* (New York: Macmillan, 1984).

[7] See David Edgerton, *England and the Aeroplane: An Essay on a Militant and Technological Nation* (London: Macmillan, 1991); id., 'British Scientific Intellectuals and the Relations of Science, Technology and War', in P. Forman and J. M. Sanchez-Rons (eds.), *National Military Establishments and the Advancement of Science and Technology* (Amsterdam: Kluwer, 1996), 1–35.

substitute technology for manpower wherever possible. It also aimed to apply the managerial techniques developed in industry to the rationalization of warfare, with the aim of maximizing scarce human and material resources.[8] Although the desire to conserve manpower sometimes meant that the Army failed to exploit tactical advantages, its combat capability improved steadily and the new doctrine brought success in several campaigns, beginning with Montgomery's victories in the Western Desert.[9]

Those who attained senior commands in the Army during the Second World War—the likes of Montgomery, William Slim, and the Adjutant-General, Ronald Adam—were keenly aware of medicine's contribution to manpower economy.[10] They also shared many of the opinions expressed in British public-health circles between the wars, especially the belief that health was a civic responsibility to be shared by the individual and the state. The Representation of the People Acts of 1918 and 1928 ushered in an age of mass democracy in which public opinion began to figure to a greater extent in policy-making. It was thought that, to be fully successful, public health could no longer be simply directive; it would have to win the hearts and minds of the people as well. Many of those involved in public health, such as the Chief Medical Officer, Sir George Newman, therefore came to stress the importance of education in hygiene and the cultivation of active citizenship in matters of health.[11] This new emphasis upon the individual in public health has sometimes been referred to as the 'decentralization of hygienic management', surveillance by the sanitary authorities being slowly replaced, or augmented, by the self-discipline of private individuals.[12] In the same spirit, Sir Ronald Adam, as Adjutant-General from 1941, did much to promote citizenship education in the British Army, including numerous lectures and demonstrations on how to prevent disease. Army propaganda made it clear that the 'citizen soldier' had certain rights and responsibilities: the right to decent medical care but also the responsibility to keep 'fighting fit'.[13]

---

[8] Jeremy A. Crang, *The British Army and the People's War 1939–1945* (Manchester: Manchester University Press, 2000).

[9] David French, *Raising Churchill's Army: The British Army and the War Against Germany 1919–1945* (Oxford: Oxford University Press, 2000).

[10] S. P. MacKenzie, *Politics and Military Morale: Current Affairs and Citizenship Education in the British Army 1914–1950* (Oxford: Clarendon Press, 1992).

[11] Jose Harris, 'Enterprise and Welfare States: A Comparative Perspective', *Transactions of the Royal Historical Society*, 5th ser., 40 (1991), 175–95; David Armstrong, *The Political Anatomy of the Body: Medical Knowledge in Britain in the Twentieth Century* (Cambridge: Cambridge University Press, 1993); Geoffrey Finlayson, *Citizen, State and Social Welfare in Britain, 1830–1990* (Oxford: Clarendon Press, 1994).

[12] David Armstrong, *A New History of Identity: A Sociology of Medical Knowledge* (Basingstoke: Palgrave, 2002), 71–3.

[13] Mark Harrison, 'Medicine and the Management of Modern Warfare', *History of Science*, 34 (1996), 379–409.

The Army's willingness to utilize medicine and medical knowledge provides further evidence, if any were needed, of its technological orientation. The Army was quick to take on board the latest developments in the medical sciences and to apply them to all areas of military life, reflecting the desire to protect its limited reserve of manpower.[14] From late 1942 the manpower situation in Britain was acute and the country could not afford to operate with the same disregard for casualties as the Russians or even the Germans.[15] This may help to explain, not only the character of British military operations—which aimed to minimize casualties—but also the greater attention paid to medical services in the British Army and the influence of medical experts in many areas of military life. Another reason for the difference in attitudes to medicine sometimes displayed by British and German forces was the greater tendency displayed in some German units towards a kind of heroic individualism that disdained such mundane matters as hygiene and sanitation. Elite German units exhibited, to a much greater degree than their British counterparts, an anachronistic masculine code that viewed sickness as a sign of weakness, and medicine as a form of pampering. Such attitudes were even more evident in the case of psychological disorders, which were sometimes concealed in many German units, or dealt with harshly, especially towards the end of the war. Although there was also a good deal of suspicion towards psychiatry in the British Army, the attitude towards medicine was generally more positive. By contrast with the Germany army, sanitation and hygiene tended to be best in elite regiments where discipline and morale was highest, and weakest in those that were poorly motivated and led. The one exception in the British case was the Chindits, which operated behind the lines in Burma. Orde Wingate, the Chindits' controversial commander, was heavily criticized for his neglect of sanitation and medical arrangements. His attitude to disease was essentially individualistic and fatalistic; he regarded disease as an inevitable part of tropical warfare and expected soldiers to endure their illnesses stoically. Such attitudes had more in common with some Victorian commanders than with the collectivist approach of a 'citizen army'.

The language of health and citizenship meshed easily with that of 'social hygiene' and 'social medicine', both of which conceived of the health of the individual in relation to society as a whole. The proponents of social medicine saw health and disease as the outcome of an individual's behaviour, his or her genetic inheritance, together with a range of social and environmen-

---

[14] The argument that follows builds on the work of Andreski and Titmuss. Andreski argued that social benefits for the less privileged expanded in relation to 'the proportion of militarily utilised individuals in the total population'; Titmuss made a similar argument with respect to health and social policy. See S. Andreski, *Military Organisation and Society* (London: Routledge & Kegan Paul, 1968); Richard M. Titmuss, *Problems of Social Policy* (London: HMSO, 1959); id., 'War and Social Policy', in *Essays on the Welfare State* (London: Allen & Unwin, 1955).

[15] French, *Raising Churchill's Army*, 242–6.

tal factors; they attempted to bridge the gap between medical specialities and to treat the patient as a 'whole' person. This humanistic view was shared by many social hygienists, who paid great attention to all factors affecting human health, from heredity to poverty. The overriding concern of social hygienists was the improvement of national efficiency and particularly the physical condition of the working class, and such ideas enjoyed broad support after the First World War, amidst talk of 'regenerating Britain'.[16] But it was in the 'citizen army' of the Second World War that the principles of social hygiene and social medicine found their fullest expression. The military environment was more conducive than civilian life to the regulation of those aspects of individual behaviour that had a bearing on health. Military medicine had long been concerned with everything from diet and physical training to personal and collective hygiene, and it is not surprising that military medical officers were among the pioneers of social medicine. The advocates of social hygiene also stressed the value of education and the Army provided them with a captive audience, which, it was hoped, would later carry their gospel into civilian life. The broad acceptance of these ideas within the Army may help to explain the great success with which it met the medical challenges posed by the Second World War.

Those who embraced the principles of social hygiene did not necessarily embrace demands for socialized medicine, however, and many prominent public-health officials rejected the idea of a free health service. But by the 1930s support for a state-funded medical service, available to all 'on the basis of common citizenship', was gaining ground in Britain.[17] The Labour Party led the way in 1934 with its proposals for a comprehensive health service, and by the early 1940s there was widespread official support for such a scheme, reflecting what appeared to be a popular clamour for free health care. Civil servants concluded that the public would not be satisfied with anything less than a scheme of hospital treatment that was free of charge and free from the stigma of the Poor Law. The establishment of the Emergency Medical Service in 1938, which was gradually extended to cover all manual workers, seemed like a sign of things to come. A free national health service thus became a touchstone of schemes for reconstruction, and was extensively discussed in Army education circles in the course of the war. Health services

[16] See Greta Jones, *Social Hygiene in Twentieth Century Britain* (London: Croom Helm, 1986); Dorothy Porter, *Health, Civilization and the State: A History of Public Health from Ancient to Modern Times* (London: Routledge, 1999), 291–6; Christopher Lawrence and Anna-K. Mayer (eds.), *Regenerating England: Science, Medicine and Culture in Inter-War Britain* (Amsterdam and Atlanta: Rodopi Press, 2000).

[17] Charles Webster, *The Health Services Since the War. Volume I: Problems of Health Care, the National Health Service before 1957* (London: HMSO, 1988), 27.

also formed an important element of wartime propaganda, which attempted to foster a sense of equality. The Blood Transfusion Service established in 1938 was vital in this respect, as it seemed to epitomize a shared sacrifice made for the common good. Although the political consequences of wartime propaganda and Army education may be questionable, there can be little doubt that they ensured a continued commitment to the health and well-being of soldiers. In a political climate in which health care was seen as a right rather than a privilege, the high-handed neglect that typified previous wars was inconceivable.

1

A Medical Service for a Modern Army?

During the Second World War medical care for British soldiers serving in the front line was provided chiefly by the Royal Army Medical Corps, a body which had been established in 1898 from the medical officers and male hospital staff of the Army Medical Department (AMD). Together with the Army Nursing Service (later the Queen Alexandra Imperial Military Nursing Service), it was part of the umbrella organization known as the Army Medical Services (AMS). The royal warrant which brought into being the RAMC was heralded as a turning point in British military medicine.[1] As well as being dignified by the royal imprimatur, medical officers now possessed substantive rank which placed them on an equal footing with combatant and other non-combatant branches of the Army. The royal warrant thus addressed one of the main grievances of medical officers in the years before 1898, when they had often complained of their lack of authority and status. But while the warrant conferred the rights and privileges of substantive rank, it did little to alter relations between medical and combatant officers. The latter continued to look upon military doctors as their social inferiors and medical arrangements were seldom a priority. Despite the well-publicized disasters of the Crimean War (1854–6),[2] some combatant officers continued to regard medical provisions as dispensable luxuries. In the Sudan campaign of 1896–8, for example, Kitchener reduced his medical staff to the bare minumum on the grounds that this improved mobility. There were only five medical officers and sixteen orderlies to care for a force of thousands.[3] The situation was little better in respect of hygiene, at least on active service.[4] *The Soldier's Pocket Book*, written by the Adjutant-General, and later Commander-in-Chief, Sir Garnet Wolseley, notoriously stated that the sanitary officer

[1] On the AMD before 1898 see Neil Cantlie, *A History of the Army Medical Department*, 2 vols. (Edinburgh: Hodder & Stoughton, 1974).

[2] See John Shepherd, *The Crimean Doctors: A History of the British Medical Services in the Crimean War*, 2 vols. (Liverpool: Liverpool University Press, 1991).

[3] W. S. Churchill, *The River War*, 2 vols. (London: Longman, Green & Co., 1899), i. 349; Cantlie, *Army Medical Department*, ii. 337.

[4] Philip D. Curtin, *Disease and Empire: The Health of European Troops in the Conquest of Africa* (Cambridge: Cambridge University Press, 1998).

was a 'useless functionary', wholly ignorant of operational matters.[5] Little had changed by the time of the South African War (1899–1902), during which the advice of medical officers generally went unheeded. Some two-thirds of the 22,000 British deaths during the war were attributed to disease and wound infection, and many could have been prevented if commanders had taken more care of sanitation and made arrangements for the evacuation of the wounded from forward areas.[6] Kitchener was, again, publicly critized after it transpired that he had drastically reduced medical supplies and transport for the force relieving Bloemfontein.[7]

Although the military authorities did their best to conceal the medical situation in South Africa, it was eventually made public following a visit by the maverick MP, William Burdett Coutts.[8] The ensuing scandal shook the government as much as the military disasters of 'Black Week', and led to the appointment of two commissions of inquiry which criticized the Army for its neglect of the sick and wounded.[9] While the RAMC did not emerge from the controversy unscathed, it largely benefited from public scrutiny, gaining improved conditions of service and a new army medical college at Millbank in London.[10] The Russo-Japanese War of 1904–5 provided another powerful stimulus to medical reform. The Japanese medical services appeared to perform with great distinction and were held up as a model for the medical services in Britain. Although the glowing reports of Japanese medical arrangements were probably exaggerated, it seemed at the time that the Japanese were far more successful at preventing disease than any other army. This led to improved training in sanitation for medical officers, as well as a number of initiatives designed to increase awareness of hygiene amongst combatants.[11]

[5] Viscount Wolseley, *The Soldier's Pocket Book for Field Service* (London: Macmillan, 5th edn., 1886 [1869]), 109.

[6] Mitchell Stone, 'The Victorian Army: Health, Hospitals and Social Conditions as Encountered by British Troops During the South African War, 1899–1902' Ph.D. thesis, University of London (1992).

[7] CMAC, RAMC 1007, Diary of F. J. W. Porter, 26 Jan. 1900; J. Stone and E. A. Schmidt, *The Boer War and Military Reforms* (New York: University of America Press, 1988), 23–4.

[8] William Burdett Coutts, *The Sick and Wounded in South Africa: What I saw and said of them and of the Army Medical Service* (London: Cassell, 1900).

[9] *Report of the Royal Commission appointed to consider and report upon the Care and Treatment of the Sick and Wounded during the South African Campaign* (London: HMSO, 1901); *Report of the Committee appointed by the Secretary of State to consider Reorganization of the Army Medical Services* (London: HMSO, 1901).

[10] CMAC, RAMC 350, J. B. Neal, 'The History of the Royal Army Medical College'.

[11] The Japanese army achieved a disease-to-battle fatality ratio of 1.6:1—Roger Cooter, 'War and Modern Medicine', in W. F. Bynum and R. Porter (eds.), *Companion Encyclopedia of the History of Medicine* (London: Routledge, 1993), 1543. On the medical significance of the Russo-Japanese War see also Louis J. Seaman, *The Real Triumph of Japan* (New York: D. Appleton, 1919); Claire Herrick, '"The Conquest of the Silent Foe": British and American Military Reform Rhetoric and

The Russo-Japanese War also highlighted the destructive power of modern weaponry, and it became clear that the British Army would have to make extensive provisions for the evacuation and reception of casualties if it went to war against a powerful industrialized nation. As a result, there were extensive alterations to the medical complement of expeditionary forces, including the formation of clearing hospitals (where the wounded could be treated or evacuated after an assessment of their injury) and provision for a limited number of motorized ambulances.[12] While moving in an appropriate direction, these provisions proved woefully inadequate when put to the test in 1914. The number of clearing hospitals and ambulances was far too low to deal with the casualties sustained by the British Expeditionary Force during the first few weeks of the war. The War Office, however, was determined that there should be no repeat of events in South Africa, and initial deficiencies in medical arrangements were soon made good. The enormous number of casualties sustained in France and Flanders meant that it was essential to return the sick and wounded to duty, if at all possible. The Casualty Clearing Station, as clearing hospitals came to be known, proved vital in this respect, since they provided facilities for the treatment of medical and surgical cases close to the front.

It was equally important to stop men from going sick—something that the British Army had found exceedingly difficult in previous campaigns. Inoculation against typhoid (still uproven during the South African War) played a crucial role in this respect, since typhoid was endemic in most theatres of the war. The establishment of sanitary sections to clean up after the armies, and of bath-houses and disinfection facilities, also played an important part in the prevention of disease. Though some combatant officers still proved negligent in matters of hygiene, disease prevention on the Western Front was largely successful and the British Army managed to keep deaths from disease below those inflicted by the enemy. This was the first time this had occurred in a major British campaign.[13]

The success of medical arrangements on the Western Front owed much to close co-operation between the medical and combatant branches of the

---

the Japanese War', in R. Cooter, M. Harrison, and S. Sturdy (eds.), *Medicine and Modern Warfare* (Amsterdam and Atlanta: Rodopi, 1999), 99–130.

[12] W. G. MacPherson, 'The Removal of the Sick and Wounded from the Battlefield', *Journal of the Royal Army Medical Corps*, 12 (1909), 78–100; F. S. Hewton, 'Motor Traction Behind the Firing Line', ibid. 499–501.

[13] For medical services on the Western Front see: W. G. MacPherson, *History of the War Based on Official Documents: The Medical Services on the Western Front, and during the Operations in France and Belgium in 1914 and 1915* (London: HMSO, 1923); Claire Herrick, 'Of War and Wounds: The Propaganda, Politics and Experience of Medicine in World War I', Ph.D. thesis, University of Manchester (1996); Ian R. Whitehead, *Doctors in the Great War* (Barnsley: Leo Cooper, 1999).

Army. Medical officers were consulted on operational matters and senior MOs and civilian consultants (given temporary commissions in the RAMC) enjoyed friendly relations with members of the General Staff. Senior MOs were regularly invited to dine with Sir John French and Sir Douglas Haig, successively the Commanders-in-Chief of the British Army in France and Flanders;[14] Haig also defended the RAMC against its critics at home.[15] Things were very different outside Western Europe, however. In Gallipoli, Mesopotamia, East Africa, and Salonika there were medical disasters on a par with those in South Africa. The main problem in all these campaigns was that they were run on the same lines as the colonial wars of the nineteenth century, with authority concentrated in the commander and his small staff.[16] This highly personalized and centralized style of command may well have been effective in the 'Small Wars' of the Victorian era, but it was wholly unsuited to large, complex operations such as those in Mesopotamia and the Dardanelles. Such campaigns required a high degree of co-ordination between the different branches of the Army, as well as between the Army and Navy—something which was evidently lacking during the first two years of the Mesopotamian campaign and during the first landing at Gallipoli.

Another unfortunate consequence of this system of command was that medical officers were seldom allowed to enter the inner sanctum of operational HQ, which meant that medical matters were rarely given serious consideration. Two commanders—Sir Ian Hamilton in the Dardanelles and Sir John Nixon in Mesopotamia—deliberately excluded medical officers from their staff. Preparations for the evacuation and treatment of the wounded were consequently based on wildly unrealistic estimates. For the same reason, matters of sanitation and hygiene were treated with indifference or contempt. Witness after witness to the commissions of inquiry set up to investigate the campaigns in Mesopotamia and the Dardanelles reported the lack of sanitary arrangements and the thousands of deaths caused by diseases such as dysentery and cholera.[17] In Mesopotamia in 1916 admissions to hospital

[14] RCSE MSS Add.458, Bowlby Papers, War Diary of Sir Anthony Bowlby, 30 Sept. 1914, 10 Dec. 1914, 16 Jan. 1916.

[15] PRO WO 32/4751, Comments of Douglas Haig on the 'Report of the Commission on the Medical Establishment in France', 10 Mar. 1918.

[16] See T. H. E. Travers, 'Command and Leadership Styles in the British Army: The 1915 Gallipoli Model', *Journal of Contemporary History*, 26 (1994), 403–42.

[17] On medical services in the Dardanelles campaign see *First Report of the Dardanelles Commission* (London: HMSO, 1918), *Final Report of the Dardanelles Commission* (London, HMSO, 1919), Michael Tyquin, *Gallipoli: The Medical War: The Australian Army Medical Services in the Dardanelles Campaign of 1915* (Kensington, NSW: New South Wales University Press, 1993). For Mesopotamia see: *Mesopotamia Commission—Report and Minority Report* (London: HMSO, 1917); Paul K. Davis, *Ends and Means: The British Mesopotamia Campaign and Commission* (Rutherford, NJ: Associated University Presses, 1994); Mark Harrison, 'The Fight against Disease in the Mesopotamia

(chiefly from disease) were as high as 1,309 per thousand troops, and in the Dardanelles the figure was only slightly better, being 1,239 per thousand, as compared with an average of 567 per thousand on the Western Front between 1914 and 1918.[18] In other words, nearly a third of men in Mesopotamia and Gallipoli were hospitalized more than once.

The reports of the Dardanelles and Mesopotamia commissions forced the government to take matters in hand. Medical arrangements for the second Gallipoli landings were far better than the first, with much better co-ordination between the combatant and medical branches of the Army, and between the Army and Navy. Once control of the Mesopotamia campaign passed from the Government of India to the War Office in 1916, significant improvements were made there too. By the end of the war sanitary discipline had been tightened and steps had been taken to prevent the transfer of disease from the civilian population to soldiers. Facilities for the collection of the wounded had also improved beyond measure, and by 1918 the RAMC was running ambulance convoys in Mesopotamia over distances exceeding one thousand miles. These tremendous achievements demonstrate that medicine now figured prominently in the planning of military operations, and that good medical services were vital to the prosecution of a modern war.

The increasing importance attached to military medicine during the First World War led many to anticipate further modernization once the war had ended. A review of salaries and conditions of service in 1919, and the cre-ation of separate branches for pathology and hygiene the same year, provided further encouragement. But the collapse of the post-war boom and wide-spread criticism of the government for excessive public expenditure dashed all hopes of a major boost to military medicine. Military expenditure was the main target of the Prime Minister Lloyd George, and all the armed services were affected to some degree by the ensuing cuts. Retrenchment seems to have affected the medical services of the Army badly, and their official historian, F. A. E. Crew, later claimed that the RAMC had been all but emasculated. Although he acknowledged that rearmament later brought a vital injection of resources, Crew claimed that the process was far too slow and that the Second World War had begun before the necessary improve-ments had been made.[19]

It is true that medical provisions left much to be desired between the wars,

Campaign', in H. Cecil and P. Liddle (eds.), *Facing Armageddon: The First World War Experienced* (Barnsley: Leo Cooper, 1996), 475–89. For East Africa and Salonika see Mark Harrison, 'Medi-cine and the Culture of Command: The Case of Malaria Control in the British Army During the Two World Wars', *Medical History*, 40 (1996), 437–52.

[18] T. J. Mitchell and G. M. Smith, *History of the Great War based on Official Documents: Medical Services—Casualties and Medical Statistics of the Great War* (London: HMSO, 1931), 59.

[19] F. A. E. Crew, *The Army Medical Services: Administration*, 1 (London: HMSO, 1953), 3.

yet Crew may have been too pessimistic. Although the medical services suffered disproportionately from cuts in the military budget, the 1920s and 1930s brought many significant improvements of a technical and organizational nature which laid sound foundations for military medicine during the Second World War. In addition to the introduction of new technologies such as the portable X-ray machine, the British Army established a blood transfusion service that was the envy of other nations. The Army also made great efforts to bridge any remaining gap between medical and combatant personnel, by providing basic instruction in hygiene and medical arrangements for all branches of the service. The medical services, like other branches of the Army, also began to prepare for a mechanized war, although the pace of mechanization remained slow until hostilities began.

The Problem of Medical Manpower

In April 1921 those who wished to see further expansion and modernization of the AMS received some encouragement from a War Office report on the reorganization of the medical services, which advocated the creation of more specialist posts and better rates of pay. It was hoped that these measures would make the AMS—historically, one of the least popular branches of the Army—more attractive to prospective recruits.[20] These hopes were soon dashed by the announcement that military expenditure was to be drastically reduced and the reorganization postponed.[21] The following year a Cabinet committee under Lord Weir was charged with identifying areas for retrenchment, and the Director-General of the Army Medical Service (DGAMS) was asked to make plans for a budgetary reduction of 15 per cent. The proposal was vigorously opposed by the DGAMS, Sir William Leishman, who argued that it would be dangerous to cut expenditure until the Army had reduced its commitments abroad. But Leishman could do no more than delay the inevitable, and in 1924 the Weir Committee decided that the RAMC should be reduced to 945 officers and 4,214 other ranks. This represented a slight reduction in the number of officers on peacetime service (which stood at 1,062 officers prior to 1914) though not of other ranks, which formerly numbered 3,887.[22]

The most significant thing about the cuts was not so much the reduction

[20] PRO WO 32/11395, 'Report of the Reorganization Committee, Army Medical Service', 26 Apr. 1921.

[21] PRO WO 32/11395, Memo. D.F. (a), 13 June 1922; Secretary to War Office to Secretary to Commonwealth of Australia, 10 Nov. 1922.

[22] PRO WO 32/11395, 'Report of the Reorganization Committee', 5.

in the number of MOs but the principles upon which medical support was now calculated. Formerly, peacetime establishments had taken into account the possibility of war and of the need to equip an expeditionary force in such an eventuality. Now the establishment of the AMS was to be determined *entirely* by the requirements of peacetime, with little thought given to mobilization or the expansion of the Army in the event of war. It was generally believed that the First World War had been an 'abnormal' event and that Britain was unlikely to become embroiled in a major conflict in the near future. This belief was enshrined in the 'Ten Year Rule', formulated in 1919, according to which the services were to plan on the assumption of no major conflict occurring in the next ten years. Although it had little influence until 1925, the rule came increasingly to dominate strategic policy until it was abandoned in 1932.[23]

The distant prospect of war also accounts for the deep cuts made to the medical branch of the Territorial Force (Territorial Army from 1921), which was reduced even more drastically than the Regular forces. A War Office committee appointed in September 1921 recommended a reduction in the number of TA field ambulances from forty-five to fifteen, and of general hospitals from twenty-three to three. All fifteen of the casualty clearing stations staffed by the TA were also to be disbanded. The announcement provoked protests from the TA and the medical profession, but to no avail. The General Staff believed that the TA would be needed only in the event of a major war; even then, it would not be required to embark until at least six months after mobilization. In the 1920s such an emergency seemed only the remotest possibility, and the TA was therefore particularly vulnerable to cuts.[24]

Retrenchment was not the only difficulty facing the RAMC. Despite the reduction in its size, the corps found it hard to attract recruits of sufficient calibre, particularly at officer level. The best young graduates normally set their sights on a prestigious position in one of the teaching hospitals or a lucrative private practice, and the RAMC was neither particularly prestigious nor well remunerated. The absence of suitable candidates, and a steady stream of voluntary retirements from the middle ranks of the service, left the Army without adequate medical cover, especially in overseas stations like India. Matters were made worse by the fact that many Regular officers had little experience of medical work in the field, having been confined to administrative duties during the war. In the belief that the absence of recruits was due to poor conditions of service, the British Medical Association approached the War Office in July 1921 to secure better terms for the military branch

[23] See Brian Bond, *British Military Policy Between the Two World Wars* (Oxford: Oxford University Press, 1980); John Robert Ferris, *The Evolution of British Strategic Policy 1919–26* (London: Macmillan, 1989).

[24] Crew, *Army Medical Services*, i. 22–4.

of its profession. It raised, among other things, the position of the DGAMS, who appeared to be at a disadvantage in relation to other lieutenant-generals. In effect, the latter were paid more than the Director-General because their salary was drawn partly in the form of allowances and was not subject to tax. The BMA argued that the lack of such benefits diminished the dignity of the medical profession; it also suggested that the RAMC was still not regarded as a 'proper' part of the Army. But in view of the economic situation, the War Office was in no mood to hear complaints from the BMA and made it clear that it would not countenance any increase in salaries, beyond honouring some modest increases announced in 1919.[25]

However, the difficulties facing the RAMC could not be swept conveniently under the carpet. In early 1923 only four candidates came forward for fifteen new commissions, prompting the Army Medical Advisory Board to seek a meeting with the Secretary of State.[26] The board pointed out that the rates of pay and pensions fixed for the RAMC in 1919 were far less generous than those for combatant branches of the Army. Sir John Goodwin, the DGAMS, also protested about the pay of middle-ranking officers, and the fact that MOs were at a disadvantage compared with other officers regarding leave and foreign service. These protests came to nothing, and in July Goodwin had no option but to plead with the universities to encourage more medical graduates to enter the RAMC. But the DGAMS was unable to alter the prevailing view that the RAMC had little to offer talented graduates, and only three candidates presented themselves for the twenty commissions on offer. His voice was drowned out by the chorus of complaint emanating from the Corps itself. The correspondence columns of the *British Medical Journal* and other professional organs regularly contained letters from disaffected medical officers.[27]

With no sign of an end to the problems faced by the RAMC, the BMA and the DGAMS held a conference in November 1923 to discuss the issues surrounding recruitment. There was a good deal of common ground between military and civilian doctors, although Sir William Leishman, the DGAMS, believed that poor morale was due more to the slowness of promotion than to poor pay. However, both the DGAMS and the BMA agreed that shorter terms of service and fewer moves between stations would address the most serious grievances of serving officers and help to attract new recruits. But still the War Office took no action, and the entrance examination in 1924 had to be cancelled when only seven candidates came forward for forty vacancies. This prompted parliamentary demands for an inquiry into the

---

[25] *Lancet*, 27 Aug. 1921, pp. 465–7.
[26] *British Medical Journal*, 7 Apr. 1923, p. 606.
[27] e.g. letters from 'Major RAMC', *British Medical Journal*, 29 Sept. 1923, p. 587, and from 'Field Officer', *British Medical Journal*, 13 Oct. 1923, p. 681.

recruitment of MOs and the low morale of those already serving.[28] By 1925 the situation was so bad that the supply of officer candidates to the RAMC had virtually dried up and the corps was ninety officers below strength.[29] The situation was now incompatible with military efficiency, and the BMA warned the War Office that the *British Medical Journal* would not publish the RAMC's terms and conditions of service until the matter had been rectified.[30]

The relationship between the medical profession and the Army was now worse than at any time since 1897, the last occasion on which the BMA and the royal colleges had threatened to withdraw their co-operation. In 1897 threats had forced the Secretary of State for War, Lord Lansdowne, to agree to certain improvements in the terms and conditions of medical officers, including the creation of the RAMC. But this time the government's response was more equivocal, merely appointing an interdepartmental committee to consider the problem of recruitment. The committee, under the chairmanship of Sir Nicolas Warren Fisher, the Permanent Secretary to the Treasury, did practically nothing to solve the problem of recruitment. The small increases in pay that it recommended resulted in a few more candidates coming forward, but even this modest revival was short-lived and hardly any candidates presented themselves for examination in 1929.[31]

The RAMC's failure to attract recruits may not have been due solely to poor conditions of service, however. Those closely involved with recruitment also blamed an 'anti-militaristic outlook' which was 'general amongst a large body of the public, notably the rank and file of the Trade Unions and a certain class of University Don and Student'.[32] Colonel H. R. Bateman, commandant of the Aldershot Depot, where medical officers completed their training after attending the College at Millbank, was convinced that such attitudes had affected recruitment to the RAMC's officer corps, since graduate entrants had probably been exposed to pacifistic ideas at university. In 1927 Bateman reported to the DGAMS, Mathew Fell, that: 'Our recruits are rapidly dwindling, to such an extent that the Corps is with difficulty finding drafts for its overseas commitments.'[33] Nor was recruitment the only problem highlighted by Bateman in his report to the DGAMS: the

---

[28] Dr F. E. Freemantle, who had worked as a civilian surgeon during the South African War, was the MP who was most vocal in representing medical officers. See *British Medical Journal*, 22 Mar. 1924, pp. 549, and 29 Mar. 1924, p. 598.

[29] *British Medical Journal*, 21 Mar. 1925, p. 577.

[30] Crew, *Army Medical Services*, i. 67–8.

[31] CMAC RAMC 1194/3, 'The Warren Fisher Report', *News and Gazette of the Royal Army Medical Corps, The Army Dental Corps and Q.A.I.M.N.S.*, 9, 7, Mar. 1934, pp. 261–4.

[32] PRO WO 222/229, Col. H. R. Bateman, 'Events and General Development of the Depot of the RAMC (Aldershot), September 1927–March 1930', 1.

[33] PRO WO 222/229, 1.

retention of recruits was an equally serious matter, since 'an appreciable number' resigned from the service, either during their period of training or immediately afterwards. The chief reason, he believed, was the 'out of date Sergeant-Major attitude' adopted towards younger officers by some of the senior officers at the depot, and the poor living conditions of the men who trained there. Once these matters had been rectified—as they had by 1930—resignations ceased almost immediately.[34]

Improvements at Aldershot may have raised morale among junior officers, but they had little effect on recruitment. By 1931 the RAMC was as many as one hundred officers below its peacetime establishment—a critical situation that led to the reappointment, in May, of the Warren Fisher Committee. In view of the financial constraints that circumscribed all aspects of military policy, the committee felt that the only way to improve recruitment was to reduce the number of Regular officers. But this reduction would be compensated by an increase in the number of higher posts (to break the log-jam in promotion) and the employment of medical officers on short-service commissions to make good any deficiency. The decrease proposed was from 865 Regular officers to 754. It was anticipated that only 420 of these would hold full service commissions and that the rest would be on short service, some of whom would be retired Regulars who would serve at home stations only.[35] As an additional incentive to recruitment, the committee recommended that there should be more opportunities for continuing in professional, as opposed to administrative, work in the higher ranks of the service; a proposal which entailed the creation of more specialist posts.

These proposals aimed to remove two of the three main causes of poor recruitment identified by the BMA in their protests to the War Office: the lack of professional opportunities and of economic attraction. Yet they neglected what some doctors regarded as a more serious problem: the low status of medicine within the British Army. The royal warrant of 1898 had addressed some of the grievances of military doctors, but the South African War showed that many combatant officers still regarded them as inferiors. Although relations improved during the First World War, some MOs still complained that they were treated more like civilians than soldiers. To make matters worse, the low status of medicine in the Army appeared to be enshrined in administrative arrangements. In 1904 a committee chaired by Lord Esher had abolished the Army Board and the War Office Council, and created a new body—the Army Council. As part of this reorganization, the AMD ceased to exist as an independent department of the War Office and

---

[34] PRO WO 222/229, 2.
[35] Crew, *Army Medical Services*, i. 262.

became part of the Adjutant-General's Department. The DGAMS was not part of the Army Council and therefore ceased to have any direct input into the body responsible for military policy and organization. This arrangement remained in force throughout the First World War, despite protests from military doctors and the BMA.[36]

Most medical officers regarded the 1904 reforms as a retrograde step, but the success of military medical arrangements on the Western Front shows that the new structure was not without its merits. Although the DGAMS was not entitled to a seat on the Army Council, he was regularly admitted to its meetings in order to inform its members about the Army's medical situation.[37] Sir Alfred Keogh, who was DGAMS for most of the First World War, was fortunately highly respected in both military and medical circles; the subordination of the DGAMS was also more than compensated by the inclusion of senior MOs in military planning at HQ level, at least on the Western Front.

The BMA continued nevertheless to press for reform at the War Office, arguing that the DGAMS should have a seat on the Army Council. But the Warren Fisher Committee took a dim view of the BMA's intervention in military affairs, and chastised it for meddling in matters beyond its competence. In its second report, the Warren Fisher Committee stated—quite reasonably—that 'The function of a Medical Board is . . . of its nature auxiliary to the main offensive purpose of a fighting force'.[38] It is also questionable whether medical arrangements during the First World War, and subsequently, would have been any better had the DGAMS been given a permanent seat on the Council. It is unlikely that he would have been able to make the case for medicine as effectively as the Adjutant-General, an officer who had progressed through the combatant branches of the service before taking his administrative position.

While some medical officers undoubtedly backed the demands of the BMA, the DGAMS was inclined to agree with the findings of the Warren Fisher Committee. Lieutenant-General J. A. Hartigan, who was appointed DGAMS at the time the committee made its report, acknowledged that it had been criticized by doctors inside and outside the service, but felt that no committee could produce a report acceptable to all. He believed that the failure of the RAMC to attract recruits was not due principally to low status or poor pay but to the lack of professional opportunities. The First World War, he claimed, had created an unfortunate impression whereby doctors on

---

[36] W. G. MacPherson, *History of the Great War Based on Official Documents: Medical Services, General History* (London: HMSO, 1921), i. 3–4.

[37] PRO WO 163/9, Minutes of the Proceedings of the Army Council, 1904.

[38] *Committee on the Medical Branches of the Defence Services—Report* (London: HMSO, 1933), 16.

temporary commissions found that Regulars had been withdrawn from professional to administrative work. These temporary officers returned to civilian life convinced that the RAMC were a bunch of pen-pushers who were of little use as doctors. The Warren Fisher proposals, which allowed for more specialist and continuing professional work, would go some way towards alleviating this problem, he believed.[39]

The DGAMS's optimism was not entirely misplaced. Following the implementation of the Warren Fisher proposals in May 1934 recruitment began to improve significantly, and forty-three short-service commissions were granted during that year and an increasing number of candidates came forward thereafter. The fact that the great majority of these eventually applied for permanent commissions provides some evidence that they were satisfied with a military career, and shows that one of the greatest disincentives to recruitment in the past may have been apprehension about signing on for a longer period.[40] This modest increase in recruitment was insufficient to fill the additional posts created following rearmament, but it did correct the disadvantage the medical services had long faced in respect to other branches of the Army. The combatant branches faced similar similar problems of recruitment for much the same reasons as the RAMC: namely, low pay, poor promotion prospects, and long overseas tours. But unlike the RAMC, there was to be no improvement: a shortfall of 176 officers in 1922 increased to 410 by 1937.[41] Placed in this wider context, the position of the medical services seems rather less bleak than is suggested by the official history; relatively speaking, their position—though far from ideal—was somewhat better than that of the Army as a whole.

Technology and Training

The prospects for military medicine immediately after the First World War seemed bright. In June 1919 new Directorates for hygiene and pathology were created in the AMS, in recognition of the important role that each had played during the First World War. Pathology, which had previously been part of the Directorate of Hygiene, came of age between 1914 and 1918, with the appointment of many pathologists to hospitals and mobile laboratories. These specialists performed many important functions, not least the identification of soldiers infected with disease.

[39] 'The Warren Fisher Report', *News and Gazette of the Royal Army Medical Corps*, 263–4.
[40] Crew, *Army Medical Services*, i. 80.
[41] David French, 'Officer Education and Training in the British Regular Army, 1919–39', in G. C. Kennedy and K. Neilson (eds.), *Military Education: Past, Present and Future* (Westport, Conn.: Praeger, 2002), 105–28.

The new Directorates were heralded in the medical press as part of a 'far-reaching scheme' for the reorganization of the medical services, and it was anticipated that they would attract more scientifically minded graduates.[42] The new departments were also supplemented by two standing committees which replaced the old Army Sanitary Committee: one each for hygiene and pathology respectively.[43] Also, in January 1921 an entirely new branch of the AMS was created in the form of the Army Dental Service, which sat alongside the RAMC and the QAIMNS, under the control of the DGAMS. Dentists had played an important role during the First World War, as many soldiers would have been disqualified from military service had it not been for dental treatment. The employment of dentists enabled the Army to deal quickly and effectively with the large numbers of men with gum infections and dental caries. It also enabled medical officers to concentrate on other duties.[44]

These developments were part of a general trend towards specialization in medicine, one which had been accelerated by the First World War. A range of specialists—including orthopaedic surgeons, physiologists, and ophthalmologists—had obtained support from the War Office because of their claims to treat casualties more quickly and efficiently than before.[45] Although they often made great progress in wartime, the gains made by specialists were not always consolidated in the very different circumstances of peace.[46] Dental officers were still judged necessary on account of the poor dental standard of many recruits, but there no longer seemed to be the same urgent need for specialists in hygiene and pathology. In 1932 the separate Directorate of Pathology was abolished and the post of Director of Pathology at the War

---

[42] *British Medical Journal,* 5 July 1919, p. 20.

[43] Crew, *Army Medical Services,* i. 41.

[44] L. J. Godden (ed.), *History of the Army Dental Corps* (Aldershot: RADC, 1971), 9.

[45] On medical specialization during the First World War, see: Steve Sturdy, 'From the Trenches to the Hospitals at Home: Physiologists, Clinicians and Oxygen Therapy, 1914–30', in J. V. Pickstone (ed.), *Medical Innovation in Historical Perspective* (London: Macmillan, 1992), 104–23; id., 'War as Experiment: Physiology, Innovation and Administration in Britain, 1914–18: The Face of Chemical Warfare', in R. Cooter, M. Harrison, and S. Sturdy (eds.), *War, Medicine and Modernity* (Stroud: Sutton, 1998), 65–84; Roger Cooter, *Surgery and Society in Peace and War: Orthopaedics and the Organization of Modern Medicine* (London: Macmillan, 1993); Christoph Gradmann, ' "Vornehmlich beängstigend"—Medizin, Gesundheit und chemische Kriegführung im deutschen Heer 1914–1918', in C. Gradmann and W. Eckert (eds.), *Die Medizin und der Erste Weltkrieg* (Pfaffenweiler: Centaurus, 1996), 131–54. For other examples of wartime specialization, see: John Turner, 'Cabinets, Committees and Secretariats: The Higher Direction of War', and Jose Harris, 'Bureaucrats and Businessmen in British Food Control, 1916–19', in Kathleen Burk (ed.), *War and the State: The Transformation of British Government, 1914–1919* (London: George Allen & Unwin, 1982), 57–83, 135–56.

[46] Many of those who made great strides in establishing medical specialisms during the war—such as in the field of orthopaedics—found it difficult to attract the institutional support necessary for the development of their disciplines in peacetime. See Cooter, *Surgery and Society.*

Office was merged with that of the Professor of Pathology at Millbank. Even though it was foreseen that the Directorate would have to be re-established in the event of major war, and that this would result in delays and inefficiency, the prospect in 1932 seemed sufficiently remote for the War Office to reject the representations of the DGAMS.[47]

Although the position of some specialist departments was precarious, the training of specialist staff improved steadily. The end of the First World War left the RAMC with few specialists. Most of the surgical and medical work had been performed by temporarily commissioned officers, and it was the responsibility of the handful of the RAMC's own specialists to train a new generation within the Regular Army. The deficit was made good by retraining middle-ranking RAMC officers in surgical and other skills, but this was merely a short-term expedient and a new cadre of specialists was clearly required. The training of surgical specialists was the work of Major-General J. W. West, Consultant Surgeon with the Army from 1920 to 1927, and Professor of Military Surgery at the RAMC College from 1932 to 1935. Despite the constraints imposed by the shortage of new recruits, West was able to boast that 'a splendid band of young Surgical Specialists' had been formed by the time war was declared, many having been admitted as Fellows of the Royal College of Surgeons.[48] He was also successful in training a new generation of radiologists (among RAMC officers) and radiographers (among NCOs). Both had been in short supply in the years immediately after the First World War, yet both were increasingly in demand, as X-rays came to play a larger part in military medicine and surgery. This was made possible by research conducted at the X-ray Research Department at Woolwich Arsenal, which produced a small portable X-ray set, capable of being carried by small medical units. These portable sets became widely available in the mid-1920s and were used extensively in the Second World War.[49]

The high rates of disease that undermined campaigns outside Europe during the First World War also suggested that combatant officers needed constantly to be reminded of their responsibilities in respect of sanitation and hygiene. The King's Regulations of 1928 stated that officers should pay particular attention to the health of their troops and that they were responsible for remedying any sanitary defects in the area under their command. This applied regardless of how long an area had been occupied.[50] But orders were not enough. The *Army Manual of Hygiene* stated that: 'In order that every . . . commander may be in a position to bear this sanitary responsibility, he must have a knowledge of the laws of health, must understand the reason

[47] Crew, *Army Medical Services*, i. 44.   [48] West, 'Progress of Surgery', 2.
[49] Ibid. 5.   [50] *Army Manual of Hygiene—1934* (London: HMSO, 1935), 9.

for them and must see that they are obeyed.'[51] With this in mind, the War Office established a new School of Hygiene at Aldershot for the training of medical staff and combatants. The new school, which opened in 1922, combined in one establishment the former RAMC Hygiene School, the Entomology Laboratory, and the Hygiene Laboratory at Aldershot.[52] Medical officers were also selected to attend the Staff College and the Senior Officers' School. Here they instructed combatant officers in hygiene and sanitation, and themselves learned much about operational planning.[53] These moves reflected the widespread view that the attainment of military efficiency rested on close co-operation between all branches of the Army, and this was more than justified by the high standard of hygiene generally maintained by the British Army during the Second World War. Between 1939 and 1945 the School of Hygiene (which moved to Mytchett, in November 1939) provided instruction for some 15,329 Regular (non-medical) officers and 98,811 other ranks.[54]

Although the school placed great emphasis on practical teaching and sanitation in the field, the parameters of military hygiene had broadened considerably since the subject was first taught in the mid-nineteenth century. As Lieutenant-Colonel J. A. Anderson, Professor of Hygiene at the Royal Army Medical College, put it: 'military hygiene in the past concerned itself chiefly with the more obvious, more immediate problems of death and disease and frequently with only a minor group of these, the infections. Concern with the welfare of the healthy many was scarcely recognized, or, if practised at all, was strictly environmental.'[55] The Army's manuals of hygiene epitomized this shift in thinking. Hygiene was seen as the science of the 'maintenance and promotion of health' as well as the prevention of disease; it was a 'progressive science that calls for continual investigation'.[56] Physiological research, in particular, was providing what many contemporaries believed to be a more scientific grounding for the enhancement of health. During the First World War the findings of physiologists led to a radical overhaul of military rations and physical training,[57] and after 1918 a number of important studies took these investigations a step further, making detailed assessments

[51] *Army Manual of Hygiene—1934* (London: HMSO, 1935), 9.
[52] Crew, *Army Medical Services*, i. 51.
[53] F. A. E. Crew, 'The Army Medical Services', in Sir A. S. MacNalty and W. F. Mellor (eds.), *Medical Services in War: The Principal Medical Lessons of the Second World War* (London: HMSO, 1968), 67–8.
[54] F. A. E. Crew, *The Army Medical Services. Administration*, 2 (London: HMSO, 1955), 35–6.
[55] Lt.-Col. J. A. Anderson, 'The Recent Trend in Military Hygiene', *Journal of the Royal Army Medical Corps*, 43 (1924), 85.
[56] *Army Manual of Hygiene—1934*, 9–10.
[57] See: Harrison. 'The Fight Against Disease'; Sturdy, 'From the Trenches to the Hospitals at Home'; id., 'War as Experiment'; Joel D. Howell, 'Soldier's Heart: The Redefinition of Heart Disease and Speciality Formation in Early Twentieth-Century Great Britain', *Medical History*, Suppl. no. 5 (1985), 34–52.

of the energy value of military rations and the load-bearing capacity of soldiers on long marches.

Some of this research was highlighted in the War Office's pamphlet on *Elementary Physiology in its Relation to Hygiene*, which was published in 1919. As Lieutenant-Colonel Anderson indicated, military hygiene was evolving in line with the principles of scientific management. Referring to research conducted by officers of the RAMC and the Royal Engineers into the effort expended in digging trenches, Anderson concluded that: 'this piece of work possesses special interest in that it is, perhaps, the example most strikingly indicative of the new association between military hygiene and industrial efficiency, and because it presents, as far as I am aware, the first application of scientific time-and-motion studies to military duties.'[58] A number of time-and-motion studies had already been conducted in casualty clearing stations during the First World War,[59] but Anderson's summary suggests that there was now a broad consensus about what constituted 'efficiency'. Personnel management was increasingly informed by scientific principles and especially by ideas derived from physiology.[60] Academic psychology was also beginning to have some impact upon management practices, the most notable innovation being the foundation in 1922 of the National Institute of Industrial Psychology by the former Army MO, C. S. Myers.[61] In a monograph entitled *The Meaning of Rationalisation* (1929), the Director of the International Management Institute at Geneva, L. Urwick, saw industrial psychology (or 'psycho-technology' as he termed it) as a natural extension of Taylorite principles of scientific management, even though the Institute itself did its best to avoid association with Taylor. Organizations in both the private and public sectors knew that Taylorism was unpopular with organized labour and disavowed any connection with Taylor's methods, even though they attempted to introduce techniques of scientific management.[62]

---

[58] Anderson, 'Recent Trend in Military Hygiene', 85.

[59] CMAC RAMC 466/8, 'Report of Surgical Work accomplished following the move of No. 1 CCS, 25 August, 1918'; Bvt.-Col. W. R. P. Goodwin, 'The Casualty Clearing Station as a Working Unit in the Field', *Journal of the Royal Army Medical Corps*, 33 (1919), 42–57.

[60] Notions of 'Scientific Management' developed first in the USA and came gradually and selectively to be applied to British industry and administration. See: Charles S. Maier, 'Between Taylorism and Technocracy: European Ideologies and the Vision of Industrial Productivity in the 1920s', *Journal of Contemporary History*, 5 (1970), 27–61; Craig Littler, *The Development of Labour Processes in Capitalist Societies: A Comparative Study of the Transformation of Work Organization in Britain, Japan and the USA* (London: Heinemann, 1982); S. Haber, *Efficiency and Uplift: Scientific Management in the Progressive Era, 1890–1920* (Chicago: Chicago University Press, 1964); H. Thistleton Monk, *Efficiency Ideals: A Short Study of the Principles of 'Scientific Management'* (London: T. Werner Laurie, 1919).

[61] For a representative sample of this work see: Charles S. Myers (ed.), *Industrial Psychology* (London: Thornton Butterworth, 1929).

[62] L. Urwick, *The Meaning of Rationalisation* (London: Nisbet & Co., 1929), 68–70.

Senior Army officers such as Sir Ronald Adam, who was to have a very important influence on the Army as wartime Adjutant-General, were keenly aware of these developments. After serving on the Western Front as a gunnery officer, he attended the Staff College at Camberley as a student and later held a post as an instructor. After moving to the War Office in 1935 to take up a staff position, he was appointed Deputy Director of Military Operations in 1936. The following year Adam took command of the 1ˢᵗ Division of the Royal Artillery, until being appointed Commandant at the Staff College in 1937. He served as Deputy Chief of the Imperial General Staff in 1938–9 and as GOC 3ʳᵈ Corps in 1939–40, in which capacity he served in France. After a brief spell as GOC Northern Command, Adam was appointed Adjutant-General in 1941, a post he held until 1946. Adam took industry as the model for many of his innovations, including personnel selection, which he helped to introduce in 1942.[63] He also recognized the importance of what he termed 'man-management' and of 'mental well being' in maintaining the morale of soldiers.[64] When considering the health of soldiers—for which he had overall responsibility—Adam stressed the need for the promotion of health as well as the prevention of disease. He was instrumental in the creation of Physical Development Centres, which aimed to remedy minor physical defects through educational campaigns and took great pains to encourage soldiers to keep fighting fit. Adam was also behind the creation of both the Army Education Corps and the Army Bureau of Current Affairs, and he saw a vital link between the promotion of health and the promotion of democratic citizenship. This may seem extraordinary for a man who became one of Britain most senior generals during the Second World War, and who was an old Etonian and hereditary baronet to boot. Yet Adam was deeply commited to health and education for the masses, and saw both as vital to the prosecution of a 'People's War'.[65]

The Army's 'No. 1 Democrat' had much in common with proponents of 'social medicine' and 'social hygiene'; indeed, some of the latter had considerable experience of military life. One of the best-known proponents of social hygiene between the wars was P. S. Lelean (1871–1956), who served in the RAMC from 1899 to 1926. After leaving the Corps, Lelean become Professor of Public Health at Edinburgh University, a position he held until his

[63] LHCMA, Adam Papers, Confidential memo from Adjutant-General on 'Selection of Personnel', 3. See also Jeremy A. Crang, *The British Army and the People's War 1939–1945* (Manchester: Manchester University Press, 2000), 9–10.

[64] LHCMA, Adam Papers 3/4/4, Secret memo from Adjutant-General to District and Divisional Commanders on 'The Soldier's Well-Being', June 1943.

[65] LHCMA, Adam Papers, cutting from *Leicester Evening Mail*, 27 Apr. 1946, p. 3: 'He looks just like the popular conception of a general but his progressive outlook is astonishingly different from the popular conception of a general's. He is the Army's No. 1 democrat.'

retirement in 1944. During his time at Edinburgh he expanded the scope of public health to include eugenics, child welfare, physical training, and hygiene based on physiological principles. Lelean held the view that health was a positive attribute and not merely the absence of disease, and taught his students to look for the social and environmental causes of illness.[66] He was also a great advocate of education in matters of public health. In the journal *Health and Empire* he wrote that: 'the outstanding need for both present and future is that of education for every individual, so that intelligent co-operation in all hygienic measures may be secured from all good citizens as it has been from all good soldiers.'[67] Fitness, he believed, was 'the citizen's first duty', and he stressed the costs of sickness in terms of industrial and military performance.[68]

The military environment was very conducive to the development of a holistic approach to health, such as that advocated by Lelean and other pioneers of social medicine. As the Army's *Manual of Hygiene* put it: 'The aim of sanitation in the Army is military efficiency and therefore everything that will maintain or improve the health of the soldier and thereby aid his military efficiency must be regarded as coming within the scope of hygiene and sanitation.'[69] This all-embracing conception of hygiene was much easier to realize in a regulated environment like the Army than it was in civilian life, for: 'The military population consists of a large proportion of young men who have all been subjected to a thorough medical examination before entering the Army, they live a disciplined communal life, which is under constant supervision and disciplined health measures can be adopted more rapidly and effectively than in a civilian community.'[70]

Nevertheless, there were many who believed that civilians could be instilled with some of the hygienic discipline exemplified by the military. In an age of total warfare the links between civilian and military populations were becoming blurred, and both would play an important part in the coming war. It therefore seemed reasonable to expect the dutiful citizen to keep him- or herself fit to serve the country in whatever capacity might be deemed necessary. During the last war Dr Charles Porter had argued, in an article entitled 'Citizenship and Health Questions in War-time', that citizenship and public health were synonymous. He insisted that all individuals owed a duty to keep themselves fit to serve in wartime, in return for which

[66] CMAC RAMC 565, Lelean Papers, Obituary of P. S. Lelean, 'Pioneer in Public Health', *The Times*, 8 Nov. 1956; extract from Edinburgh Senatus Academicus minutes, 8 Nov. 1944.

[67] P. S. Lelean, 'The Evolution of Public Health', *Health and Empire* (Dec. 1929), 10.

[68] CMAC RAMC 565, P. S. Lelean, 'National Physical Unfitness and Some Remedies', Presidential Address to the Sanitary Association of Scotland; id., *How to Feed the Family* (Edinburgh and Glasgow: William Hodge & Co., 1927).

[69] *Army Manual of Hygiene—1934*, 10.   [70] Ibid. 12.

the state not only protected them, but would provide to some extent for their health and welfare.[71] It was a vision that many shared during the 1920s and 1930s, including the Chief Medical Officer of the newly formed Ministry of Health, Sir George Newman. He believed that there was a clear link between public health and active citizenship, and believed firmly in the value of education in health. Newman also saw a role for the state in the promotion of health, in the form of infant welfare clinics, health visitors, and the like, although he did not envisage a comprehensive state medical service. Like Lelean and many proponents of hygiene in the military, Newman's conception of public health was holistic, in that it embraced the clinician, the laboratory scientist, and the sanitarian. He believed, too, that doctors should consider the moral and social as well as the biological dimensions of medicine. His overall aim was to conciliate social differences and to bring health to the body politic as well as to each individual.[72]

These developments amounted to a shift in emphasis in public health from the environment to the individual, from sanitarianism to social hygiene. The apostles of hygiene now sought to regulate all aspects of the individual's behaviour and social relations. It was a dynamic conception of society that had an affinity with the dynamic conceptions of the human body that had emerged from physiology and experimental psychology.[73] The wide currency of such ideas in Britain between the wars, and their compatibility with military values, helps to account for the intelligent interest in medicine and hygiene shown by many British officers during the Second World War. The overriding concern in British military doctrine was to avoid casualties, as it was generally believed that the nation would not countenance losses on the scale experienced in the First World War. Should another war occur, most senior offices expected the next generation of soldiers to be less deferential and of questionable loyalty. Every attempt was therefore made to substitute technology for manpower, or at least to enhance manpower by using scientific and technological resources. British doctrine 'attempted to bring the same order and regularity to the battefield . . . as industrialists had brought to the modern factory'.[74] Medical knowledge played an important part in

---

[71] Charles Porter, 'Citizenship and Health Questions in War-time', *Journal of State Medicine*, 25 (1917), 300–6.

[72] See Jose Harris, 'Enterprise and Welfare States: A Comparative Perspective', *Transactions of the Royal Historical Society*, 5th Series, 40 (1991), 175–95; Geoffrey Finlayson, *Citizen, State and Social Welfare in Britain, 1830–1900* (Oxford: Clarendon Press, 1994); Steve Sturdy, 'Hippocrates and State Medicine: George Newman Outlines the Founding Policy of the Ministry of Health', in C. Lawrence and G. Weisz (eds.), *Greater Than the Parts: Holism in Biomedicine 1920–1950* (New York and Oxford: Oxford University Press, 1998), 112–34.

[73] See David Armstrong, *The Political Anatomy of the Body: Medical Knowledge in Britain in the Twentieth Century* (Cambridge: Cambridge University Press, 1993).

[74] David French, *Raising Churchill's Army: The British Army and the War Against Germany 1919–1945* (Oxford: Oxford University Press, 2000), 19.

this endeavour, as it offered a way of understanding the soldier and of improving his physical and mental suitability for battle. Effective medical provisions were also recognized as vital to the maintenance of social and military cohesion.

The 1920s and 1930s thus brought many important developments in medicine and hygiene, and an increasing awareness among combatant officers of their military value. There were, however, few opportunities to put this training into practice. Small imperial campaigns on the North-West Frontier of India, and the suppression of the Burma Rebellion in 1931, presented no major challenges to the medical services.[75] In Britain, too, there were few opportunities to test the co-ordination of medical and combatant arms, as field medical units did not exist in peacetime. In 1928 proposals were made to establish an annual training camp for the RAMC, and this was afterwards enshrined in the RAMC's training manual.[76] But due to the financial climate, no training exercise was held until 1937, and only sixty-nine officers and 940 other ranks passed through the camp before war was declared.[77] Another factor affecting training was the shortage of Regular officers, which meant that few could be released from duties.[78] As Major-General R. W. D. Leslie put it in 1939: 'The tactical handling of several field ambulances—say of a division—can rarely, if ever, be efficiently practised as the peace-time establishment of the RAMC will not permit the liberation of more than a few officers and other ranks from their normal hospital duties.'[79] In view of this, the RAMC created skeleton ambulances for the purposes of field training. These required only a quarter of the usual personnel, with one man taken to represent an entire stretcher squad, for example.[80] This situation was typical of that in the Army as a whole: training exercises were both too infrequent and too unrealistic to prepare the Army for the trials it was to encounter in 1940.[81]

Although the RAMC learned relatively little from the small colonial campaigns of the 1920s and 1930s, there was one conflict from which it learned a great deal: the Spanish Civil War of 1936–9. It was in this war that Josep Trueta, Director of Surgery in the General Hospital at Barcelona and future Professor of Orthopaedics at Oxford, revolutionized the treatment of fractures by perfecting what became known as the 'closed method' of treatment. After any damaged tissue had been removed and the bone had been set,

[75] West, 'Progress of Surgery', 10–12.

[76] *Royal Army Medical Corps Training—1935* (London: HMSO, 1935), 14.

[77] Crew, *Army Medical Services*, i. 87.

[78] Maj.-Gen. J. A. Hartigan, 'Training of the R.A.M.C. Officer in Medical Duties in the Field', *Journal of the Royal Army Medical Corps*, 42 (1934), 1–5.

[79] Maj.-Gen. R. W. D. Leslie, 'R.A.M.C. Field Training—The Casualty Card Scheme', *Journal of the Royal Army Medical Corps*, 72 (1939), 145.

[80] Ibid. 146.   [81] French, *Raising Churchill's Army*, 169–70.

Trueta encased the patient's limb completely in plaster so as to render it absolutely immobile. In place of frequent dressings and examination of the wound, as in older methods, the wound was left to heal on its own without antiseptics. Trueta achieved remarkable results with this method, successfully treating thousands of civilian and military casualties. Infections such as septicaemia and gas gangrene, which were formerly prevalent in Catalonia, were comparatively rare. Trueta recorded only one case of gangrene in 1,073 patients treated; another surgeon, using the same technique, recorded only twenty among 5,000.[82]

Trueta's methods were not widely known in Britain before the start of the Second World War, and it was not until 1939 that his work was published under the title of *The Treatment of War Wounds and Fractures*. At the outbreak of the war most senior orthopaedic surgeons still looked back to the First World War for guidance.[83] But as war approached, a number of articles and editorials began to appear in medical journals popularizing Trueta's work, and these impressed many of the younger surgeons who went out to France in 1939–40.[84] Unfortunately the military situation there did not enable them to put Trueta's method into practice, but during the Western Desert campaigns it came into its own, saving the limbs of many casualties who had to make a long and often arduous journey back to base. The Spanish Civil War also provided the inspiration for the medical service of the Home Guard. Some of those involved in setting up the Home Guard medical service had served in the International Brigades, which relied heavily on medical services improvised from civilian sources.[85]

It was at the time of the Spanish Civil War that sulphonamide drugs first came to be used in the British Army to treat a variety of bacterial infections, raising hopes that many diseases common in wartime might be controlled in the event of a future conflict. The discovery in the mid-1930s of the anti-bacterial effects of sulphonamides (synthetic chemical compounds) spurred the Army to introduce trials against a range of common military infections, including gonorrhoea. A study conducted in Egypt during 1937 concluded that 'Sulphonamide in doses sufficient to produce a certain degree of toxicity is shown to be a most powerful agent in the treatment of gonorrhoea, two-thirds of the cases leaving hospital in less than nineteen days'. Encouraged by these results, the author of the report believed that the

[82] A. M. Low, *Benefits of War* (London: Scientific Book Club, 1945), 137–40.

[83] Cooter, *Surgery and Society in Peace and War*, 220.

[84] 'Treatment of War Wounds and Fractures', Editorial, *Journal of the Royal Army Medical Corps*, 73 (1939), 302–3.

[85] G. B. Shirlaw and C. Troke, *Medicine versus Invasion: The Home Guard Medical Service in Action* (London: Secker & Warburg, 1941), p. x.

'barometer is set fair for further progress'.[86] These trials, together with those conducted by respected bodies such as the Medical Research Council (MRC), proved that sulphonamides were also likely to be effective against a range of common wound infections, including streptococcal infections and the bacteria causing gas gangrene. At the outbreak of the Second World War, the War Office recommended that all wounds likely to become the site of secondary infection should receive a prophylactic course of sulphonamides for forty-eight hours, providing the patient had recovered from shock.[87]

More effective measures were also available against tetanus. The prophylactic use of tetanus antitoxin during the First World War saved thousands of lives, but the antitoxin could not always be administered in time if heavy fighting prevented casualties from being collected. Experiments with active immunization against tetanus, conducted during the mid-1920s, offered hope of a prophylactic that could be administered to troops before they went into battle. A series of trials with active immunization at the Royal Army Medical College revealed that doses of tetanus toxoid given at intervals of six weeks produced a concentration well above that needed to confer protection.[88] As a result, immunization became routine in the British Army throughout the Second World War.

Preparing for War

From 1934 to 1939, as Britain began to reconsider its strategic commitments, the AMS began to prepare for a possible war in Europe. Up to 1933, when military members of the Army Council reviewed the position of the Army and its readiness for war, it was thought that the most likely theatre for any future conflict would be in the East. The basis for Britain's strategic commitments had therefore been the 'Defence of India Plan', which provided for a period of mobilization lasting six months and the dispatch of only two divisions in the first four months, and small contingents thereafter. The organization and equipment of the medical services, as for the Army more generally, were also designed for 'undeveloped' terrain such as India's North-West

[86] Majs. D. W. Beamish and L. B. Clarke, 'Treatment of Gonorrhoea and Soft Chancre in Egypt by Sulphonamide', *Journal of the Royal Army Medical Corps*, 73 (1939), 103.

[87] 'Memorandum Concerning the use of Sulphonamide Derivatives for Prophylaxis and Treatment of Wound Infections', issued by Army Directorate of Pathology, 11 Oct. 1939, *Journal of the Royal Army Medical Corps*, 73 (1939), 298–300; 'Supplementary Memorandum No. 1 Concerning the use of Sulphonamide Derivatives for Prophylaxis and Treatment of Wound Infections', issued 1 Nov. 1939, ibid. 301.

[88] Maj. J. S. K. Boyd, 'Active Immunization against Tetanus', *Journal of the Royal Army Medical Corps*, 70 (1938), 289–307.

Frontier. The state of the medical services was, moreover, so parlous that they were unable to meet their peacetime commitments, let alone those of a small expeditionary force.

After Hitler came to power in 1933 it soon became evident that planning would have to take into account the possibility of a war in Europe and the commitment of an expeditionary force of at least eight divisions (four Regular and four Territorial). It was also decided to embark on a thorough modernization of Britain's defences, to be completed within a period of five years. This plan was supported by the Army Council and approved by the Committee of Imperial Defence in 1934. Of the £20 million allotted to the Army, the largest part was to be spent on the expeditionary force, and on increasing the peacetime establishments of both the Regular Army and the Reserve. The programme was regarded as provisional and subject to adjustment as circumstances dictated.

The deficiencies of the rearmament programme were obvious as early as 1935, when it became apparent that the Warren Fisher reforms had been insufficient to attract the larger number of recruits it now required. In that year it was estimated that the expeditionary force would require 650 MOs, with 320 ready for service at home, but the RAMC found itself over 300 officers short. A similar situation existed in respect of other ranks: 6,345 were required for the first contingent of an expeditionary force (2,395 for medical units at home, and a further 1,000 for the expansion of hospitals), but there was a deficit of around 2,800 men.[89] These shortages persisted right up to 1939, when the RAMC still lacked 210 Regular officers. Had it not been for the introduction of limited conscription in April 1939, and arrangements made in July for 16,000 men to join the Army every other month to serve for a period of six months, the expeditionary force would have been without its complement of medical staff. By August 1939 these measures had raised the number of MOs to 1,453 and other ranks RAMC to 9,321: sufficient to supply the expeditionary force and to maintain commitments elsewhere.[90]

In the years running up to the Second World War it also became clear that the medical services would have to adapt to a heavily mechanized form of warfare. As late as 1935 the RAMC's training manual envisaged a system of evacuation little changed from that on the Western Front during the First World War. Medium-sized and relatively immobile units such as the main dressing stations of field ambulances and CCSs still played a pivotal role in sorting and treating casualties. In the coming years their role came increasingly to be questioned, and in an article of April 1939 Lieutenant-Colonel J. C. A. Dowse concluded that: 'The cumbersome, over-equipped field ambulance will have to be modified and, in my opinion, modified to such

[89] Crew, *Army Medical Services*, i. 10.   [90] Ibid. 15.

an extent as to be scarcely recognisable as such. Possibly the name might be changed to a "Field Evacuating Unit". This can only be done by remembering that the main duty of a field ambulance is to evacuate the casualties as rapidly and comfortably as possible.'[91] This new unit was modelled on the mechanized cavalry field ambulances already used by some overseas garrisons. The staff of these field ambulances spent a great deal of time anticipating the demands of mechanized warfare: practising the loading and unloading of vehicles and perfecting methods of transporting the wounded.[92] Some ordinary field ambulances were also given extra vehicles so that they could accompany motorized infantry divisions. But most medical units were still too sluggish for mechanized warfare, and in the conflict that was to follow most would be radically overhauled or rendered obsolescent.

In addition to Regulars and Reservists, the Army was able to count on the support of the medical branch of the Territorial Army. In 1927 the medical complement of the TA consisted of 768 officers and 2,136 men, and this did not change substantially until 1937, twelve months after the reorganization of the TA. In the run-up to the Second World War the TA built up its medical support to thirty-eight field ambulances and four casualty clearing stations. Plans to build twenty-nine stationary TA general hospitals in the United Kingdom, however, did not progress very far, and only four large institutions were constructed. The DGAMS proposed instead that some of these be replaced with smaller units of 600 beds, and fifteen of these were ready by the beginning of the war. TA hospitals thus became available in two sizes (600 and 1,200 beds), like the rest of the Army's general hospitals.

Plans for the expansion of military hospitals in the United Kingdom were shelved because the civilian medical profession, local authorities, and the Ministry of Health objected to the diversion of resources from civilian to military use. They protested that few military casualties were likely to occur during the first few months of the war—prior to the dispatch of an expeditionary force—but warned that heavy civilian casualties due to air raids could be expected from the very beginning. The ministry therefore proposed that the Army should fall back on civilian hospitals if it required additional beds. This met with strong opposition from the DGAMS, who drew attention to the fact that the medical needs of the Army during the first two months of the war would amount to no more than 2,140 doctors out of 43,500 registered practitioners, and 1,200 nurses out of 89,000—hardly a major drain upon medical resources. He also drew attention to the desirability—on disciplinary grounds—of treating military casualties separately.

[91] Lt.-Col. J. C. A. Dowse, 'Mechanization and the Modern Field Ambulance', *Journal of the Royal Army Medical Corps*, 72 (1939), 376.
[92] Maj. J. Bryan Fotheringham, 'Training a (Mechanized) Cavalry Field Ambulance—Egypt, 1936', *Journal of the Royal Army Medical Corps*, 72 (1939), 151–63.

It was eventually decided that the Army should depend largely on civilian hospitals in the United Kingdom, and that any expansion of military hospitals should be restricted to special needs.[93] Many of the sick and wounded evacuated from France and Norway in 1940 were treated in special wings of Emergency Medical Service (EMS) hospitals. The EMS was originally established to provide treatment for service personnel and air-raid casualties, but the remit of EMS hospitals was gradually expanded to cover all manual workers employed in industry, as the number of casualties from air raids was lower than expected. The situation that obtained in the United Kingdom during the Second World War was therefore quite different from that in 1914–18, when the government took control of civilian hospitals solely for the use of the armed services.[94]

Much of the work at the larger military hospitals was performed by women rather than RAMC orderlies, in order to release the latter for active service. In peacetime the Army's female nurses were drawn exclusively from the QAIMNS. The QAIMNS was an amalgamation of the old Army and Indian Nursing Services, and was a product of the military medical reforms that followed the South African War.[95] It was to some degree independent of the DGAMS, though the latter was a member of its management board and was, as head of the AMS, ultimately responsible for its effectiveness.[96] QAIMNS nurses prided themselves on their professionalism and took readily to military discipline: by involving themselves in work of national importance, they hoped to improve the status of nursing as a profession.[97] Although there had always been some friction between military doctors and military nurses,[98] the QAIMNS were generally admired for their professionalism and technical competence.[99]

As in the First World War, the British Army also made use of supplementary nursing assistance in the form of Voluntary Aid Detachments. On mobilization, members of VADs (who were mostly, but not entirely, female) reported at the medical units to which they had been previously allocated.

[93] Crew, *Army Medical Services*, i. 102–3.

[94] See R. M. Titmuss, *Problems of Social Policy* (London: HMSO, 1950), 54–86; C. L. Dunn (ed.), *The Emergency Medical Services*, 2 vols. (London: HMSO, 1952); Brian Abel-Smith, *The Hospitals, 1800–1948* (London: Heinemann, 1964), 426–39.

[95] For the Army Nursing Service, see Anne Summers, *Angels and Citizens: British Women as Military Nurses 1854–1914* (London: Routledge, 1988).

[96] PRO WO 30/114, 'Report of the Committee appointed . . . to consider the Reorganization of the Army and Indian Nursing Service' (1901).

[97] See Penny Starns, 'Fighting Militarism? British Military Nursing During the Second World War', in Cooter, Harrison, and Sturdy (eds.), *War, Medicine and Modernity*, 189–202.

[98] The story of female nursing in the First World War is recounted in Lyn MacDonald's *The Roses of No Man's Land* (Harmondsworth: Penguin, 1993).

[99] IWM, Papers of Mrs D. Boys. Memoirs of various VADS of service in Army hospitals.

Although they retained the distinctive status, conditions of service, and uniforms of the VADs, and were organized by the VAD Council, they were under the orders of the military authorities. This duality of control created some confusion at first, but most of the problems were ironed out within a few months. Despite moves to merge the VADs with the Auxiliary Territorial Service, they retained a separate identity throughout the war: a testament to the status and influence of parent bodies such as the Red Cross and the Order of St John of Jerusalem.[100] The VADs were organized into two classes: 'mobile' and 'immobile'. The former undertook to serve overseas if required, while the latter agreed to home service only; in 1942 there were 4,150 'mobile' and only forty-eight 'immobile' members of VADs.[101]

As in 1914–18, the main purpose of the VADs was to replace RAMC orderlies, who were needed for front-line service. But not all volunteers seem to have been aware of this fact, nor was it clearly stated to them that they would be employed under essentially the same conditions as an RAMC orderly. This gave rise to a certain amount of misunderstanding and dissatisfaction, and during the first winter of the war there were many complaints from VADs about conditions of service. The main causes of complaint were poor accommodation and the preponderance of menial tasks among their duties. Many VAD nurses felt these conditions were demeaning, even though their professional qualifications were generally inferior to those of RAMC orderlies. As a result of these criticisms, the War Office issued an order in 1940 limiting the duties of VADs, but this meant they could not so easily replace the orderlies of the RAMC.[102]

There was also some tension between the VADs and the Queen Alexandra's Imperial Military Nursing Service, which was a Regular branch of the AMS. While VADs respected the superior training of the QAIMNS nurses, the latter tended to look down on the former's lack of experience and professional qualifications. Only a handful of the VAD nurses had a background in nursing, and most were formerly shop assistants or secretaries. But, despite their lack of experience, medical officers generally got on better with VAD nurses than with the Regulars, whom they respected but treated more formally. This was also true of patients, who had to salute the QAIMNS as they would their own officers, but were on much more friendly terms with the VADs.[103]

---

[100] See Starns, 'Fighting Militarism?', 192–3.
[101] PRO WO 222/275, Memo. on VAD Members and their Employment in the Army, 26 Aug. 1942, 2.
[102] PRO WO 222/275, 3.
[103] IWM, Papers of Mrs D. Boys.

One novel feature of medical provisions during the Second World War was the recruitment of female doctors into the Army, although they were admitted into the Auxiliary Territorial Service (ATS) or the Blood Transfusion Service (BTS) rather than the RAMC. During the First World War women doctors had not been permitted to work in the British Army, but had served as volunteers in general hospitals on the Western Front and other theatres.[104] These hospitals were not run by the Army but by voluntary organizations under the overall control of the Joint War Coordinating Committee of the British Red Cross and the Order of St John of Jerusalem. Although women doctors were not permitted to enter the Army during or after the First World War, a precedent of sorts had been set, for it had been shown that women could work very effectively as doctors in military hospitals, even relatively close to the firing line. This was the basis of the plea by the Medical Women's Federation (MWF) to the War Office in 1937, when it requested that women doctors be allowed to serve in the Army in the event of war breaking out. But the DGAMS believed that any employment of female doctors within the Army should be strictly limited, and that they were better employed in a civilian capacity in order to release male doctors for the services. After another twelve months the matter was raised again, this time by the BMA. The DGAMS now conceded that some women doctors could be employed in the ATS with the pay and relative rank of lieutenant, or as replacements for RAMC officers in the BTS.[105]

The wartime Director-General, Sir Alexander Hood, was not unsympathetic to the demands of the MWF, but he insisted that there were 'insuperable' legal obstacles to granting women commissions in the RAMC. He pointed out that women were unable to fulfil the combatant and disciplinary duties that men were called upon to perform, and that this effectively barred them from holding a commission in the RAMC, because it had to work in forward areas.[106] These remarks reflected the Army Council's policy that there should be only one female corps within the Army (the ATS), and female doctors were excluded from the RAMC for the duration of the war.[107]

The British Army was mobilized immediately after the declaration of war against Germany on 3 September 1939. On the same day the TA was embodied and all men of the Army Reserve were ordered to rejoin the Regulars, and many were posted to the expeditionary force being assembled for deploy-

---

[104] Leah Leneman, *In the Service of Life: The Story of Elsie Inglis and the Scottish Women's Hospitals* (Edinburgh: Mercartor Press, 1994); Eileen Crofton, *The Women of Royaumont: A Scottish Women's Hospital on the Western Front* (East Linton: Tuckwell Press, 1997).
[105] CMAC SA/MWF/A49, Meeting of Committee [of the Medical Women's Federation] on Medical Women and War Service, 13 Feb. 1940.
[106] CMAC SA/MWF/A49, 207–8, 213–14.
[107] CMAC SA/MWF/A29, Meetings of the Committee on Medical Women and War Service, 10 Sept. 1941; 2 Mar. 1942; 20 May 1942.

ment in France. Mobilization brought with it a number of organizational changes, including the reconstitution of the Directorate of Pathology, which had been removed for financial reasons in 1932. As the DGAMS had warned, this entailed much unnecessary work and expense. There were some innovations too: a new statistical section of the Army Medical Directorate was formed in 1940 to process information received from the front, and other branches of the AMD came into being as circumstances required, such as the Directorate of Psychiatry, which was established in 1942 at the insistence of the new DGAMS, Lieutenant-General Alexander Hood.[108] But the most important new department to be created within the AMD was the Army Blood Transfusion Service, which became the envy of all combatant nations during the coming war.

The DGAMS—Lieutenant-General Sir William MacArthur—and the Royal College of Surgeons discussed the possibility of establishing a BTS in the autumn of 1938, soon after the Munich crisis. The college agreed to design the necessary organization and procure staff and equipment. By April 1939 a core staff drawn from the laboratories of the college and the Middlesex Hospital had been earmarked for the purpose and was placed under the direction of the War Office's Director of Pathology. The headquarters of the BTS was the new Army Blood Supply Depot based at Southmead Hospital in Bristol, where collection of blood from local donors began in the summer of 1939.[109] During the campaign in France in 1940 the Blood Supply Depot provided nearly all the blood and plasma needed by the expeditionary force, but in subsequent campaigns most had to be obtained from soldiers stationed overseas. Britain was the only nation that went to war with a fully functioning transfusion service, which meant that transfusion in the field was far better organized than in the armed forces of other combatant nations, especially Germany. This advantage was adroitly exploited by British propagandists, who seized upon blood transfusion as an example of successful voluntary co-operation, epitomizing the values of freedom and national unity.

The other great change at the beginning of the war was the introduction of full conscription in June 1940, which removed medical practitioners from the category of reserved occupations. After considerable deliberation, it was decided that the War Office and other relevant departments should inform the BMA's Central Medical War Committee (CMWC) of their requirements. The CMWC decided upon the quota of practitioners to be found from each district of the country and its local committees chose the practitioners they considered most suitable for military service. The names of these men were

[108] LHCMA, Adam Papers 3/13, narrative of work as Adjutant-General, 'Chap. IV—Medical Problems', 1–2.
[109] Crew, *Army Medical Services*, ii. 372–3.

then submitted to the CMWC, which allocated doctors to each of the three armed services. As in the First World War, there were frequent disagreements over priority between the War Office on the one hand and the BMA and civilian authorities on the other. The Secretary of State for War received numerous deputations from the CMWC and the royal colleges stating their concerns about staffing levels in civilian hospitals, and seeking assurance that the best use was being made of medical manpower.[110]

This conflict between military and civilian interests reached crisis-point during 1943, when an outbreak of influenza created an emergency situation that overshadowed the requirements of military expeditions overseas. F. A. E. Crew, the official historian of the Army Medical Services, claimed that they were at a 'continual disadvantage' because government was insufficiently apprised of military needs. The medical requirements of the Army, he argued, could not be calculated purely on the basis of its strength, as they varied massively according to the military situation.[111] It is certainly true that the medical services were sometimes overstretched, but the Army was never seriously understaffed, at least not for long periods. At the same time, there is no evidence of overmanning—an allegation made by some members of the civilian medical profession. Indeed, one of the most impressive aspects of British military medicine during the Second World War was the ability of the medical services to make the best of scarce resources and to maintain a standard of medical care that matched and often exceeded that of other combatant nations.

Conclusion

There can be little doubt that the AMS suffered a marked decline in its fortunes between the wars, to the extent that it was unable to provide adequate cover for the Army in its garrisons overseas. From 1922, following the decision to cut all branches of the armed services, the size of the AMS was progressively reduced. At the same time, it experienced great difficulty in attracting candidates to its few remaining posts, and especially to the officer ranks of the RAMC. While the RAMC had always found it difficult to recruit men of high calibre, the situation between 1922 and 1934 was more serious than at any time in its history, with the Corps one hundred officers and thousands of men below its peacetime establishment. The failure of the service to attract recruits can be attributed in part to its unattractive rates of pay, but the financial rewards of a military medical career had never been remarkable.

---

[110] Crew, *Army Medical Services*, i. 206–14.   [111] Ibid. 194–5.

Most young doctors probably rejected the idea of military service because it offered relatively few opportunities for advancement in specialist areas of medicine. The perception was that promotion to the upper ranks of the RAMC meant giving up professional work for a dull administrative routine. This negative image was also, perhaps, compounded by the prevailing sentiment of anti-militarism. Although this affected all branches of the armed services to some degree,[112] the medical branches may have suffered disproportionately because they had direct civilian counterparts, unlike combatant branches of the service. Pay and pensions in the former were also thought to be less generous than in the latter, so the RAMC was at a disadvantage in this respect too.

But from 1934 the tide was beginning to turn in the RAMC's favour, and from this point the RAMC appears to have fared better than other branches of the service. The second Warren Fisher Report offered more opportunities for promotion and specialist work, and the introduction of short-service commissions proved popular with those who were unsure about making a long-term commitment to the Army. The fact that many signed on for a further term suggests that a career in military medicine still offered some attractions. Although it is true that the expansion of the AMS during rearmament left many posts unfilled, the introduction of limited conscription meant that the expeditionary force dispatched to France possessed a full complement of medical staff. The reconstruction of the AMS between 1935 and 1939 was therefore less half-hearted than the official history has claimed. In addition, the British Army was the only army to enter the war with an established blood transfusion service, and it possessed a cadre of medical officers who had been trained as specialists in military surgery, themselves assisted by newly trained specialists in radiology and radiography. In the sphere of preventive medicine, the scope of military hygiene had been expanded to include measures designed positively to promote health, rather than simply to prevent disease. More importantly, there had been strenuous efforts to improve co-operation between medical and combatant officers, the lack of which had been the chief cause of medical disasters in previous campaigns. Combatants were now trained in the rudiments of preventive medicine at the Army's new School of Hygiene, and officers received instruction on medical planning at the Staff College and the Senior Officers' School. This training gave the British Army a crucial advantage over its opponents in several future campaigns.

---

[112] LHCMA, Adam Papers 2/1, *Report on the Staff Conference held at the Staff College, Camberley, 13th to 16th January, 1930* (London: HMSO, 1930). The Army was said to have lost its popularity due to 'trends in modern thought', the lack of financial attraction compared to business and other careers, the expense of service in India, distaste for discipline, etc. See ibid. 23–4.

2

Medicine in Retreat, 1940–1942

Norway

The German invasion of Scandinavia in April 1940 put an end to the 'Phoney War' that had lasted since September 1939. Pushing up through Denmark, the Germans landed 2,000 troops at the Norwegian port of Narvik on 9 April, marking the start of their conquest of that country and of open hostilities with Britain. The British response to this unexpected invasion was, at first, a naval one. Several destroyers, which arrived too late to prevent the German landing, succeeded in eliminating the German naval force in the area. A few days later an Allied force landed at three points along the Norwegian coast, at Narvik, Namsos, and Andalsnes. At Narvik a combined force of Norwegian, British, French, and Polish troops attempted to oust the Germans, and succeeded in doing so by the end of May. The other two landings were intended as a pincer movement for the capture of Trondheim, but these never came close to achieving their objectives. The latter operations were frustrated by poor planning and organization, as well as by a hostile climate and mountainous terrain. Indeed, the whole campaign, including its medical aspects, suffered from a singular combination of poor preparation and bad luck.[1]

The performance of the medical services during this short campaign was not without merit, especially given the unfavourable conditions in which medical personnel had to work, but poor planning and organization hindered medical work throughout. The main problem was the dire shortage of medical supplies, most of which had failed to reach Norway because they had been loaded onto the wrong vessels or not at all. Medical equipment was also lost to enemy action—on land and at sea—and because medical units were diverted at the last minute from their original destinations.[2] As a result, the force that landed at Andalsnes arrived without any transport and all arrangements for evacuation had to be carried out by the Norwegian medical

---

[1] See J. Adams, *The Doomed Expedition: The Campaign in Norway 1940* (London: Mandarin, 1989).

[2] PRO WO 222/1480, 'Campaign in Norway, April–June 1940', 11.

services. The force at Namsos was also devoid of medical transport and had to rely on vehicles acquired locally; these were often trucks rather than proper ambulance cars.

Medical arrangements also suffered because of the difficulty of communicating by telephone, signal, and wire. The lines had to operate through civilian exchanges, and there were often long delays; it was also feared that German spies had overheard telephone conversations.[3] These difficulties were compounded by poor co-ordination between the three services. Naval units initially signalled their casualties independently of the Army, which caused much unnecessary work. Very often there were two or more journeys for the collection and evacuation of the wounded, when one would have sufficed. This difficulty was partly overcome by the appointment of a naval MO ashore at Harstad—the HQ of medical operations in Norway—in order to co-ordinate casualty collection with the land forces. The other communication problem was language: British MOs had to deal not only with their own wounded, but also with those of the Norwegians, Polish, and the French Foreign Legion. Luckily, many Norwegians in the coastal areas spoke some English and so co-operation with the civilian medical services and those of the Norwegian army was of a high order. Mutual respect and sympathy also managed to prevent a total breakdown of medical arrangements between the Allied forces,[4] although relations were sometimes strained. Colonel Ernest Scott, commanding a Territorial field ambulance at Narvik, recorded in his diary that the chief MO of a French aid post was 'a supercilious perisher' who had tried to make Scott's ambulance carry a number of healthy men, despite his protests that he was only to carry the wounded.[5]

There was no easy solution, either, to the problem of transporting casualties across the snow-capped mountains and valleys around Namsos and Andalsnes. In these areas, the regimental staff of the respective national forces, plus detachments from British field ambulances, provided medical cover for the expeditionary force. The latter evacuated the sick and wounded using a relay system, with resting posts established en route. But the rugged terrain made carrying stretchers very laborious, especially once the snow had begun to melt. One medical officer engaged in evacuating the wounded from around Namsos recalled that he had taken 'seven casualties by one motor ambulance to Snasa, a terrible journey as the road was in a shocking condition due to combined effects of thaw and military traffic. It was more like a farm track than a main road. The 40 kilometres took 3½ hours.'[6]

[3] Ibid. 19.   [4] Ibid. 20–1.
[5] CMAC RAMC 478/1, Diary of Col. Ernest Scott, 14 May.
[6] PRO WO 222/1480, quoted in 'Campaign in Norway', 9.

Fortunately, casualties were not too heavy, despite a number of soldiers falling victim to frostbite.[7]

Once the wounded had been brought down to landing posts on the fjords they were carried by one of the small steamers ('puffers') to one of the two ships which acted as dressing stations, to the CCSs at Taorstad, or to the General Hospital at Harstad. Casualties requiring immediate evacuation were sometimes taken directly to waiting destroyers, although most were retained for evacuation en masse by hospital ship. The transportation of casualties by water had immense advantages in a mountainous area like the Norwegian coast, but it was often difficult to find vessels to carry casualties, as many were requisitioned for rations and military equipment. These boats were also very slow (averaging 6 to 8 miles per hour) and suffered from frequent breakdowns, and so were sitting ducks for German aircraft. The report on the medical aspects of the campaign stated that:

It should be borne in mind that the water evacuation was at all times liable to interference by bombing. The Germans took no notice whatever of the Red Cross with which the larger ships were marked, and ultimately it was found necessary to substitute trained naval crews for the Norwegians, who deserted rather than face the fierce and frequent air attacks to which all the craft were subjected.[8]

Throughout the war many similar allegations were made against the German forces, although it was not always clear that violations of the Red Cross were deliberate. The campaign in Norway alerted the British Army to the practical problems involved in the evacuation of the wounded, especially when transport was subjected to aerial attack. It also demonstrated the vital importance of proper planning and organization, which the Norwegian campaign manifestly lacked. Perhaps the only valuable lesson of a specific kind was the need to provide resuscitation facilities for all wounded troops at the earliest possible opportunity. In Norway, facilities for blood transfusion were available only in the general hospital at Harstad and one of the casualty clearing stations, so wounded men often had to wait some time before resuscitation.[9] Medical officers involved in this and subsequent campaigns agreed that blood transfusion needed to be early and plentiful if it was to be effective in alleviating wound shock.

[7] PRO WO 222/1480, quoted in 'Campaign in Norway', 35.
[8] Ibid. 8.
[9] CMAC, RAMC 1816/6/1/3, Major R. V. Facey, 'Report by Pathologist, 22 GH on Mobile Blood Bank'.

France and Belgium

A few months after war was declared in September 1939 the British Expeditionary Force (BEF) was dispatched to forward positions in France and Belgium, running north from Maulde on the Belgian–German border and then southwest along the River Lys to Armentières. The numbers of men deployed mounted steadily, and by the end of April the total strength of the British Army in France was 394,165. Approximately 250,000 troops—the main fighting force—were stationed in forward areas and the rest in the rear, preparing installations for what was intended to be a much larger force to come.[10] Front-line troops in the corps area were served by their regimental medical establishment plus twenty-five field ambulances, while general hospitals (fifteen in total), convalescent depots, and medical stores were located along the lines of communication. These were served by six ambulance trains and motor ambulance convoys (MACs), which were controlled by GHQ. Headquarters was also in direct charge of the mobile laboratories and a number of hygiene sections and casualty clearing stations (CCSs). Major-General J. W. F. Scott, the Director of Medical Services (DMS), was based at the HQ near Arras, but the main base for medical purposes was Dieppe, where there were several specialist hospitals and store depots.[11]

In many respects medical arrangements for the BEF resembled those that had developed on the Western Front during the First World War. The chain of evacuation extended, as in 1914–18, from the regimental aid post to the general hospitals at the base, via field ambulances and casualty clearing stations. The sick and wounded were to be evacuated, as before, by a combination of ambulance trains and motorized transport. Unlike in 1914, however, these were provided in what seemed to be adequate numbers from the very beginning (based on estimated casualties of 38,000).[12] Experience gained in the First World War also showed the value of forward treatment, rather than the evacuation of cases to the United Kingdom. In 1914 the Director of Military Operations had opposed plans for forward treatment on the grounds that evacuation to Britain would be good for morale,[13] but heavy casualties forced the Army quickly to abandon its policy. As the manpower crisis intensified, it became necessary to return casualties to duty as quickly

---

[10] L. F. Ellis, *History of the Second World War: The War in France and Flanders 1939–1940* (London: HMSO, 1953), 19–20.

[11] PRO 222/1479, 'Movements of British Field Ambulances, B.E.F. from 10 May to Evacuation, Dunkirk'; '[Medical Cover for BEF] 1st Phase: 3 September 1939–9 May 1940', 2–5.

[12] PRO WO 177/1, 'Report of Committee on Evacuation of Casualties, 28 October 1939'.

[13] PRO WO 106/49A/2, 'Outline of the Scheme and Details regarding Mobilization and Staff Arrangements, chapter XI—Medical'.

as possible; forward treatment also appeared to be more effective. In 1939–40 it was decided from the outset to treat the bulk of casualties as near the front as possible. The only cases to be evacuated back to England were those requiring an absence from duty of more than twenty-eight days. Complex injuries, such as maxillo-facial and some orthopaedic cases, would be given preliminary treatment in special hospitals or wards in France and then sent back to England from Dieppe.[14]

Another difference was that medical units were more widely dispersed than they had been in 1914–18. The threat posed to ground forces by aircraft meant that there could be no large concentrations of troops, either on the front line or in rest areas to the rear. British troops were therefore scattered in small contingents all over the countryside, as were the smaller medical units. The same policy also applied to the General Staff, who were dispersed throughout a number of villages around Arras. Though necessary from a military point of view, the dispersal of medical personnel created problems. Despite the assistance of the French authorities, communication by telephone proved—as in Norway—to be unreliable, quite apart from the danger of a beach of security. Commanders and senior medical staff found that the only way to gain effective control over medical units was to visit them in person, which entailed a considerable waste of time.[15]

The wide dispersal of soldiers aggravated other problems confronting the medical authorities. Not the least of these was the prevention of venereal disease, which had been responsible for many of the non-battle casualties in France and Flanders during the First World War.[16] The problem in 1939–40 was potentially even worse because the battle area was no longer denuded of its civilian population, as it had been for much of 1914–18. British troops were now scattered across the country in small numbers and billeted close to, or even with, civilians. As well as increasing the likelihood of soldiers meeting sexual partners, dispersal made it more difficult to keep them under effective control. Since most were not quartered in camps but in billets, soldiers also lacked the Army's usual recreational facilities, and boredom quickly set in. According to many MOs, this contributed largely to the high incidence of drunkenness and VD among troops during their first months on the Continent. By contrast with 1914–18, the VD rate was actually higher in Corps areas nearer the front than at the base and along the lines of communications; a fact which some MOs ascribed to the larger number of fit,

[14] PRO WO 177/1, '[Medical Cover for BEF] 1st Phase', 7; Col. Hood for DMS to Cmdt., Medical Base and DDMS Lines of Communication, 7 Oct. 1939.

[15] Ibid. 11–12.

[16] Mark Harrison, 'The British Army and the Problem of Venereal Disease in France and Egypt During the First World War', *Medical History*, 40 (1996), 437–52.

virile young men in forward areas. Others said that it had more to do with the downturn in trade close to the front, 'where the population was poor and partly Polish' [immigrant labourers], and where 'the unemployed shop-girl frequently became the fully employed prostitute'.[17]

The first month in France was undoubtedly the worst as far as VD was concerned, with an admission rate of three per thousand troops—equivalent to a yearly rate of thirty-six per thousand (the highest rate recorded for the BEF in 1914–18 was thirty-two per thousand). But the authorities acted quickly to combat the disease, attacking a number of fronts simultaneously. Although the BEF in 1918 had found it necessary to abandon medically regulated prostitution on account of public criticism, the old system of regulated brothels was instituted in France and Belgium in 1939 and continued until the evacuation. The effectiveness of these measures was called into question when it was revealed that the civilian doctors charged with inspecting women in the brothels (and sending them for compulsory treatment if necessary) took a relaxed attitude to their work. The situation apparently improved when French military doctors took over the inspection of brothels used by the French and British armies, but any subsequent improvement in VD rates may well have been due to other factors.[18] These 'tolerated houses' were also, as in 1914–18, the target of the purity lobby in Britain, which denounced the use of licensed brothels on the grounds that they encouraged immorality. The British Social Hygiene Council (BSHC) bemoaned the absence in the Army of 'any positive teaching on sex [*sic*] behaviour, and any recognition . . . of the need for giving full effect to the expectation of a high moral standard of conduct'.[19] In this endeavour it received support from a handful of military medical officers, including the venereologist L. W. Harrison, who assisted the BSHC in drafting its propaganda.[20]

There was, however, one matter on which the Army and the BSHC saw eye to eye, and that was the desirability of 'contact tracing', whereby VD patients were ordered to report the woman who infected them and to encourage her to seek treatment. The latter course of action had been the established practice of civilian clinics in Britain for some time.[21] From November 1939 medical officers with the BEF were issued with forms to be completed during interviews with each VD patient and designed to ascertain the whereabouts of 'diseased prostitutes'. The MO had to ask his patient for details

[17] PRO WO 35.
[18] Ibid. 36.
[19] CMAC SA/BSH A.2/19, Meeting of the British Social Hygiene Council (BSHC), War Executive Committee, 6 May 1940.
[20] Ibid., Meeting of the BSHC, 1 Apr. 1940.   [21] Ibid.

regarding the date upon which he exposed himself to infection, the occurrence of the first symptoms, the location of the woman's house or brothel, and her name, nationality, and appearance.[22]

Though the Army and civilian groups placed considerable emphasis on contact tracing, many MOs doubted its practicality. The likelihood, as they saw it, was that the woman could not be identified, or that the soldier had exposed himself to infection on more than one occasion. The most effective method of keeping VD under control, according to the Deputy Director of Hygiene for the BEF, Colonel Hepple, was through propaganda in the form of leaflets, and lectures by NCOs and commanding officers. The Army also established ablution centres where men could disinfect themselves after sexual intercourse, and organized entertainment to relieve men of the boredom that had apparently led many into vice.[23] Condoms were also freely available from regimental MOs. These measures owed much to the efforts of Colonel L. W. Harrison, who had distinguished himself as a venereologist during the First World War. Harrison was a realist as well as a moralist: while he was critical of the absence of moral teaching within the Army, he tried to ensure that soldiers reduced their risk of infection during intercourse. He also emphasized the need for effective treatment and, at his request, all regimental MOs received training in the prevention and treatment of VD before they were dispatched to France.[24]

The War Office *Memorandum on Venereal Diseases* epitomized Harrison's approach. While it advised lectures on abstinence and sexual morality (construed widely to include the soldier's duty to his family, country, and regiment), it made detailed provisions for so-called 'ablution rooms', which were to be established in all large military stations and brothels. Each ablution room was to be manned by two trained attendants and equipped with plentiful supplies of the disinfectants potassium permanganate and perchloride of mercury, which were to be rubbed into the genitalia following sexual intercourse. Condoms were an optional extra, but it was noted that those regiments that made them available had the lowest rates of VD. Those men who bothered to disinfect themselves after intercourse were likely to be confronted with an unfamiliar array of equipment and disinfecting creams, and a set of instructions which read:

Direction 1.—Take three pieces of wool from the box. Pour lotion into the bowl. Soak the wool in lotion and with one piece thoroughly wash the penis and parts

[22] PRO WO 177/1, 'Medical Administrative Instructions', No. 12, 23 Nov. 1939.

[23] Ibid., Col. Hepple, 'Memorandum on Hygiene', 16 Oct. 1939.

[24] Communication to the author from Dr R. S. Morton, MBE—a distinguished venereologist who served six years in the RAMC in Europe and the Middle East.

around it. With the second piece wash the knob, ring and bridle string and with the third piece the mouth of the pipe. Throw the used wool in the bucket.

Direction 2.—Take a tube out of the left-hand bowl and insert it into the end of the rubber tubing, open the clip and let the lotion flow. Wash out the mouth of the pipe with the lotion. Close the clip. Take the tube from the rubber tubing and place it in the right-hand bowl.

Direction 3.—Thoroughly dry the penis with a clean piece of wool.

Direction 4.—Rub the ointment well in, especially in to the knob, round the ring or girdle and the bridle string. Rub in for five minutes.

Direction 5.—Open the mouth of the pipe and insert a little ointment.

Direction 6.—Wash your hands and scrub your nails.

Direction 7.—Write on the ticket: Date and time of using the room. Time since having connection [sexual intercourse]. Last four figures of your number. Get the orderly to initial your ticket, keep your half, *i.e.* the half with your number on it.[25]

Studies of VD prevention indicated that these procedures were seldom carried out thoroughly, if at all, but combined with other measures they appear to have been more effective than punishment. At first, any British soldier who contacted VD faced a reduction of pay while absent from duty, together with postponement of leave for six months. This was soon abandoned when it became clear that punishment led men with VD to conceal their infections and to attempt to treat it themselves with dubious preparations available in local pharmacies. In this, the British followed the French, whose army had abandoned punishment for VD infection some years before. As a deterrent to infection, the DMS decided to treat all VD cases as close to their units as possible, rather than sending men to the base or to England.[26] Forward treatment was intended as a disincentive to malingering as well as a more effective means of returning soldiers to duty.

Once punishment was abandoned, and propaganda and other 'positive' measures had been established, the VD rate in the BEF began to decline. By the beginning of May, on the eve of the German attack, the monthly rate had fallen to just over two per thousand—equivalent to an annual rate of nearly twenty-six per thousand.[27] Though much higher than the annual military rate in the United Kingdom (almost nine per thousand[28]), it was significantly lower than in 1939. The BEF was also fortunate in that new forms

[25] *Memorandum on Venereal Disease—1936* (London: HMSO, 1936), 146.

[26] PRO WO 222/12, Consulting Venereologist, 'Summary of Policy and Action, September 1939–August 1943, 5–8; WO 177/1, 35–6.

[27] PRO WO 177/1, 37.

[28] PRO WO 222/12, Consulting Venereologist, 'Summary of Plan and Action', 5.

of treatment for venereal diseases had reduced the period in which a soldier was normally absent from duty. The treatment for the most serious venereal disease—syphilis—was founded on the concurrent and intermittent use of neo-arsphenamine (an arsenical preparation similar to the established drug Salvarsan) and bismuth, a treatment that had been used with some success in the United Kingdom. For early syphilis the minimum amount of treatment was four weekly courses of 5.85 grammes of neo-arsphenamine, but this was reduced to 4.05 grammes following concerns that the drug might occasionally cause jaundice. The drugs normally used to treat the most common venereal disease—gonorrhoea—were sulphonamide preparations, the dose varying according to the doctor concerned. It was found that intensive treatment with 20 grammes of sulphonamide drugs, over four or five days, gave the best results.[29] With the exception of chronic cases, which were referred to general hospitals, all VD patients in the BEF were treated in field ambulances and CCSs, thus preventing the serious drain of manpower from front-line units that had occurred during the First World War.[30]

After VD, the health problem that gave greatest cause for concern in the BEF was the poor state of the men's teeth. As in the First World War, the dental condition of many members of the BEF was far from satisfactory. Disease, dietary deficiency, and oral sepsis abounded, and only a small proportion of new recruits had received regular dental attention. This state of affairs was due partly to the poor nutritional state of some sections of the working class, and partly to the lowering of the Dental Standard of 1930 and its final abolition in 1938. This lowering of standards allowed into the Army many men who would formerly have been excluded from military service. To make matters worse, quite a few of the medical officers charged with examining new recruits were indifferent to matters of dental health.[31]

All men entering the Army were entitled to free dental treatment, including free dentures.[32] Given the number of men with severe dental problems, this placed a great strain on the dental services of the BEF. In the Pioneer Corps, for example, almost 75 per cent of the men required extensive dental treatment. Although the British Army now had the benefit of the regular dental service that had been established in 1921, the number of dentists attached to the BEF was far too few, and the shortage of dental surgeons and technicians was still acute in the spring of 1940. Writing soon after the war,

29 PRO WO 222/12, Consulting Venereologist, 'Summary of Plan and Action', 10–11.

30 PRO WO 222/1479, 'Conference on Venereal Disease held at G.H.Q., 9 December 1939', in papers collected by Col. J. Ingram, Consultant Venereologist, BEF.

31 PRO WO 177/1, 38.

32 Ibid., Maj.-Gen. J. W. C. Scott, 'Medical Arrangements During the Period of Assembly', 14 Sept. 1939, 7.

the Adjutant-General, Sir Ronald Adam, recalled that: 'The need for a national health service was brought home by the condition of many of the recruits joining the army. The state of teeth of soldiers was terrible. It was estimated that some 90% of all intakes required some dental treatment, 40% extensive dental treatment and some 10% were unable to eat properly without dentures.'[33] The situation in 1940 was such that the DMS was forced to issue an order permitting temporary treatment only, or a set of dentures if necessary. His aim was to treat all men in forward areas and therefore to prevent a massive haemorrhage of manpower from front-line units.[34] The full range of treatment was to be completed later, but this did not become possible until after the Lend-Lease agreement of 1941, which gave dental surgeons the latest equipment from the United States.[35]

Apart from the high incidence of VD and dental problems, the health of the BEF was good and hospital admissions never exceeded 2.8 per cent of total strength.[36] This was a remarkable achievement, considering the hard winter of 1939–40 and some early problems with sanitation and hygiene. During the first few months in France and Belgium sanitary conditions were poor: many MOs had no previous knowledge of the Army or preventive medicine, and the urgent need for the construction of defensive works meant that men were not available for sanitary fatigues. Some officers in command of units—particularly those holding temporary commissions—also cared little for hygiene and sanitation, so conservancy arrangements and personal cleanliness often left much to be desired.[37] In September, for example, the Assistant Director of Hygiene with the BEF reported that the sanitary condition of Chanzy Barracks, occupied by British and French troops, was wholly unsatisfactory and that it represented a constant source of danger to the men.[38] The BEF's Deputy Director of Hygiene (DDH) also complained that the precautionary blackout had 'added to the temptation of men to go no further than outside the billets [to relieve themselves], and hard though it is to believe it, men urinated from their beds and some actually defecated into their blankets'.[39]

Despite this unpromising situation, there were marked improvements in both sanitation and personal cleanliness in the months before the German invasion. In part this can be attributed to a continuous stream of propaganda

[33] LHCMA, Adam Papers 3/13, narrative of aspects of work as Adjutant-General, 'Chap.IV—Medical Problems', 3.
[34] PRO WO 177/1, '[Medical Cover for BEF] 1ˢᵗ Phase', 38–40.
[35] LHCMA, Adam Papers 3/13, 'Chap.IV—Medical Problems', 3.
[36] PRO WO 177/1, '1ˢᵗ Phase', 34.
[37] Ibid. 16.
[38] Ibid., 'Monthly Report by DDH', Sept. 1939, 1.
[39] Ibid., 'Monthly Report by DDH', Oct. 1939, 1.

emphasizing the soldier's duty to keep 'fighting fit', and in part to the insistence that officers should take sanitary matters seriously. Unit commanders were reminded that it was they, and not their medical officers, who were ultimately responsible for the health of their men. This was especially true of skin infections, like scabies, which were common among newly mobilized troops (most military hospitals in France had special scabies wards in order treat these patients in isolation).[40] Colonel Hepple, the DDH, noted that:

A considerable proportion of sick wastage in the Field is due to skin diseases, scabies and infestation with lice. These conditions are brought about by a failure to maintain a satisfactory degree of personal cleanliness. All junior officers should be taught how to spot them and when discovered the men suffering should be ordered to report to their Medical Officer for treatment. The Regimental Medical Officer will also inspect the men at frequent intervals but it should be fully understood that the responsibility for maintaining cleanliness in the unit falls solely on Unit Officers.[41]

This 'FFI'—the 'Free From Infection' examination—was viewed as mandatory at agreed intervals and was designed primarily to detect scabies and lice. It was essentially a relic of the First World War and some MOs were sceptical that it did much good, but when it was used in conjunction with frequent baths and changes of clothing, it may have had some impact upon the incidence of louse-borne infections. Mobile bathhouses arrived in France in November, after which the incidence of skin diseases began to fall from its peak in September–October.[42]

Eight months of uneasy peace were shattered on 10 May 1940, when the Germans invaded the Low Countries through the densely forested and weakly defended Ardennes. The BEF moved forward into Belgium, to the River Dyle, to meet the German attack, but on 16 May it was forced to retreat to the frontier defences and to defend the GHQ at Arras. These positions were held until 28 May, when the BEF withdrew to Dunkirk. From 10 to 18 May casualties were dealt with more or less according to the medical plan, with men being evacuated from field ambulances to the base via CCSs. After 18 May the rapid German advance meant that a greater degree of flexibility and improvization was necessary, so CCSs were placed under the control of deputy directors of medical services (DDsMS) in the corps areas, rather than centrally at GHQ, as before. The CCSs were increasingly called upon to function as small general hospitals, holding casualties for a longer time than expected, especially after 21 May, when hospitals in the Dieppe and Étaples areas were cut off by the German advance. This led the DMS,

[40] IWM 73/58/1, W. L. McWilliam, 'Civil and Military Medical Services of World War II' (Account as Nursing Orderly with RAMC, France and UK, 1940–4), 46.

[41] PRO WO 177/1, Col. Hepple, 'Memorandum on Hygiene', 5.

[42] Ibid., '[Medical Cover for BEF] 1st Phase', 20; communication from Dr R. S. Morton, MBE.

Major-General Scott, to revise plans for the evacuation of casualties from Dieppe and to concentrate on Calais instead, but the establishment of medical units in Calais was soon found to be impossible due to enemy action and difficult communications between the port and forward areas. Scott then decided that his only course of action was to evacuate casualties from CCSs in the rear—by road or rail—straight to hospital carriers waiting off Dunkirk. This scheme functioned up to 24 May, but the heavy German bombardment meant that trains were frequently delayed.[43]

It is difficult to generalize about the fate of medical units in the few weeks between the German invasion and the evacuation of the BEF; not only did their experiences vary widely, but many documents relating to the AMS were lost or destroyed during the final evacuation. Those unit histories that have survived do, however, provide an insight into the panic and confusion created by the German advance and its effects on the treatment and evacuation of casualties. Typical of the experiences of forward medical units was that of No. 10 Field Ambulance, which was ordered on 14 May to move into Belgium to provide medical support to front-line troops facing the German invasion. On arriving at Vilvorde, a small town a few miles south of Brussels, the staff of No. 10 found it full of refugees and the tattered remnant of the Belgian army. The field ambulance then moved on to Brussels itself, where it established its Main Dressing Station (MDS) in what had formerly been a school. Within three days the ambulance was on the move again, withdrawing to the town of Neuemarre and ultimately back to France. By the 29 May No. 10 had arrived on the Normandy coast, at the seaside resort of Coxyde-les-Bains, and established its MDS in the Grand Hotel Regina. Here, like other field ambulances, it was called upon to play the role of a large CCS, taking incoming casualties who could not be absorbed by larger units.[44]

Some idea of the work done by this and other medical units can be gained from the description given by its commander, Colonel Arthur Cox:

All cases on arrival were taken into a large room on the ground floor, which was also used as a ward capable of holding eighty stretcher cases. In this room, they sorted those requiring immediate and urgent treatment, [these] being taken into a large MI room, where three MOs were continuously at work. From this room cases requiring operation were taken to the kitchen of the hotel, where a surgical team was at work all night.[45]

[43] PRO WO 22/1479, '[Medical Cover for BEF] 2nd Phase: 10 May to Evacuation', 2–3.

[44] CMAC RAMC 801/13/3, Col. Arthur Cox, 'Notice of Events 10. Field Ambulance, 10 May–1 June 1940', entries for 10 May, 14 May, 15 May, 22 May, 29 May.

[45] Ibid., entry of 29 May.

By noon on 30 May all three floors of the hotel were full and every room and corridor was packed with stretchers; but relief came the following day, when all the patients were removed to Rosendal, a few miles from Dunkirk, to await evacuation.[46] By this time the German bombardment of the town had intensified and Dunkirk had become an inferno. Medical staff feared for their patients, but the vast majority were evacuated safely by 1 June. Evacuation from the beach-head initially created some anxiety, as it was soon realized that there were not enough boats to ferry casualties to the waiting ships. Like many other units, the staff of No. 10 were forced to improvise, pulling down rowing-boats from the dunes above the beach and rowing out with casualties to a paddle-steamer anchored offshore. Others waded or swam out to other ships, and at least two members of the unit rowed over to Margate with their patients.[47]

Field ambulances found it possible to adapt quite easily to mobile warfare, but this was not the case with clearing hospitals such as No. 133 CCS. On May 10 No. 133 was forced by the German advance to withdraw from its site 15 kilometres north of Amiens, and while most of the patients were accommodated within motor transport, around forty had to make the journey to St-Pol by foot. The movement of this and other clearing hospitals was painfully slow, as they were overburdened with equipment and patients. Many, including No. 133 CCS, found themselves cut off from the rest of the BEF by the rapid movement of German units. The commander, Colonel Morris, felt that their only chance of escape was to divide the unit into three parts, one of which was headed by Major D. I. McCallum, who later recounted the following story of his escape from France.

McCallum's column made its way slowly westward for a few miles to the Doullen–Aux-le-Chateau Road, which they dashed across under fire from the machine gun of a tank. Their escape was only assured after swimming across a nearby river. Afterwards the column travelled by night and slept by day, surrounded all the time by German motorized units. Some of the men had to be left behind owing to exhaustion, although they were generally left in farm buildings and provided with ample food. The rest pushed on for four or five nights through the forests of Crécy, narrowly avoiding discovery by German patrols. On the sixth night they waded thigh-deep through marshland and luckily found shelter with a French official. Here they remained for one week, surrounded by Germans but with plenty to eat and a much-needed opportunity for rest.

After receiving a warning that the Germans were coming, the party moved off again, and on the following day reached the River Somme, both banks

[46] CMAC RAMC 801/13/3, entries of 30 May, 31 May.   [47] Ibid., entry of 1 June.

of which were already lined with German machine-gun posts. After waiting for several days until conditions were right, they decided to cross the river at low tide. Those who could swim across did so, while non-swimmers were placed inside the inflated inner tubes of motor tyres and pulled across by a rope attached to the stronger swimmers. Nine of the eleven managed to cross the river but two became separated in the dash across the banks; McCallum was unable to say what had happened to them. For the next five or six hours the remaining men walked barefoot and almost naked, until they happened upon some kit and clothing abandoned by the Highland Regiment. The next few nights were spent walking through German-occupied territory until they reached the River Seine, which they crossed in a raft made of inflated inner tubes. Shortly afterwards the group narrowly avoided capture by German sentries by posing as French refugees. Fortunately, the Germans were less fluent in French than McCallum and his men. After several more days of walking, they reached the coast opposite Jersey, only to find that the Germans had occupied the island. So the decision was made to proceed south to the Pyrenees, which seemed to be the only route by which they could hope to escape from France. McCallum and his party got as far as Marseilles where, exhausted, they surrendered themselves to the French authorities. Having obtained false passports from a Polish ex-serviceman's organization, the party managed to escape on a ship bound for Casablanca, and then went on to Lisbon, where they made for the British Consulate, after which their return to Britain was arranged.[48]

Unlike Major McCallum and his men, most medical personnel and their patients escaped from France via Dunkirk, or in lesser numbers from points further south. But the experiences of No. 133 CCS illustrate the confusion that gripped almost all forward medical units in the weeks after the German invasion. Many had no idea of their position in relation to enemy forces.[49] In the rush to withdraw, some were forced to abandon much of their equipment, while others were overrun by the Germans or suffered attacks from the air.[50] Sharing their flight along the roads were civilian refugees, fleeing the fighting further to the north and east. As civilian services had broken down all over the northern invasion area, many of the refugees were in a pitiful condition, lacking medical or any other form of assistance.[51]

The evacuation area itself afforded little relief from this grim spectacle. Dunkirk witnessed many pitiful scenes, as desperate civilian refugees

[48] PRO WO 222/16, Maj. D. I. McCallum, RAMC, 'Escape from France, May–June 1940'.
[49] PRO WO 177/2, Col. A. D. Stirling, 'Medical Situation Report No. 3—1200 hours, 10 June 1940'.
[50] PRO WO 177/3, Col. H. Walker, 'Account of Events May–June 1940', 2.
[51] 'Gun Buster', *Return Via Dunkirk* (London: White Lion, 1975; first edn., 1940), 135.

clamoured around the ships' gangways and the wounded on the beaches were subjected to constant aerial attack. One British soldier recalled that: 'Down on the beach you immediately felt yourself surrounded by a deadly evil atmosphere. A horrible stench of blood and mutilated flesh pervaded the place . . . We might have been walking through a slaughter house on a hot day.'[52] W. L. McWilliam, a nursing orderly, told a similar story: 'As we went along the beach we saw many who had been blown to pieces, and we walked along searching for any living amongst the dead and found one at the back of a sand hill. He was a soldier, half buried in the sand, breathing feebly, and blood coming from ears, nose and mouth . . .'[53] The soldier, who had a fractured skull, died before he reached hospital. Another wounded man, anxious that the truth about the operation be told, protested that: 'The newspapers are full of the story of the evacuation from Dunkirk, of its discipline, of its wonderful organisation. Well it didn't seem particularly well organised to me.'[54] If the experiences of most medical units are anything to by, he was correct, for the success of the final evacuation owed a good deal to chance. As is well known, the evacuation was only possible because of Hitler's decision to concentrate his ground forces on other objectives.[55]

For medical reasons it was impossible to evacuate all the British wounded from France. Apart from those captured during the German advance, many had to be left behind because they could not be moved without endangering their health. In view of this regrettable necessity, some medical personnel remained in France to care for the wounded, and to see that they were well treated in the likely event of their being discovered by the Germans. In some units the medical staff drew lots to decide who should remain.[56] Major E. R. C. Walker was one of those who stayed in France, and his experiences shed some light on the fortunes of those who entered captivity. He, his patients, and other medical staff were captured near the small Normandy town of St-Valery-en-Caux on 11 June. They were treated well by the German medical officers and the latter arranged their disposal to hospitals in Rouen, where many stayed until February 1941. Walker then accompanied the patients to a hospital in Germany, which was soon visited by a commission of medically trained observers. The task of the commission was to assess medical arrangements for POWs and to judge whether any should be repatriated on medical grounds. The commission found conditions at this

---

[52] 'Gun Buster', *Return Via Dunkirk* (London: White Lion, 1975; first edn., 1940), 245.

[53] IWM 73/58/1, McWilliam, 'Civil and Military Medical Services', 66–7.

[54] Capt. Sir Basil Bartlett, *My First War—An Army Officer's Journal for May 1940* (London: Chatto & Windus, 1940), 127.

[55] See N. Harman, *Dunkirk: The Necessary Myth* (London: Hodder & Stoughton, 1980); P. Turnbull, *Dunkirk: Anatomy of Disaster* (London: Batsford, 1978).

[56] IWM 73/58/1, McWilliam, 'Civil and Military Medical Services', 67.

hospital 'disgracefully inadequate', and noted that patients received only 1,200 calories per day, which had caused all of them to lose weight. After frequent protests and the arrival of Red Cross parcels, conditions at the hospital began to improve, but Walker was far from satisfied with arrangements for medical care. 'With one or two exceptions, the Germans doctors appeared to be astonishingly ignorant medically', he claimed.[57]

Walker remained with his British patients until June 1941, when he appears to have returned to Britain. Medical staff were among those persons designated 'protected personnel' under the Geneva Convention, and as such were to be sent back to the country to which they belonged as soon as the military situation permitted. The Convention also allowed some medical staff to remain with prisoners, provided that a special agreement had been concluded between belligerent nations. Such an agreement existed between Britain and Germany, but both sides claimed that it was abused by the other and that doctors were sometimes detained against their will. A War Office memorandum on the fate of medical officers in captivity stated that: 'When those who were "detained" in Germany over a period of years pointed out this breach to the German authorities they were met with the counter accusation that the British Government was likewise detaining German "protected personnel".'[58]

In the absence of any impartial assessment, it is impossible to judge how far this agreement was breached; in any case, it is far more important to establish whether arrangements at the camps met the conditions of the Geneva Convention, which stipulated that medical care for POWs should be equal to that given to combatants. As Major Walker's experiences suggest, the picture was mixed, and the international medical commissions that regularly inspected POW camps in Germany confirm this. Some camp hospitals, like Lazaret Freising, which served POWs in Wehrkries VII, were efficient institutions, with clean, well-equipped wards and cheerful staff.[59] But in other camps, such as Sandbostel, which was later to become a notorious camp for political prisoners, there were complaints that patients were forced to leave hospital to do heavy manual labour,[60] and that relations between British and German medical staff were poor, owing to the draconian regime imposed by their commandants.[61] Another common cause of complaint was that patients received insufficient quantities of medicine, despite pleas from British MOs.

[57] PRO WO 222/245, Maj. E. R. C. Walker, 'Account of 500 British Wounded POW, June 1940–June 1941'.

[58] Ibid., 'Memorandum on Position of British MOs in Captivity'.

[59] PRO WO 222/1361, 'Report on Reserve Lazaret Freising', 22 Oct. 1941, Medical Quarterly Reports, POW Camps, Germany, 1941.

[60] Ibid., 'Report on Lazaret of Stalag X B, Sandbostel', 21 Nov. 1941.

[61] Ibid., 'Report on Oflag IV', 20 Oct. 1941.

British doctors at Rottenmuenster POW camp complained constantly that they did not possess sufficient supplies of vitamin B to treat cases of beriberi among British troops, or sufficient drugs to treat cases of malaria among soldiers captured in the Mediterranean.[62] But the worst POW camp, as far as the medical care of British soldiers was concerned, was Stalag XVII D. Inspectors visiting the camp in October 1941 reported that toilet facilities were primitive and that the camp was generally unhygienic. The hospital used by British POWs was overcrowded and there were no provisions to separate contagious from non-contagious cases. There were also reports that British medical staff were beaten by their German colleagues. The commissioners concluded that: 'Stalag XVIII D is absolutely inadequate for its purpose. Everything is in disorder and very badly organised. The sanitary conditions are deplorable . . . The camp is a real danger to the health of the prisoners, and it is to be hoped that very serious measures will be taken before the winter to improve the present conditions.'[63] The quarterly medical reports on POW camps did record some improvements, but the increasing scarcity of food and medical supplies towards the end of the war caused conditions to deteriorate badly.

When they evacuated France, the medical services, like other branches of the Army, were compelled to leave behind much of their equipment, despite attempts to salvage essential stores in the last days before evacuation.[64] Some general hospitals were left more or less intact, with all their stores and the personal belongings of their staff.[65] But those who returned from France did not leave entirely empty-handed, for they had learned some valuable lessons about the organization of medical services in mechanized warfare. One of the most important of these—which was to be emphasized again in subsequent campaigns—was the limited effectiveness of the old-style CCSs. These units were capable of treating a large number of casualties using the 'twin table' system of surgery developed in the First World War.[66] One patient was anaesthetized as another underwent surgery: a process that had been developed in response to a number of time-and-motion studies conducted towards the end of the war. But CCSs had evolved in the static conditions of the Western Front, and were too heavy to be shifted as often as they needed to be in a fully mechanized conflict. The rapidity of the German Blitzkrieg also prevented medical officers from following what many believed to be the best practice in the evacuation of wounded men; namely, primary treatment and

[62] PRO WO 222/1361, 'Report on Reserve Lazaret, Rottenmuenster', 5 Nov. 1941.

[63] Ibid., 'Report on Stalag XVIII D', 3, 23 Oct. 1941.

[64] PRO WO 222/244, Brig. R. Ogier Ward, 'Last Days in France, 1940: Diary of the Offanville CCS, Dieppe Medical Base Area'.

[65] CMAC RAMC 877, T. D. Pratt and G. A. Bramley, 'The Story of the 18th General Hospital 1939–45', 13.

[66] IWM 87/9/1(P), Diaries of Miss E. M. Luker, QAIMNS, Diary of 1940, No. 12 CCS, France.

the immobilization of wounds using the method developed by Trueta in the Spanish Civil War. Although most surgeons in the BEF were impressed by Trueta's work, there was not enough time in most cases to perform primary suture or to place wounded limbs in plaster casts.[67] The general method of dealing with wounds in forward units was to dress them with the antiseptic solution EUSOL (Edinburgh University Solution of Lime), and to administer morphia for pain relief.[68]

France in 1940 was also the testing ground for the Army's new Blood Transfusion Service. From the very beginning of the war it was recognized that blood transfusion was vital in the prevention of wound shock—a circulatory failure that closely resembled the effects of haemorrhage in its clinical features. If conducted early enough, before blood pressure had fallen below 90 millimetres, transfusion could restore the patient's blood volume, preventing the usual symptoms of wound shock: pallor, increased pulse rate, falling body temperature, vomiting, and in extreme cases, heart failure. The MRC's Committee on Traumatic Shock and Blood Transfusion, which reported in 1940, recommended that transfusion be carried out as far forward as possible, in resuscitation wards attached to CCSs, and even as far forward as the dressing stations of field ambulances.[69]

In line with current thinking, blood transfusion for the BEF was provided by Field Transfusion Units (FTUs) and a number of mobile refrigeration units that carried stores of blood. These units were assisted by a Blood Transfusion and Surgical Laboratory situated in the rear. FTUs were deployed in forward areas soon after the arrival of the BEF, but their duties were not clearly defined and there was initially some uncertainty as to the part they would play in the organization of the units (such as CCSs) to which they were attached.[70] Most of these problems were solved before the German invasion, but the transfusion service still found it difficult to cope, because of a shortage of blood. Up to 10 May only four FTUs had been able to open, and these were stocked with only enough blood required for routine surgery.[71] Immediately after the German invasion was announced all resting units were put into action, and the Blood Supply Depot at Bristol did its best to provide the necessary stocks of whole blood. In the nine days following the German invasion the Bristol depot supplied 990 bottles of whole blood and 116 of plasma, the production of which was still at an experimental stage.[72] Field trials with plasma during the summer of 1940 showed that it was effective in reducing wound shock and that it had no apparent

[67] Maj. J. S. Jeffrey, 'Treatment of War Wounds in France, May–June 1940', *Journal of the Royal Army Medical Corps*, 74 (1940), 347.
[68] IWM 73/58/1, McWilliam, 'Civil and Military Medical Services', 64.
[69] MRC, *The Treatment of Wound Shock* (London: HMSO, 1940), 3–5.
[70] PRO WO 222/1479, 'The Army Transfusion Service', 5.
[71] Ibid. 7.   [72] Ibid. 8.

side effects, although later experiences were to show that whole-blood trans-fusions were preferable in cases of severe injury.

The rapid response of the Bristol depot undoubtedly saved the lives of many of those wounded on the battlefield, but only a small number of cases actually benefited from transfusion compared with later campaigns. This was due to several factors: the rapidity of the German advance; the fact that some medical staff had not been properly trained; and the length of time taken for some casualties to reach a CCS at which transfusion was available. Owing to the breakdown of the chain of evacuation, many cases died before they reached a properly equipped unit.[73]

The British Army learned from these mistakes when organizing blood transfusion for the British force during the Western Desert campaigns. Among the main points it bore in mind were the need for an advanced blood bank (which, in France, had to be improvised from an FTU), and the need to maximize the full potential of the FTU, since too little advantage had been taken of its mobility. Too many FTUs were attached to cumbersome CCSs, which were unable to keep pace with the retreating army. The experiences of transfusion officers in France also demonstrated that such units were poorly equipped and that orderlies often lacked training in general nursing, as opposed to other technical skills. Generally, however, the experience had been a positive one, which proved that blood transfusion could be organized in the field on a much grander scale than had been attempted during the First World War. It also demonstrated the usefulness of blood and plasma in the prevention of wound shock. If the full benefits of transfusion were to be obtained in future, it became clear that all medical officers, orderlies, and nurses would require some knowledge of transfusion therapy, and that equip-ment and supplies of blood needed to be stored in all medical units and not just specialist ones.[74]

Casualties sustained by the BEF in France also showed that the treatment of burns was likely to form an important part of medical work in future cam-paigns involving armoured fighting vehicles. During May 1940 hospitals in Britain received many cases of severe burns, some so bad that veins could not be found in their bodies to insert the needles of saline drips.[75] Fortunately, injuries caused by flash burns and igniting fuel had been anticipated before the force was dispatched, and each tank crew had been provided with tannic jelly preparations in their first-aid kits. Surgeons who treated burns cases in hospitals back in the United Kingdom reckoned that men who had applied

[73] PRO WO 222/1479, 'The Army Transfusion Service', 10–11.   [74] Ibid. 12–17.
[75] IWM 89/19/1, See Mrs A. Radloff, 'Going in to Gooseberry Beach: Travels and Adventures of a Nursing Sister', 5.

these preparations fared better than those who had not. Within three to five days of wounding, the burnt area had usually coagulated and the loss of serum had been stemmed.[76] In early burns cases some surgeons also used intravenous morphia, which had the advantage of killing pain and ensuring the co-operation of the patient.[77]

In 1940 there was no generally agreed method of how to treat burns and no consensus over which specialists should be in charge of such cases. S. M. Cohen, a surgeon at an EMS hospital, observed that there had been a tendency to see burns treatment as lying within the domain of skin specialists, some of whom had begun to form special 'burns clinics'. This was not a development that Cohen welcomed. He believed that burns cases should be the responsibility of surgeons—like himself—who had more experience of sepsis, deformities, and sick patients, and some knowledge of how to perform blood transfusions and skin grafting.[78]

Cohen's preferred method was to administer an anaesthetic such as evipan or pentothal intravenously, and then to combat any bacterial infections with sulphonamide drugs. Diet was also important, according to Cohen, who gave his patients plenty of protein in order to replace lost serum. In addition to these medical treatments, burns patients were treated in the surgical theatre with preparations of silver nitrate and tannic acid, which were applied to the burnt area in order to stem further loss of serum and aid healing. Cohen claimed that the healing time of his patients was, on average, three-and-a-half weeks.[79]

Cohen's recommendations were subsequently endorsed by a special committee of the MRC, which also stressed the vital importance of first aid in the treatment of burns cases. However, the MRC advised that gauze impregnated with sterilized Vaseline was more suitable for application to facial burns than tannic acid, because of the deep stains which the latter left on the skin. Mrs Mary Morris, a nurse at the Kent and Sussex Hospital in Tunbridge Wells, recalled that the skin of burns patients treated with tannic acid set into a 'hard black cement'.[80] Once a patient had reached hospital, the MRC recommended that burns should be cleaned carefully with soap and water, followed by saline solution. After cleaning, the burnt area was to be dried and dusted with an antibacterial sulphonamide powder, and a coagulant was applied to all areas except hands, feet, and face. This coagulant was typically

[76] S. M. Cohen, 'Experience in the Treatment of War Burns', *British Medical Journal*, 24 Aug. 1940, p. 251.
[77] Communication from Dr R. S. Morton, MBE.
[78] Cohen, 'Treatment of War Burns', 251.
[79] Ibid. 252–3.
[80] IWM 80/38/1, Mrs Mary Morris, 'The Diary of a Wartime Nurse', I, 2, entry of 1 June 1940.

a mixture of 10 per cent each of silver nitrate and tannic acid, or alterna-
tively gentian violet or brilliant green. Areas of the body, such as the face,
which ought not to be tanned were to be dusted with sulphonamide powder
and covered with layers of gauze soaked in paraffin, kept moist by the constant drip of saline solution.[81] Despite some dissent, these remained the basic
principles of burns treatment until the advent of penicillin in military hospitals during the North African campaign.[82]

The return of men from France and Norway also provided some indication of the types of psychiatric casualties that could be expected in mechanized warfare. Even before the campaign began, psychiatric specialists had
speculated that 'active warfare' would produce fewer psychiatric casualties
than the trench warfare of 1914–18, which offered fewer opportunities for
soldiers to escape from enemy fire. Nevertheless, some cases of war neurosis
were expected to occur as a result of battle stress (particularly fear of hidden
dangers such as land mines)[83] and guilt over killing.[84] Provisions for psychiatric casualties were, therefore, made well in advance of the German invasion. The model was essentially that of the Western Front during 1917–18,
with the emphasis upon the forward treatment of all neurotic cases; psychotic
cases were to be evacuated straight to the United Kingdom on account of
their potentially disruptive influence. The medical plan provided for a specialist psychiatric centre—a kind of CCS—established close to one of the
railheads, in which there would be 300 beds to retain patients for observation and simple treatment. Those requiring further treatment would be sent
in the first instance to a 600-bed psychiatric hospital at the base and then,
if necessary, to the United Kingdom.[85] But these provisions proved to be
rather inadequate, and the disruption caused by the German blitzkrieg rarely
allowed psychiatric cases to receive specialist treatment in forward areas. The
vast majority of such casualties could not be treated until they returned to
Britain.

Much of British military psychiatry during the Second World War was
predicated on the assumption that war did not affect all men equally: that
is, that certain individuals were predisposed, by virtue of heredity or upbring-

[81] EMS Memorandum on 'The Local Treatment of Burns', *British Medical Journal*, 29 Mar.
1940, p. 489.

[82] See e.g. Maj. M. C. Oldfield, 'Burns in Wartime', *Journal of the Royal Army Medical Corps*,
77 (1941), 1–13.

[83] E. Wittkower and J. P. Spillane, 'Neuroses in Wartime', *British Medical Journal*, 10 Feb. 1940,
p. 224.

[84] For more on this matter see Joanna Bourke, *An Intimate History of Killing: Face-to-Face Killing
in Twentieth-Century Warfare* (London: Granta Books, 1999).

[85] PRO WO 222/1513, Maj.-Gen. R. Priest, 'Memorandum on Treatment of Psychiatric Cases
on Active Service Overseas'; 'Scheme for Medical Arrangements for Treatment of Psychiatric Cases
in Active Service Areas'.

ing, to suffer from mental breakdown. Though the First World War had led to an increasing emphasis on the trauma of combat as the most significant cause of war neuroses, the role of predisposing factors was not entirely eclipsed. In their study of war neuroses, published in 1917, the psychiatrists E. D. Adrian and L. R. Yealland wrote of a 'hysterical type of mind', characterized by weakness of will, hyper-suggestibility, and negative emotions. The majority of such cases, they felt, could be attributed either to low intelligence or to a history of personal or family instability.[86] Hugh Crichton Miller, one of the most distinguished psychiatrists of the First World War, also believed that there was such a thing as a 'hysterical disposition', which commonly stemmed from 'association with timorous or cruel parents, and harmful experiences in early life'.[87] Such opinions were echoed in the report of the War Office Committee on Shell-Shock, issued in 1922,[88] and in postwar literature on war neuroses such as F. C. Barlett's study, *Psychology and the Soldier* (1927). Bartlett, a Reader in Experimental Mental Psychology at Cambridge University, acknowledged, along with many Great War psychiatrists, that the roots of mental breakdown in wartime generally lay in the conflict between a man's instinct for self-preservation and the demands of wartime service. Yet he also maintained that there was a 'type of personality which can triumphantly survive such incompatibility, and there is another type which cannot do this'. One 'very important predisposing condition', according to Bartlett, was 'an unusual degree of shyness, or lack of sociability', which meant that such a man had few outlets for his feelings.[89]

On the eve of the Second World War the question of predisposition was still very much alive. Dr Francis Prideaux, the psychiatric expert at the Ministry of Pensions, reopened the issue in a memorandum of 1939, in which he argued that it had been a mistake, in the last war, to assume that most cases of neuroses were due primarily to the strain of combat. He believed that the policy of granting pensions to those discharged from the Army with war neurosis had provided soldiers with an incentive to maintain neurotic symptoms. Furthermore, he argued that most of the 40,000 men still drawing pensions had a 'constitutional predisposition' to nervous disorders. This view prevailed in official circles, where there was widespread concern over the cost of pensions in a future war. In 1939 it was therefore agreed that no pensions for war-related neuroses would be paid during the war, but that

[86] E. D. Adrian and L. R. Yealland, 'The Treatment of Some Common War Neuroses', *Lancet*, 9 June 1917, pp. 867–72.

[87] Hugh Crichton Miller, *Functional Nerve Disease: An Epitome of War Experience for the Practitioner* (London: Hodder & Stoughton, 1920), 53.

[88] PRO WO 32/4748, 'Report of the War Office Committee on Shell-Shock, 1922', 95.

[89] F. C. Bartlett, *Psychology and the Soldier* (Cambridge: Cambridge University Press, 1927), 196–9.

there would be a review once the war was over to make sure that 'genuine' cases were provided for.[90] Later in the war this policy was relaxed, but few very pensions were awarded to psychiatric casualties.

Although some psychiatrists took issue with the views aired by Prideaux, there were many—even on the liberal or progressive wing of British psychiatry—who broadly supported them, or at least who agreed that the matter of predisposition was important. E. Wittkower and J. P. Spillane, researchers at the Tavistock Clinic in London, concluded in March 1940 that individuals of a depressive, anxious, or timorous nature were generally unable to withstand the stresses of combat, although those with other mental problems, such as mild psychosis or so-called high-grade mental defectives, could make good soldiers.[91] The Tavistock Clinic had been founded after the First World War to treat soldiers suffering from war neuroses, and many of its staff were inclined towards psychoanalysis. They tended to search for the causes of mental illness in family circumstances, and particularly in traumatic events during childhood. Even though such ideas were far from pervasive, most psychiatrists and neurologists acknowledged the importance of family background or individual peculiarities in how a soldier coped with the stress of battle. Lieutenant-Colonel J. A. Hadfield at No. 41 General (Neuropathic) Hospital, who treated many of the psychiatric cases returning from France, concluded that: 'A striking feature of the cases in this war is the fact that so many of our patients *volunteered* the statement: "I have been nervous all my life: I have had depressed turns as long as I can remember." '[92] Hadfield claimed that out of a total of 326 cases treated in the course of 1940, there was 'predisposition of a constitutional or acquired type' in 82 per cent. In 69 per cent of cases this predisposition seemed to have its roots in early childhood and was therefore deep-seated.[93] Hadfield came to these conclusions after interviewing his patients, and there is little reason to doubt that many of those suffering from war neuroses did have a history of 'nervousness', if not mental instability. But this distinction between 'constitutional' and 'psychological' predisposition was spurious, to say the least. Although Hadfield stated precisely that 49.4 per cent of those predisposed to psychiatric breakdown were 'constitutional' cases and the remainder 'psychological', he provided no explanation of how he managed to separate physiological factors from the effects of upbringing.[94] Such vagueness was a hallmark of much of

---

[90] Ben Shephard, *Soldiers and Psychiatrists 1914–1994* (London: Jonathan Cape, 2000), 165–7.
[91] PRO WO 222/1513, 'Scheme for Medical Arrangements', 225.
[92] J. A. Hadfield, 'War Neuroses: A Year in a Neuropathic Hospital', *British Medical Journal*, 28 Feb. 1942, p. 283.
[93] Ibid. 283.　　　　[94] Ibid. 284.

the writing on predisposition to mental disorders, yet most military psychiatrists were convinced that predisposition played some role, however ill-defined, in the production of war neuroses.

Another common feature of military psychiatry that emerged in the aftermath of Dunkirk was the observation that the vast majority of cases were unlike those encountered on the Western Front during 1914–18. Most of the psychiatric casualties from the BEF in 1940 (some 53 per cent) were cases of 'anxiety neuroses' and not of 'hysteria', which allegedly predominated among the rank and file during the First World War. Only 24 per cent of the psychiatric casualties dealt with by Hadfield, for instance, were classified as hysterical.[95] Like many others, Hadfield attributed the profile of cases from Dunkirk to the very different conditions of warfare that obtained then and in 1914–18. There were 'far more traumatic cases in the last war', he wrote, and 'traumatic experiences, owing to their physical accompaniments, are more likely to produce somatic symptoms of the hysterical type than are ordinary conditions of danger'.[96] While Dunkirk, Norway, and civilian air raids had produced some hysterical cases, they were negligible by comparison with the thousands of 'shell-shocked' patients who returned from the Somme and other great battles during the First World War.[97] Hadfield, and psychiatrists who studied subsequent campaigns during the Second World War, felt that most of the 'anxiety' cases they treated were simply showing exaggerated signs of fear and other normally healthy emotions.[98]

The mobile warfare that typified most of the campaigns in which the British Army was involved during 1940–5 did not engender the feelings of helplessness characteristic of the killing fields of the Somme or Ypres. Anxiety states arose from fear, which was seen as a natural reaction to danger and, to some degree, as indispensable in combat, since the release of adrenaline stimulated the body and mind. Fear was counter-productive only when it inhibited aggression or disrupted unit discipline; that is, when it became 'contagious'. Hysterical symptoms such as mutism and paralysis were thought to be typical of those subjected to traumatic experiences from which there

[95] Ibid. 282.   [96] Ibid. 281.

[97] On the different types of war neuroses recorded during the First World War, and their treatment, see: Keith Simpson, 'Dr James Dunn and Shell-Shock', in H. Cecil and P. Liddle (eds.), *Facing Armageddon: The First World War Experienced* (Barnsley: Leo Cooper, 1996), 502–22; Ben Shephard, ' "The Early Treatment of Mental Disorders": R. G. Rows and Maghull 1914–1918', in G. Berrios and H. Freeman (eds.), *150 Years of British Psychiatry, Volume 2: The Aftermath* (London: Royal College of Psychiatrists, 1996), 434–64.

[98] See Joanna Bourke, 'Disciplining the Emotions: Fear, Psychiatry and the Second World War', in R. Cooter, M. Harrison, and S. Sturdy (eds.), *War, Medicine and Modernity* (Stroud: Sutton, 1998), 225–38.

appeared to be no escape; they were a subconscious form of release from an intolerable situation. Cases of hysteria were comparatively rare during the Second World War, or at least very few were diagnosed. Nor were they associated particularly with the rank and file, unlike the First World War, when the supposed preponderance of hysterical symptoms among other ranks was commonly attributed to their supposedly inferior constitution or upbringing. While class distinctions were by no means absent from psychiatric writing and practice during the Second World War, the tone was generally more egalitarian, and individual differences in responses to trauma were explained more in terms of 'personality types' than social class.

Greece and Crete

British troops were first dispatched to Greece in November 1940, following Italian incursions into Albania, and remained in the country through 1941 in order to assist the Greeks in the event of future attack. The first British contingent numbered just a few thousand men and consisted mostly of non-combatant personnel, including men of the RAMC, who established hospitals in the vicinity of Athens. They remained there during March 1941, when Greek forces countered an attempted Italian invasion on the Albanian front. Although Mussolini's army was repulsed, it looked increasingly likely that the Germans would launch an attack on Greece following their advance into Yugoslavia. This led to the deployment of a larger force of British and Commonwealth troops, which joined the existing contingent to constitute 'W' Force. Most of these soldiers were deployed in the north of Greece, along a natural defensive line known as the Aliakmon Line—a mountainous barrier with only four passes.

Medical units were situated close to the front and at various points along the lines of communication to Athens and the port of Piraeus. It was planned from the outset that the evacuation of casualties would be completed in stages, so that the seriously ill and wounded could be given rest in the dressing stations of field ambulances. Otherwise the journey across the mountains by ambulance car from Edessa, at the front, to Elasson, the location of the nearest CCS, would have taken at least twenty-four hours. Patients arriving at the CCSs at Elasson and Larissa were then to be evacuated, if necessary, by train to general hospitals in the rear.[99] There were two rather primitive ambulance trains operating in Greece, running north from Athens on

---

[99] PRO WO 222/1481, Col. D. T. M. Large, '[Report on Medical Aspects of] Campaign in Greece', 1941, 3–6.

alternate nights to pick up sick and wounded from Lamia, a country station south of Larissa. The journey to Athens from the front could take up to twenty-four hours, and certainly not less than fourteen, but it became shorter as the Germans advanced and the front contracted.[100]

The anticipated German attack began in the second week of April, out-flanking the Aliakmon Line and forcing 'W' Force to withdraw to a second defensive position. Badly mauled during the retreat through the Olympus Pass, and facing a continued heavy onslaught, 'W' Force was soon compelled to withdraw from this position too. It soon became clear that there was no prospect of stopping the German advance, and by 21 April the British government decided to evacuate its forces from Greece. During this rapid retreat the medical services did their best to keep to the original plan of evacuation, and an ambulance train ran for some days after 16 April, by which time the force had abandoned its position around Larissa. This was a remarkable feat, for the driver and guards had abandoned the train, leaving it to be run by the medical staff and patients.[101] Most of the evacuation, however, was by motor ambulance convoy, the RAMC being assisted by Quaker volunteers from a Friends' Ambulance Unit, which had made its way to Greece after the fall of Norway via Eastern Europe.[102]

The situation was now completely fluid, and it was impossible for the DDMS, Colonel D. T. M. Large, to keep track of all medical units and to maintain contact with his Assistant-Directors of medical services (ADsMS). The latter were left to their own devices when deploying medical units and arranging evacuation. One common complaint in Greece, as in France in 1940, was that CCSs were too cumbersome for mechanized warfare. At least two three-ton lorries were required to move each CCS, and the packing and loading of equipment took far too long when confronted with a rapid enemy advance. It was generally considered that the field ambulance, with the addition of a surgical team and extra vehicles, was in a better position to accomplish the main task of the CCS—the short-term retention and sorting of casualties. One such unit was actually improvised in Greece and worked well, as field ambulances were lighter and more mobile than CCSs.[103]

Back in Athens the general hospitals were crammed with wounded men from the Macedonian front. This was worrying, not only because of the medical situation, but because such a concentration of men made them vulnerable to enemy bombardment. Although the Germans did not deliberately

[100] Communication from Dr R. S. Morton, MBE.
[101] PRO WO 222/1481, Col. D. T. M. Large, 'Campaign in Greece', 9; communication from Dr R. S. Morton, MBE.
[102] IWM PP/MCR/10, Second World War memoirs of Dr L. E. Le Souef, 77–8.
[103] PRO WO 222/1481, 'Campaign in Greece', 17.

target the hospitals, German POWs later explained that the red crosses on hospitals and ambulance cars were not always clearly visible from the air.[104] The decision was therefore taken to remove 400 patients and convalescents from hospitals in Athens to Magara, where they would be hidden in the nearby woods until they could be evacuated by sea. Another 400 wounded, together with nursing sisters, were handed over to the American Red Cross and moved to Argos in the Peloponnese to await evacuation.[105] Most patients and medical staff managed to escape to Crete and other islands before the Germans arrived in Athens, but evacuation was often risky. One lifeboat full of walking wounded capsized as it went out to meet the cruiser HMS *Orion*. It was a stormy, pitch-black night, and all were lost.[106]

Those who could not be evacuated from Greece faced an arduous journey back to POW camps in Germany. The first train sent from Greece to Germany carrying wounded British POWs comprised only cattle- and baggage-cars. The captives were locked inside them for five days and the American Red Cross at Belgrade supplied the only refreshments. Toilet facilities in the cars were non-existent and the stench was practically unbearable; at least one British POW died en route. Conditions on board subsequent trains were somewhat better, though far from adequate for the carriage of sick and wounded men.[107]

Most of those successfully evacuated from Greece arrived on the island of Crete. This placed an enormous strain on the island's medical services, since most of the medical units had abandoned their equipment and supplies. In the majority of cases medical staff brought with them nothing more than the clothes they were wearing and what little they could carry in their haversacks.[108] Aside from the shortage of medical stores, which proved to be a great handicap during the forthcoming battle, the influx of men from Greece completely overwhelmed such hospital accommodation as existed. Hundreds of sick and wounded men had to be housed in transit camps and tended as conditions permitted. In most cases the wounded were in very poor condition and badly in need of medical attention; many had not had their dressings changed for over a week.[109]

The German bombardment of the island and the invasion by sea and air, which began on 20 May, placed a great additional strain on the British hospitals. No. 7 General Hospital was hit by a bomb, killing several of its staff,

[104] PRO WO 222/1481, 16; IWM PP/MCR/10, Second World War memoirs of Dr L. E. Le Souef, 79–80.
[105] PRO WO 222/1481, 'Campaign in Greece', 10–13.
[106] Communication from Dr R. S. Morton, MBE.
[107] PRO WO 222/1361, 'Report on Reserve Lazaret, Rottenmuenster', 5 Nov. 1941.
[108] PRO WO 222/1481, '[Report on Medical Services in the] Battle of Crete, May 1941', 5.
[109] Ibid. 6.

and some MOs felt that hospitals had been deliberately targeted, despite the red crosses displayed prominently on their roofs. On 20 May No. 7 General Hospital was subjected to

A most severe attack lasting about two hours, during which time the wounded were machine-gunned in their tents by low-flying aircraft. At 11.30 hours the hospital was over-run by German troops who marched off some of the staff and those of the wounded and sick capable of walking a distance of about four miles to the region of Galatas prison where they were promptly employed in making a landing ground.[110]

Later on heavy bombing forced the hospital to retreat to some caves along the coast, where a pretty effective medical service was maintained for five days until threatened by the German advance.[111]

Following the invasion, the medical situation on the island was at breaking point. Field ambulances were forced in many cases to function as general hospitals, some handling as many as 500 patients. By 23 May nearly all units had exhausted their stores,[112] and these deficiencies were only partly remedied by occasional drops by air and sea.[113] The medical services were also undermined by a severe shortage of transport. The British Army on Crete possessed only six motor ambulance cars and the Navy five, which meant that there was little ambulance cover for the island. In any case, much of the terrain was unsuitable for motor vehicles and, as in Gallipoli in 1915, many of the wounded were carried by hand or by pack animals. Not surprisingly, those able to walk chose to do so, but like the ambulances, they moved only during the hours of darkness, lest they were mistaken for combatants.[114] The fighting on the island was very fierce and both sides seldom gave a man the benefit of the doubt. There were, however, many cases of conspicuous bravery, in which medical staff attended the wounded at considerable risk to themselves. On one occasion a medical team drove an ambulance across the runway of Maleme airfield in the middle of a German bombing raid in order to tend a group of badly wounded men.[115]

By 26 May it had become clear to the island's commander, Lieutenant-General Freyberg, that the position was hopeless. The following afternoon, after having gained permission to evacuate Crete, he ordered a retreat to Sphakia on the southern side of the island, where part of the force was to be evacuated to Egypt. Another evacuation was planned from Heraklion on the

---

[110] Ibid. 7.
[111] Ibid. 13; Lt.-Col. R. K. Debenham, 'A R.A.M.C. Hospital in Crete', *Journal of the Royal Army Medical Corps*, 78 (1942), 183–5.
[112] PRO WO 222/1481, 'Battle of Crete', 7.
[113] Ibid. 10.   [114] Ibid. 10.
[115] Antony Beevor, *Crete: The Battle and the Resistance* (Harmondworth: Penguin, 1992), 106.

northern coast. The latter was accomplished without any casualties, but the former encountered harassment from the Luftwaffe, which resulted in the loss of several ships. A substantial number of men, including most of the severely wounded, had to be left behind. After news of this difficult decision filtered down through the ranks, many seriously wounded men attempted, unsuccessfully, to be reclassified as walking wounded in order to avoid becoming POWs. The decision to leave the seriously wounded behind cannot have been easy, but it was clear that the Navy was unable to embark stretcher cases in the conditions that obtained during the evacuation. The wounded were not completely abandoned, however, for a skeleton staff of RAMC remained to tend to them and to ensure they were adequately cared for once captured.[116]

The Germans did not treat the wounded harshly, but rations in POW camps fell short of that required for the maintenance of health, and some sick and wounded men died as a result. The nourishment of patients therefore relied very largely on the generosity of the local inhabitants.[117] Some British doctors were also surprised at the readiness of German doctors to amputate limbs, and warned their patients not to consent to an amputation unless a British doctor agreed. L. E. Le Souef, a medical officer interned in Maleme POW camp, believed that the Germans 'considered conservative surgery a long term wastage of their immediate war effort, whereas amputations healed quickly and the patients could be quickly discarded'.[118]

Hong Kong

The reverses suffered by the British Army in Europe during 1940–1 were followed, at the end of 1941, by a series of catastrophes in the Far East. Beginning with the invasion of North-Eastern Malaya and Hong Kong in early December, the British Army was subjected to a series of humiliating defeats, culminating in the fall of Singapore and the capture of 130,000 British and Commonwealth troops.[119] The fall of Singapore—a strategically important island commanding sea-routes to Australia and the Far East—dealt the British a major blow, and one from which their eastern empire never recovered. Leaving the British disheartened, it raised the hopes of those struggling for independence in British possessions such as India. From a medical point of view, the campaigns in Malaya and Singapore proved testing in the

---

[116] PRO WO 222/1481, 'Battle of Crete', 11.
[117] IWM PP/MCR/10, Second World War memoirs of Dr L. E. Le Souef, 135.
[118] Ibid.
[119] On the fall of Singapore see Louis Allen, *Singapore 1941–42* (London: Frank Cass, 1993).

extreme. The swiftness with which the Japanese achieved victory meant that lines of communication were broken and units isolated. Doctors and nurses were forced to work in exceptionally arduous conditions at great risk to their lives—a risk many continued to run long after the fighting had finished.

The British colony of Hong Kong consisted of the island of Hong Kong, together with the Kowloon Peninsula, Stonecutter's Island, and the New Territories. The latter bordered the Chinese province of Kwantung, parts of which had been occupied by the Japanese since 1938, but the colony's garrison—consisting of two British, two Canadian, and two Indian battalions—offered little in the way of protection. When the Japanese invasion began on 8 December 1941, the mainland brigade was forced quickly to retreat to the island of Hong Kong. During the next five days the island was bombarded by Japanese artillery, and shelling intensified on the morning of 18 December to coincide with an amphibious assault across the narrow straits. The invading force quickly overwhelmed the defences on the north part of the island, and after sixteen days of fighting without relief its garrison finally surrendered on the afternoon of Christmas Day 1941.

In view of the colony's isolation, it was clear that the medical services would have to rely on their own resources in the event of an invasion, since evacuation and the importation of supplies would be impossible if the enemy controlled the mainland and sea lanes. As a contingency measure the military medical services had worked out a plan to utilize civilian medical support, and had stockpiled up to a year's supplies. In addition to the British Military Hospital at Bowen Road (188 beds) and the Indian General Hospital in Kowloon (120 beds), the military were able to fall back on several large civilian hospitals, such as the 400-bed St Albert's Convent Hospital in Stubbs Road. Arrangements were also made to convert buildings such as the Hong Kong Hotel into hospitals in the event of an emergency.[120] In theory both beds and stores were plentiful, but the medical services were acutely aware of the problems they would face should the Japanese overrun the hospitals and supply depots.[121]

Once it became apparent that an invasion was imminent, the medical services placed themselves in a state of readiness and volunteers were called up and deployed according to the medical plan. Hospitals at Bowen Road and St Albert's convent were enlarged and the Indian Military Hospital in Kowloon was cleared prior to its removal to the island—an Advanced Dressing Station (ADS) was established in its place. But before the move could be

[120] CMAC RAMC 2062/2, P. H. Starling, 'In Oriente Fidelis: The Army Medical Services in the Battle of Hong Kong, December 1941', 3.
[121] F. A. E. Crew, *The Army Medical Services. Campaigns, Volume II: Hong Kong, Malaya, Iceland and the Faroes, Libya, 1942–1943, North-West Africa* (London: HMSO, 1957), 9–10.

completed the hospital came under heavy fire and a number of the Chinese orderlies were killed.[122] All casualties on the mainland were ferried back across the straits, to the hospital at Bowen Road in the case of major surgical cases, and to St Albert's in the case of the sick and lightly wounded. A hospital established at St Stephen's College functioned as a convalescent centre.[123] Evacuation proceeded smoothly at first, but from 13 December the medical situation became increasingly difficult. Any movement invited attack from Japanese aircraft, and evacuation could only be conducted safely under the cover of darkness. By this time the roads had become so pitted by shellfire that driving at night was scarcely less hazardous than evacuation by day.[124]

After the Japanese began their assault on the island medical arrangements were thrown into turmoil and the chain of evacuation was severed. Owing to the concentration of medical units within a restricted area, the Japanese were able quickly to overrun several of the dressing stations and larger hospitals. The remaining hospitals worked under constant fire; the Bowen Road Hospital alone received 111 hits during the initial bombardment.[125] As a result, the upper floors of the hospital became unsafe and it was forced to reduce its functions to those of a CCS, all patients fit to move being transferred soon after their operation.[126] The Indian General Hospital, however, continued working until it was overrun on 20 December; an Indian wing was then created at St Albert's and remained open until the surrender.[127]

Once it became clear that the colony was lost, hospital staff grew apprehensive about their treatment should they and their patients be captured. The Japanese were already notorious for the atrocities they had committed in China, though in the majority of hospitals in Hong Kong they did not indulge in murder or rapine. Following the surrender, staff were normally permitted to continue their work and relations with the Japanese were, in some cases, even cordial.[128] But some medical units were not so lucky. On the night of 18–19 December the Japanese captured the Army Medical Store at Shaukiwan, which was staffed by the RAMC. The captured men were forced to strip and were marched up a nearby hill. Here they were divested of their rings and watches by Chinese civilians, taken into a small clearing, and butchered by the Japanese with bayonet and sword, most of the survivors

---

[122] CMAC RAMC 2062/2, 'In Oriente Fidelis', 3.   [123] Ibid. 6.
[124] Crew, *Campaigns*, ii. 14.
[125] CMAC RAMC 2062/2, 'In Oriente Fidelis', 7.
[126] CMAC RAMC 1291/3, 'Report on Military Surgery in Hong Kong', 5.
[127] See Charles G. Roland, *Long Night's Journey into Day: Prisoners of War in Hong Kong and Japan, 1941–1945* (Waterloo, Ontario: Wilfred Laurier University Press, 2001), 50–5.
[128] CMAC RAMC 1510, Notes by Warrant Officer E. Sims, giving an account of the Japanese occupation of the British Military Hospital, Hong Kong, 2–3.

being finished off with a revolver. In the midst of this slaughter two British soldiers—Corporal Norman Leath and Captain Thomas—managed to escape. Captain Thomas was shot in the back and played dead until his assailants had left. Corporal Leath, after taking a blow to the head by a sword, also feigned death and later rolled down into a gully, along which he crawled in the direction of the medical store. Next morning he moved on and hid in a deserted house until 26 December, surviving on only one pint of water and no food. His poor health meant that he had no alternative but to come out of hiding, and he presented himself at an internment camp at North Point, where he received medical attention. Luckily, the Japanese authorities took no action against him.[129] Leath survived this ordeal and internment in a Japanese POW camp to give evidence against Colonel Tanaka, the commander of the Japanese 229th Regiment, on whose orders the nine RAMC men had been killed. Tanaka was sentenced to twenty years imprisonment by a war crimes tribunal.[130]

This was not the only atrocity committed by the Japanese during the invasion of Hong Kong. In the final days of the fighting many of the staff and patients at St Stephen's were transferred to the hospital at Stanley Prison, after several had been killed in heavy artillery fire. At dawn on 25 December, as the padre was about to conduct the Christmas service, the Japanese burst into the hospital. The commander, Lieutenant-Colonel George Black, and Captain John Whitney RAMC went to stop them, reminding the Japanese that they had entered a hospital. Black was shot in the head and bayoneted as he lay on the floor, as was Whitney. The Japanese then began to kill the patients in their beds, together with nurses, orderlies, and anyone else who got in their way. The survivors were herded into a storeroom and some were later killed; the female nurses were kept separate and were repeatedly raped before being killed. More than sixty patients and twenty-five hospital staff met their deaths on this occasion. No one was really sure why the Japanese had acted with such cruelty, but it was suggested that they were angry because they had lost many men (including the brother of one of the Japanese officers) in the capture of the college grounds, which had been defended vigorously by Canadian troops. Others said that many of the Japanese were drunk.[131] Both explanations may contain an element of truth, but they do

---

[129] CMAC RAMC 1291, D. C. Bowie, 'Captive Surgeon in Hong Kong: The Story of the British Military Hospital, Hong Kong 1942–1945', repr. from the *Journal of the Hong Kong Branch, Royal Asiatic Society*, 15 (1975), 168, RAMC 2062/2, 'In Oriente Fidelis', 7; Crew, *Campaigns*, ii. 23.
[130] For a fuller account, see CMAC RAMC 2062/2, 'In Oriente Fidelis', 8; Charles C. Roland, 'Massacre and Rape in Hong Kong: Two Case Studies involving Medical Personnel and Patients', *Journal of Contemporary History*, 32 (1997), 43–61.
[131] CMAC RAMC 2062/2, 'In Oriente Fidelis', 9.

not explain why similar atrocities occurred in other territories captured by the Japanese. The Japanese often killed hospital patients whose immobility would have made them a burden, nor did they countenance the least sign of resistance to their authority, such as the attempts made by medical staff to protect their patients and equipment.[132] Hong Kong and other British colonies were, however, spared the slaughter that followed the capture of Nanking in 1937. It may have been the case that the troops who attacked Hong Kong were soon transferred elsewhere, whereas those who had captured Nanking remained in the city for longer. The atrocities committed against patients and medical staff in Hong Kong, and later in Singapore, were carried out by men fresh from battle and who had nothing but contempt for the defeated.

With the surrender on 25 December, the British and Commonwealth forces in Hong Kong passed into a long period of captivity. For nearly four years they were imprisoned in camps on a near-starvation diet and compelled to perform hard manual labour. The regime of these camps was brutal: discipline was severe and summary beatings were common. Even in hospital, patients and staff were forbidden to play music and games or to dance and sing. Japanese guards even had orders to shoot on sight any individual seen with hands in his pockets.[133] But the medical staff at Bowen Road—which continued to function as a hospital—and the smaller, makeshift hospitals established in the camps had more pressing concerns. Due to filthy conditions at the camps, dysentery and diarrhoea reached epidemic proportions during August–December 1942.[134] Sanitation and fly-proofing of huts was difficult to arrange because of the scarcity of building materials and the damage caused by the Japanese bombardment. Deficiency diseases such as beriberi were also widespread in the Hong Kong POW camps, and were the main cause of admissions to hospital during 1943.[135] The meagre rations issued by the Japanese had to be supplemented by food purchased by commissioned officers among the POWs. From August 1942 officers received wages from the Japanese and most set aside a large amount in order to contribute to a Comfort Fund and an Extra Diet Fund. The POWs also received Red Cross parcels, but despite these supplements to their meagre rations, their health was precariously balanced for most of their captivity, placing great strain on the facilities of camp hospitals.[136]

---

[132] CMAC RAMC 2062/2, 8; RAMC 1291, 'Captive Surgeon', 161–2; Roland, 'Massacre and Rape'.
[133] CMAC RAMC 729/10, Orders for British Military Hospital, Hong Kong, 1942–16 Jan. and 20 May 1942.
[134] CMAC RAMC 1393, Capt. A. J. N. Warrack, RAMC, 'Conditions Experienced as a Japanese POW, from a Medical Point of View', 4–7.
[135] CMAC RAMC 1291, 'Captive Surgeon', 172–7.
[136] Ibid. 166.

Malaya and Singapore

Uncertainty over the likelihood of war meant that British forces in Malaya were inadequately prepared for the Japanese invasion. There was not enough time to move all medical units forward and soldiers on the mainland had to make do with general hospitals. As in France, these proved too cumbersome to be packed up and moved quickly as the military situation demanded. On Singapore Island the problems were of quite a different nature, and similar in some respects to those faced by medical staff in Hong Kong. The crowding together of hospital units amidst targets of tactical importance, such as ammunition dumps and artillery batteries, meant that surgery had to be performed in the heat of battle. It was in such circumstances that the medical services had to deal with exceptionally heavy casualties, most of which ended up being evacuated to the island of Singapore. By the fall of Singapore on 15 February, British casualties amounted to as many as 38,496, together with 18,490 Australian, 67,340 Indian, and 14,382 among local volunteers.

Medical work in forward areas at the beginning of the Malaya campaign was undertaken largely by men of the Indian Medical Service (IMS), who were attached to the Indian infantry brigades deployed in the north of the peninsula. In the absence of CCSs, casualties had to be taken to the nearest British or Indian general hospital—and some to larger civilian institutions—but these had ultimately to be evacuated to Singapore, as the Japanese were advancing quickly down the eastern and western coasts. As the army retreated, the medical services sent back to Singapore whatever supplies they could find in abandoned civilian hospitals, and some 150,000 tablets of the anti-malaria drug mepacrine were salvaged in this way.[137] Not all patients and medical staff managed to return to Singapore, however, for the speed of the Japanese advance was such that many units were overrun.[138] Although large numbers of wounded were captured by the Japanese, forward units meeting the Japanese invasion were fortunate in that they were often able to utilize the railway network as an aid to evacuation. Initially there was only one ambulance train available, but three were in service by 16 December, each consisting of thirteen specially fitted coaches and equipped with its own operating theatre. In some cases ambulance cars were able to take casualties straight from MDSs to the nearest railhead, bypassing the military and civilian hospitals.[139]

By 31 January all British and Commonwealth forces had withdrawn across

---

[137] Crew, *Campaigns*, ii. 75.
[138] Ibid. 79–80.
[139] CMAC RAMC 1613, 'No. 1 Ambulance Train—Malaya, 1941'.

the causeway to the island of Singapore. Fewer than 9,000 hospital beds were available at this time, and nearly all were full even before the Japanese attack on the island. Furthermore, many of the hospitals had lost their equipment during the rapid retreat through Malaya,[140] and nearly all were lacking assistance from female nurses. The decision to evacuate the female nursing staff of military hospitals was made immediately after the withdrawal to Singapore, and was wise in view of events in Hong Kong. Several contingents of Australian, Indian, and British nurses managed to leave the island—well over 2,000 in total. In spite of persistent air attacks, most of the evacuees managed to reach Batavia and sailed on from there to Australia, but one vessel carrying Australian nurses and physiotherapists was hit off Banka Island and sunk.[141] Despite the evident dangers, some medical staff felt that many patients could also have been evacuated by ship, thus relieving the pressure on medical facilities. There were apparently several occasions on which the Japanese had permitted ships bearing the Red Cross to sail unmolested.[142]

The Japanese assault on Singapore began on 5 February with a naval and aerial bombardment. This was followed, on the night of 8 February, by the landing of Japanese troops, who quickly made progress inland. Further landings the next day resulted in the causeway sector being abandoned, leaving the main road to Singapore City uncovered, and by 13 February the bulk of the defending force had withdrawn inside the city's perimeter. These were trying times for the medical services. As the official historian, Francis Crew, rightly comments: 'Never before in their history were the Army Medical Services called upon to discharge their functions in circumstances more difficult and more disadvantageous than those that obtained in the island and city of Singapore.'[143] The swiftness of the withdrawal into the city meant that medical units outside the perimeter had constantly to pack up and move backwards, leaving staff and patients bewildered and anxious. Meanwhile, hospitals in the town were subjected to a massive bombardment and some were totally destroyed. Towards the end of the battle casualties had to be hawked from unit to unit until beds could be found for them. Hospitals still in service faced not only the hazards of operating under heavy fire, but also a lack of piped water, as the mains had been damaged by the Japanese bombardment. Such water as was available had to be carried to wards and operating theatres in buckets.[144] These difficulties might have been avoided if a designated hospital area had been created at the start of the invasion, as suggested by officers of the Australian Army Medical Service. As the official history records, however, 'the general situation was such that it could not be accepted';[145] a verdict that seems reasonable in view of the dislocation that

---

[140] Crew, *Campaigns*, ii. 95.   [141] Ibid. 103–4.   [142] Ibid. 105–6.
[143] Ibid. 98.   [144] Ibid.   [145] Ibid. 105.

wholesale movement of medical units would have caused at the time when they were most needed.

It was during the retreat into Singapore City that its defenders received the first intimations of the brutality that was to be inflicted by the Japanese. The most notorious incident occurred on 14 February at the Alexandra Military Hospital, located just outside the city's perimeter. At 1 p.m. the Japanese entered the hospital grounds, prompting one of its MOs—Lieutenant Weston—to claim protection for the hospital under the Geneva Convention. Carrying a white flag, and wearing a Red Cross brassard, he walked out of the hospital in order to signify its surrender, only to be bayoneted to death.[146] The Japanese then entered the hospital and advanced along the corridor, firing as they went. According to one eyewitness: 'They collected the staff at Reception, less two men—one shot in the thigh and one bayoneted through the chest—and the RSM who had his arm blown off with a grenade. They bayoneted the surgeon and his patient in the theatre.'[147] The Japanese then continued along the corridor and collected the patients from the medical ward; another party went into the other wards and wounded a number of the patients, and then killed an RAMC private in the hospital kitchens.[148]

After the Japanese had searched the hospital, the remaining staff and patients were rounded up and tied together by the wrists in groups of three to five, during which several more patients were bayoneted. The rest were confined in three small rooms, from where groups were taken out periodically into the open and killed. As in Hong Kong, a lucky few escaped the attempt to kill them. One of the survivors, Major Corbitt, recalled that:

a Jap jumped into the theatre and motioned us out—when we were lined up outside against the wall about 12 Japs faced us and set upon us with bayonets. [Private] Sutton was beside me—a Jap came for me and hit a silver cigarette case in my left breast pocket (I still have the case). He then came back and I knocked the bayonet down and it went into my left groin. The third time into my right hand . . . I then decided to pretend to be dead and shouted at Sutton who was behind me to do the same. Sutton and I lay for quite a few minutes and the Jap moved off . . .[149]

Another survivor—a corporal—received a bayonet thrust through his back as he went out of the hospital door. Left for dead, he got up, and when everybody had gone, managed to stagger back to the surgical ward.[150]

By 16 February this episode of barbarity had ended, leaving four officers

---

[146] CMAC RAMC 840/1, Col. W. J. Irwin, RAMC, 'The Alexandra Outrage', 4.
[147] CMAC RAMC 840/2, Letter from Maj. Corbitt to Irwin.
[148] Ibid., Report by Pte. Ray.   [149] Ibid., Corbitt to Irwin.
[150] Ibid., Sgt. Saye, RAMC, to Irwin, 8 Sept. 1968.

and six British other ranks officially classed as dead and a further ten British officers and seventy-three other ranks as 'missing'. As in Hong Kong, the survivors of these outrages struggled to comprehend the actions of the Japanese. Some thought that the Japanese believed that the hospital had sheltered combatant troops, and that the massacres were carried out by way of retribution. But the only basis for this was a rumour that Indian sappers digging a tunnel at the rear of the hospital had made their escape through the building when the Japanese advanced.[151] Although some survivors confirmed this, the story was never fully substantiated.[152] In view of similar incidents in Hong Kong and Burma, it is likely that the brutality meted out by the Japanese at Alexandra Hospital was gratuitous, reflecting the contempt felt by the Japanese for those they had defeated.

On 15 February 1942 those who had survived the Japanese attack on Singapore passed into captivity. Two days later they were marched from Singapore City to the Changi area at the eastern tip of the island, where they were interned, each national group being housed separately. At Changi the normal pattern of military life was gradually restored and morale began slowly to improve, at least amongst the Australian and British POWs. However, many Indian troops—some 40,000 of the 45,000 captured by the Japanese—were persuaded to join the newly formed Indian National Army and to fight with the Japanese for the downfall of the British Empire. These men, mostly raw recruits who were bewildered and dispirited by recent events, were particularly susceptible to the blandishments of the Japanese.[153] Those who remained in captivity at Changi were spared the worst excesses of brutality seen in some other Japanese camps, but the regime was nevertheless a harsh one. Prison guards routinely beat the inmates, and overcrowding and poor sanitary conditions encouraged the spread of infectious diseases. The former military camp at Changi normally housed 3,000 men and accommodation could be expanded to take a maximum of 6,000. But now 50,000 POWs were crammed into this relatively small area, and sanitary conditions, which had previously been excellent, quickly deteriorated.[154] At one point the prison area housed a population equivalent to 84,000 per square mile. The situation was aggravated by the destruction of sanitary facilities during the Japanese bombardment and by the fact that hygienic discipline among the POWs from Malaya was poor. These men brought with them the germs of amoebic dysentery, which had hitherto been rare in

---

[151] CMAC RAMC 840/2, Report by Pte. Ray.   [152] Ibid., Saye to Irwin.

[153] See Peter Ward Fay, *The Forgotten Army: India's Armed Struggle for Independence 1942–1945* (Ann Arbor: University of Michigan Press, 1993).

[154] IWM, Papers of Brig. L. R. S. MacFarlane, CBE, 'Unusual Aspects and Therapy in Amoebic Dysentery', 1.

Singapore. Attempts to stem the spread of the disease by establishing wards solely for dysentery patients were frustrated by the Japanese, who insisted that all the sick should be centralized in one small barrack area, thus infecting the rest of the hospital.[155] The result was that as many as 39,000 men were admitted to hospital during 1942 (equivalent to 944 admissions per thousand), 42 per cent of whom were suffering from dysentery (amoebic and bacillary) and diarrhoea.[156] This situation did not improve until after October 1942, when a large number of prisoners were sent out in labour detachments to other camps in South-East Asia, leaving only 6,000 inmates at Changi.[157] Slowly sanitary arrangements at the camp began to improve, and the inmates became increasingly 'fly conscious', which began to bring dysentery and other intestinal diseases under control. The Japanese also later permitted a dysentery ward to open, which meant that infectious patients could be isolated. Many were treated effectively with drugs such as Emetine and various arsenical preparations.[158]

By the end of their first year of captivity the health of prisoners at Changi was reasonably good, but there was one remaining medical problem—malnutrition. In spite of numerous representations to the Japanese, rations were inadequate for the preservation of health, and deficiency diseases were common among the prisoners. Although Japan had signed the Geneva Convention regulations of 1929, which stated that POWs should be fed at least to the standard provided by the captor nation for its own troops, they were seldom obeyed.[159] During May 1942 beriberi was widespread at Changi, and did not begin to diminish until yeast was cultured on a large scale in order to supplement the rations. The peanut meal supplied by the Japanese as manure for the camp's garden was used as an additional source of B vitamins, and the arrival of Red Cross parcels from October also proved invaluable.[160] Rations issued by the Japanese improved somewhat during 1943, but they were still inadequate and extra food had to be purchased locally out of deductions from the inmates' working pay.[161] These supplements became increasingly expensive, however, as supplies grew scarce towards the end of the war. The dietary deficiencies suffered by prisoners were recorded in detail in the annual medical report for 1944, which shows that the protein intake of

[155] IWM, Papers of L. R. S. MacFarlane, 'Amoebic Dysentery', 1–2.
[156] CMAC RAMC 1016/2, 'Annual Medical Report for Changi Camp', Feb. 1942–Feb. 1943, 13.
[157] Ibid. 5.
[158] IWM, Papers of L. R. S. MacFarlane, 'Amoebic Dysentery', 2.
[159] Charles G. Roland and Henry S. Shannon, 'Patterns of Disease Among World War II Prisoners of the Japanese: Hunger, Weight Loss, and Deficiency Diseases in Two Camps', *Journal of the History of Medicine*, 46 (1991), 65–85.
[160] CMAC RAMC 1016/2, 'Changi Camp,' 1942–3, 3–7.
[161] CMAC RAMC 1016/3, 'Annual Medical Report for Changi Camp, 1943–4', 2–4.

prisoners fell to half that normally required; thiamine also remained consistently below the level needed to prevent beriberi, while the calorific value of the rations fell short of that required for men doing even light work.[162] The scarcity of food gave particular cause for concern given the state of the prisoners who had returned in early 1944 from labour camps in Thailand and elsewhere. These men were suffering extensively from beriberi, and 80 per cent were infected with malaria.[163]

Throughout their captivity at Changi British medical cases were cared for in a hospital at Roberts Barracks; other nationalities were also treated here from March 1942, after the Japanese ordered that all the sick should be concentrated in one area. The hospital staff had been hastily transferred from the former Alexandra Military Hospital, and for the first month or so it was in a state of disarray. Dr Robert Hardie of the Australian Army Medical Service, who arrived at Roberts Barracks to offer his services, recalled a scene of utter confusion: 'Sick and wounded were arriving constantly, before accommodation was ready. The chaos was indescribable.' He claimed further that there 'appeared to be little organising ability among the higher ranks'. It seems likely that much of the confusion was due to the difficult circumstances in which the MOs had to work,[164] but Hardie claimed that an Australian (Colonel Glyn White) had been entrusted with the hospital because the RAMC were 'apparently unequal to the task'.[165] This harsh verdict was, perhaps, a measure of the ill feeling created by the refusal of Malaya Command to create a designated hospital area in Singapore, as the Australians had suggested. For the rest of their internment in Changi, however, the medical services of both nations appear to have worked together in a spirit of friendly co-operation.

Whether or not there is any basis for Hardie's criticism of the administration of the barracks hospital, there can be no doubt that conditions left much to be desired. There was gross overcrowding, and wards designed for sixty patients were holding more than double that number. By the end of March there were no fewer than 2,600 patients being treated at the hospital. The scarcity of clean water for drinking, cooking, and washing also caused serious problems during the first few months, before the mains to the hospital were repaired.[166] Nor was any electricity available in the hospital until August, so the staff had to make do with hurricane lamps

[162] CMAC RAMC 1016/4, 'Annual Medical Report for Changi Camp', 1944–5, 10.
[163] CMAC RAMC 1016/1, 'Changi Camp, 1943–4', 3.
[164] Robert Hardie, *The Burma–Siam Railway: The Secret Diary of Dr Robert Hardie 1942–45* (London: Imperial War Museum, 1984), 21.
[165] Ibid. 20.
[166] CMAC RAMC 1016/1, 'Changi Camp', 1942–3, 2.

for lighting the wards and operating theatres.[167] Medical stores were obtained from local stocks but were later supplemented by Red Cross supplies shipped from South Africa. The latter prevented a grave shortage of medicines and other necessities, but medical staff complained that Red Cross supplies were often unevenly balanced.[168] Fortunately, the only period during which the hospital was severely taxed, apart from the first few months, was after the return of the labour detachments at the end of 1943, when levels of overcrowding returned to those of February–March 1942. Careful nursing and attention to diet fortunately restored most of the survivors to health.[169]

Of the prisoners sent out to work on the construction of the Burma–Siam railway, nearly one-half had died before returning to Changi.[170] David Jones, who had been an RAMC orderly on one of the ambulance trains in Malaya, claimed that prisoners in Changi had been told they were going to a sanatorium in the hills; the Japanese had even suggested that the internees should send their sick, as it would help them recuperate. Consequently, quite a few patients were sent out of Changi with the labour force in April 1943; sick and healthy alike were crammed—thirty-five to a car—into metal goods wagons with poor ventilation and no sanitary facilities. The train proceeded through the stifling humidity of Malaya for five days before arriving at Themat Bampura in Thailand. Those who survived were in a sorry state, with most of the prisoners suffering from heat exhaustion and dysentery.[171] After a brief rest, the working parties left Bampura by foot, marching over 200 miles to labour camps on the Thai–Burma border—a journey which took up to twenty-one days. Conditions at staging posts on the journey north to the Burma–Siam railway were very poor. POWs were given little to eat except for plain rice, and there were few arrangements for the care of the sick. Dysentery and diarrhoea were rife in all parties, and exhaustion was universal; many men also suffered from ulcerated feet.[172]

The ultimate destination for many POWs was Sonkrai. David Jones was one of a party of 1,680 POWs placed in No. 2 Camp at Sonkrai, which he later described as the 'horror hell of prison camps'. Out of his party, less than 250 survived twelve months later to tell their tales of neglect and brutality. Some idea of what it was like to work on the Burma–Siam railway can be gained from the recollections of Major Courtney Lendon, RAMC:

[167] Crew, *Campaigns*, ii. 124.
[168] CMAC RAMC 1016/1, 'Changi Camp, 1942–3', 12.
[169] Crew, *Campaigns*, ii. 125.
[170] CMAC RAMC 2060, Dr Alex Sakula, 'The Bridge on the River Kwai: Medical Reminiscences of 1945', 15.
[171] CMAC RAMC 1613, David Jones, 'Japanese Holiday'.
[172] CMAC RAMC 982, 'Report on Conditions of POW in Thailand May–December 1943', 15.

After a breakfast of unsweetened rice porridge, working parties were on parade a few minutes before dawn—punctually at dawn parties moved off to the railway and began to work at once—heavy manual labour of all kinds. There was no protection from either sun or rain and speed (never skill) was the keynote of the Japanese engineer's drive. Ill-defined periods of about 10 minutes' rest were ordered approximately every hour and about 1 hour was allowed for the mid-day meal (a haversack ration of cold rice with, possibly, onions and dried meat) . . . The average hours of labour . . . were 9–10 hours but might be extended up to 12–16 hours daily. Light sick were employed on tasks such as digging latrines, road making, water-carrying, etc.[173]

Disease of all kinds was rampant, and deadly infections such as cholera and amoebic dysentery sometimes killed as many as fifty prisoners per day; to make matters worse, the Japanese refused to distribute rations to those too sick to work.[174] In some camps, where the number of fit men fell below that demanded, the engineers came into the hospitals and forced the sick from their beds to work. Officers were usually exempt from labour outside the camp, but at Sonkrai where conditions were worse than anywhere else, one Japanese engineer officer—Lieutenant Abe—came into the officers' quarters asking to see the six patients who were most seriously ill and said: 'Unless men are produced from tomorrow I will send my soldiers to take these officers out to work.' Despite the heavy death-toll among the prisoners, Abe treated all appeals on behalf of the inmates with contempt. By July more than half the workforce was without boots and many were suffering from poisoned feet and trench foot; there were many cases of malaria, and most of the men were suffering from amoebic dysentery and avitiminosis. Conditions would probably have deteriorated even further had it not been for the arrival, in August 1943, of Lieutenant Wakabayshi of the Japanese Malayan POW Administration, who instituted a more humanitarian regime.[175] But these improvements came too late for many prisoners, who were already dead or dying. Of the 7,000 POW who left Changi in April, nearly 3,000 were already dead by December 1943 and around the same number were in hospital, where many perished in the coming months.[176] When the remnants of 'F' Force returned to Changi in April 1944, 3,100 men, or 45 per cent of the original working party, had died.[177]

Thailand was not the only destination for POWs formerly interned at Changi. Working parties were also dispatched to camps in Borneo, Burma,

---

[173] CMAC RAMC 1042, Maj. Courtney Lendon, 'Disease Among Prisoners of War', 22–3.
[174] CMAC RAMC 1613, 'Japanese Holiday'; IWM, Papers of L. R. S. MacFarlane, 'Amoebic Dysentery', 6. In his MD thesis on amoebic dysentery, MacFarlane later claimed that the disease had been responsible for more deaths than any other amongst POWs in Thailand.
[175] CMAC RAMC 982, 'Report on Conditions of POWs in Thailand May–December 1943', 18–19.
[176] Ibid. 19.   [177] Crew, *Campaigns*, ii. 141.

and Japan, while officers of the rank of colonel or above were sent to a camp in Formosa (Taiwan).[178] Conditions at the latter camp were undoubtedly better than in Thailand, but still fell far short of that stipulated by the Geneva Convention. Officers appear to have been spared hard labour in the nearby copper mines, but many unfit men were compelled to perform lighter tasks. Those who did not work well were punished by being forced to run up and down a hill, being beaten as they ran; the Formosan guards beat all the sick men who could not work,[179] and the Japanese medical sergeant regularly assaulted any prisoner who got in his way.[180] Colonel J. F. Crossley, the administrative officer of No. 1 POW Camp on Formosa, recalled that

Each morning the Jap medical Sergeant would appear and start the day's work by severely beating up the Doctor and his orderlies. Sick parade was held by the Jap Sergeant and the cure in nearly all cases was to be knocked to the ground with a big stick; as a consequence, men who were really sick did not report . . . The Doctor managed to slip round the huts at the risk of a good beating and attend to the seriously ill.[181]

Crossley claimed in his report on the camp that there had been a 'general policy of beating and ruthlessness', at least until the arrival of a new commander in December 1943, who not only stopped the beatings but allowed the prisoners to participate in sports and other recreational activities.[182]

The brutal treatment meted out to POWs in Japanese-run camps is well known, but it is worth examining more closely what Crossley might have meant by a 'policy' of ruthlessness. The official report on the Thai camps declared that 'it is our firm belief that our present experiences have not been in accordance with the intentions or policy of the Imperial Japanese Government in Tokyo or the Japanese Red Cross, who cannot have been aware of the actual state of affairs in Thailand'.[183] It is true that conditions were somewhat better in POW camps in Japan—notwithstanding a high incidence of deficiency diseases[184]—but if the imperial government was not complicit, brutality was endemic in most Japanese camps. How is one to account

---

[178] Ibid. 117.
[179] CMAC RAMC 1016/1, Col. J. F. Crossley, 'Report on No. 1 POW Camp, Formosa, December 1942–1945', 4–5.
[180] Ibid. 7.   [181] Ibid. 16.   [182] Ibid. 2.
[183] CMAC RAMC 982, 'Report on Conditions in POW Camps in Thailand', 15.
[184] IWM 87/12/1, William Muir Stewart, 'Experiences as a Prisoner of War, 1942–1945', typescript of interview by Dr Charles Roland, 14 Aug. 1985. Stewart recalled that the POW camps in Japan were inspected by doctors from neutral countries. The main problem in these camps appears to have been the shortage of food and medicines, which was partly a reflection of the shortages facing Japan as a whole towards the end of the war. For a very detailed study of conditions in the Japanese camps see Roland, *Long Night's Journey*.

for this? One common explanation is that the Japanese thought surrender ignoble because of their warrior code (*bushido*), and thus POWs were deemed unworthy of respect. But to this must be added the brutal treatment that Japanese soldiers routinely faced from their comrades. In the Japanese army it was customary for an officer to chastise a NCO physically and for the latter then to thrash his subordinates. The lowest ranks, in turn, vented their rage on civilians and POWs. In each case the physical assault was seen as an act of punishment, akin to a parent chastising a child. But this cannot account for the arbitrary beatings inflicted by the Koreans and Formosans who, in some camps, replaced the Japanese as guards. These men were notorious for their brutality and corruptibility, and routinely confiscated the Red Cross parcels sent to prisoners.[185]

Compared to Japanese POW camps, conditions in camps run by the Germans for British and other western POWs were fairly good. At the beginning of the war western POWs received a standard of medical care not far below that available to combatants. Though the regime at German camps could be harsh, commandants generally complied with the Geneva Convention and permitted regular inspection by neutral monitors. The Germans were more respectful of the Red Cross in battle, too. Although hospitals and ambulances were sometimes deliberately targeted, most attacks on hospitals were probably accidents of war. It is not surprising that medical units were accidentally hit by both sides, given that many were located close to legitimate military targets such as runways, railways, and fuel depots. The Japanese, by contrast, displayed on several occasions a callous disregard for the wounded and for the rights of medical personnel under the Geneva Convention. Atrocities like those that occurred in Hong Kong and Singapore can only be understood in terms of the Japanese warrior code and the prevalence of physical violence within the Japanese army itself. The contrast between the German and Japanese armies should not be drawn too starkly, however, since many Japanese did take seriously their responsibilities towards the sick and wounded. By the same token, the Germans dealt brutally with POWs from Russia and Eastern Europe, many of whom were regarded as racially inferior or politically dangerous. Of the 5,700,000 Red Army soldiers captured by the Germans, no fewer than 3,300,000 had died by the end of the war. Many were executed soon after capture, but most perished in POW camps from starvation, exposure, and disease.[186]

---

[185] CMAC 1016/1, 'Report on No. 1 POW Camp', 1.
[186] Omer Bartov, *Hitler's Army: Soldiers, Nazis, and War in the Third Reich* (Oxford: Oxford University Press, 1992), 83.

Conclusion

Capture was only one of the hardships suffered by the British Army as it retreated in Europe and Asia. Many of those who escaped the clutches of the enemy returned in a pitiful condition, often with hideous wounds and burns, or deeply traumatized as a result of their ordeal. The level of care available to such men in the field was inevitably less than perfect, owing to the fact that the Army was in rapid retreat. Medical units often found themselves cut off from lines of evacuation, or unable to receive supplies, so that casualties in need of blood transfusion or surgical attention were sometimes unable to receive it in time. But in no theatre of the war did the medical services suffer a complete collapse, and most of their patients had nothing but praise for their work in difficult and dangerous circumstances. The planning of medical arrangements may have left much to be desired (as in Norway and Malaya), but there was no need for commissions of inquiry, such as those which had followed the campaigns in Gallipoli and Mesopotamia during the First World War.

Although the early campaigns of the Second World War permitted little in the way of innovation, they at least provided some valuable experience. During the campaigns in Norway and France it became apparent that blood transfusion apparatus needed to be available in all forward units, and not just in specialist ones, so that transfusion could be conducted as early as possible. From now on, it was axiomatic that early and plentiful transfusion was crucial to success in resuscitation. The other main lesson learnt from these early campaigns was that larger field hospitals such as CCSs were of limited use in mobile warfare. Clearing and general hospitals were supposed to be mobile units, but their equipment was so plentiful and so heavy that they could seldom be packed up in time, and transported quickly enough, to keep pace with a mechanized army. The British Army's experiences in Europe and Malaya thus pointed the way to a new era of forward treatment, in which much greater reliance would be placed upon field ambulances and mobile specialist units.

3

The Western Desert, 1940–1943

The Western Desert campaigns were fought in Egypt and Libya under the auspices of the Middle East Command, which had its headquarters in Cairo. It was the most important of the three campaigns fought by British and Commonwealth forces in the region, the others being in East Africa (Ethiopia and Somaliland) and the Balkans. Operations in this theatre were extremely mobile and covered vast expanses of territory, creating severe logistical problems. Fighting broke out in September 1940, when Marshal Graziani was ordered to launch the Italian 10th Army in an invasion of Egypt. After making a tactical withdrawal, the small British Western Desert Force, under the Commander-in-Chief, Middle East, Field-Marshal Sir Archibald Wavell, made a surprise attack on the Italians, inflicting heavy losses. The British advanced beyond Tobruk and cut off the Italian retreat at Beda Fromm, where most of the Italian army surrendered on 7 February 1941. On 12 February the remnants of the Italian force were reinforced by the first of two German divisions that later achieved notoriety as the Afrika Korps. Nevertheless, no counter-attack by Axis forces was anticipated at this stage and many British troops were withdrawn from the theatre to meet the threatened German invasion of Greece. This left the British forces critically weakened and, finding little resistance, Field-Marshal Erwin Rommel drove the Afrika Korps and the Italian Ariete Division deep into Cyrenaica. This created disorder and confusion amongst the British, whose two field commanders, Neame and O'Connor, were subsequently captured. Hasty British counter-attacks were ineffectual owing to the fact that the British were outgunned and poorly equipped. This led to Wavell being replaced in July by Sir Claude Auchinleck.

Auchinleck was able to delay further offensives until November, by which time his force had been reinforced with armour. The newly formed 8th Army, consisting of the old Western Desert Force plus 30th Corps, conducted the attack. It was designed to pre-empt an assault by Rommel's Panzergruppe Afrika (the Afrika Korps plus 21st Italian Corps) on the crucial base at Tobruk. The 8th Army suffered such heavy losses in these engagements that it had to withdraw, though Rommel's lines of supply were overstretched and he was forced to retreat. Having secured extra tanks and fuel, Rommel launched another offensive in January 1942, driving the British rapidly before him until he had taken Benghazi. This left the vital Cyrenaica airfields under German control, with the notable exception of Tobruk, which was not taken until 21 June. The British now retreated further to Mersa Matruh, where Rommel inflicted another defeat, causing 8th Army to fall back again to the El Alamein line. This was the lowest point in the campaign for the British, who were thoroughly dispirited. Despite this, a precipitate attack by Rommel was held off in what subsequently became known as the first battle of El Alamein.

A stalemate ensued until the appointment of Montgomery as GOC 8th Army in August 1942, and Auchinleck's replacement by Field-Marshal Alexander in the same month. Montgomery made a number of crucial changes to 8th Army's defensive arrangements and devised modern tactics of attrition uniquely suited to the Western Desert. He also benefited greatly from improvements in ULTRA intelligence which revealed Rommel's battle plans, and, putting this intelligence to good use, Montgomery inflicted a morale-boosting defeat on Rommel's forces at Alam Halfa. It is worthy of note that Rommel was now suffering from hepatitis—a disease that twice caused him to be evacuated to Germany—while Montgomery remained in rude health throughout the campaign.[1] On 23 October Montgomery launched what would become the second battle of El Alamein, which culminated in British victory and the capture of 30,000 POWs. While Montgomery was criticized for allowing Rommel's best forces to escape, he led a well-executed advance across Libya to take Tripoli on 23 January 1943.[2] Rommel subsequently withdrew to Tunisia, precipitating what would become the North African campaign.

Excepting the account given in the official medical history, British historians have never explored the medical aspects of these operations in detail.[3] Even less is known of medicine in the Italian army, but there are a number of historical works that describe the medical situation of the Afrika Korps. This chapter will draw on these and various contemporary sources to illustrate crucial differences between medical arrangements in the Allied and Axis forces. In the Western Desert these differences were striking: sanitary

[1] IWM Ancillary Collections—20, Montgomery Collections, Montgomery to Mrs Smirely, 10 Oct. 1942.
[2] On the war in the Western Desert, see: David Fraser, *Knight's Cross: A Life of Field Marshal Erwin Rommel* (London: Harper Collins, 1993), pt. 4; Robin Neillands, *The Desert Rats: 7th Armoured Division 1940–1945* (London: Weidenfeld & Nicolson, 1991); B. Pitt, *The Crucible of War*, 2 vols. (London: Jonathan Cape, 1980–2); Alan Morehead, *Montgomery* (London: Hamish Hamilton, 1946), chs. 8–9; David French, *Raising Churchill's Army: The British Army and the War Against Germany 1919–1945* (Oxford: Oxford University Press), chs. 7–8.
[3] F. A. E. Crew, *The Army Medical Services: Campaigns*, 1 (London: HMSO, 1956).

measures in the British Army were markedly superior to those in the German and Italian armies, as were arrangements for field surgery and blood transfusion. Together, these medical provisions gave the British a crucial edge, particularly during the climactic battle at El Alamein.

The War Against Disease

The campaign in the Western Desert provides what is probably the best modern example of the operational importance of disease control. It demonstrates that superior medical arrangements can confer a significant advantage in battle; in this case enabling British and Commonwealth forces to field a larger proportion of their force than their opponents. The statistics speak for themselves: as is shown clearly in Table 3.1, the British enjoyed a marked and consistent advantage over the Germans when it came to the prevention of disease, sickness rates being less than half those in the Wehrmacht. The absence of medical statistics for the Italian force does not permit a similarly precise comparison, but intelligence reports and the condition of Italian POWs suggest that disease was an even greater problem in the Italian than in the German army. The comparative absence of disease amongst the British was quite remarkable in view of the prevalence of infectious diseases in major centres of concentration such as Cairo and Alexandria. This proved to be a significant factor in 8th Army's victory over the Afrika Korps, as the opposing forces were otherwise evenly balanced.

Despite its advantage over the German and Italians, losses from disease in the British Army were still higher than in some other theatres. During 1941 the rate of sickness in the British Expeditionary Force was 585 per thousand,

Table 3.1. Sickness rates in the British and German armies in the Western Desert (per 1,000 men per month)

Months	Year	German	British
Oct.–Dec.	1941	154	52
Jan.–Mar.	1942	95	51
Apr.–June	1942	105	42
July–Sept.	1942	158	67
Oct.–Dec.	1942	153	48
AVERAGE		133	52

Sources: H. Fischer, *Der deutsche Sanitätsdienst 1921–1945* (Osnabrück: Biblio Verlag, 1984), 1517, 1535; F. A. E. Crew, *The Army Medical Services: Campaigns*, 1 (London: HMSO, 1956), 359, 362, 365, and id., *Campaigns*, 2 (London: HMSO, 1957), 250.

declining gradually to 506 and 442 per thousand in 1942 and 1943, respectively. Battle casualties, by contrast, amounted to only forty-eight and forty-nine per thousand men per annum over the same period. Or, to put it another way, in the Middle East sickness was responsible for almost twenty times as many casualties as actual combat. The chief causes of sickness in 1941–2 were, in descending order: diseases of the digestive system, skin diseases, venereal diseases, malaria, inflammation of the tonsils, and sand-fly fever.

The prevention of disease in the Western Desert had four main elements. Perhaps the most visible of these was the sanitary work performed by specialist hygiene sections, which cleared away refuse and constructed privies and latrines. Medical personnel, together with military police, were also involved in the sanitary policing of civilian populations, in an attempt to prevent the spread of disease to soldiers. Specific preventive and prophylactic measures aimed at individual soldiers also played an important part in the prevention of disease in the Western Desert. These measures ranged from the inoculation of troops against diseases such as tetanus, to prophylactic treatment with anti-malarial drugs such as mepacrine and quinine. Last but not least, there was a concerted attempt to instil hygienic habits through sanitary propaganda in newspapers and radio broadcasts. In the prevention of bowel infections like dysentery and diarrhoea, all four elements were vital. Experience in previous wars had shown that sanitary provisions, such as fly-proof latrines, could not alone prevent the spread of diseases like typhoid and dysentery, especially in conditions of mobile warfare. In such circumstances individual measures were essential, be they inoculation, personal cleanliness, or simple precautions against the contamination of food and water. The British Army was fortunately accustomed to improvisation and was able to construct basic sanitary apparatus with little difficulty. Over a century of colonial campaigns in Africa and Asia had led to the development of portable water-filters and incinerators for the disposal of refuse and excreta.[4] However, the sanitary discipline of British forces in previous wars had often left much to be desired, Gallipoli and Mesopotamia being two recent examples. In both these campaigns, officers had set a very poor example to their men and had taken few precautions against the spread of disease.

British commanders in the Western Desert were determined not to make the same mistake. Many had passed through the Army's School of Hygiene at Mychett and some had learned at Staff College and the Senior Officers'

---

[4] Philip D. Curtin, *Death by Migration: Europe's Encounter with the Tropical World in the Nineteenth Century* (New York: Cambridge University Press, 1989); id., *Disease and Empire: The Health of European Troops in the Conquest of Africa* (New York: Cambridge University Press, 1998).

School to pay close attention to medical arrangements.[5] Keeping 'fighting fit' was now a prominent part of propaganda at home and in overseas theatres, and it was said that the maintenance of health was among the foremost duties of the 'citizen soldier'. A health memorandum designed for soldiers serving in hot countries put it succinctly: 'We have all undertaken to serve in the army. It should be up to each one of us to keep ourselves fit to carry out that undertaking. We have an Empire, which extends right round the world, and our service may be, and often is, in many queer and uncivilised countries. Our job is to be fit, and keep fit to serve and to fight anywhere at any time.'[6] This entailed learning a few simple rules about the causation of disease, with the aid of numerous leaflets and memoranda, not to mention films and radio broadcasts. Soldiers became familiar with the 'cycle' of different diseases: the communication of germs from 'carriers' to the healthy and back again. They learnt, for example, that:

The dysentery germs leave the sick man in his excreta (urine and dung). Flies feed on the excreta and pick up some of those dysentery germs. The infected flies feed on some cooked food and leave some dysentery germs in the food. A healthy man eats that food and those germs. The germs now attack his intestines and make him a case of dysentery. He in his turn passes out dysentery germs which are taken to some other healthy person in the same manner.[7]

Thus, in order to prevent dysentery soldiers were instructed to protect food from flies, to purify their drinking water, and to prohibit known sufferers from handling food.[8] 'Mobile bogs' were also constructed from petrol tins surrounded by a wooden frame and a lid to prevent flies from entering.[9]

The distribution of health memoranda was often accompanied by practical demonstrations in field hygiene.[10] Lest these lessons be forgotten, soldiers were reminded constantly of their duty to keep fit by posters bearing such messages as 'Camp Cleanliness' and 'Don't Murder Your Mates'. British forces' newspapers were also bombarded with hygienic propaganda such as the 'Health Quiz', a light-hearted attempt to get across the message of the communicability of germs. The deluge of propaganda was such that *Parade* magazine refused at one point to take any more inserts on matters of hygiene, for fear of boring its readers.[11] Aside from personal cleanliness and care in

    [5] F. A. E. Crew, *The Army Medical Services. Administration*, 2 (London: HMSO, 1955), 35–6.
    [6] CMAC RAMC 762/8, 'Health Memorandum for British Soldiers in the Tropics', 2.
    [7] Ibid. 4.
    [8] Ibid. GCRO D.4920/8/17, Sgt. John Vaughan, 'Experiences with "G" Squadron, 2 Royal Gloucestershire Hussars', 13.
    [9] Communication from Dr R. S. Morton, MBE.
    [10] CMAC RAMC 2046/1, War Diary of DDH Middle East, 30 Nov. 1942.
    [11] Ibid., March 1942.

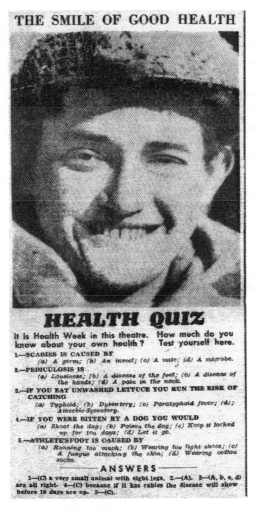

THE SMILE OF GOOD HEALTH

HEALTH QUIZ

It is Health Week in this theatre. How much do you know about your own health? Test yourself here.

1.—SCABIES IS CAUSED BY
   (a) A germ; (b) An insect; (o) A mite; (d) A microbe.

2.—PEDICULOSIS IS
   (a) Lousiness; (b) A disease of the feet; (c) A disease of the hands; (d) A pain in the neck.

3.—IF YOU EAT UNWASHED LETTUCE YOU RUN THE RISK OF CATCHING
   (a) Typhoid; (b) Dysentery; (c) Paratyphoid fever; (d); Amoebic dysentery.

4.—IF YOU WERE BITTEN BY A DOG YOU WOULD
   (a) Shoot the dog; (b) Poison the dog; (c) Keep it locked up for ten days; (d) Let it go.

5.—ATHLETE'S FOOT IS CAUSED BY
   (a) Running too much; (b) Wearing too tight shoes; (c) A fungus attacking the skin; (d) Wearing cotton socks.

—————— ANSWERS ——————

1.—(C) a very small animal with eight legs. 2.—(A). 3.—(A, b, c, d) are all right. 4.—(C) because if it has rabies the disease will show before 10 days are up. 5.—(C).

1. 'Health Quiz', Middle East Theatre, CMAC RAMC 651/3

the handling of food and water, soldiers were encouraged to think of themselves as at war with Nature as well as the Axis powers. Men travelling into the Canal Area of Egypt, for example, were warned that they were entering a war zone where the fly was their principal enemy.[12] But the campaign against the fly was less successful than that against the Germans and Italians. J. D. P. Graham, who served as an MO with 7th Armoured Division, recalled

[12] Ibid., 29 Jan. 1942.

that: 'We killed them [flies] by the ten thousand but there were no effective sprays and the main thing to do was to keep moving and instruct every man to bury his personal contribution with a spadeful or two of sand.'[13]

Another way of breaking the disease 'cycle' was to avoid contact with persons thought to be carriers. As disease was known to be rife among the indigenous population, soldiers were warned to avoid contact with locals or at least to ensure that care was taken in handling materials touched by them.[14] The unavoidable proximity of local carriers meant that sanitary discipline had to be strict in order to be effective, but this was not always the case. In September 1940, for example, 16th Infantry Brigade was said to have suffered heavily from dysentery on account of the proximity of a native labour detachment. The DDMS, Brigadier Joseph Walker, was pessimistic about the prevention of such outbreaks. He warned in 1941 that large labour camps erected at Matruh and Bagush, in the vicinity of British troops, meant that the stage was set for further epidemics; an opinion which may well have reflected his previous experience as a medical officer in Egypt from 1926 to 1931.[15] The Assistant Director of Hygiene, Lieutenant-Colonel McKinley, was equally concerned by conditions at Amiyra military camp. 'I cannot exaggerate the potential dangers existing here at present,' he stressed in March 1941: 'With flies and warmer weather dysentery in epidemic form is inevitable . . . There are thousands of Bedouins in the Area. Some within 50 yards of the camp. These Bedouins mean wholesale dysentery and looting, they must be got rid of somehow.'[16] In some camps, fear of infection also led to the replacement of locals with European personnel. Men of the 18th General Hospital, stationed at Al Kantara, recalled that: 'We got rid of the mess contractor and the natives in the kitchen because of the general filth and flies.'[17]

In general, however, the incidence of bowel infections in the British Army compared favourably with that in the Axis forces. Dysentery accounted for much of the sickness in the Afrika Korps prior to the crucial second battle of Alamein, during which nearly one in five Germans were listed as sick. During the months running up to the battle most German regiments (equiv-

[13] CMAC RAMC 1762, J. D. P. Graham, 'A Time in the Sand: A True Account of Some Personal Experiences with the RAMC in the Western Desert 1941–1943' (c.1982), 77.

[14] CMAC RAMC 762/8, 'Health Memorandum', 4, 10.

[15] PRO WO 177/92, Memo. from Brig. J. Walker, DDMS, WDF, 5 July 1941; Sir Robert Drew, *Commissioned Officers in the Medical Services of the British Army 1660–1960*, 2 (London: Wellcome Historical Medical Library, 1968), 169–70.

[16] CMAC RAMC 538, Lt.-Col. R. McKinley, 'Report on a Visit to No. 1 Line of Communication Area, 19–22 March 1941', 2.

[17] CMAC RAMC 877, T. D. Pratt and G. A. Bromley, 'The Story of the 18th General Hospital 1939–45', 21.

alent in size to British brigades) had between 500 and 1,000 men hospitalized, with hundreds more sick and struggling to perform their duties.[18] In
October the Afrika Korps carried the burden of 9,954 sick out of a total
strength of 52,000, and 5,860 sick out of 41,000 troops in November.[19] Even
elite units such as the 15th Panzer Division were markedly under strength,
with only 3,840 men operational out of a total strength of around 10,000.[20]
After a tour of the Middle East in early 1943, the Adjutant-General, Sir
Ronald Adam reported that: 'It is not surprising to hear that the sanitation
of the Italians was about as bad as the native, but we hardly expected to learn
that in this respect the Germans were not much better, which has proved to
be the case. As a result, dysentery was much more prevalent in their armies
than in our own.'[21] The official medical historian of the campaign concluded
that: 'It is not improbable that the complete lack of sanitation among both
the Germans and the Italians did much to undermine their morale in the
Alamein position.'[22] This advantage may have proved crucial, as the opposing forces were fairly evenly matched in terms of manpower and weapons.[23]

Eyewitness accounts confirm that sanitary conditions in the German
camps were very poor and that the incidence of sickness was much higher
than among British troops. In 1944 Colonel H. S. Gear, an assistant director of hygiene in the Middle East, claimed in the *British Medical Journal* that
enemy defensive localities were:

obvious from the amount of faeces lying on the surface of the ground . . . This contempt for hygiene became such a menace to the enemy as to affect from 40 to 50
percent of his front-line troops, as interrogation of captured medical officers revealed.
The enemy appears to have no conception of the most elementary sanitary measures,
and has a dysentery rate so very much higher than ours that [it] is believed that the
poor physical condition of these troops played a great part in the recent victory at
El Alamein.[24]

German sources also indicate that their sanitary services were in a state of
disarray due to the lack of co-operation between medical personnel and the
officers of the armoured divisions, who regarded sanitary matters as beneath

[18] Hanns Gert von Esebeck, *Afrikanische Schicksalsjahre: Geschichte des Deutschen Afrika Korps
unter Rommel* (Weisbaden: Limes Verlag, 1949), 160–1.
[19] H. Fischer, *Der deutsche Sanitätsdienst 1921–1945* (Osnabrück: Biblio Verlag, 1984), 1535.
[20] R. F. Bellamy and C. H. Llewellyn, 'Preventable Casualties: Rommel's Flaw, Slim's Edge',
Army (May 1990), 54.
[21] LHCMA, Adam Papers 3/3, 'Notes for Secretary of State Estimates Speech—February 1943',
16.
[22] F. A. E. Crew, *The Army Medical Services: Campaigns*, 2 (London: HMSO, 1957), 254.
[23] Nigel Hamilton, *Monty: The Making of a General 1887–1942* (London: Hamish Hamilton,
1981), 662.
[24] H. S. Gear, 'Hygiene Aspects of the El Alamein Victory', *British Medical Journal*, 18 Mar.
1944, p. 383.

them.[25] The incidence of dysentery and diarrhoea seems to have been just as high among the Italians. J. D. P. Graham observed that POWs from the Ariete Tank Division 'were not in very good physical shape, suffering from attacks of diarrhoea that I attributed to their poor and untreated supply of water'.[26] Again, on the matter of Italian field hygiene he reported that: 'If the camp was a stationary one only strict observance of the rules could minimise the inevitable outbreaks of dysentery; in the case of the Italians and their hapless POWs these were severe.'[27]

Rommel was fully aware of the incidence of sickness in his army, and his failure to address the problem constitutes one of the great mysteries of the campaign. One can only surmise that he regarded sanitary matters as the responsibility of others. Rommel, certainly, had little understanding of the causes of dysentery and other bowel infections, ascribing these diseases solely to the poor quality of rations consumed by the Afrika Korps. Two months before the second battle of El Alamein, Rommel complained that:

Rations . . . were beginning to be a problem, now that we were coming to the end of the stocks we captured in the Marmarisca. On my visits to the front I was continually hearing of growing sick parades caused by bad rations. Casualties from this cause were particularly heavy in divisions which contained troops who had also been too long in Africa, or who had not been tested for fitness for tropical service.[28]

There is no mention here, or elsewhere in Rommel's diaries, of the problems of fly-borne disease or contaminated water, or of organizing hygiene in military camps. This is all the more surprising in view of the fact that Rommel was labouring under the effects of hepatitis, a disease that had also claimed several members of his staff. In September he wrote to his wife lamenting that: '[General] Gause is unfit for tropical service and has to go away for six months. Things are also not looking too good with Westphal, he's got liver trouble. Lt.-Col. von Mellenthin is leaving today with amoebic dysentery.'[29] Some of Rommel's contemporaries—such as Kesselring—believed that Rommel's illness had fatally weakened his resolve during the later stages of the desert campaign,[30] although Rommel's critics may have placed too much emphasis on his personal failings, as opposed to the chronic shortage of supplies from which his forces suffered.

[25] Rolf Valentin, *Die Krankenbataillone Sonderformation der deutschen Wehrmacht im Zweiten Weltkrieg* (Düsseldorf: Droste, 1981), 22.

[26] Graham, 'Time in the Sand', 35.

[27] Ibid. 77.

[28] B. H. Liddell Hart (ed.), *The Rommel Papers*, trans. P. Finlay (London: Collins, 1953), 289.

[29] Rommel to his wife, 9 Sept. 1942: ibid. 290.

[30] Mathew Cooper, *The German Army 1933–1945: Its Political and Military Failure* (London: Macdonald & James, 1978), 386.

Ultimately, though, the difference in sickness rates between the Allied and Axis armies in the Western Desert was due to two main factors: the British Army's greater experience of fighting in hot climates, and the two very different styles of leadership epitomized by Rommel and Montgomery. From the eighteenth century the British had regularly dispatched sizeable expeditionary forces to fight in hot climates and maintained large overseas garrisons, most notably in India. As a result of bitter experience, the Army had evolved strict rules and regulations governing such matters as the cleanliness of barracks, the preparation of wood, and the purification of water supplies. Mortality rates in British overseas consequently plummeted during the second half of the nineteenth century, and sickness rates also began to fall from around 1900. It was harder to maintain hygiene on active service than in military stations—where hygiene was enshrined in standing orders—but most experienced officers did their best to ensure compliance.[31] The Germans, by contrast, had acquired fewer colonies than the British and these were lost after the First World War. This meant that the German army had no experience of hot climates in the two decades preceding the Second World War.

This cumulative experience gave the British Army an edge when fighting the Germans in the Western Desert, but perhaps even more decisive were the different attitudes displayed by the two principal commanders to sanitation and hygiene. Montgomery and Rommel fought as young men in the First World War, and both had been appalled at the deadlock and wastefulness of war on the Western Front. Yet they had learned very different lessons from their experiences. Whereas Rommel concentrated overwhelmingly on tactics—on personal leadership in battle and on the element of surprise— Montgomery was preoccupied with organizational matters and the preservation of material and human resources. Though Montgomery was more sceptical than some generals about the effects of education and propaganda, his emphasis upon sanitary discipline and organization ultimately paid dividends when it came to the prevention of disease.[32] With these precautions, life in the desert, according to Montgomery, was 'wonderfully healthy'.[33] As he remarked in a letter to his friend Frank Simpson, at the end of the Western Desert campaign: 'The morale [of 8th Army] is right up on the top line and

---

[31] See Curtin, *Death By Migration*; id., *Disease and Empire*; Mark Harrison, *Public Health in British India: Anglo-Indian Preventive Medicine 1859–1914* (Cambridge: Cambridge University Press, 1994), 60–72; Sumit Guha, 'Nutrition, Sanitation, Hygiene, and the Likelihood of Death: The British Army in India c.1870–1920', in *Health and Population in South Asia: From Earliest Times to the Present* (London: Hurst & Co., 2001), 110–39.

[32] Fraser, *Erwin Rommel*, 352–3; French, *Raising Churchill's Army*, ch. 8.

[33] IWM, Ancillary Collections—20, Montgomery Collections, Montgomery to Lt.-Col. Trumbull Warren.

the sick rate is 1 man per 1,000 per day; you cannot want anything better than this.'[34]

Low rates of sickness were not due entirely to hygienic and sanitary arrangements: the advent of new therapies also played a significant role in reducing the time spent in hospital. This was particularly true of the treatment of dysentery with the drug sulphaguanadine, which was introduced during 1942.[35] One medical officer serving in the theatre claimed that it had 'transformed the dysentery scene . . . duration and recovery times were slashed'.[36] Before the drug became widely available in Egypt patients had to be evacuated all the way back to hospitals in the Nile Delta, and spend about three weeks being nursed back to health on a liquid diet.[37]

Science was also the key to the prevention of typhoid, traditionally one of the British Army's greatest foes. As in the First World War, all British soldiers who agreed to submit to inoculation against the disease received the vaccine before being sent overseas, but, in contrast to the German army, inoculation against typhoid was never compulsory—a legacy of Britain's liberal attitude to such matters as vaccination. However, most British soldiers agreed to accept inoculation, and the vast majority of men serving in the Middle East received two injections with the TAB vaccine before leaving the United Kingdom. This provided them with protection against typhoid fever and the more common infections, paratyphoid A and B. The combined vaccine had been developed in 1916, when it immediately became available to British troops; indeed, the experience of the British Army during the First World War demonstrated that the TAB vaccine conferred a high degree of protection on those who had undergone inoculation. This was also true of the Second World War, and near universal inoculation with the TAB vaccine ensured that British troops suffered a lower rate of infection than their opponents. Intelligence reports received in the latter part of 1940 stated that enteric infections were very common among German and Italian troops. This was confirmed following the first Libyan campaign of 1940–1, when the British captured an unexpectedly large number of Italians, many of whom were found to be suffering from the disease. Indeed, a serious outbreak of typhoid occurred in one of the POW camps at Geneifa. Captured Italian MOs also stated that there had been 'a considerable amount of sporadic enteric fever, possibly para-typhoid, among the troops prior to their capture'.[38] In the overcrowded conditions of the POW camps the number

[34] IWM, Montgomery Collections, Montgomery to 'Simbo' [Sir Frank Simpson], 6 Feb. 1943.
[35] LHCMA, Adam Papers 3/3. 'Notes for Secretary of State', 18.
[36] Communication from Dr R. S. Morton, MBE.
[37] GCRO D.4290/8/17, Vaughan, 'Experiences with "G" Squadron', 16.
[38] CMAC RAMC 1816/4, Boyd Papers, J. S. K. Boyd, 'Report by DDH on the Occurrence of Enteric Fever in the POW Camp, Geneifa, 23/1/41', 1.

of cases quickly multiplied. The Assistant Director of Hygiene, Lieutenant-Colonel R. McKinley, warned in January 1941 that:

I consider the pens very overcrowded. Although the pens were originally designed for 480 European prisoners, it was agreed that they could accommodate 600 Italians or 800 Libyans. At present approximately 1,500 is the average number in each pen. The tents are mostly of the 160-lbs variety, the number of men per tent being 16 Italians or 20 Libyans, and this is very tight packing. An outbreak of respiratory or infectious disease will be uncontrollable.[39]

Although improved sanitary arrangements and inoculation with TAB eventually contained the spread of typhoid, the outbreak among Italian POWs was an acute embarrassment to the British medical services. Colonel J. S. K. Boyd, the Deputy Director of Pathology for the Middle East Command, admitted that 'the sanitation of the P.O.W. camps was inevitably of a makeshift type', but in the same breath blamed the Italians. 'The complete lack of sanitary conscience which is common to the Latin races made control a matter of very considerable difficulty', he claimed. 'In the circumstances', he concluded, 'it is surprising that a large-scale outbreak of bowel disease was avoided.'[40] A large part of the problem, however, was due to overcrowding, which overwhelmed such sanitary facilities as existed. Although sanitary conditions had improved at the camps, cases of typhoid occurred with alarming frequency during the summer of 1941. Another reason why the Italians were plagued by typhoid was that their TAB vaccine was less effective than that used by the British. The British vaccine was made from strains of bacteria rich in the Vi antigen, but Italian vaccines were made from non-virulent strains that had less protective power.[41] Having discovered this difference, the British embarked on a programme of re-vaccination, after which the number of cases rapidly declined; by October the outbreak had ceased altogether.[42] The same method was used again to control another outbreak of typhoid that occurred among Germans and Italians captured after the second battle of El Alamein. The hospital captured at Mersa Matruh, for instance, contained two wards—one Italian, one German—which were full of patients suffering from typhoid.

Compared with typhoid and dysentery, typhus accounted for very few cases of sickness among British troops stationed in the Western Desert, the

---

[39] CMAC RAMC 538, Lt.-Col. R. McKinlay, 'Visit to Geneifa Area by ADH, BTE, 14/1/41'.

[40] CMAC RAMC 408, J. S. K. Boyd, 'Enteric Group Fevers in Prisoners of War from the Western Desert, with Special Reference to Prophylactic Inoculation, Jan. 1941, to Feb. 1943', *British Medical Journal*, 12 June 1943, p. 719. On conditions at Geneifa camp see also Col. P. S. Tomlinson, 'Notes on a Visit to the Canal Zone by the DDMS, BTE on 5–6th July 1940', DDMS War Diary.

[41] CMAC RAMC 408, 'Enteric Group Fevers', 721.

[42] CMAC RAMC 538, Lt.-Col. R. McKinlay, 'Visit by ADH to 306, 309 and 310 POW Camps, 13/9/41'.

sickness rate amounting to only 0.56 per thousand troops in 1942 and 0.29 per thousand in 1943. Yet typhus was one of the greatest fears of the medical authorities in Egypt and Libya on account of its potential fatality. A louse-borne disease, typhus was endemic in the Middle East, and it was feared that troops might contract the disease from native labour detachments or local civilians. As one health memorandum put it: ' "Lousiness" is common among the poorer class of the native population in most Eastern countries and therefore it is most essential that particular care should be shown by all troops in regard to their personal hygiene, as lousiness is associated with dirt.'[43] Soldiers were therefore urged to wash carefully and to change clothing regularly or, if that was impracticable, to inspect their clothing for the small eggs or 'nits' of the louse.[44]

Lectures, posters, and films were employed to educate soldiers in the dangers of lice, and NCOs conducted regular inspections to check for infestation. Sergeant John Vaughan of the Royal Gloucestershire Hussars recalled that 'Twice per week all work in camp stopped whilst its inhabitants went out with blow lamps and louse powder in search of these little fellows'.[45] Anti-lice powder for rubbing into the seams of underwear was also supplied to every man operating in a typhus area, along with 'anti-lice belts'—cotton pleats impregnated with chemicals.[46] These measures of personal protection were combined with sanitary policing and conducted in co-operation with the civilian authorities. House-to-house inspections were carried out in suspect areas to locate those suffering from typhus; once identified, infected individuals were removed to hospital and their houses, and all persons with whom they were believed to have had contact, were disinfected. Infected towns were placed out of bounds to troops and quarantines were established around them.[47]

The British Army also followed the practice that it developed during the First World War of routinely disinfecting all 'native' labourers and POWs.[48] Delousing of POWs and their clothing using chemical disinfectants and mobile steam baths was carried out routinely in forward areas before they arrived at camp.[49] The process was repeated at regular intervals on account

[43] 'Health Memoranda for British Soldiers in the Tropics', 15.
[44] Ibid.
[45] GCRO D.4920/8/17, Vaughan, 'Experiences with "G" Squadron', 13.
[46] CMAC RAMC 762/12, 'The Control of Typhus, 1942', 3–4.
[47] Ibid. 6, 9.
[48] CMAC RAMC 538, Lt.-Col. R. McKinlay, 'Report on a Visit to POW Camp at Tabag, 17/3/41', 1.
[49] PRO WO 222/24, 'Medical Administrative Instructions, No. 5, WDF, 18/8/40', War Diary of ADMS, F. G. A. Smyth, WO 177/92; DDMS East Africa, 'Some Medical Aspects of the Campaign in Somaliland and Ethiopia, 1914', 12.

2. Axis POWs lining up for disinfection, Middle East Theatre, CMAC 594/3

of the generally poor sanitary conditions and overcrowding in the camps.[50] Minor outbreaks of relapsing fever in some Indian units also led to their personnel being disinfected.[51] Similar action was taken to prevent outbreaks amongst Allied troops elsewhere in the Middle East, such as among the Polish 10th Army stationed in Persia. The outbreak amongst Polish troops was attributed to poor general hygiene and to the fact that they were allowed to mingle freely with the civilian population.[52] But while localities with typhus were placed out of bounds to British troops, it seems more likely that personal cleanliness was the crucial factor in preventing the disease, as the British, who suffered little from typhus, often frequented the red-light districts of Cairo and Alexandria.

The British Army's long experience of fighting in the Middle East and India meant that it was also aware of the dangers of heat exhaustion and heat stroke. These experiences led the Army to develop appropriate uniforms and headgear; the Army also took note of research conducted between the wars into the physiology of heat stroke and heat exhaustion. This research, which

---

[50] CMAC RAMC 1816/4, 'Enteric Fever in the P.O.W. Camp, Geneifa', 3.
[51] PRO WO 177/92, 'Quarterly Report by DDMS, WDF, for Qtr. ending 30 Sept. 1940'.
[52] CMAC RAMC 1816/4, J. S. K. Boyd, 'Notes, 16/4/42', 8.

was conducted by RAMC officers, drew attention to the electrolytic im-balance of body fluids that was caused by loss of salt through sweating. It emphasized the need to provide soldiers serving in hot climates with ade-quate supplies of salt—in the form of tablets if necessary—as well as water.[53] But the only sure means of preventing these conditions was to prevent over-exposure to the sun. Standing orders for the Middle East dictated that: 'Severe disciplinary action will be taken if casualties are allowed to occur through disregard of these orders. OsC Troops and Draft Conducting Offi-cers will therefore study them immediately after sailing and will take imme-diate steps to put them into action.'[54] All men were instructed to wear light clothing and appropriate headgear, and to ensure that they took salt and water regularly. Initially, men were forbidden to sunbathe or to work bare backed,[55] but by 1942 this was positively encouraged in order to prevent the skin condition 'prickly heat', which was caused by sweating. By this time most soldiers had also abandoned their sunhats, following research under-taken by an MRC team in the Persian Gulf states, where it was found that heat stroke could be avoided simply by taking sufficient quantities of salt and water. On his first tour of the Middle East, the Adjutant-General, Ronald Adam, was astonished to see soldiers throwing their sunhats overboard, but he soon came to accept prevailing opinion.[56]

It had always been assumed that European soldiers who had recently arrived in hot climates could acclimatize to some degree, provided they took proper precautions.[57] As the War Office manual for *Service in Hot Climates* put it: 'Because of our variable climate, we as a race accommodate ourselves fairly well to extremes of hot and cold.'[58] This assumption appeared to be confirmed by British physiologists, who had recently found that humans could become partially acclimatized to tropical temperatures in about a week and fully acclimatized in three weeks. Conducting experiments with volun-teers in artificially heated chambers, they concluded that this could best be achieved by daily bouts of exercise of between ninety minutes and two hours. It was recommended that all those sailing to tropical climates should have

[53] See Lt.-Col. T. B. Nicholls, 'Heat Stroke and Allied Conditions', *Journal of the Royal Army Medical Corps*, 73 (1939), 73–84.

[54] CMAC RAMC 792/1/2, 'Standing Orders for Disembarkation of Personnel and Unit M.T.', 1.

[55] Ibid. 10–12.

[56] LHCMA, Adam Papers, 3/13, narrative covering aspects of Adam's work as Adjutant-General, 'Chap. IV—Medical Problems', 5.

[57] In the course of the previous two centuries a vast amount had been written about the vul-nerability of Europeans in hot climates and attempts to acclimatize them. See Mark Harrison, *Cli-mates and Constitutions: Health, Race, Environment and British Imperialism in India, 1600–1850* (New Delhi: Oxford University Press, 1999). For the Second World War, see CMAC RAMC 792/1, 'Medical Memo., 5—DDMS Persia and Iraq Force', 1–2.

[58] *Service in Hot Climates—1943* (London: HMSO, 1943), 4.

daily exercise during the voyage, and that after disembarking they should be given carefully regulated bouts of exercise.[59] It was often impracticable to follow these guidelines to the letter, but most men were permitted a period of up to one month in which to acclimatize.[60] Later in the war it was thought that acclimatization could be achieved by sunbathing on the deck of troop ships before their arrival in hot climates, beginning with ten minutes per day for the first three days, building up to longer periods in the course of three weeks.[61] In the Western Desert adherence to medical advice meant that there were comparatively few cases of heat stroke, but in India, Iraq, Persia, and the Red Sea ports the incidence was much higher.[62] Between May and September 1942 there were 2,364 cases of heat stroke in the Persian Gulf, for example, whereas in Egypt the number was negligible.[63] One base hospital in Egypt received only one case of heat stroke between March 1941 and September 1942, out of a total of 13,542 casualties admitted.[64] Those cases that did occur often received treatment quickly at the front. Mobile heat stroke centres—three-ton lorries with plentiful supplies of water and special equipment—travelled with all large formations.[65]

Another unpleasant feature of desert warfare proved harder to prevent— the 'desert sore'. These sores occurred in large numbers among British troops in the Middle East, often as a result of fleabites or minor injuries that became infected. In most cases the affliction was merely annoying, but in a few cases, if the sores became infected with diphtheria germs, it could prove fatal. The sores tended to be worse among soldiers who were to some degree malnourished, and these chronic cases could only be cured by evacuation to the Delta, where they could enjoy a diet rich in fresh fruit and vegetables. However, most emphasis was placed on prevention and particularly on preventing fleas from biting soldiers. As a result, the men were provided with puttees into which they could tuck their trousers. But the degree of flea infestation in some areas of the desert was such that prevention was difficult to achieve. One soldier even complained to his MP about the fleas at Tobruk, and questions were asked about the matter in the House of Commons. An entomologist was dispatched forthwith, but the problem was never really solved.[66]

[59] Ibid. 4–5.
[60] CMAC RAMC 792/1, DDH, War Diary, 17 Sept. 1942.
[61] CMAC RAMC 163, 'Selections from the Army Medical Department Bulletin, August 1943', 1.
[62] Ibid. 35.
[63] *Service in Hot Climates*, 9.
[64] Ernest Bulmer, 'Military Medicine in the Middle East. An Experience of 13,542 Cases', *British Medical Journal*, 27 Mar. 1942, pp. 374–7.
[65] *Service in Hot Climates*, 13.
[66] Communication from Dr R. S. Morton, MBE.

The stubborn prevalence of desert sores was one of the few real failures in disease control in the British Army during the Western Desert campaign. The other—far more important in terms of lost manpower—was the high incidence of sexually transmitted diseases; a common problem in time of war and one that affected all theatres to varying extents. In the first two years of the war the incidence of VD among British servicemen and male civilians more than doubled, and among women it rose by 63 per cent. In addition to the likely consequences for national efficiency, these figures seemed to indicate a national moral decline, going hand-in-hand with a rise in the number of births outside of wedlock. The government's decision to increase the number of treatment centres for VD, and to introduce compulsory treatment for women suspected of having the disease, were reminiscent of its response during the Great War, which had been criticized by many as authoritarian. But the frankness of anti-VD propaganda was quite unlike anything during 1914–18 and marked a shift towards a more secular, scientific view of the problem. In 1942 the Ministry of Health launched a campaign to make the facts about VD and its treatment more widely known, and for the first time in Britain the subject was deemed appropriate for a radio broadcast.[67] As the new Central Council for Health Education (the successor to the British Social Hygiene Council) put it, 'hush-hush was being banished'; in other words, the causes, effects, and treatment of VD were to be discussed more openly than before.[68]

The idea that VD could be fought effectively through a combination of education and propaganda stemmed from the belief that it thrived among the poorly motivated and the ill-informed. Lieutenant-Colonel Robert Lees, the Consulting Venereologist for British Middle East Forces, insisted that:

control of V.D. is a matter of discipline and 'morale' much more than of medical measures. Self-discipline comes first, with pride in being fit to fight, and fit to serve. Secondly comes unit discipline which depends on the C.O., officers and senior N.C.Os. It is my impression that the units with the highest reputation as crack fighting men and famous for good discipline have a low rate of V.D. and base units have a high V.D. rate.[69]

There was, it seemed, a need to provide soldiers with wholesome forms of recreation, and to dispel the ignorance that still surrounded VD. But propaganda had to be of the right kind. According to Lees, that which aimed to frighten the soldier by describing in graphic detail the symptoms of gonorrhoea or syphilis was likely to fail, since modern forms of treatment had

[67] Angus Calder, *The People's War: Britain 1939–1945* (London: Pimlico, 1992), 313.
[68] Ministry of Health and Central Council for Health Education leaflet, *A Great Black Snowball.*
[69] PRO WO 222/1302, Lt.-Col. Robert Lees, memo on prevention of VD, 14 Apr. 1942.

robbed VD of much of its horror. He suggested that 'the impairment of military efficiency of the soldier, and his duty to his unit, the Army and the country by keeping "fighting fit" should be the basis of the appeal'.[70] While the emphasis had changed considerably since the Great War, the Army continued to regard venereal disease as a moral and disciplinary problem, although there were clearly different views on the matter. In a letter to the *British Medical Journal* in August 1941, Colonel P. F. Chapman, a retired colonel of the Indian Medical Service, denounced appeals to chastity as 'worse than useless', advocating frank discussions instead: 'Men are surprisingly shy about these matters', he claimed.[71] But his comments met with an indignant response from a serving officer of the RAMC, who stressed that chastity was still 'strongly encouraged' in the Army. He insisted that troops received lectures on 'maintaining a high moral standard and on abstention from illicit sexual relations'.[72]

These exchanges took place against the backdrop of more general concerns about venereal disease and sexual behaviour in wartime.[73] The NSPVD (successor to the National Council for the Combating of Venereal Disease), and Left-leaning organizations like the Progressive League and the National Social Hygiene League, were engaged throughout the war in a battle against what they perceived as 'obscurantism': an unholy alliance between Church and State which drew a veil over sexual matters. Their principal opponent was the Archbishop of Canterbury, William Temple, who was appointed president of the Central Council for Health Education in 1942 in an attempt to assuage religious opinion. The Archbishop had angered the Society and many military doctors by his opposition to the compulsory treatment of women with VD, as well as to chemical and mechanical prophylaxis. At a meeting on VD convened in London in 1943 by the Central Council for Health Education, Temple spoke out against the distribution of prophylactics to troops on the grounds that it would be an inducement to fornication. Army education, he insisted, should stress the sacredness of sex and the possibility of chastity.[74]

For most advocates of prevention, the moral or religious approach to VD control was *not* incompatible with the medical or secular, although many

---

[70] Ibid., Lees, Report for Jan.–Mar. 1941, 6.

[71] Col. P. F. Chapman to editor, *British Medical Journal*, 3 Aug. 1940, p. 169.

[72] Lt.-Col. T. E. Osmond, RAMC, to editor, *British Medical Journal*, 17 Aug. 1940, p. 236.

[73] For a fuller discussion see Mark Harrison, 'Sex and the Citizen Soldier: Health, Morals and Discipline in the British Army During the Second World War', in R. Cooter, M. Harrison, and S. Sturdy (eds.), *Medicine and Modern Warfare* (Amsterdam and Atlanta: Rodopi Press, 1999), 229–54.

[74] The Most Revd W. Temple, 'The Church's Approach', *Proceedings of the Central Council for Health Education Conference on Health Education and the Venereal Diseases, 26 February, 1943* (London: CCHE, 1943), 9–10.

progressives viewed the moralizing of the Church as unworldly and restrictive.[75] Organizations like the Progressive League and the Communist Party of Great Britain went so far as to accuse the government of giving way to religious opinion and of failing to make chemical prophylaxis readily available to civilians.[76] Nor were such suspicions confined to the Left. *Reynolds News*, a lowbrow London newspaper, carried a story alleging a 'behind the scenes fight at the Ministry of Health', one section stressing the need for 'clean living', the other for greater frankness about VD. The former, it lamented, had won.[77] These suspicions appear to be borne out by the fact that the Ministry of Health actively discouraged local authorities—many of which were subscribers to the NSPVD—from disseminating information about chemical prophylaxis.[78]

Yet the debate over VD prevention cannot be characterized simply as one between 'moralists' and 'pragmatists', since the meaning of 'morality' had changed. Morality in sexual matters was now construed not so much in religious terms, as in terms of civic responsibility. Posters exhorted soldiers to 'Guard against VD. Keep straight—keep sober. You owe it to yourself, your comrades, your efficiency.'[79] As the British forces newspaper in the Middle East, the *Union Jack*, put it in July 1942: 'As for the moral aspect, well, we leave it to you, but remember the women folk waiting at home—will you be able to face them with a clear conscience on your return?'[80] The soldier was also made aware of his responsibility to future generations. A Central Council for Health Education leaflet distributed to soldiers in the Middle East described VD as 'a great black snowball which, unless we check it, will go rolling down the years of peace and reconstruction . . . The problem is one which the community as a whole must face seriously and resolutely because it affects the whole nation and the future of our race'.[81] Films such as *Sex Hygiene*, which were shown to all Allied servicemen in overseas theatres, underscored the possible effects of venereal diseases on soldiers' wives and children.

It is necessary to distinguish between what were termed, respectively, health 'education' and health 'propaganda'; the former appealed to reason, while the latter sought to elicit a more emotional response. Appeals to

---

[75] Discussion point by Dr Maitland Radford, MOH St. Pancras: ibid. 19.

[76] CMAC SA/PVD, 'We Demand Prophylaxis', *PLAN*, 11 (1944), 1. Secretary to J. B. S. Haldane, University of London Dept. of Biometry, to NSPVD, 28 Nov. 1942, re. article on VD by Haldane in the *Daily Mail*.

[77] CMAC SA/PVD, *Reynolds News*, 27 Feb. 1944, p. 2.

[78] CMAC RAMC SA/PVD/11, H. R. Hartwell, on behalf of Minister of Health, to Town Clerk, Bournemouth, 31 July 1944 and A. Lindsay Clegg, Town Clerk of Bournemouth, to Ministry of Health, 15 Aug. 1944.

[79] CMAC RAMC 1542, copy of poster.

[80] 'Health Hints for Soldiers', *Union Jack*, 5 July 1942.

[81] Ministry of Health and Central Council for Health Education leaflet, *A Great Black Snowball*.

chivalry, pride of self, and patriotism all fell into the category of 'propaganda', which distinguished the morality of the British soldier from what Ernest Cowell referred to as the 'wanton promiscuity' of the Germans and Italians.[82] It is questionable how far British servicemen thought of themselves as morally or psychologically superior to their Axis counterparts, but propaganda that instilled a sense of duty to comrades and country was invaluable, according to the Consulting Venereologist Lieutenant-Colonel Lees. In his opinion, it reached 'the man to whom reason does not appeal—the rather stupid sensual fellow who indulges most of his appetites and who is the type most commonly infected'.[83] Lees was referring mainly to the rank and file, whose education and upbringing had not instilled the virtues of self-discipline and sexual restraint expected of the officer class.[84] It was alleged that other ranks were more likely to include persons with 'inadequate personality', as psychologists then described them.

A study conducted by the psychiatrists Major E. Wittowker and Captain J. Cowan in 1942 found that VD patients were far more likely than other categories to include persons with a history of mental instability or indiscipline. Contrasting 200 VD patients with a control group of eighty-six patients with the skin disease impetigo, they found that 59 per cent of VD patients were classified as 'immature personality types' as against only 19 per cent of impetigo patients. Some 54 per cent of VD patients were classed as discontented with military life, as against only 29 per cent of impetigo patients. The classification was made on the basis of a questionnaire and a simple psychiatric interview. A supposedly typical VD case was 'Corporal A.B.', aged 28, and described as an 'unaggressive dependent' personality. He was supposedly a 'selfish individual whose role in life is to make money and to have personal comforts. Has never been able to hold his own. Married two-and-a-half years and got on well with his wife who mothered him a good deal.'[85] The study is interesting for two reasons. First, it draws a picture of the typical VD patient as a selfish mother's boy, who shirks his responsibility to comrades and country in his desperate search for comfort. He is, in many respects, the antithesis of the model British citizen, lacking both independence and self-control. Secondly, virtually every case discussed in the report is drawn from the other ranks, giving the impression that such behaviour was class-based. Thus, despite echoing the inclusive rhetoric of citizenship, psychiatry may have occasionally served to confirm latent ideas of a dependent working class.

[82] CMAC RAMC 466/38, Cowell, 'Report on the Health of the Army in North Africa', 7.

[83] PRO WO 222/1302, Lees, 'Methods of Prevention of Venereal Disease', 14 Apr. 1942.

[84] CMAC RAMC 1849, Medical report on the Italian campaign.

[85] CMAC GC/135/B.1, MacKeith Papers, Maj. E. Wittowker, and Capt. J. Cowan (with the assistance of Lt. D. C. T. Sullivan), 'Some Aspects of the V.D. Problem in the British Army'.

Table 3.2. Incidence of VD amongst British troops in the Middle Eastern Force (per 1,000 troops)

Type of VD	1939	1940	1941	1942	1943	1944	1945
Gonorrhoea	30.20	22.40	16.0	8.5	—	4.3	7.2
Syphilis	2.50	4.13	4.3	2.4	—	3.0	5.4
Other VD	6.26	7.60	19.7	14.7	—	8.4	11.8
TOTAL	39.00	34.20	40.0	25.6	15.9	15.7	24.4

Source: W. Franklin Mellor (ed.), *Medical History of the Second World War: Casualties and Medical Statistics* (London: HMSO, 1972), 119, 192, 264, 282, 334.

Most health educators believed that appeals to sexual abstinence would make little impact on the immature and self-centred. So, in the event of their urges being too strong to control, Major-General Ernest Cowell urged soldiers to use a condom or prophylactic packet, both of which were provided from the very beginning of the war.[86] He also warned them to report sick at once if symptoms appear: failure to do so was a crime under military law, and those reporting sick with VD faced the loss of wartime proficiency pay. Those engaged as tradesmen or acting NCOs also lost their rank and position.[87] Measures against VD, then, were never entirely free from penal stigma, but the sanctions against contracting these diseases were far less severe than during the First World War, when all pay was stopped during the period of hospitalization and leave cancelled for up to twelve months.[88] This more tolerant attitude reflected the observation, made during the First World War, that punishment tended to produce concealment and was therefore counter-productive.[89]

This combination of discipline and health propaganda met with mixed success. In the Middle East there was some improvement, as admissions from VD fell from almost forty per thousand troops per year in 1941 to just under sixteen per thousand in 1944, increasing somewhat in 1945. However, in other theatres, such as Italy, the rise in VD was almost inexorable, climbing from the already high figure of nearly fifty-one per thousand in 1944 to just over seventy-one per thousand in 1945.

The high incidence of VD in the British Army overseas was attributed to a combination of sexual opportunity and the lack of alternative recreations.

[86] PRO WO 177/1, Monthly report of Deputy Director of Hygiene, France, Sept. 1939, p. 2.
[87] CMAC RAMC 466/36, Cowell, 'Health Memorandum', 16 Dec. 1943.
[88] Mark Harrison, 'The British Army and the Problem of Venereal Disease in France and Egypt During the First World War', *Medical History*, 39 (1995), 139.
[89] See L. W. Harrison's comment on E. T. Burke in his 'Venereal Disease: Its Prevention and Treatment on Active Service', *Bulletin of War Medicine*, 1 (Sept. 1940), 41.

But in which circumstances, precisely, was VD contracted? Overseas, it was generally acknowledged that most infections were contracted at brothels and from so-called 'amateur prostitutes' operating on the streets of cities such as Cairo or Alexandria. In Britain, the situation was more complex. A survey of 200 VD military patients showed that the majority (76 per cent) had contracted VD from sexual partners 'picked up' at public houses, cinemas, and so forth. Some 22 per cent of these were married women whose husbands were serving overseas, over 4 per cent were 'service girls', and 1 per cent were men. Only 6 per cent of patients claimed to have been infected by a prostitute.[90] Well over half those interviewed owned up to not using a condom, the majority because they had regarded it as unnecessary; in other words, because their partner had 'looked respectable'.[91]

In some cases, however, fear of venereal infection did engender caution. Letters from servicemen and women to organizations such as the NSPVD, requesting further information on prophylaxis, indicate that venereal infection was a risk not accepted lightly. In the first years of the war the Society claimed it had received 'many thousands' of such requests, and although the number of letters in its archive suggests this may have been an exaggeration, letters from servicepeople were fairly common. One young man from Renfrewshire wrote: 'As I expect to be called up for military service in the near future, I should be grateful if you would inform me of the best prophylactic measures against venereal disease.'[92] Another, from London, asked for information on the grounds that: 'I am about to join the army and I may possibly find myself in the category of those many men who find palliative relief from the strains of war in occasional promiscuity.'[93]

The high rates of venereal infection that existed in the Middle East and some other theatres indicate that few British soldiers were so well informed. Throughout the war the NSPVD continued to receive complaints from soldiers that they had not been told about prophylaxis: not because the Army disagreed with the practice, but simply because medical officers were overwhelmed with other tasks. In 1943 John Finlayson, Organisational Secretary and Lecturer of the National Social Hygiene League, told Herbert Jones of the NSPVD that: 'It is certainly untrue to say that Medical Officers lecture to all units, many men tell me that they have not had a lecture at all and they have been in the army three years.' He also claimed that:

In many units there are no facilities whatever for the men to keep themselves free from Venereal Diseases should they take risks. No condoms are provided even at a

---

[90] CMAC GC/135/B.1, Wittkower and Cowan, 'Some Aspects of the V.D. Problem', 2.
[91] Ibid. 9.
[92] CMAC SA/PVD/6, Hector MacKenzie to Secretary, NSPVD, 28 Nov. 1940.
[93] Ibid., Mr A. Deaner, Bethnal Green, London to Secretary, NSPVD, 6 Dec. 1940.

price, or douche departments. I am very often able to give the Commanding Offi-cers . . . the address of condom manufacturers and they readily avail themselves of the chance to purchase and supply their men at about 3*d* each.[94]

A greater obstacle to VD prevention was posed by the Army's policy of regulated prostitution. Brothels were numerous in the Middle East, and while there were none in Sudan and Eritrea, there were plenty of so-called 'ama-teurs' who plied their trade in the streets and bazaars.[95] These 'amateurs' were said to be the product of a society that possessed no moral or religious bar to sexual intercourse outside of marriage.[96] In other countries the abundance of prostitutes was attributed largely to poverty and the economic dislocation caused by the war. Whatever the reason, it was generally believed that prostitution was a complex social and economic problem, and that the only effective means of controlling it was to place it under medical and military control.[97]

In most overseas theatres the British attempted to contain the problem by establishing regulated brothels in which prostitutes could be inspected for venereal disease.[98] This was a continuation of practices which had become widespread during the nineteenth century, and which had received a new lease of life during the First World War in France and Egypt, until the broth-els were closed under pressure of public opinion.[99] In the Middle East, however, the Army established only one new brothel of its own. It was estab-lished in Tripoli at the behest of Montgomery, who was quoted as saying that his men 'deserved it'. Condoms, washing facilities, and mercury ointment were provided for all those who used the brothel;[100] elsewhere British sol-diers appear to have used existing institutions. Inspection of these brothels was usually carried out by military MOs, but in some areas, such as Eritrea, the British Army resurrected the Italian system of inspection by a municipal doctor. The Consultant Venereologist in Eritrea, Captain Bell RAMC, paid surprise visits to test the effectiveness of the system and to investigate all instances where military personnel claimed to have been infected.[101]

The inspection of brothels was accompanied by a crackdown on unregu-lated and 'amateur' prostitution. In Egypt, reported Robert Lees: 'The civil

---

[94] CMAC RAMC SA/PVD/9, John Finlayson to Herbert Jones, 18 Jan. 1943.
[95] PRO WO 222/1302, Lees, 'Report of Consulting Venereologist', 28 Apr. 1941, p. 5.
[96] Ibid., Lees, 'Report on Visit to Eritrea', 15 Nov. 1941, p. 6.
[97] Ibid., Lees, 'Report on Methods of Prevention of Venereal Disease', 14 Apr. 1942, p. 1.
[98] Such practices were common in other armies, e.g. the establishment of 'soldaten Bordellen' for German soldiers. See Franz Seidler, *Prostitution, Homosexualität, Selbstverstümmelung. Problem der deutschen Sanitätsführung 1939–1945* (Neckargemünd: Kurt Vowinkel, 1977); Christa Paul, *Zwangs Prostitution: Staatlich Errichte Bordelle im Nationalsozialismus* (Berlin: Hertrich, 1994).
[99] Harrison, 'Problem of Venereal Disease'.
[100] Communication from Dr R. S. Morton, MBE.
[101] PRO WO 222/1302, Lees, 'Report on Visit to Eritrea', p. 6.

and military police are constantly vigilant and active against streetwalkers and other clandestine prostitutes. During the first quarter of 1941, the Cairo police arrested 732 such women and, on medical examination, 175 (twenty-four per cent) were found to suffer from venereal disease.'[102] Many prostitutes were arrested on the basis of information supplied by soldiers who had contracted VD. As in France, VD patients were supplied with a form that requested information that would enable military policemen to identify 'diseased prostitutes'. They were required to furnish details of the date of exposure, the first occurrence of symptoms, the location of the woman's house or brothel, and her name, nationality, and appearance.[103] The system remained in place wherever the British Army was permitted to operate it.

The contradiction between this system of officially tolerated prostitution and exhortations to sexual restraint became increasingly apparent. Although some MOs favoured the continuation of regulated prostitution, the majority, including most senior officers and venereologists, denounced the practice for undermining their efforts. The existence of medically inspected brothels created a false sense of security, they claimed. The Deputy Director of Hygiene (DDH) for the Middle East noted in January 1942 that: 'the idea is extremely prevalent that . . . the brothels are safe, and it is considered that far larger numbers of men are consequently visiting these places than would otherwise associate with loose women.' He claimed that over 45,000 men were visiting the Cairo brothels every month.[104] Surveys of those admitted to hospital with VD also revealed that very few soldiers had bothered to wear condoms or perform chemical prophylaxis after intercourse.[105] The Consulting Venereologist, Lieutenant-Colonel Lees, reported in 1943 that only one soldier in twenty who contracted VD had carried out any form of personal disinfection.[106] Attendance at brothels also raised the spectre of infection with deadly diseases such as typhus, which had broken out amongst the civilian population on several occasions. The DDH reported that: 'The state of these brothels, although much has been done to improve them, is still sordid, degrading, and insanitary in the extreme, and in close proximity to forbidden areas, the conditions of which are indescribably filthy.' Further, the effects of brothels on the 'mental hygiene, discipline and morale' of a 'young, raw, civilian army' were such as to corrode military authority.[107]

[102] Ibid., Lees, 'Report of Consulting Venereologist', 28 Apr. 1941, p. 5.
[103] PRO WO 177/1, Medical administrative instructions, No. 12, 23 Nov. 1939.
[104] CMAC RAMC 2048/1, DDH MEF, 'Notice for DMS', 19 Jan. 1942.
[105] PRO WO 222/1300, Report of Brig. Robert Lees, Consulting Venereologist CMF, 13 Apr. 1945.
[106] PRO WO 222/12, Consulting Venereologist—Summary of Policy and Action, Sept. 1939–31 Aug. 1943.
[107] CMAC RAMC 2048/1, DDH MEF, 'Notice for DMS', 19 Jan. 1942.

Other officers had similar concerns, but many—including Montgomery—regarded sexual relaxation as essential to morale, and military brothels appeared to be the lesser of two evils. These opposing viewpoints can be clearly discerned in the debate over regulated prostitution in Cairo. At the beginning of 1942 the DDH pressed for the closure of licensed brothels on disciplinary grounds, and because they would provoke an outcry 'of the first magnitude' in Britain and the Dominions should their existence become known.[108] Medical opinion at this stage was virtually unanimous that brothels in Cairo and Alexandria should be placed out of bounds to British troops, and that alternative recreational facilities should be provided. But the Deputy Adjutant-General was firmly opposed to this and doubted whether such moves would reduce the incidence of VD, despite the allegedly beneficial effects of an experimental closure of brothels in the Canal Zone.[109] The case made by the DDH was further weakened in March 1942 when, at a conference on VD, several MOs previously committed to the closure of brothels, including the DDMS himself, sided with the Deputy Adjutant-General.[110] The DDH suspected that pressure had been exerted upon them, and wrote in 'the strongest possible terms' to the Deputy Adjutant's superior.[111]

By the late summer, however, the tide was beginning to turn in favour of closure. The political storm of which the DDH had warned had broken, and 'numerous charges had been made against the Army by 'dignitaries of the Church, morality societies and others of encouraging the soldier in fornication'.[112] Some combatant officers had also begun to share his concerns. At the beginning of August the DDH received a copy of a letter from the commander of Cairo Area to all zone and unit commanders declaring that the Berka—a military brothel—would shortly be placed out of bounds.[113] The so-called 'Battle of the Berka'—a fight between large numbers of British, Australian, and New Zealand troops—had precipitated the decision.[114] Although the commander faced considerable resistance from other officers, he stood firm in his decision to close the brothel. The DDH recorded in December 1942 that: 'It is gratifying to record that the Commander . . . thinks that the closing of the Berka has removed a grave blot on British prestige in Egypt; that the behaviour of the troops has improved to a very mate-

---

[108] CMAC RAMC 2048/1, DDH MEF, War Diary, 19 Jan. 1942.
[109] Ibid., 13 Feb. and 16 Feb. 1942.
[110] Ibid., 19 Mar. 1942, RAMC 2048/1, CMAC.
[111] DDH MEF, War Diary, 20 Mar. 1942.
[112] PRO WO 222/12, Consulting Venereologist, Summary of policy and action, Sept. 1939–41 Aug. 1943, p. 9.
[113] CMAC RAMC 2048/1, DDH MEF, War Diary, 4 Aug. 1942.
[114] Communication from Dr R. S. Morton, MBE.

rial extent since the closure; that, even if a slight increase in V.D. did occur as a result, it is quite offset by other advantages . . .'[115] However, the Berka appears to have reopened after a decent interval, and other lower-profile establishments continued to operate unmolested, masquerading as dinner-and-dance establishments. This was true of the brothels which catered for British officers, one of which was located near Cairo, close to the pyramids; the other—'Mary's House'—did a steady trade in the city itself. 'Mary' also had a branch at Alexandria.[116]

The Berka affair is significant because it illustrates the importance of preserving the image of British discipline and 'good form'. The DDH's statement shows that such considerations outweighed anxieties caused by manpower wastage from VD, as does the eventual agreement of the commanding officer, who took the decision to close the Berka only after a fight had broken out between British and Commonwealth troops. After all, treatment with sulphonamides and later with penicillin massively reduced the time taken to treat most forms of VD.[117] The need to maintain an air of moral superiority was especially important in those countries under Allied military government, and particularly in Egypt, where anti-British sentiment had increased during 1942.[118]

The methods used to control venereal disease in Egypt were therefore guided by more than the need to prevent loss of manpower. Although sexually transmitted diseases constituted a serious military problem in the Middle East, it was the political and disciplinary dimensions of VD that were ultimately the most important. Its association with vice and intemperance blackened the reputation of British forces overseas—a vitally important consideration in view of the awkward relationship that often existed between the Allies and civilian administrations. VD and rampant promiscuity also dealt to a blow to prevailing images of 'Britishness', as expressed in wartime propaganda. Although this propaganda seems to have had little impact on the behaviour of troops, it tells us a great deal about the ways in which national identity was represented during the war. It also reveals a decided shift away from religious strictures upon sexual behaviour to ones that were predomi-

[115] CMAC RAMC 2048/1, DDH MEF, War Diary, 1 Dec. 1942.

[116] Communication from Dr R. S. Morton, MBE.

[117] Before the introduction of penicillin, treatment for gonorrhoea could last up to 25 days, and for syphilis as many as 40–50 days. However, gonorrhoea could be treated in only 24 hours using intramuscular injections of penicillin and over 4–5 days in the case of syphilis. See WO 222/1300, Lees, 'Report of the Consulting Venereologist, July–Sept. 1944, 2; CG/135/B.1, Wittkower and Cowan, 'Some Aspects of the V.D. Problem', 1; Report on Penicillin in Cases of Venereal Disease, *British Medical Journal*, 23 Mar. 1944, pp. 428–9.

[118] P. J. Vatikiotis, *The History of Modern Egypt: From Muhammed Ali to Mubarak* (London: Weidenfeld & Nicolson, 1991), 352–4.

nantly secular. But this is not to say that those on the 'progressive' wing of the anti-VD campaign had fully succeeded in ridding these diseases of their stigma. Although fewer people now regarded illicit intercourse as an offence against God, to have risked infection with VD was to have failed in one's duty as a soldier, spouse, parent, and above all, as a British citizen.

Casualty Disposal and the Challenge of Mechanized Warfare

The lines of communication in the Western Desert campaigns were precarious, to say the least. For much of the time the only established routes between the front and the bases in the Nile delta were the single-track road and railway running along the Mediterranean seaboard. To the south lay an inhospitable expanse of open desert, strewn with mines and traversed by only a few rough tracks. The evacuation of casualties was therefore a risky business, as the narrow lines of communication were congested and frequently subjected to hostile fire. It was also difficult to treat casualties along the lines of communication, as few places possessed supplies of water sufficient for a hospital. This unfortunate situation meant that the main hospitals of the British-led force were concentrated in the Nile Delta at Alexandria, Cairo, and in the Canal Zone. Only two general hospitals usually existed at any one time outside the Delta area, such as those located at Tobruk and Granola. Terrain and transportation therefore dictated that a new system of treatment and evacuation be developed, capable of dealing with the majority of cases in forward areas.

The need for forward treatment grew steadily more apparent as British forces penetrated deeper into Libya, when the lines of communication lengthened to over 500 miles. As one report pointed out, the situation was comparable to: 'having the Base Hospital area in London when the country between that city and York is almost uninhabited and uninhabitable—the two places connected by one single narrow road and one line of railway. Fighting is taking place near Edinburgh and the connection between York and Edinburgh being one road and many tracks over dusty rock strewn desert.'[119] Although ambulance trains were endowed with ample accommodation and medical facilities, and although they were given priority on the railway, patients were always at risk from delays and enemy attack.[120] Hospital ships operating out of Tobruk and Mersa Matruh helped to relieve the

---

[119] CMAC RAMC 466/36, Covell Papers, Report on casualty disposal in the Western Desert, 1942, p. 6.
[120] Communication from Dr R. S. Morton, MBE.

strain on the lines of communication, but evacuation by sea was hazardous because the ships were too large to enter the harbour at Tobruk. This meant that they had to be loaded by small craft called 'lighters'—a time-consuming and dangerous procedure. The RAF also removed a few casualties, but at this stage there was no regular evacuation by air.[121]

The enormity of the task facing the medical services is evident from the sheer number of casualties that had to be transported back from the front. Between 18 November 1941 and 26 May 1942 (beginning with Auchinleck's offensive, Operation CRUSADER, and ending with the start of Rommel's offensive at Gazala), some 32,694 casualties—both sick and wounded—were evacuated to hospitals in the Delta. Despite the fact that ambulance trains were supposed to run daily between Mersa Matruh and Alexandria,[122] casualties evacuated by rail took on average six days to reach their destination, by contrast with those evacuated by air (no more than 2,000) who normally reached their destination within six hours. Heavy traffic on the line meant that hospital trains were subjected to frequent and lengthy delays, during which the wounded were often left lying at way-stations without proper nursing or feeding.[123] The journey by road was little better: the route was bumpy, slow, and ill-suited to the carriage of surgical cases. It was fortunate indeed that the Army now used the 'Tobruk Splint', a conventional Thomas splint (as used in 1914–18) reinforced by plaster of Paris to immobilize limbs without impeding circulation. This followed the procedure developed by Trueta during the Spanish Civil War.[124] Nor were these difficulties compensated by facilities available in forward areas. CCSs were practically immobile due to lack of transport, and could usually be brought no nearer than 50 miles from the firing line.[125] Units close to the front also lacked much basic equipment: the ADMS, F. G. A. Smyth, reported in July 1941 that field ambulances were rationed to one three-inch tin of Elastoplast per week, and that similar restrictions were placed on the use of cotton wool.[126] Surgery in forward areas was further hindered by the lack of electricity, which meant that most operations were conducted using paraffin lamps, which did not give off sufficient light.[127]

---

[121] CMAC RAMC 466/36, Report on casualty disposal in the Western Desert, p. 6.

[122] PRO WO 177/92, Medical Administrative Instruction, No. 1, WDF, 18 Aug. 1940, p. 1.

[123] PRO WO 177/92, Memo. from ADMS regarding ambulance trains, 3 Oct. 1940.

[124] J. C. Watts, *Surgeon at War* (London: George Allen & Unwin, 1955), 32; Lt.-Col. A. McMillan, 'Surgical Experiences at a Base Hospital in Egypt', *Journal of the Royal Army Medical Corps*, 78 (1942), 300–6.

[125] CMAC RAMC 466/36, Report on casualty disposal in the Western Desert, p. 6.

[126] PRO WO 17/92, Memo. from ADMS on medical stores, 16 July 1941.

[127] 'Surgery in Libya', leading article, *British Medical Journal*, 4 July 1942, p. 16.

Desert surgeons were fortunate in that they were working in a relatively sterile environment, otherwise the long delays to which the wounded were subjected would have allowed wound infection to develop before many casualties had reached the base. In fact, the conditions in which surgeons operated in the Western Desert permitted them to return to the conservative methods of surgery developed during the South African War of 1899–1902.[128] Eighth Army surgeons seldom resorted to debridement (radical excision of the wound), as practised on the Western Front during the First World War, and removed only that tissue which was obviously dead—a procedure known as 'wound trimming'. The sterile conditions, together with antibacterial sulphonamide drugs, also allowed surgeons to leave the wound open so as to facilitate drainage. Clean 'through-and-through' bullet wounds were left alone, save for a dusting of sulphonamide powder, and were simply covered with vaseline gauze. Conservatism was even the watchword in more difficult cases, such as abdominal and chest wounds.[129]

The first step taken to rectify the twin problems of evacuation and forward surgery was to make the CCS more mobile. This was achieved by adding one platoon of Royal Army Service Corps (RASC) and more large trucks (up to a maximum of thirteen) to each CCS. The light section of the CCS could now be lifted in one move and the whole in three, the former serving as an advanced operating centre or Field Surgical Unit (FSU). Like most other medical units, the FSU developed from an improvisation made in the thick of battle. During Wavell's desert campaign of 1941 a team of surgeons working at the MDS of a field ambulance under Bernard Williams RAMC, together with some men from the light section of a CCS, used looted Italian lorries to make a mobile surgical unit. The FSU, which could be attached to any CCS, Field Dressing Station (FDS), or Field Ambulance (FA), enabled casualties to receive surgical attention within six to twelve hours.[130]

The demands of mechanized warfare also led to radical changes in the organization of field ambulances. The old, heavy sections of FAs did not lend themselves to highly mobile operations such as those in the Western Desert, so their commanding officers began to make piecemeal changes to improve their manoeuvrability. By the end of the desert campaign the typical field ambulance consisted of one MDS providing shelter for up to 200 patients and two mobile companies, each of which were divided into three sections.

---

[128] G. H. Makins, *Surgical Experiences in South Africa 1899–1900: Being a Clinical Study of the Nature and Effects and Injuries produced by Bullets of Small Calibre* (London: Hodder & Stoughton, 1913); L. J. Ramsey, 'Bullet Wounds and X-rays in Britain's Little Wars', *Journal of the Society for Army Historical Research*, 60 (1982), 91–102.

[129] 'A Note on Surgery in the Eighth Army' *British Medical Journal*, 28 Aug. 1943, p. 274.

[130] Watts, *Surgeon at War*, 28.

One of these sections (transported by two three-ton lorries) formed the ADS and the other two were light sections that could each be moved by one three-ton truck. These composite units could easily keep pace with an advancing armoured formation. One company or part thereof was usually placed in the vicinity of the main brigade headquarters, while the reserve company advanced to take the place of the first, as it went forward with the brigade.[131] In addition to the extra trucks, the field ambulances received more ambulance cars, so that each had at least twenty vehicles.[132]

Despite these improvements, medical transport in forward areas was still deficient. Regimental MOs with armoured divisions were handicapped by the fact that they had no armoured vehicle to enable them to get close to the fighting. The only vehicles allocated to regimental medical units were generally fifteen-hundred weight trucks, which afforded little protection from bullets, let alone artillery shells.[133] The inability of MOs to reach wounded men led on several occasions to long delays in their treatment and evacuation.[134] The only options for injured tank crew at that time were to remain in the tank or to lie on the ground, exposed to hostile fire and the cold of the desert night. MOs insisted that the only solution was to supply them with armoured scout cars, or similar vehicles, so that they could keep pace with rapidly moving forces and thus always be in a position to tend to the wounded.[135] These were eventually supplied and became a characteristic feature of medical work in the Western Desert.[136] However, the provision of scout cars did not alter that fact that RMOs were often poorly informed about the order of battle, and in some cases had no idea that an attack was about to be launched. Recalling the battle of Sidi Rezegh in November 1941, J. D. P. Graham, an MO with 7th Armoured Division, wrote: 'there I sat in my Dingo [Daimler scout car], deafened, without orders or any conception as to which way to turn to be of assistance or to withdraw to a healthier patch.'[137] Such confusion was common until the appointment of Montgomery, who ensured that MOs were adequately briefed.[138] By the second battle of El Alamein there were clear instructions stating that senior medical officers were to be informed of the divisional commander's plan; a move that dramatically improved co-ordination between medical and combatant branches at all levels.[139]

---

[131] Lt.-Col. R. Johnston, 'The Divisional Field Ambulance in Mobile Warfare', *Journal of the Royal Army Medical Corps*, 82 (1944), 168–76.
[132] CMAC RAMC 466/36, Report on casualty disposal in the Western Desert, pp. 6–7.
[133] CAMC RAMC 498, Maj.-Gen. M. D. Moore, Commander Armoured Division, Egypt, 'Medical Arrangements for Armoured Divisions—Western Desert, 1 January 1940', 2.
[134] CMAC RAMC 466/36, Report on casualty disposal in the Western Desert, p. 7.
[135] Ibid. 12.   [136] Graham, 'Time in the Sand', 29.
[137] Ibid. 44.   [138] Ibid. 24.
[139] PRO WO 222/89, 'Reorganisation of Medical Services in the Field', 3 Nov. 1942.

Next to the collection of the wounded from the firing line, the most pressing need was for improved evacuation from the CCSs, which could only be effectively carried out by air. The main stumbling-block was the lack of aircraft, but the problem was also an organizational one. A medical report on the theatre in 1942 lamented the fact that there were no designated aerodromes to which casualties could be brought, leaving MOs uncertain as to whether a plane was available. The report suggested that: 'If some scheme could be evolved whereby a more regular service of returning [transport] planes could be made use of from one or more selected aerodromes, then it would be possible to ensure that medical holding units could be established near the aerodromes and cases sent to these units to await evacuation by air.'[140] These recommendations amounted to a reversal of the standing orders laid down in 1939, which stated that evacuation by air would be 'reserved for dangerously ill patients and cases of extreme urgency'.[141] But as Colonel Wallace, the ADMS to 7th Armoured Brigade, explained to his superior in August 1941: 'There is a general feeling amongst senior officers and men, which is increasing as time goes on, that after two years of war, air evacuation of casualties should be available, and I am constantly being asked when it will be possible and what is being done about it.'[142] Having special responsibility for the welfare and medical care of the Army, the Adjutant-General was greatly concerned by what he heard during his first tour of the Middle East. In his report, he noted that:

An important point in morale is the removal of the wounded. It is unbelievable that, at this stage of the war, the United Kingdom has not one single air ambulance. Although much use was made of returning transport aircraft, it meant that the wounded had to be taken to the aircraft and not the aircraft to the wounded. It is to my mind essential . . . that at the earliest possible moment some air ambulances should be provided. It is impossible to get accurate facts and figures as to the number of lives lost and the suffering inflicted through the non-provision of ambulance aircraft.[143]

The lack of such a facility contrasted starkly with provisions made by the Germans and Italians, who had been evacuating their casualties by air from the beginning of the war.[144] Medical sections (*Sanitätsflugbereitschaft*) had been organized in the Luftwaffe early in the war, and each unit had between

---

[140] CMAC RAMC 466/36, Report on casualty disposal in the Western Desert, p. 9.
[141] CMAC RAMC War Diary of Col. P. S. Tomlinson, DDMS, 24 Aug. 1939, 1.
[142] PRO WO 177/92, Col. Q. V. B. Wallace, ADMS 7th Armoured Brigade to DDMS, 11 Aug. 1941.
[143] LCHMA, Adam Papers, 3/6/1, 'Report by the Adjutant-General on his Tour of the Middle East, India, and West Africa, August, 1942', 3.
[144] PRO WO 177/92, Wallace to DDMS, 11 Aug. 1941.

five and six Junker transport aircraft, each capable of carrying up to twelve sitting or four lying casualties.[145] This early superiority in air evacuation was one of the few advantages that Axis forces enjoyed over the British when it came to the disposal and treatment of casualties.

Few British casualties were evacuated by air until the end of 1942, after the second battle of El Alamein,[146] but the Army was able to compensate for this by treating more of its wounded close to the front. We have already seen how the Army responded to the challenge of mechanized warfare by making its medical units more mobile. To achieve this, the DMS, Sir Percy Tomlinson, had recommended that special surgical units (FSUs) be constructed, complete with transport of their own.[147] This process was already under way by October 1941, when the War Office convened a special committee to examine the role of the medical services in mechanized warfare. The committee, chaired by W. C. Hartgill, who was to become DMS for the Middle East in 1943,[148] endorsed most of the changes that had already taken place in the Western Desert and stressed further the importance of moving surgical and other specialists down to the front.[149] The new consensus in medical circles was summed up by the DGAMS, Alexander Hood, in his introduction to the committee's report, when he stated that: 'Modern war and the reorganization of the Army has necessitated changes in the Field Medical Units. The object has been to produce a flexible organization of mobile and elastic Units capable of treating and evacuating casualties under any conditions.'[150]

To be successful, forward surgery required far more than the provision of additional transport: it depended equally on a plentiful supply of blood, which was a vital element in the resuscitation of the wounded. In earlier campaigns blood transfusion had saved many lives, but its effectiveness was limited due to lack of technical knowledge and apparatus in medical units near the front. In the Western Desert blood was in short supply at first, and often had to be obtained at the moment of transfusion. What was needed was an efficient method of storage and distribution near the front: a task that was enthusiastically taken up by a British physiologist, Colonel G. E. Buttle. J. C. Watts, a surgeon with the 8th Army, recalled that:

---

[145] E. Guth, 'Der Sanitätsdienst der Wehrmacht im Zweiten Weltkrieg. Ein überblick', in E. Guth (ed.), *Vorträge zur Militärgeschichte, Band II. Sanitätswesen im Zweiten Weltkrieg* (Bonn: E. S. Mittler & Sohn, 1990), 14.
[146] Crew, *Campaigns*, ii. 257.
[147] CMAC RAMC 408/1/35, P. Tomlinson, 'Surgical Service in the Field'.
[148] Ibid. 262.
[149] F. A. E. Crew, *The Army Medical Services: Administration*, 2 vols. (London: HMSO, 1953), i. 465.
[150] PRO WO 22/89, 'Reorganisation of Medical Services in the Field', 3 Nov. 1942, p. 1.

In 1940 transfusion had involved finding a donor, cross matching his blood to ensure against incompatibility, then withdrawing the blood into a complicated transfusion apparatus. . . . The whole procedure was time consuming, taking about half an hour, and the field surgeon had had to do it himself. All this had changed [by 1943] thanks to the masterly organization of Colonel (now Professor) Buttle. Each group of surgical teams had a field transfusion unit attached, with highly trained personnel and supplied with bottles of blood by air from the base transfusion unit.[151]

Transfusion was essential to effective surgery in wartime, since all previous attempts to maintain blood volume using substitutes like saline solution and gum acacia had proved disappointing. The experiences of the First World War had shown that blood transfusion was the only truly effective method of treating cases of profound shock, and that saline and other non-blood solutions were useful for maintaining blood pressure in only the mildest cases. Ordinary saline solution could not, for example, prevent acidosis or 'air hunger'—a condition that develops in cases of low blood pressure, causing shortage of oxygen.[152] Thanks to the work of Walter B. Cannon and

3. Mobile Operating Theatre, Middle East Theatre, CMAC RAMC 801/22/31

[151] Watts, *Surgeon at War*, 42.
[152] J. Fraser and E. M. Cowell, 'A Clinical Study of the Blood Pressure in Wound Shock', 1–26; W. B. Cannon, 'Acidosis in Cases of Shock, Haemorrhage and Gas Infection', 41–57, Cowell, 'The

other physiologists towards the end of the First World War, the mechanism of shock was now better understood. It was known that 'shock' was not caused simply by loss of blood from the wound—as previously thought—but also by its tendency to concentrate in the capillaries, which effectively removed blood from circulation.[153]

Although a small number of refrigerators had been issued for the storage of blood, transfusion in the first phase of the Western Desert campaign was usually arm-to-arm, as required. The method was essentially the same as that conducted during the later stages of the First World War, when it had been possible to carry out only a limited number of transfusions. Each surgical team in the Western Desert possessed lists of voluntary donors, but these were sufficient only for short emergencies, and in some cases surgeons had to fall back on saline solution. The threat of contamination also loomed large. The Deputy Director of Pathology, J. S. K. Boyd, warned in October 1940 that: 'should malaria ever reach epidemic proportions transfusion from local donors will become impossible.' In the short term, he anticipated that any shortage of blood would have to be made good by the use of glucose saline solution.[154] Another crucial factor was manpower: in quiet times blood transfusion could be conducted in forward units, but under battle conditions it was practically impossible.[155]

By the middle of 1941 the evolution of forward surgical units had led to important changes in the way in which transfusion was organized. A number of Mobile Blood Transfusion Units had come into being and were operating in forward areas, which greatly assisted dressing stations and the fledgling FSUs.[156] By the end of the year many forward units were also receiving blood from base transfusion units, which were under the overall charge of Colonel Buttle. 'Buttle's Bottled Blood' was flown to advanced medical stores and kept there until required in oil-burning refrigerators.[157] In the run-up to the second battle of El Alamein it became obvious that much larger quantities of blood would be required in forward areas, and so the Army made a desperate appeal for donors among troops in the rear. Despite the urgent need for more blood, only men from Britain and the 'white' Dominions were invited to come forward. 'Coloured' troops were never used as donors for

Initiation of Wound Shock', 58–66; Cannon, Fraser, and Cowell, 'The Preventive Treatment of Wound Shock', 84–93, in Medical Research Committee, *Reports of the Special Investigation on Surgical Shock and Allied Conditions, No. 2.* (London: HMSO, 1917).

[153] W. B. Cannon, 'A Consideration of the Nature of Wound Shock', ibid. 67–83; MRC Committee on Traumatic Shock and on Blood Transfusion, *The Treatment of Wound Shock* (London: HMSO, 1940).

[154] CMAC RAMC 1816/4/1, J. S. K. Boyd, 'Report on the Pathological Service, Middle East', 9 Oct. 1940, p. 6.   [155] Ibid., Boyd, Notes, 30 May 1941.   [156] Ibid.

[157] Ibid., 1 Dec. 1941; J. S. G. Blair, *Centenary History of the RAMC 1898–1998* (Edinburgh: Scottish Academic Press, 1998), 268–9.

whites because they were deemed more likely to be infected with malaria and other diseases.[158] Luckily, a great many soldiers from Britain and the Dominions were willing to donate blood, no doubt in view of the likelihood that they would soon be needing it themselves.[159] The discovery of the rhesus factor in blood by American scientists in 1939 also removed much of the risk formerly involved in transfusion and inspired confidence amongst recipients. Although mass testing of British troops was never conducted, because of the possibility of error, blood was obtained from group 'O' donors (whose blood was compatible with all groups) and tested, individually, before issue to ensure compatibility and the absence of syphilitic infection.[160]

The expansion of blood transfusion was largely a response to the demand created by the development of forward surgery, but demand often exceeded supply, especially when it came to personnel skilled in the techniques of transfusion. In fact, many MOs possessed only a limited knowledge of how to deal with wound shock. As late as May 1943 many units were without any officer who had attended a blood transfusion course. By the time of second Alamein, in October, all units had at least one trained officer, but afterwards postings to other units left some without any medical personnel experienced in transfusion.[161]

Transfusion with whole blood remained the norm in the British Army, but some surgeons were also beginning to experiment with plasma.[162] In 1939 American scientists had made the discovery that unfiltered blood plasma was a useful substitute for whole blood in transfusion, and it had been used to a limited extent during the fighting in France and Belgium.[163] Although whole blood was generally used at the larger British hospitals (CCSs and upwards), most forward units tended increasingly to use plasma, which in dried form could be stored and transported regardless of temperature.[164] This was clearly an advantage when fighting in desert conditions, but plasma had its limitations. The commanding officer of No. 1 Base Transfusion Unit acknowledged that 'Plasma is undoubtedly of great value and plasma alone is sufficient for

[158] CAMC RAMC 1816/6/1/5, 'A Report on the Work of No. 1 Base Transfusion Unit, July 1942–June 1943', 2.
[159] Ibid. 6.
[160] PRO WO 222/68, 'Blood-grouping of Military Personnel'.
[161] CMAC RAMC 1816/6/1/5, Memo. on resuscitation in the 8ᵗʰ Army, March–May 1943.
[162] CMAC RAMC 1816/6/1/6, Capt. George Lumb, No. 10 FTU, to Brig. L. E. H. Whitby, ABSD, Bristol, undated.
[163] See F. H. K. Green and Sir Gordon Covell (eds.), *Medical Research: Medical History of the Second World War* (London: HMSO, 1953), 103–9.
[164] CMAC RAMC 1861/4/1 Boyd, Notes, 1 Dec. 1941; PRO WO 222/57, Army Pathology Committee, 'Report on the use of dried Blood Plasma, Middle East—16th January 1942', 1–2. During 1941 almost all of the blood obtained by the Army Blood Transfusion Service—some 400–500 pints per day—was converted into dried plasma: 'Army Blood Transfusion Service, 1941'; see PRO WO 222/38.

the resuscitation of large numbers of the less seriously wounded men'. But he cautioned that 'there are, however, a number of severely wounded men for whom blood is essential', and believed that 'This opinion is universally held by the responsible medical officers of the Eighth Army'.[165] Plasma could do no more than restore blood volume, which was often all that was required, but cases with severe blood loss required whole blood to restore the oxygen in their blood.

The rapid expansion of blood transfusion was an achievement of which the British Army could be proud, and its significance was immediately apparent to propagandists. A BBC correspondent at the second battle of Alamein reported that: 'blood transfusion on a big scale is one of the biggest and finest medical service developments in this war. It's a thoroughly well-organized business, and it's saving very many lives on the battlefield itself, as well as at base hospitals—lives which would have been lost from loss of blood.'[166] In fact, blood transfusion was better organized in the British forces than in either the Axis armies or those of Britain's allies. The British Blood Transfusion Service was established in 1938, but the US Army entered the war without the benefit of a national blood programme and whole blood was in short supply during some of the early campaigns. In North Africa, for example, over-reliance on plasma led to a number of unnecessary deaths.[167] Advocates of whole-blood transfusion found few supporters in the US government or the armed forces, because they were overawed by the logistical difficulties of supplying blood in the field. Nevertheless, from 1943 the US Army began to emulate the British and established blood banks in Sicily and Italy, but it was not until the middle of 1944 that American troops received large supplies from the United States itself.[168]

In the German army blood transfusion was performed in military hospitals from 1940,[169] and blood refrigeration wagons were sometimes used in the field to preserve supplies brought from Germany.[170] But whole blood seems to have been in short supply in the Western Desert, presumably because blood donation failed to receive the priority it deserved. Supplies of

[165] CMAC RAMC 1816/6/1/5, 'Report from Officer Commanding No. 1 Base Transfusion Unit, Middle East Forces, to WO, on Blood Transfusion Arrangements during the El Alamein Battle', 2.
[166] CMAC RAMC 801/21/10, Godfrey Talbot quoted in Army Blood Transfusion Service leaflet.
[167] Brig.-Gen. Douglas B. Kendrick, *Medical Department, United States Army Blood Program in World War II* (Washington DC, Office of the Surgeon-General's Department of the Army, 1964), pp. ix–x.
[168] Albert E. Cowdrey, *Fighting for Life: American Military Medicine in World War II* (New York: Free Press, 1994), 165–73.
[169] Johannes Bringmann, *Problemkreis Schussbruch bei der deutschen Wehrmacht im Zweiten Weltkrieg* (Düsseldorf: Droste Verlag, 1981), 36.
[170] Hans Käfer, *Feldchirurgie: Leitfaden für den Sanitätsoffizer der Wehrmacht* (Dresden and Leipzig: Verlad von Theodor Steinkopf, 1944), 212–13.

blood—like the other supplies upon which the Afrika Korps depended—were also hindered by Allied interdiction of transport by air, road, and sea. Heavy bombing also disrupted work at the main blood supply depot and laboratory in Berlin. As far as blood substitutes were concerned, the Wehrmacht relied until 1943 upon a synthetic substance called 'Periston', which most German MOs complained was unsatisfactory. It was not until after the capture of dried plasma from the British at Tobruk in June 1942, that natural blood substitutes were issued to German medical units. The extreme pallor of many patients in captured German hospitals appeared to confirm intelligence reports that both whole blood and plasma were in short supply throughout the desert campaign.[171] This was a gift to British propagandists, who emphasized the contrast between medical provisions in the British and German armies. In a radio broadcast in the summer of 1943, the DGAMS, Sir Alexander Hood, declared that:

There is no doubt that what you donors have done and what the scientists and doctors have done with your gift has been one of the greatest life-saving measures ever provided for any Army. The enemy have nothing like it—not that they've poor medical equipment, far from it . . . but they depend on a synthetic product to take the place of blood transfusion in forward medical units, and I know that the German doctors themselves envy us our blood transfusion.[172]

The success of blood transfusion in the British Army undoubtedly did much to reassure the public that its soldiers received the best available care. Relying on voluntary donations, transfusion epitomized national solidarity at a time of crisis—the willingness of soldier and civilian alike to contribute unselfishly to the war effort.

The expansion of blood transfusion in forward areas undoubtedly made a great contribution to the recovery of surgical cases in the Western Desert, but it was not the only innovation of note. Another important feature of the desert campaigns was the development of specialist surgical provisions, such maxillo-facial surgery, both in forward areas and at the base. During the First World War it had been noted that maxillo-facial surgery was vitally important, not only in preventing the wastage of manpower, but also for the morale of soldiers and their families. As the *Field Surgery Pocket Book* put it: 'The effect on dependants and relatives at home must not be overlooked.'[173] In

[171] Kendrick, *United States Army Blood Program*, 23; Brig. Sir Lionel Whitby, 'Blood Transfusion in the Field: Organisation of Supplies', in Sir H. Letheby Tidy (ed.), *Inter-Allied Conferences on War Medicine 1942–1945* (London: Staples Press, 1947), 183–6.
[172] Lt.-Gen. Sir Alexander Hood, 'Army Medical Services in Action', *Journal of the Royal Army Medical Corps*, 38 (1943), 287–90.
[173] CMAC RAMC 50, 'A Field Surgery Pocket Book: Memorandum Based on the Experience of the Present War', 9.

1914–18 this realization had led to the development of what was essentially a new surgical specialism, due to the pioneering work of Harold Gilles at the military hospital at Sidcup, in Kent.[174] In the First World War maxillo-facial surgery was seldom practised in forward areas, but in 1940–1 it became standard practice to conduct preliminary operations at the CCS and even the MDS, involving close co-operation between MOs and dental surgeons. Here, displaced hard and soft tissues were corrected and fixed in position until a major operation could be conducted.[175] Although forward units were only capable of conducting minor operations, early surgical intervention was vital to success. 'It is only by the earliest treatment of these cases', insisted the Army's standing committee on maxillo-facial surgery, 'that serious deformity and loss of function can be obviated or mitigated.'[176] As soon as the patient had recovered from his preliminary operations, he was transported from the MDS or CCS to a special maxillo-facial (MF) hospital, or another hospital where a specialist team was available.

Plans for specialist MF hospitals were drawn up as early as 1935, when the War Office had decided that at least one such hospital should be established in all theatres, in the event of a future war. After arriving at these institutions, patients first received the attention of a dentist, before undergoing other repairs to soft and hard tissue. Sometimes these operations required skin or bone grafting, although the latter was comparatively rare. In its report of December 1941, No. 1 MF Unit, which was attached to No. 8 General Hospital (GH) in Cairo, reported only four bone-grafting operations during the previous six months, out of a total of 188 operations.[177] The most difficult plastic surgery cases were dealt with at larger institutions in the United Kingdom. Aside from the greater facilities possessed by these hospitals, it was found that wounds were generally slower to heal in the Middle East than at home, and that plastic operations conducted in Egypt tended to leave less satisfactory scars. To combat this, No. 1 MFU (known locally as the 'Max Factor Outfit') pioneered a therapy using vitamin C that seemed markedly to improve the healing of wounds. Pathologists subsequently confirmed this, and the administration of ascorbic acid to patients awaiting plastic surgery became the norm in most MFUs.[178] By the end of the Western Desert

---

[174] Andrew Bamji, 'Facial Surgery: The Patient's Experience', in H. Cecil and P. Liddle (eds.), *Facing Armageddon: The First World War Experienced* (Barnsley: Leo Cooper, 1996), 490–501.
[175] CMAC RAMC 1816/4/4/1, WO memo. on the preliminary treatment of maxillo-facial wounds, 30 Feb. 1941.
[176] *Report to the Army Council of the Army Advisory Standing Committee on Maxillo-Facial Injuries* (London: HMSO, 1940 [1935]), 3.
[177] CMAC RAMC 1816/4/4/1, 'Quarterly Report of No. 1 Maxillo-Facial Unit', 31 Dec. 1941.
[178] Ibid., Maj. Champion, OC No. 1 MFU, 'Report on a Visit to Jerusalem, October–November 1941', 3–4.

campaign nearly all surgeons—including non-specialists—had become 'skin-minded', and performed their own grafting.[179] But professional co-operation between surgeons was not all that it might have been. The officer commanding No. 1 MFU informed the DDMSs of the Cairo and Alexandria areas that a dispute had occurred over the treatment of a patient at No. 1 and No. 2 MFUs, which had culminated in the patient not wishing to return to No. 1. 'In future,' he wrote,

> except in emergency, no case which has been under treatment at any time by one Maxillo-Facial Unit will be operated on by a second M.F.U., without the written permission of the former, which must be in possession of full particulars . . . All correspondence . . . between such units will be couched in strictly professional terms. Childish bickerings of this sort serve no useful purpose and waste important time.[180]

Plastic surgery was also essential to the treatment of severe burns, of which there were many in the Western Desert, due to the mechanized nature of the campaign. Burns were one of the chief causes of injury among the crew of AFVs (especially General Grant, General Stuart, and Cruiser Mark VI tanks) and caused 27 per cent of all admissions to hospital. The incidence of burns was so high because tank crews seldom wore protective 'anti-flash' clothing, of the kind issued to the Royal Navy. In the heat of the desert the atmosphere inside a tank was already stifling, and crews tended to wear as little as possible.[181] But while many burns were caused by explosions in AFVs, a surprisingly large number were the result of accidents caused by the widespread use of petrol as a cooking fuel. Following procedures developed in Britain in 1940, burns were dressed with sulphonamide gauze and pressure bandages of crêpe applied over cotton wool (or preferably sterilized cotton waste, which was more elastic than wool). Correctly applied, these bandages minimized the loss of serum from burnt areas. At a later date sulphonamide gauze was replaced by penicillin gauze, but not before one or two deaths had occurred as a result of the absorption of a toxic dose of sulphonamide from the dressings, or from an allergic reaction to the drug.[182]

Maxillo-facial surgery and burns treatment were two of three specialisms that underwent a rapid process of development during the Western Desert campaign. The third was military psychiatry, or at least the development of psychiatry in forward areas. When he arrived in Egypt, in September 1940,

[179] Watts, *Surgeon at War*, 35.
[180] CMAC RAMC 1816/4/4/1, OC No. 1 MFU to DDMS Cairo and Alexandria Areas, 4 June 1942.
[181] PRO WO 222/65, 'Report on Casualties in AFVs', 2, 20 July 1942.
[182] Watts, *Surgeon at War*, 43; 'Surgery in the Desert', editorial, *Journal of the Royal Army Medical Corps*, 80 (1943), 266–9.

the psychiatric consultant to the Middle East Force, G. W. B. ('Jimmy') James, found that there were no specialist psychiatric provisions for troops fighting in the Western Desert, and that there was a general level of ignorance amongst regimental medical officers about the causes of psychiatric breakdown and its treatment.[183] Many regimental doctors were very suspicious of psychiatric specialists and insisted that front-line doctors should possess general surgical and medical skills. There was also a widespread belief—shared by many medical staff—that most 'nervous' cases were malingerers or cowards.[184] This belief was enshrined in the diagnosis 'Lack of Moral Fibre' (LMF). Though normally associated with the RAF, the label also seems to have been used by regimental medical officers in the early stages of the Western Desert campaign. Every soldier thus classified was likely to be left out of battle, downgraded in medical category, and sent to the base; inevitably, many such cases felt they had been posted in disgrace. But, as their experience of combat increased, most MOs came to feel that the label was inappropriate. J. D. P. Graham, serving with the 7th Armoured Division, later admitted that:

I felt that no man who had fought with a tank or gun or worked in close support deserved the designation of L.M.F. It was a contradiction in terms. I had to 'smuggle' one major, one sergeant and five other ranks out of harm's way. This way they retained their self-respect and came back for more after a rest. To have applied the label would have upset the tank crews and aroused a feeling of distrust and resentment that would have had the worst possible effect on morale.[185]

In some cases Graham labelled cases of anxiety neurosis as 'Pyrexia of Unknown Origin', a diagnosis he justified on account of the fact that anxiety sometimes produced physical symptoms akin to fever, such as an increased pulse rate. The men preferred this diagnosis, as it indicated that their problem was organic rather than mental.[186]

The label of LMF was short-lived, however. Aside from opposition from MOs who thought the term clinically inappropriate, the designation led to an avoidable loss of manpower, because men were unnecessarily excluded from active service. The same was true of the classification that appears immediately to have replaced it: 'Not Yet Diagnosed Nervous.' James felt that this diagnosis was inappropriate because many of the cases he examined

---

[183] Ben Shephard, *War of Nerves: Soldiers and Psychiatrists 1914–1944* (London: Jonathan Cape, 2000), 183.
[184] R. H. Ahrenfeldt, *Psychiatry in the British Army in the Second World War* (London: Routledge & Kegan Paul, 1958), 5; R. L. Crimp, *Diary of a Desert Rat*, ed. A. Bowlby (London: Leo Cooper, 1971), 61.
[185] CMAC RAMC 1762, Graham, 'Time in the Sand', 65.
[186] Ibid. 64–5.

appeared to be due to physical exhaustion rather than some deep-seated trauma or nervous disposition. His preferred diagnosis was 'battle exhaustion', a term which conveyed to the patient the idea that his condition was temporary and that it could be easily rectified given sufficient rest. From the middle of 1942 the most common diagnosis became 'exhaustion' rather than 'NYDN',[187] though by no means all casualties were simple cases of 'exhaustion'. The trauma suffered by combatants often left psychological scars that remained unhealed, despite an outward appearance of normality and continued service at the front. The development of forward psychiatry was driven, above all, by the need to return men as quickly as possible to active service; long-term care was, at best, an afterthought.

Forward psychiatry dealt principally with those men who were classified as 'neurotic', rather than the less tractable 'psychotic' cases or so-called 'mental defectives'. 'Neurosis' was an umbrella term embracing a number of different pathological states, including hysteria, obsessive/compulsive disorders, anxiety, and 'neurasthenia'—a nineteenth-century term used to describe chronic nervous exhaustion. Some of these neuroses were attributed directly to battle, while others appeared to stem from sexual anxiety, separation from one's family, and so forth. Whatever the cause, the neurotic patient was not generally regarded as permanently infirm or 'mad'. Notwithstanding ideas of predisposition, which were still widespread in military psychiatry, it was generally thought that anyone could suffer from an anxiety neurosis if subjected to sufficient strain. Combat neuroses—of which 9,000 cases were recorded in the British Army in the Middle East during 1942[188]—manifested themselves in a number of ways, including panic reactions such as screaming, laughing, or crying; hysterical fits; stupor or coma; gross tremors; and staring cataleptic states.[189] These symptoms could appear before, during, and even some time after a battle. Those reactions that occurred during a battle were likely to be simple psychological responses to fatigue, fear, and danger, and could usually be treated quickly with rest and reassurance. Post-battle reactions were usually more complex, being related not only to fear but also to guilt over killing. They manifested themselves in a variety of ways, such as the so-called 'campaign neurosis', a form of mild, chronic anxiety state indicated by tremor and loss of appetite; or what were known as 'personality reactions', including mild hysteria, alcoholism, and delinquency.[190]

[187] Shephard, *War of Nerves*, 185.
[188] Crew, *Campaigns*, ii. 491.
[189] CMAC RAMC 1652, 'Psychiatric Casualties: Hints to Medical Officers in the Middle East Forces, September 1942', 4–6, 11–13.
[190] CMAC GC/135, MacKeith Papers, GHQ, MEF, 'An Experimental Forward Psychiatry Unit', Dec. 1943, pp. 9–10; interview with S. A. MacKeith, OBE.

Many forward medical units were initially reluctant to deal with psychiatric casualties, and passed them further along the line of evacuation. As one RMO put it: 'During two years of war in the Middle East, the neurosis rate was four per thousand. This may not sound so terrible, but the amount of time and trouble in dealing with them is out of all proportion to the actual numbers involved.'[191] Medical officers were instructed in 1942 to treat as many psychiatric casualties as possible near the front. A report of that year declared that: 'In an Army in the Field it is important that psychiatric casualties are diagnosed and dealt with as early as possible. Some of the conditions are "contagious" and being liable to spread in a unit, may cause serious loss of efficiency. Others render the sufferers dangerous.'[192] The most common treatments in forward areas were rest and reassurance, mild purgatives, or, in more severe cases, a strong sedative drug, especially barbiturates. Suggestion therapy was also recommended in hysterical cases, although MOs were instructed never to adopt a bullying tone.[193] Cases of anxiety neurosis that did not respond to these simple treatments were sent to one of the new neuro-psychiatric centres established in the theatre in 1942; here a full case history was taken and specialist treatment provided. Treatments included psychotherapy, prolonged narcosis induced by drugs, and electro-convulsive therapy.[194]

The Consultant Psychiatrist, Brigadier James, began to press for more neuro-psychiatric centres in May 1941, but the ebb and flow of battle in the Western Desert meant that it was impossible to establish psychiatric units west of Alexandria. Most cases had to be evacuated either to Cairo or Alexandria, to psychiatric centres in the Delta and Palestine, or later to No. 41 Neuropathic Hospital at Kantara. When the battle zone stabilized following the withdrawal of the British Army from Cyrenaica, an Army Rest Centre was established by 200th FA not far to the west of Amiriya, to relieve forward units of simple 'exhaustion' cases; a special centre was also established at No. 23 GH to deal with cases of 'effort syndrome'—minor nervous or cardiac symptoms brought on by prolonged stress. These events were said to mark 'the beginning of Forward Psychiatry'. After the second battle of Alamein, however, the number of psychiatric casualties was low due to improved morale. There was no need for further units to be established until the advance to Tripoli in 1943.[195]

[191] Anthony Cotterell, *R.A.M.C.* (London: Hutchinson, 1944), 95.
[192] CMAC RAMC 1652, 'Psychiatric Casualties', 1
[193] Ibid. 20–1.
[194] Crew, *Campaigns*, ii. 457.
[195] CMAC GC/135, 'An Experimental Forward Psychiatry Unit', 1–2.

The first hospital that arrived in Tripoli functioned as a casualty clearing station, dealing with early casualties from Tunis, including exhaustion cases. It was here that Major H. A. Palmer pioneered his controversial treatment of stubborn neuroses by rapid abreaction, aided by ether. Abreaction was a cathartic treatment that aimed to cure the patient by inducing him to relive the traumatic experience that had caused his disorder—it was a kind of therapeutic release. As we shall see in the next chapter, Palmer's methods may have been controversial but they succeeded in returning the majority of psychiatric cases to duty within a matter of days. For this reason, Palmer commanded the respect of many regimental medical officers, most of whom were initially suspicious of psychiatrists.[196]

The premise that underlay forward treatment was that the vast majority of cases requiring psychiatric treatment were basically sane, and could be returned to active service given adequate rest and reassurance. This, at any rate, was the opinion of Brigadier James, who had treated many psychiatric casualties during the First World War. According to his obituary, James—a former regimental MO—possessed 'an intimate knowledge of the soldier, and the stress and squalor he endured in forward conditions, the utter boredom and loss of regimental roots he often experiences in base depots'.[197] Despite the introduction of more rigorous selection, there was still concern that many unsuitable men, such as 'psychotics' and 'mental defectives', were gaining entry into the armed forces. While a few mild psychotics were deemed tolerable in an infantry regiment, 'low-grade' mental defectives were thought to make poor soldiers and be more likely to break down under pressure. In September 1942 a report on psychiatry in the Western Desert stated that:

It is remarkable how many of such men succeed in gaining admission to the army and how long they remain undetected. Such soldiers are anxious to conceal their true condition for fear of being discharged. Under the stress of active service conditions they eventually break down, frequently appearing to be neurotic or even psychotic as they readily imitate the symptoms of other cases.[198]

The failure of the Army to remove such men during training meant that MOs were instructed to get to know the men in their unit, and to weed out the 'less stable and feebleminded individuals'.[199] The tell-tale signs, according to the official instructions given to MOs, were that:

Dull and backward men are sometimes subjected to continual teasing, ragging or ridicule. They may be bedwetters, inclined to excessive masturbation, given to sense-

[196] Communication from Dr R. S. Morton, MBE.
[197] Obituary of Brig. G. W. B. James, *British Medical Journal*, 2 Nov. 1968, p. 333.
[198] CMAC RAMC 1652, 'Psychiatric Casualties', 2.
[199] Ibid. 25.

less destruction of property, cruelty to animals, outbursts of tearfulness or to suspicion of others . . . Persistent petty theft, drunkenness, temper tantrums, overstaying leave, absence from duty, leaving parades without permission, such are the disorders of conduct which point to congenital weakness.[200]

Such duties fell less and less upon the ordinary RMO and increasingly upon the Directorate for Personnel Selection, which was responsible for the battery of intelligence and aptitude tests introduced in the British Army during 1942.[201] From July 1942 all men recruited by the Army underwent series of tests designed to assess their general intelligence, aptitude for different tasks, and psychological fitness for combat. The tests were followed by an interview with a Personnel Selection Officer. In total, it was estimated that around ten hours were spent on each man during the selection process, after which men were allocated to various branches of the army, some being selected for training as officers or tradesmen. As Jeremy Crang has observed, personnel selection tests 'revolutionized the utilisation of manpower in the army and brought them the recognition that recruits had different capabilities, temperaments and job needs'.[202] It was but one of several ways in which the Army was becoming more responsive to the individual needs and abilities of its soldiers.

The testing of new recruits was first proposed at the end of the First World War, and was often discussed between the wars, although the Army remained sceptical and was reluctant to introduce it. Unlike the German army, which did introduce intelligence testing, and which placed great emphasis upon psychiatric reports in officer selection, the British Army was a volunteer rather than a conscript force, and in peacetime the recruits were self-selecting. The shortage of volunteers also meant that the Army could ill afford to turn away potential recruits, provided they met its physical criteria. Though a volunteer force, the US Army had also introduced personnel selection, but it had a much bigger pool of potential recruits.[203] The British Army's antipathy to any kind of testing was still evident on the eve of war, in early 1939, when Dr J. R. Rees of the Tavistock Clinic proposed unsuccessfully that the Army introduce some of the psychological tests then being developed in industry. It was only after Ronald Adam became Adjutant-General in 1941 that psychological and intelligence testing was seriously

---

[200] Ibid. 26.
[201] J. R. Rees, 'Three Years of Military Psychiatry in the United Kingdom', *British Medical Journal*, 2 Jan. 1943, p. 4.
[202] Jeremy A. Crang, *The British Army and the People's War 1939–1945* (Manchester: Manchester University Press, 2000), 16–17.
[203] LHCMA, Adam Papers, 3/4/2, Confidential memo from Adjutant-General, Jan. 1943, 'Selection of Personnel', 3, 15.

considered in military circles. Adam was sympathetic to the suggestions made by Rees and other Tavistock psychiatrists, as they shared essentially the same objectives: namely, to make the Army more meritocratic, technically orientated, and specialized.[204] Personnel selection—through intelligence, aptitude, and psychololgical testing—appeared to be the key, as it ensured that the optimum use was made of an individual's skills. Adam wanted the British Army to follow the lead of the Germans and Americans, but his real model was industry, which, he felt, had long reaped the rewards of 'personnel selection by intelligence and aptitude'.[205]

The introduction of intelligence tests suggests that the mental calibre of recruits was a much greater concern than in the First World War, when lower intelligence was generally deemed acceptable among recruits to nontechnical branches of the Army.[206] In 1939–45 this was no longer the case, and even the humble infantryman was expected to demonstrate a reasonably high level of intelligence and technical ability. But while a consensus existed over the value of intelligence and aptitude testing, there was great scepticism about the value of psychological examinations designed to reveal the personality of potential officers. Many serving officers felt that these tests were too subjective and that they had resulted in the loss of many good men. Also, the Brigade of Guards, which placed more emphasis on traditional values such as 'character' and upbringing, refused to participate in the General Service Selection Scheme.[207] The sceptics had a powerful ally in Churchill, who was instrumental in downgrading the psychiatrists' role: from April 1943 psychiatrists examined only those candidates who were referred to them, rather than every man who presented himself for selection.[208]

Conclusion

The campaign in the Western Desert during 1940–3 provides one of the clearest illustrations of medicine's importance in modern warfare. Higher standards of hygiene and sanitation, and facilities for blood transfusion and forward surgery, gave the British a crucial edge over their opponents, enabling them to maximize the potential of their forces in the Middle East. During

[204] Shephard, *War of Nerves*, 187–9.
[205] LHCMA, Adam Papers, 3/4/2, 'Selection of Personnel', 3.
[206] See Mathew Thomson, 'Status, Manpower and Mental Fitness: Mental Deficiency in the First World War', in R. Cooter, M. Harrison, S. Sturdy (eds.), *War, Medicine and Modernity* (Stroud: Sutton, 1998), 149–66.
[207] Crang, *The British Army and the People's War*, 17.
[208] Shephard, *War of Nerves*, 195.

the second battle of El Alamein the British managed to keep disease at manageable levels, while around one-fifth of the German force had reported sick. The British Army enjoyed this advantage because it paid far more attention to hygiene and sanitation than its opponents. The fact that many British officers and NCOs had undergone thorough sanitary training prior to, or during the campaign made an enormous difference, as did the British Army's long experience of fighting in hot climates. Even more important, perhaps, were the contrasting styles of command epitomized by Montgomery and Rommel. Montgomery placed far more emphasis upon organizational matters than Rommel, who concentrated overwhelmingly on tactics. Neither he nor his officers had much interest in, or knowledge of, preventive medicine. They appear to have regarded disease as an occupational hazard rather than an unnecessary burden.

The success of medical arrangements in the Western Desert also depended upon the professionalism of medical officers, especially the DMS, Percy Tomlinson, who was later chosen to preside over the medical services for the D-Day landings. Tomlinson won the praise of all who served with him. The Australians, for example, acknowledged that: 'The medical organization of the Eighth Army made it possible for Australian soldiers to be cleared from the Front, to be resuscitated and treated in forward units, and to be admitted to Australian General Hospitals with utmost expedition.' In a letter of thanks to Tomlinson, the HQ of Australian forces in the Middle East stated that 'this highly satisfactory result . . . was due in great part to the whole hearted cooperation and good organisation of the Medical Service under your command'.[209] As the Australian Army had been highly critical of British management of the medical services on other occasions, it is likely that this expression of gratitude was sincere. Tomlinson had effected a remarkable transformation in the medical services of the British Army and for the first time they were truly equipped to meet the demands of mechanized warfare.

[209] CMAC RAMC 408/1/15, HQ, AIF (ME) to Tomlinson, 11 Nov. 1942.

4

North Africa, Sicily, and Italy

With the second battle of Alamein over but a few days, a combined Allied force landed further west along the African coast in Morocco and Algeria. The first landing in November 1942 (operation TORCH) was primarily an American affair, under the overall command of Lieutenant-General Eisenhower. But the Americans were soon reinforced by a British contingent that became the British 1st Army, under the command of Lieutenant-General K. A. N. Anderson. The objective of 1st Army was to push into Tunisia in order to sever the forces of General Arnim from those of Rommel, who was then withdrawing into southern Tunisia. The ensuing battle for Tunisia took the form of a series of engagements fought by 1st Army and American formations in the north, and a push northwards through Tunisia by the British 8th Army under Montgomery. Having been reinforced by some 17,000 men, Axis forces mounted a formidable defence and inflicted a number of heavy defeats on the Allies, but their position became steadily weaker as Allied naval superiority enabled an effective blockade against vital supplies. In April the Allies mounted a decisive attack on Tunis, and by 13 May the last pockets of resistance had been mopped up. Although Allied losses had been quite heavy—some 76,000 casualties—they had succeeded in taking more than 238,000 prisoners of war. Rommel, who had been appointed Commander-in-Chief of Army Group Africa in February, was not among them—he had returned to Germany on 9 March, suffering from hepatitis.

Before the North African campaign drew to a close the decision had already been taken in principle to invade Sicily, although not without considerable scepticism on the part of the Americans. The British insisted that an invasion of Italy would distract German forces from the Eastern Front and from France (in preparation for an Allied invasion), but the Americans were rightly concerned that the operational objectives of the campaign had not been clearly stated. Some also harboured suspicions of British imperial ambitions in the Mediterranean once the war was over. However, the only alternative to such an invasion was to transport the entire Allied force back to the United Kingdom, leaving battle-hardened men in idleness for at least twelve months.

The campaign began with the invasion of Sicily by a combined Allied force in July 1943, and continued with further invasions of the mainland in September. The British force, which landed at the Reggio di Calabria and at Taranto, was unopposed, but the American force, which landed at Salerno, met with fierce resistance and almost failed to establish a beach-head. Thereafter, with the exception of the American and British landing at Anzio in January 1944 and commando raids along the Italian coast, the campaign took the form of a slow advance northwards through difficult terrain. The Apennine mountains—the spine of Italy—provided the Germans with a series of superb defensive positions, most notoriously at Monte Cassino, which withstood three successive Allied attacks. The Allied advance was also impeded by marshes and rivers, which traversed the coastal plains to the east and west of the central mountains. These environmental barriers, adroitly exploited by the German commander Kesselring, meant that a quick and decisive victory in Italy eluded the Allies, despite having achieved air superiority early in the campaign. The campaign resulted in 188,746 casualties for the American 5th Army and 123,254 for the British 8th Army; the Germans sustained 435,000. Whether this counts as a successful outcome is still a matter of controversy. Although the Allies succeeded in pushing up to the Alpine border in May 1945—keeping many German troops pinned down in Italy during decisive phases of the battles in Normandy and on the Eastern Front—some claimed that the campaign had been an expensive diversion. Certainly, there is no evidence that it had a significant impact on operations to the east or west, as the Germans were still able to find over twenty divisions for their counter-attack in the Ardennes, for example.

If the strategic significance of the Italian and even the North African campaigns remains questionable, the medical significance of these operations is not. The campaigns in North Africa and Italy demonstrate clearly the connection between health, discipline, and morale. They provided ample opportunities for dalliance with civilians and hence for the spread of sexually transmitted disease. Prevailing ideas of masculinity also worked against appeals to self-restraint and responsibility. Many commanders continued to regard sexual relations as vital to morale, and there was widespread suspicion of anti-malarial drugs, which were rumoured to cause sexual impotence. Rates of VD in Italy were among the highest recorded in any theatre of the war, and continued to increase throughout the campaign. The battle against malaria was more successful, but its effective control in Italy from 1944 owed as much to the arrival of the powerful insecticide DDT as to any improvement in anti-malaria discipline.

On the curative side, there were marked improvements in the treatment of bacterial infections such as gonorrhoea following the introduction of penicillin; this meant that manpower wastage from VD was much lower than it otherwise would have been. Penicillin was also a considerable boon in forward surgery and the control of wound infections, which were potentially a more serious problem in Italy than in North Africa or the Western Desert. Another notable feature of these campaigns was the development of forward psychiatry, which was still very much in its infancy during operations in Egypt and Libya. In North Africa and in Italy psychiatry was placed on a much firmer footing, and a number of innovations—including group therapy—were attempted in the treatment of those suffering from psychiatric disorders. But the most significant aspect of these campaigns, from a medical point of view, was the increasing use of aircraft for evacuation. This heralded a new era in the disposal and treatment of casualties, in which the most serious surgical cases were filtered out of the normal chain of evacuation and sent directly to large hospitals in the rear.

The Burden of Disease

The editor-in-chief of the British official histories of the medical services during the Second World War, Sir A. S. MacNalty, wrote of the Mediterranean campaigns that 'the antagonists were . . . evenly matched and any considerable unilateral manpower wastage through uncontrolled disease or through mismanagement of the facilities for treatment and repair could have turned the scale'.[1] This was, indeed, the case in the Western Desert, but in North Africa and Italy the Allies enjoyed only a marginal advantage over the Germans, at least in terms of ordinary sanitation and hygiene. DDT, which made its first appearance in the winter of 1943, proved a tremendous boon to the Allies, but it saved them from disaster rather than providing a decisive edge over their opponents. One of the reasons why the Allies no longer enjoyed the sanitary advantage they had gained in the Western Desert was that most of the troops fighting in North Africa were new to desert warfare, and the campaign—which lasted only five months—was not sufficiently long to permit the lessons of tropical hygiene to be learnt. With the onset of the hot weather, bacillary dysentery became common amongst Allied troops new to the theatre, by contrast with the more experienced 8th Army fighting to the south.[2] It was only through bitter experience, and continual education in hygiene, that sanitary conditions began to improve in British 1st Army.[3] Disease therefore sapped the strength of both Allied and Axis forces,

---

[1] A. S. MacNalty, 'Forward' to F. A. E. Crew, *The Army Medical Services. Campaigns, Volume III: Sicily, Italy, Greece (1944–45)* (London: HMSO, 1959), pp. v–vi.

[2] F. A. E. Crew, *The Army Medical Services. Campaigns. Volume II: Hong-Kong, Malaya, Iceland and Faroes, Libya 1942–1943, North West Africa* (London: HMSO, 1957), 369.

[3] *British Medical Journal*, 10 July 1943, p. 59.

with a wastage rate from disease in the British Army approximately four times higher than from wounds inflicted in battle.[4] The only area in which Allied forces had a consistent advantage over the Germans was in the prevention of typhoid, as intelligence reports revealed that the German vaccine was still of inferior quality.[5]

The British Army attempted to improve the situation by bombarding its troops with sanitary propaganda in newspapers and posters.[6] In North Africa and Italy there were also regular 'Health Weeks', during which the Army Education Corps gave lectures on the prevention of disease.[7] It was a learning experience for many medical officers, as well as for the men under their charge. E. Grey Turner, a medical officer with the 2nd Battalion Coldstream Guards in North Africa, recollected that: 'My Army medical career made me very "hygiene conscious", and I must say I was horrified on returning to civil life to observe the low standard of hygiene in the average restaurant at home.'[8] There is no reason to suspect that hygiene was taken any less seriously in the German army, but the conditions it had sometimes to endure militated against effective sanitation. Such was the case at Monte Cassino, where Allied bombing of the town had reduced it to ruins. German troops had been forced to occupy cellars and foxholes, and the whole area was littered with stinking corpses and faeces.[9]

While standard hygienic precautions could be effective against diseases such as dysentery, it was more difficult to prevent multi-causal complaints such as the ear disease otitis media. Otitis media was a common cause of sickness in North Africa and Italy, and especially in Sicily, where it reached epidemic proportions. The ENT departments of general hospitals were flooded with cases. The prevalence of the disease was ascribed to many factors, including dirt, sand, infected bathing pools, sweat running into the ear, sea-water, and dirty towels. Although the military environment was, in this sense, identical to the Middle East, such complaints had been managed more successfully there than in North Africa. In the Middle East an ENT specialist had been on hand as an Adviser since 1942, and had overseen facilities for the treatment of such infections. The well-organized facilities meant that manpower wastage from ENT infections was kept to a minimum. In North Africa and Italy, however, there was no specialist on hand to oversee arrangements,

---

[4] LHCMA, Adam Papers, narrative of work as Adjutant-General, 'Chap. IV—Medical Problems', 4.

[5] CMAC RAMC 466/38, Ernest Cowell, 'War Diary', Feb. 1944. Cowell reported that typhoid was very prevalent in the German army in both Sicily and the Italian mainland.

[6] Ibid., Cowell to Maj-Gen. D. T. Richardson, Director of Hygiene, CMF, 27 Sept. 1943.

[7] CMAC RAMC 651/3, *Union Jack*, 10 Apr. 1944.

[8] CMAC GC/96/1, E. Grey Turner, Diary of RAMC Service in World War II, 1942–5, reflections on diary entry of 11 Feb. 1943.

[9] Ibid., 4 Apr. 1944.

and when the Army's Consulting Oto-Rhino-Laryngologist, Brigadier Myles Formby, toured the theatres in 1943 and 1944, he noted that cases were detained in hospital for much longer than was necessary due to the lack of trained staff and special treatment centres. The incidence of otitis media was actually lower in some parts of Italy and North Africa than it was in the Middle East, but with a less efficient machinery to deal with such cases they took longer to treat.[10] Formby explained that: 'The widely expanding responsibilities of the Command and the large number of different nationalities included in the Force made it difficult adequately to provide for E.N.T. cases (and many others) on all occasions.'[11]

A more formidable problem was presented by 'infective hepatitis', which occurred in all the armies in North Africa and, to a lesser extent, in Italy. At the beginning of the war knowledge of 'infective hepatitis', or 'epidemic jaundice' as it was sometimes known, was limited, although it was generally believed to be contagious to some degree. The disease began to appear amongst British and Commonwealth troops fighting in Egypt and Libya (the incidence was highest among Australian and New Zealand soldiers), where 4,000 cases occurred in 1941–2. A further 12,000 cases appeared in the British Army the following year, and there were almost as many among American troops arriving in North Africa.[12] In the last six months of 1943 'jaundice' also became epidemic in Italy, where the admission rate in the British Army was equivalent to 120 cases per thousand troops per annum. The onset of hepatitis was characterized by anorexia, weakness, nausea, aches, and fatigue. The jaundice was of variable intensity and duration, in some instances lasting only a few days but as long as three months in the more serious cases. Although mortality was low, those suffering from the disease could be hospitalized for from three to six weeks.[13] During 1943 as many as 340,000 days were lost in the US Army in North Africa as a result of sickness from hepatitis,[14] and 150,000 days in the Canadian Army, between July 1943 and September 1944—the numerical equivalent of the loss of a whole division for ten days.[15] In the British Army the losses from infective hepatitis remained more or less stable in each year of the North African and Italian

---

[10] AMSM M/32 2001:06, 'Tour abroad by Consulting Oto-Rhino-Laryngologist Nov. 1943–Jan.'44', 5, 'Tour in M.E., C.M. and N.A. by the Consulting Oto-Rhino-Larygologist to the Army', 1–3.

[11] Ibid., 'Third Annual Report (1944) by the Consulting Oto-Rhino-Larygologist to the Army', 6.

[12] F. H. K. Green and Sir Gordon Covell (eds.), *Medical Research: Medical History of the Second World War* (London: HMSO, 1953), 150.

[13] CMAC RAMC 466/38, Cowell, 'Infective Hepatitis', 14 Dec. 1943.

[14] Ibid., Cowell, 'Appreciation of the Medical Situation, AFHQ, 29 Jan. 1944, 2.

[15] CMAC RAMC 827, Lt.-Col. R. C. Dickson, RCAMC, 'Infective Hepatitis', Proceedings of the Conference of Army Physicians, CMF, Rome, 29 Jan.–3 Feb. 1945, pp. 39–43.

campaigns, the admission rate being thirty-four per thousand troops per annum in 1943, and thirty-two per thousand in 1944 and 1945.[16]

The debilitating effects of this disease—which appears to have affected the Germans as much as the Allies—caused grave concern and led to concerted efforts in Britain and America to establish its cause.[17] The infective character of the disease and its seasonal incidence (it reached its peak in the September–January period) suggested a virus like the common cold, although some believed that it was a bacterial disease spread by flies.[18] In view of this, the Consulting Surgeon with Allied forces, Ernest Cowell, recommended that all utensils be sterilized in boiling water, that men should be given plenty of space in sleeping quarters, and that those suspected of having the disease should be isolated.[19] But these sensible precautions were based on little more than guesses: throughout the war teams of scientists from the United States and the Commonwealth laboured to unravel the mystery of infective jaundice, but establishing the aetiology of the disease proved difficult owing to its long incubation. It was only in 1944 that W. H. Bradley and others in the United Kingdom, and R. H. Turner and his team in the United States, demonstrated that the jaundice appearing amongst troops was in fact of two kinds.[20] One of these—serum jaundice (later termed hepatitis B)—was shown to be a viral disease spread by the use of poorly sterilized syringes, as in the vaccination against yellow fever, for example. This explains why many outbreaks had apparently followed the vaccination of troops or treatment with intravenous injections of drugs. The other, more common, form of the disease (hepatitis A) was shown to be a virus excreted in faeces. These findings have been rightly described as 'an outstanding event in the medical history of the war',[21] but coming as they did towards its conclusion, they had little or no practical effect upon strategies of prevention, and no vaccine against serum hepatitis was available until 1969.

Another disease that posed a particular problem in both North Africa and Italy was typhus, which raged in epidemic form throughout 1942 and 1943.

---

[16] W. Franklin Mellor (ed.), *Medical History of the Second World War: Casualties and Medical Statistics* (London: HMSO, 1972), 239, 242, 245.

[17] E. Guth, 'Der Sanitätsdienst der Wehrmacht im Zweiten Weltkrieg', in E. Guth (ed.), *Vorträge zur Militärgeschichte. Band II: Sanitätswesen im Zweiten Weltkrieg* (Bonn: E. S. Mittler, 1990), 17.

[18] CMAC RAMC 827, Maj. S. C. Truelove, 'Infective Hepatitis', Proceedings of the Conference of Army Physicians, pp. 44–9.

[19] CMAC RAMC 466/38, Cowell, 'Infective Hepatitis' and Medical Circular, 11 Dec. 1943.

[20] W. H. Bradley, J. F. Lolit, and K. Maunsell, 'An Episode of Homologous Serum Jaundice', *British Medical Journal*, 26 Aug. 1944, p. 268; R. H. Turner, J. B. Snavely, E. B. Grossman, R. N. Buchanan, and S. O. Foster, 'Some Clinical Studies of Acute Hepatitis Occurring in Soldiers after Inoculation with Yellow Fever Vaccine: With Special Consideration of Severe Attacks', *Annals of International Medicine*, 20 (1944), 193.

[21] Green and Covell, *Medical Research*, 152.

While the number of cases was small, the high fatality rate made it one of the most feared diseases in North Africa. Measures to prevent typhus in Algeria proceeded in much the same way as in Egypt and Libya, with most control measures aimed at civilians rather than soldiers. Lieutenant-Colonel H. D. Chalke, RAMC, noted that: 'It has long been appreciated that a close connection exists between the health of an Army overseas, and the presence of civilian communicable diseases. This is particularly true in modern warfare, but its vital importance is, perhaps, not fully realised. Hygiene control must be applied even more rigidly to the civilian than to the soldier.'[22] The delousing of all civilians in North Africa was clearly impossible, but the French medical authorities were urged to proceed with the disinfection of all the villagers and nomads with whom they came into contact. They were further reminded that: 'The supervision of nomadism, the ejection of lice infested from public transport . . . is a measure of first importance.'[23] But the Vichy sympathies of many officials in the Algerian public health department meant that they could not be expected to comply with Allied requests.[24] In towns where the disease was reported (such as Philippeville), soldiers were forbidden from travelling on public conveyances, from attending cinemas and other public places, and from fraternizing with civilians.[25] The Germans took similar precautions.[26] However, some soldiers were permitted to ignore these rules in order to combat the disease among civilians. In one battle zone in Algeria the staff of No. 11 Field Ambulance were allowed to enter villages in which typhus had been reported in order to disinfect the inhabitants and their dwellings.[27] It is not clear whether there was any resistance to their actions, but MOs assumed that the local population would be grateful and they looked upon disinfection as 'the most motherly of duties'.[28]

In North Africa the Allied armies were able to utilize another weapon in the battle against typhus—the inoculation developed at the Rockefeller Institute in 1940. Almost all US troops were inoculated on arrival, and inoculation progressed rapidly amongst British troops in the theatre. As the official medical history of the campaign put it, 'so great was the dread of this disease that all save a few of the troops consented to inoculation'.[29] But inoculation against typhus was not widely available in the German army until late 1943:

[22] CMAC RAMC 651/1, Papers of Lt.-Col. H. D. Chalke, 'Typhus', 1.
[23] Ibid., H. D. Chalke, 'Typhus Prophylaxis, winter 1942–3'.
[24] Ibid., 'Typhus', 1.
[25] Ibid., H. D. Chalke, 'Report on Typhus at Philippeville, March–April 1943', 2.
[26] Ibid., German Memorandum on Typhus.
[27] Crew, *Campaigns*, ii. 369.
[28] CMAC RAMC 466/36, Sir Ernest Cowell on typhus control in North Africa.
[29] Crew, *Campaigns*, ii. 369.

too late for the campaign in North Africa, but of some use for the campaign on the Eastern Front.[30] The protection conferred by inoculation is illustrated by that fact that there were fifty cases of typhus amongst British troops in North Africa (leading to fourteen deaths) before inoculation, and only four cases afterwards, none of which was fatal.[31] The protection rate was estimated at over 90 per cent, and serum treatment was used as a prophylactic for anyone bitten by a louse.[32] Attempts were made to popularize the inoculation amongst civilians, but suspicion and delays in supplying the vaccine meant that the level of coverage was low.[33] In some cases, however, inoculation was less than voluntary. On at least one occasion several thousand villagers were forcibly inoculated at gunpoint.[34]

By the time the Allies had embarked upon the Italian campaign a new resource was at their disposal—the insecticide DDT. DDT (dichlorodiphenyl-trichloroethane) had been synthesized by a German chemist in 1874, but it was not until much later, in 1939, that the Swiss Geigy Corporation discovered that it was a powerful insecticide. DDT was subjected to further trials in the United Kingdom and the United States in 1942–3, which showed that the substance was effective against the body louse, as well as mosquitoes and flies. In Britain most of the investigations into the efficacy of DDT were carried out at the London School of Tropical Medicine and Hygiene, while parallel research into its toxicity was conducted at the Chemical Defence Experimental Station at Porton Down.[35] The first full-scale employment of DDT during the war occurred in early 1944, during an epidemic of typhus in Naples. Conditions in the city were ripe for an epidemic: the sanitary condition of the poorer parts of the town had been notorious for generations, and damage caused by Allied bombing caused further dislocation and overcrowding. It was estimated that as many as 20,000–30,000 people were living huddled together in tunnels, air-raid shelters, and caverns.[36]

The dilapidated state of Naples led AFHQ to fear an outbreak of typhus in the city. Their preparations were based on the findings of two American organizations which had been engaged since 1943 in studying typhus in

---

[30] The vaccine had first been tested on the inmates of the Buchenwald concentration camp, under the director of the tropical hygiene specialist Prof. Gerhard Rose. For every 20 people forced to take part in the trial, six died. See Karl-Heinz Leven, 'Fleckfieber beim deutschen Heer während des Krieges gegen die Sowjetunion (1941–45)', in E. Guth (ed.), *Sanitätswesen im Zweiten Weltkrieg,* 127–66.

[31] Crew, *Campaigns,* ii. 369.

[32] CMAC RAMC 651/1, Chalke, 'Typhus Prophylaxis'.

[33] Ibid., Chalke, 'Typhus at Philippeville', 1.

[34] Crew, *Campaigns,* ii. 370.   [35] Green and Covell, *Medical Research,* 160–1.

[36] C. R. S. Harris, *History of the Second World War: Allied Administration of Italy 1943–1945* (London: HMSO, 1957), App. IV, 'Notes on Public Health', 419.

Egypt and North Africa: the US Army Typhus Commission and the typhus team of the Rockefeller Foundation, whose experiments in mechanical dusting with insecticide powder had revolutionized anti-typhus measures. The head of the Rockefeller team, Dr F. L. Soper, had been an ardent supporter of the 'delousing' strategy that had been pursued with vigour in some parts of Algeria. However, immediately after the occupation of Naples in October 1943 the head of the city's public health service declared it to be free from the disease; a statement that was blatantly untrue, as cases had been recorded there as early as March.[37] In July further cases were reported from a bathing house used by soldiers and from Poggioreale jail, where the disease had appeared among Serbian prisoners.[38] Typhus soon spread to three other prisons in the town, and before leaving Naples the Germans freed their inmates, allowing carriers to mingle freely with civilians. It is believed that many sought refuge in the air-raid shelters.[39] By November the disease had spread to the civilian population and some sixty cases had been reported, and thus it became clear that the local public health authorities were incapable of dealing with the problem.[40]

The first steps were to place the city out of bounds to troops, and to warn them to take great care in personal cleanliness and to avoid all contact with civilians.[41] But it was almost impossible to avoid infestation with lice, even with regular disinfection of clothing and kit,[42] so the process of inoculation and re-inoculation had to be speeded up.[43] In the longer term it was also deemed necessary to control lice amongst the civilian population, and to this end the Rockefeller team was brought in from Algiers to organize a programme of disinfection, under the operational control of the US Army Typhus Commission. A Typhus Control Board, chaired by the British DDMS, oversaw the whole enterprise, which brought together representatives of the various military medical services and the civilian public health service.[44] Following the arrival of the Rockefeller team in December, supplies of DDT were brought in and vehicles were requisitioned; civilian personnel were screened and paid by the Allied Military Government, which also furnished an ambulance service and hospitals. These men were formed

[37] C. R. S. Harris, 419–20.
[38] CMAC RAMC 651/1, H. D. Chalke, 'Report on Typhus in Naples', 26 Nov. 1943, 1.
[39] Harris, *Allied Administration*, 420.
[40] CMAC RAMC 651/1, Chalke, 'Report on Typhus', 2.
[41] CMAC RAMC 651/3, 'Special Warning' issued to British troops in Italy.
[42] CMAC RAMC 466/36, 'The Control of Epidemic Typhus 1944', Army Council Instructions, 16 Feb. 1944, p. 4; IWM 91/16/1, Capt. H. H. Jones, 'Memoirs of Service in North Africa and Italy'.
[43] CMAC RAMC 651/1, H. D. Chalke, 'Report on Typhus in Naples', 28 Nov. 1943, 3.
[44] CMAC RAMC 466/38, Memo. from Col. Harry Bishop, AFHQ, to Maj-Gen. Sir Ernest Cowell, 3 Mar. 1944, p. 2.

into six field sections under specialist officers: a case-finding section; a contact delousing section; a mass delousing section; an immunization section; a flying squad section; and a refugee section. The functions of each are largely self-explanatory, except perhaps those of the flying squads, which were to go to areas outside Naples where cases had been reported in order to conduct diagnosis, delousing, and immunization.[45]

The city of Naples was divided into twenty-four districts, each with at least one mass delousing station. Work began on 15 December, with case finding, contact tracing, and a limited amount of delousing; on 27 December compulsory delousing of all inhabitants of air-raid shelters marked the beginning of larger operations. However, delousing did not begin in earnest until after the arrival of the US Typhus Commission on 28 December.[46] By the end of the first week of mass delousing over 70,000 people were being disinfected daily. From 3 January to 20 February 1,750,000 million delousing operations and 50,000 inoculations had been conducted in Naples and its environs. By the end of the second week of January the number of cases began to level off, and by the end of February the number of new cases reported daily was usually no more than five.[47]

In Italy the control of typhus had none of the sinister connotations that it had on the Eastern Front, and aroused none of the suspicion that later dogged attempts to control typhus amongst displaced persons in Germany at the end of the war.[48] There was complete co-operation from the civilian population and no coercive measures were necessary to enforce disinfection. The clamour for disinfection was such that police protection was necessary at delousing stations to prevent them from being mobbed.[49]

The whole episode was celebrated as one of the greatest medical achievements of the war. The newspaper *Union Jack* reported proudly in March 1944 that 'Military and civilian doctors, nurses and sanitation officials in Naples have won a two-months battle against the typhus epidemic'.[50] Lieutenant-Colonel H. D. Chalke, who was intimately involved with the campaign in Naples, went so far as to claim that 'The mechanical use of insecticide powder was the outstanding single method of control and one that opens up a new era in the prevention of typhus epidemics'.[51] In retrospect this unbridled

[45] Ibid., Bishop to Cowell, Mar. 1944, p. 2.
[46] CMAC RAMC 651/1, H. D. Chalke, 'Report on the use of Louse Powders—Naples Typhus Epidemic', Apr. 1944.
[47] CMAC RAMC 466/38, Bishop to Cowell, 3 Mar. 1943, pp. 3–4.
[48] See Paul Weindling, *Epidemics and Genocide in Eastern Europe, 1890–1945* (Oxford: Oxford University Press, 2000).
[49] CMAC RAMC 466/38, Bishop to Cowell, 3 Mar. 1943, p. 5.
[50] CMAC RAMC 651/3, *Union Jack*, 7 Mar. 1944.
[51] CMAC RAMC 651/1, H. D. Chalke, 'Report, May 1944', 1.

enthusiasm for DDT may seem rather naive—especially as the epidemic may already have peaked—but at the time there were very few who doubted its causal role in arresting the spread of typhus.

DDT also had a decisive role in the control of malaria in Italy and other theatres of the war, but not until the disease had wreaked havoc amongst Allied troops in North Africa, Sicily, and the Italian marshes. Malaria was a disease that often increased in wartime, due to population movement and ecological disruption; indeed, the famous malariologist Ronald Ross once mused that the history of war and the history of malaria were inseparable.[52] As Major J. C. MacKillop, Adviser on malaria to British forces in North Africa, pointed out: 'The circumstances of war expose to Malaria risk large numbers of troops who have no immunity to the disease, introduce, through incidental movements of populations, exotic parasitic strains to which local inhabitants have no immunity and produce, through damage to drainage and irrigation plants and systems, a wide extension of mosquito breeding places.'[53] This was certainly true of North Africa and Italy, where malaria was already present in both its relatively benign (*vivax*) and malignant (*falciparum*) forms.[54] Along with sexually transmitted diseases, malaria was one of the two chief causes of sickness in both campaigns: in 1943 it was responsible for eighty-three admissions to hospital per thousand troops, and sixty-six and twenty-one per thousand in 1944 and 1945 respectively.[55] These figures are probably on the low side, owing to the fact that uncertain cases were generally classified as 'Not Yet Diagnosed' (NYD) fever, rather than malaria. Once diagnosed, only the mildest cases could be treated in forward areas—at the MDS—and the more severe cases, including all cases of *falciparum* malaria, had to be treated at the CCS or at the base, entailing an absence from duty of more than three weeks.[56]

These heavy losses occurred despite the precautions taken by AFHQ. Anti-malaria training of a rudimentary kind was given to all medical personnel before the invasion of North Africa, and suppressive treatment with anti-malaria drugs began one week before embarkation. The invasion itself was also fortuitously timed from a medical point of view, as active malaria transmission ceased in North Africa late in October or early in November, and

[52] IWM 77/1119/1, Maj. J. C. MacKillop, 'Anti-Malaria Campaign, British North African Force 1943–1944', 1.

[53] Ibid., MacKillop, the Adviser in Malaria, was a somewhat unorthodox figure. After taking his medical degree at Glasgow, he joined a homeopathic practice in London and eventually became Consultant Physician to the Royal London Homeopathic Hospital. In North Africa he was several times mentioned in dispatches for acts of bravery.

[54] CMAC RAMC 2063/34, 'Memorandum on the Clinical Aspects of Malaria in the Middle East, GHQ, Middle East Forces, May 1942', 5. Malaria was hyper-endemic in the Atbara region: Boyd, 'Notes, 14/10/40'.

[55] Franklin Mellor, *Medical Statistics*, 237, 242, 245.

[56] CMAC RAMC 1816/4, J. S. K. Boyd, 'Notes, 21/9/41'.

did not begin again until May.[57] After the invasion, and in advance of the malaria season, plans were made for what most regarded as a thorough campaign against the disease. An Anti-Malaria School was established in January 1943 at the HQ of No. 8 Field Hygiene Section, and offered intensive seven-day courses for medical and combatant officers, as well as the NCOs of all field hygiene sections. Those attending the school were told that: 'Malaria control in the Army is as important as Musketry and in future military operations in Southern Europe and in the East the Army that fights malaria will win the war.'[58] Malaria Control Units (MCUs) set the pace of anti-malaria work in the British Army. They were raised from labour hired locally, and charged with clearing vegetation in the vicinity of military camps, with larviciding and canalizing rivers, and with the clearance of drains to deprive mosquitoes of breeding sites. In addition, every combatant unit was required to form an anti-mosquito squad, which was assisted and directed by Station Malaria Committees, Malaria Field Laboratories, and special malaria officers. The whole system of control was co-ordinated by the Malaria Advisory Board, which assisted the DMS at AFHQ.[59]

Anti-malaria education began well in advance of the malaria season: posters and slogans were displayed prominently in officers' and unit quarters; signs warning of the dangers of malaria were placed along roads; and RMOs delivered lectures to troops, explaining the basic facts about malaria and the necessity of strict anti-malaria discipline.[60] Much attention was also given to chemical prophylaxis against malaria—a precaution that had been largely ignored during the first years of the war. A memorandum on malaria prevention, issued in 1941, made no mention of chemical prophylaxis, reflecting uncertainty over the effectiveness of anti-malarial drugs and their possible side-effects. At the outbreak of the Second World War most MOs endorsed Ross's opinion that quinine could only suppress malaria, rather than prevent it. This had become evident during the First World War, as many cases of malaria continued to occur among troops taking the drug prophylactically.[61] Consequently, most attempts at malaria control in the British colonies between the wars consisted of mosquito destruction and the drainage of breeding pools rather than the mass distribution of quinine.[62] When the war started MOs were advised not to rely too much on 'suppressive treatment', as

[57] IWM 77/1119/1, MacKillop, 'Anti-Malaria Campaign', 2–3, 6.

[58] CMAC RAMC 466/36, Ernest Cowell, 'War Diary', 7 Dec. 1943.

[59] IWM 77/1119/1, MacKillop, 'Anti-Malaria Campaign', 7.

[60] Ibid. 11; IWM 83/52/1, Frank Seabrook, 'Field Ambulance. Some Memoirs of a Private Soldier in the RAMC 1940–1946', 33.

[61] Mark Harrison, 'Medicine and the Culture of Command: The Case of Malaria Control in the British Army During the Two World Wars', *Medical History*, 40 (1996), 437–52.

[62] Gordon Covell, *Anti-Mosquito Measures with Special Reference to India* (Calcutta: Government of India Central Publications Branch, 1931).

the prophylactic use of quinine was now termed, and a memorandum issued to British forces in the Middle East in 1942 stated that it should be considered an emergency measure, to be contemplated only when other methods were impracticable.[63] In many theatres of the war supplies of quinine were, in any case, unreliable, especially during mobile campaigns.[64]

The shortage of quinine intensified after the Japanese invasion of the Dutch East Indies in 1942, when the main source of the drug was closed to the Allies. However, attention began to turn to synthetic substitutes such as mepacrine (also known as atebrin), which had been synthesized by German chemists in the early 1930s and which were subsequently used by the Wehrmacht.[65] Small quantities of the drug had been produced in Britain and America before the war, but following the entry of America into the war in 1941, and the fall of Java, production of mepacrine was stepped up and it became available to front-line units from 1942.[66] This left the problem of how to encourage troops to take the drug, for anti-malarials had always been very unpopular with soldiers because of their tendency to induce nausea if taken in irregular doses. It was also rumoured that quinine caused sexual impotence, and as there was no reason to suspect that mepacrine would be regarded any differently, a concerted effort was made to overcome any prejudice on the part of British soldiers. The *Union Jack* newspaper stressed the responsibility that each soldier owed to his comrades. 'Every soldier', it insisted, 'should be aware that in becoming a malaria casualty, through neglect of precautions, he is wilfully endangering his healthy neighbour because of his own infection.'[67] Neglecting to take one's mepacrine amounted to a crime against one's fellows: 'Any soldier who steals from a comrade has sunk pretty low,' it declared; 'Yet that is exactly what scores are doing right now in this theatre of war . . . Through thoughtless stupidity and not through malice. But that doesn't let them out.'[68]

Radio Algiers lent a hand to the campaign and did much to publicize 'Atebrin Day' on 22 April. In preparation for this event, the Malaria Advisor delivered a broadcast concluding with the following message from General Eisenhower:

---

[63] CMAC RAMC 2063/34, 'Memorandum on the Clinical Aspects of Malaria', 41.

[64] CMAC RAMC 1939, 'Medicine in Jungle Warfare', repr. from *Procs. Royal Society of Medicine* (Mar. 1945), 38, 195–8.

[65] Atebrin was used on both the Western Front and in North Africa. See H. Vondra, 'Die Malaria—ihre Problematik und Erforschung in Heer und Luftwaffe', in E. Guth (ed.), *Sanitätswesen im Zweiten Weltkrieg*, 109–25; report on the 'Office of Foreign Relief and Rehabilitation Operations', *Journal of the Royal Army Medical Corps*, 82 (1944), 48–9.

[66] CMAC 466/38, Covell Papers, Circular letter on the health of the Army in 1942, p. 8.

[67] CMAC RAMC 651/3, *Union Jack*, 22 Apr. 1943.

[68] Ibid., 13 Aug. 1943.

From April 22nd onwards, every soldier in North Africa will be taking two tablets, twice weekly, of the valuable and expensive Anti-Malaria Medicine known as (Mepacrine) Atebrine. This regulation applies equally to every officer, N.C.O. and man in the Allied Forces . . . It must be understood that from this date onwards our troops must be equipped to fight malaria as well as the enemy.[69]

Suppressive treatment got off to a good start, but very soon it was to receive a setback from which it took many months to recover. On Friday 30 April— 'Black Friday' as it became known—following the third dose of atebrin, reports of a serious outbreak of sickness began to arrive at AFHQ. The dosage had been 0.4 grammes (four tablets) weekly, administered twice a week, and the vast majority of men experienced no upset until the third dose, but thereafter almost half were afflicted with vomiting and diarrhoea.[70] While the weekly dosage remained the same, it was soon found that sickness could be avoided if the tablets were administered singly; but by now the men were so wary of the drug that many refused to take it.[71] By July, three months into the malaria season, the disease was already 'quite prevalent', despite the fact that mepacrine was standard issue.[72]

This did not augur well for the invasion of Sicily, where malaria was endemic. Seventh Army had to leave behind several hundred men who were suffering from malaria and 8th Army over a thousand.[73] This might have served as a warning to those planning the Sicily invasion, but instead there was complacency over the threat posed by malaria. It is true that British troops were instructed to take mepacrine regularly and that protective clothing had been distributed; after a bridgehead had been established in Sicily, they were also provided with fly-proof bivouacs and their encampments were sprayed with insecticide.[74] But much of the anti-malaria training before the invasion was 'too theoretical', according to the 8th Army's Assistant-Director of Hygiene, Lieutenant-Colonel A. W. S. Thompson. Although 1st Army had gained some experience of malaria in North Africa, 8th Army arrived late in the theatre and had very little. Inadequate training manifested itself in the irregular taking of mepacrine and in carelessness over the selection of camps and clothing. Most soldiers went into action wearing shorts and were often unable to change into long trousers after sundown, when mosquitos were

[69] IWM 77/1119/1, MacKillop, 'Anti-Malaria Campaign', 11.
[70] Ibid. 12–14.
[71] CMAC RAMC 651/2, H. D. Chalke, 'Notes on the Incidence of Malaria in Algiers—1943', 1.
[72] IWM 91/16/1, Jones, 'Memoirs of Service in North Africa and Italy', 25 July 1943.
[73] CMAC RAMC 466/36, Ernest Cowell, 'Malaria in the Sicilian Campaign, 9 July–10 September 1943'.
[74] PRO WO 222/159, Lt.-Col. A. W. S. Thompson, ADH 8th Army, 'Malaria Control in Mobile Warfare—Italian Campaign 1943–5', 4.

prevalent. There was also a good deal of carelessness. British troops were mistakenly issued with the old Mark I anti-mosquito cream—universally disliked because it was too greasy—rather than the lighter Mark II variety. This was apparently the origin of a prejudice against repellents of all kinds, which lasted to the end of the war. Men who had been in Sicily swore that anti-mosquito cream actually attracted mosquitoes![75] The decision to supply mosquito nets to units rather than directly to individuals also proved to be a mistake, as unit supplies arrived too late. One brigade was without nets for up to a month after landing. The anti-malaria organization on Sicily was deficient for the same reasons. Malaria control units (MCUs) were thrown together haphazardly and their personnel were poorly trained. Their transport often arrived late, and their operations were uncoordinated because their parent formations were constantly on the move.[76]

The chief reason why medical transport and supplies failed to arrive in Sicily is that RAMC units were allotted to 8th Army while still in an operational role in North Africa. As a result, many arrived late in the concentration area and required almost a complete refit before they could be sent to Sicily. There was also confusion over whether responsibility for anti-malaria work lay with corps or divisions. Anti-malaria units normally belonged to the former, but, owing to the forward stage of planning, they had been allotted to divisions.[77] But while problems with transport and supply can be attributed to General Staff, the chief responsibility for the failure of anti-malaria measures in Sicily lay with junior officers and NCOs who set a bad example to their men. Few kept up their suppressive doses of mepacrine or could be bothered to use mosquito nets. Many senior officers, too, were far from blameless in this regard.[78]

The widespread neglect of anti-malaria precautions was revealed during the interrogation of 200 patients who contracted malaria in Sicily. Only 65 per cent claimed they had taken mepacrine regularly, 4 per cent said they had taken none, and the rest took the drug at irregular intervals. Answers to further questions suggest that fear of harmful side-effects was not the chief reason for their failure to take mepacrine. While 8 per cent did experience mild side-effects, all agreed that the ill effects were so mild they did not affect fighting efficiency.[79] It therefore seems likely that the failure of many soldiers to take mepacrine regularly was simply a failure of discipline, of a permissive and casual attitude that affected all ranks to varying degrees. This may have

[75] PRO WO 222/159, Lt.-Col. A. W. S. Thompson, ADH 8th Army, 5–6.   [76] Ibid. 6–7.

[77] CMAC RAMC 471/6, Col. Robert G. Atkins, 'Report on Operation Husky', 1, 7.

[78] PRO WO 222/159, Thompson, 'Malaria Control', 7.

[79] CMAC RAMC 1900/14/2, Report of Brig. Stanley Smith, Consulting Physician on Tropical Medicine, MEF.

been compounded by German propaganda leaflets, which played upon fears of mepacrine and sexual impotence. But such propaganda was also used by the Japanese in Burma, and appears to have made comparatively little impact there.[80] The crucial difference was that in Burma malaria was kept within reasonable limits 'because the contraction of the disease is virtually regarded as a Court Martial offence'.[81]

The failure of anti-malaria work in Sicily was a failure of command—one that cost the Allies dearly. There were some 11,590 cases of malaria recorded in 8th Army during the Sicilian campaign, as against 7,798 men admitted to hospital with battle casualties. There were a further 9,892 malaria cases in 7th Army.[82] This amounted to an incidence of malaria equivalent to 275 per thousand troops per annum. While this was lower than the incidence recorded in the notorious Macedonian campaign in the First World War (460 per thousand per annum), it was substantially higher than in most theatres in 1939–45. The situation was so bad that whole platoons had to be evacuated to hospital, prompting *Crusader*, the 8th Army's organ in Italy, to comment that: 'Since the start of the Sicily campaign, the tiny mosquito has been a more powerful enemy than the German.'[83]

Although casualties from malaria do not appear to have had any appreciable effect upon military operations in Sicily, the disease continued to take its toll on the invading Allied armies. From 4 September to 27 November there were a further 15,547 cases of malaria and Not Yet Diagnosed Fevers among British troops, at least 8,000 of which were attributed to infection in Sicily.[84] With such a high rate of infection, and the prospect of passing through intensely malarial areas on the mainland, the medical outlook for 8th Army appeared grim. Italy had an extensive canal system and many areas of marshland which provided ideal breeding grounds for malaria-bearing mosquitoes. The canals draining the reclaimed areas (*bonfiche*) south of Salerno were badly blocked, and the Germans had sabotaged the *bonfiche* north of Naples. Leonard Melling, serving with the 8th Army near Naples, recollected that: 'The country around these parts bred mosquitoes by the millions and we suffered heavy casualties from malaria. We were also covered all over with huge lumps from the mosquito bites, and our lads cursed these infernal creatures more than they did Jerry.'[85] The same conditions obtained

---

[80] LHCMA, Adam Papers, narrative of work as Adjutant-General, 'Chap. IV—Medical Problems', 4.

[81] CMAC RAMC 1900/14/1, Memo. on Anti-Malaria Discipline.

[82] CMAC RAMC 651/3, *Crusader* (8th Army weekly newspaper), 16 Apr. 1944; RAMC 466/36, Cowell, 'Malaria in the Sicilian Campaign'.

[83] CMAC RAMC 651/3, *Crusader*, 16 Apr. 1944.

[84] PRO WO 222/159, Thompson, 'Malaria Control', 8.

[85] Leonard Melling, *With the Eighth in Italy* (Manchester: Torch, 1955), 12.

over much of lowland Italy. The whole drainage system of the Pontine Marshes—one of Mussolini's few undisputed achievements—was deliberately destroyed before the Allied advance on Rome. The Tiber delta had also been flooded earlier in the year and water from the river had been diverted into low-lying areas; sabotage had also taken place in the *bonifiche* around Grosseto and on the delta of the Arno. On the east coast, war damage had destroyed many of the drainage canals around Foggia and the *bonifiche* of Ravenna, close to the malarious Po delta, had been deliberately flooded.[86] Much of the destruction had been carried out on the orders of Kesselring, although it is unclear whether he intended the flooding of the Pontine Marshes and other areas simply to obstruct the mobility of Allied armies, or whether he had hoped to encourage the spread of malaria. If the latter, then it is a decision which backfired on the Germans, who themselves suffered high rates of malaria as a result of their actions.[87]

While circumstances favoured a major epidemic of malaria in the Allied armies and amongst civilians in the flooded areas, it did not occur. This fortunate outcome may be attributed to a gradual improvement in anti-malarial discipline and new methods of control evolved by the Allied armies in conjunction with the Italian public health authorities. Planning for the malaria season of 1944 began in September 1943, under the direction of an Anglo-American Malaria Board chaired by the Deputy Director of Hygiene, Thomas Young.[88] 'Everyone', wrote the Consultant Surgeon, Ernest Cowell, was becoming 'more malaria minded'.[89] From 21 September, training in anti-malaria prevention for all troops was prescribed in a War Office circular and anti-malaria discipline appears to have been more strongly enforced as a result.[90] The circular warned that commanding officers were to be held personally responsible if their men neglected anti-malaria precautions such as mepacrine.[91] By the second and third malaria seasons of the campaign it was obvious, according to Lieutenant-Colonel Thompson, that 'the vast majority of troops were mepacrine-minded and took their daily tablet regularly'.[92] But while training and education appears to have induced more soldiers to take their mepacrine, it seems to have done little to overcome their dislike of anti-mosquito creams, and most soldiers still believed they were of little use.[93]

[86] Harris, *Allied Military Administration*, 424.
[87] CMAC RAMC 651/3, *Union Jack*, 4 May 1944.
[88] CMAC RAMC 466/36, Ernest Cowell to Lt.-Gen. Sir A. Hood, DGAMS, 27 Sept. 1943.
[89] Ibid., Cowell to Richardson, 27 Sept. 1943. See also RAMC 478/5, diaries of Col. Ernest Scott, 6 Aug. 1943.
[90] CMAC RAMC 466/36, Ernest Cowell, 'Malaria in the Sicilian Campaign', 26 Nov. 1943.
[91] CMAC RAMC 2063/38, Anti-malaria campaign leaflet, CMF, 1945.
[92] PRO WO 222/159, Thompson, 'Malaria Control', 14.
[93] Ibid. 14.

The improvement in anti-malaria measures in the British Army during the last two years of the Italian campaign is illustrated in Table 4.1, which shows malaria casualties in relation to battlefield casualties. That malaria was eventually brought under control was, as Thompson observed, a testament to 'the informed and intelligent cooperation of the individual soldier'. 'Discipline alone is not enough,' he insisted: 'What matters is his response when he is not under supervision, not the disciplined observance of rules but action based on knowledge and understanding and a sense of personal responsibility.'[94] The whole enterprise seemed to vindicate those who had placed their faith in the 'citizen soldier'.

It was fortunate that the Allies did not have to rely solely on individual soldiers, however. From March 1944 the introduction of DDT and power-sprayers greatly assisted in the prevention of malaria. Spraying was the task of the MCUs, which were welded together into an efficient organization by Lieutenant-Colonel J. Morgan of the Indian Medical Service, who was the Assistant Director of Hygiene for 8th Army. This was not an easy task, for, as Morgan pointed out: 'The officers and men are so poor . . . that we have to keep ringing the changes constantly. They have gifts and vino thrust upon them on all sides and their round frequently degenerates into a bibulous, hiccoughing procession in which the B.O.R. is carried along by the Italian labour.'[95]

The MCUs were eventually transformed into keen and efficient units, and contributed much to the control of malaria in Italy. Their work, and other aspects of anti-malaria prevention, was conducted in parallel with civilian anti-malaria measures and co-ordinated by a malaria control unit under Colonel Paul F. Russell of the US Army Medical Corps. The unit was under the Allied Commission (effectively the Allied Military Government in Italy), that was itself subordinate to AFHQ.[96] One of its most impressive achievements was the control of malaria in areas such as the Pontine Marshes, Cassino, and the canal systems near Prugia and Arezzo, which it achieved by organizing the aerial spraying of DDT. Even these operations paled into insignificance by comparison with the mass aerial spraying of both DDT and Paris Green in preparation for the Lombardy Plain offensive in 1945. This enormous task required in the region of 30 tons of Paris Green and 50,000 gallons of DDT solution.[97] However, Thompson cautioned that: 'Treatment by means of aircraft is so spectacular . . . and is so simple to lay on, that as a weapon against malaria it is liable to be misapplied. The number of areas really suitable for air treatment is limited, and great care in selecting sites and frequent ground checks are necessary if it is to be employed to full

---

[94] Ibid. 21.   [95] Ibid. 10.
[96] Armfield, *Organization and Administration*, 296.
[97] Ibid. 12; Harris, *Allied Military Administration*, 425–6.

Table 4.1. Admissions to hospital from malaria and battle injuries, 8th Army, 1943–1945

Year	Quarter	Malaria	Battle casualties	Ratio of malaria to battle casualties
1943	3rd	12,532	6,415	2 : 1
	4th	4,178	8,637	1 : 2
1944	1st	901	3,500	1 : 4
	2nd	3,037	15,516	1 : 5
	3rd	3,288	19,975	1 : 6
	4th	927	10,995	1 : 11
1945	1st	365	3,679	1 : 10
	2nd	600	6,210	1 : 10

Source: PRO WO 222/159, Lt.-Col. A. W. S. Thompson, 'Malaria Control in Mobile Warfare—Italian Campaign 1943–45', 20.

advantage.'[98] In other theatres, such as Russia, the Germans also sprayed DDT from the air, but they do not appear to have done so in Italy, probably as a result of Allied air superiority.[99]

Of even greater value to the military was the discovery that DDT conferred protection against mosquitoes for up to two months if sprayed inside buildings, which enabled mobile forces to protect themselves in forward areas, and in places inaccessible to aircraft.[100] 'By the close of the campaign', concluded Lieutenant-Colonel Thompson, 'the control of malaria in mobile warfare had emerged as a practical proposition for the first time in military history. Given the necessary discipline and training, there is no reason why mobile operations in Europe should ever again be attended by heavy casualties from malaria.'[101] Yet one wonders if confidence in DDT was such that it induced soldiers to relax individual precautions. While there is no evidence of this in Italy, it seems to have been a common complaint in Burma.

Next to malaria, the diseases that caused most consternation in the Central Mediterranean theatre were gonorrhoea and syphilis, which proved even more difficult to control than in Egypt. On 12 January 1943, just two months after the invasion of North Africa, an Allied working party was set up to investigate the incidence of venereal disease in the theatre and to consider measures for its control. The rate of infection was then around thirty per thousand troops per annum, being lowest among forward troops (eight

[98] PRO WO 222/159, Thompson, 'Malaria Control', 12.
[99] Vondra, 'Die Malaria', 123.
[100] Harris, *Military Administration*, 425.
[101] PRO WO 222/159, Thompson, 'Malaria Control', 1.

per thousand) and highest among soldiers at the base. These figures prompted the DMS with AFHQ to issue a directive to all commanders reminding them of Eisenhower's order, of February that year, that all formation commanders were responsible for the health of their troops. He suggested, too, that wholesome recreations be provided for the troops and prophylactic centres established for all those who could not be tempted from vice. The DMS also stressed the need to maintain close co-operation with the provost marshal and civilian police in order that 'clandestine prostitutes' (those not registered at established brothels) could be arrested. Prostitutes, clandestine or otherwise, found to be suffering from VD were to be compulsorily treated by the French authorities, in consultation with military venereologists.[102] There was initially no intention of copying British practice in Egypt, where brothels had been placed out of bounds, albeit temporarily. To do so would have been difficult in the extreme, owing to the fact that even very small settlements usually had one or two registered prostitutes (registration was insisted upon by the French authorities in Algeria, as in France itself).[103] American forces were, however, prohibited from frequenting the 'native brothels' in Algeria and were confined to brothels containing European women only.[104] It was still commonly believed that non-Europeans were more likely to be infected with venereal diseases.[105]

In Sicily and on the Italian mainland prostitution could not be regulated, even to the limited degree that it had been in North Africa. As the Adjutant-General, Ronald Adam, pointed out in a circular letter of December 1943:

Promiscuity, and venereal disease resulting from it, always increase under wartime conditions, and more particularly in occupied countries where the social system is upset, hunger and want prevail, morals go by the board and many are selling themselves for a loaf of bread or a tin of 'bully'. There are many professional prostitutes plying their trade in Europe in war as in peace, but there are also many women who have been reduced to selling their bodies in order to avoid starvation.[106]

Adam's observation was confirmed by many eyewitness accounts of conditions in Italy following the Allied invasion. Leonard Melling, recalled that:

Many young and beautiful girls—in some cases with parental consent—would consort with Allied soldiers to obtain money or food to keep themselves and their

---

[102] Crew, *Campaigns*, ii. 366–7.
[103] T. H. Sternberg et al., 'Venereal Diseases', in L. D. Heaton, *Medical Department, US Army. Preventive Medicine in World War II, Volume V: Communicable Disease* (Washington DC: Office of the Surgeon-General Department of the Army, 1960), 206.
[104] Ibid. 208.
[105] Levine, Philippa, 'Venereal Disease, Prostitution, and the Politics of Empire: The Case of British India', *Journal of the History of Sexuality*, 4 (1994), 579–602.
[106] CMAC RAMC 466/38, Adam, circular letter on 'The Health of the Army', Dec. 1943.

families from starving. Also, many girl students of the University [Rome], unable to maintain their studies with the inflated cost of living, entered on the fringe of this meretricious activity in order to continue their studies.[107]

Although all possible measures were being taken to discourage troops from indulging in unprotected sex, the Adjutant-General acknowledged that 'these alone would not be effective if our troops were to take advantage of these hideous conditions . . . and indulge in wanton promiscuity—as the Germans have done'. He stopped short, however, of recommending a ban on contact with prostitutes or the closure of official brothels.[108] In this respect, British measures differed little from those of the Germans, who also relied on a system of medically regulated prostitution in licensed brothels (*soldaten Bordellen*).[109]

Reports from the Sicilian and Italian theatres indicate that Adam's faith in British troops was ill-founded, and that they too had indulged in 'wanton promiscuity'. Since the invasion of Sicily the incidence of VD in the British Army had climbed to twenty times that of the United Kingdom. In December 1943 there were nearly 4,000 cases admitted to hospital with VD, the average time spent under treatment being just over a week in cases of syphilis and two days in uncomplicated cases of gonorrhoea.[110] This amounted to a considerable loss of manpower, second only to that caused by malaria. This sorry state of affairs had come about despite continual propaganda of the kind used in the Middle East, which portrayed British soldiers as exemplary citizens. 'Continence is a duty to oneself, to one's family and one's comrades,' read a note to convalescent soldiers: 'A man can keep fit without a woman.'[111] The rhetoric of responsible citizenship harmonized with the emphasis put on training and education in other areas of military life. 'The modern soldier is not a body,' insisted Major-General Ernest Cowell, the DMS, 'he is a highly trained individual specialist, a man taught to think for himself.'[112] But Cowell believed that appeals to individual responsibility were not enough. 'If one decides to be a fool', he wrote, one should ensure that both a condom and prophylactic packet are used. If the soldier disregarded these instructions, and became infected with VD, Cowell warned that he would face financial penalties in the form of hospital stoppages and the loss of wartime and special proficiency pay, or the loss of acting rank or tradesman status.[113]

---

[107] Melling, *With the Eighth in Italy*, 134.
[108] CMAC RAMC 466/38, Adam, 'The Health of the Army'.
[109] Sternberg et al., 'Venereal Diseases', 211; Franz Seidler, *Prostitution, Homosexualität, Selbstverstümmelung. Problem der deutschen Sanitätsführung 1939–1945* (Neckargemünd: Kurt Vowinkel, 1977); Christa Paul, *Zwangs Prostitution: Staatlich Errichte Bordelle im Nationalsozialismus* (Berlin: Hertrich, 1994).
[110] CMAC RAMC 466/36, Ernest Cowell, 'Memorandum on Health to Convalescents', 2, 16 Dec. 1943.
[111] Ibid. 2.   [112] Ibid.   [113] Ibid.

These penalties were comparatively mild when compared with the First World War, and Cowell believed they were insufficient to discourage promiscuity. He therefore recommended that drinking hours in bars should be restricted and that brothels be placed off limits. 'The V.D. rate', he warned, 'now seriously threatens to limit the effectiveness of Armies and Formations. In some instances the V.D. rate is equal to the malaria rate, larger than the infective hepatitis rate and is the chief cause of sickness.'[114] These recommendations were submitted to the Commander-in-Chief, General Harold Alexander, with requests for further powers to examine prostitutes and to treat them if necessary.[115] Colonel Hume of the US Army also favoured placing brothels out of bounds, after having visited 'licensed houses' in Naples, where he found prophylactic facilities dirty and badly staffed. In some brothels there were no condoms available and only half the men performed prophylactic ablutions. Given that the average brothel contained around a dozen women servicing hundreds of men per day, it was hardly surprising that rates of VD were so high.[116] By the end of the month it had become the policy of the British Army Council and the US Government to place all brothels in occupied territories out of bounds to troops, although this order was more honoured in the breach than the observance. Powers were also granted to permit the medical examination and compulsory treatment of prostitutes at 'lock hospitals', such as the Della Place Hospital in Naples.[117]

As in North Africa, the military authorities were concerned not only with the wastage of manpower but the maintenance of good relations with the civil administration. As the consultant venereologist, Brigadier Robert Lees, pointed out on arriving in Italy:

An Army, especially one occupying a country, is judged by the conduct of its troops, both on duty and off duty, and we noted with regret very lax discipline evidenced by careless drinking and insulting attitudes to apparently respectable civilian women, who obviously resented any approaches made. Troops with bad discipline are more prone to expose themselves to V.D. and ignore all advice on prophylaxis.[118]

As far as Lees was concerned, the only way to prevent VD was to tighten military discipline; this would also have the effect of improving the situation in military hospitals, where lax discipline had led to loutish behaviour, especially among VD patients. Several of the latter were court-martialled in Italy

[114] Ibid., Ernest Cowell, recommendations on VD prevention, 6 Dec. 1943.
[115] Ibid., Cowell, War Diary, 10 Dec. 1943.
[116] Ibid., 17 Dec. 1943.
[117] PRO WO 222/1300, Brig. Lees, 'Report of the Consulting Venereologist for the First Quarter of 1945', 13 Apr. 1945', 1.
[118] CMAC RAMC 466/36, Brig. Lees to Cowell, 'Recommendations for the Prevention of VD amongst Allied Forces in the CMF', Dec. 1943, 1.

for theft, and persistent offences led to many VD patients being treated separately when facilities permitted.[119] But troops could not be expected to submit to military discipline if their officers failed to set a good example. Too many officers, according to Lees, were tolerant of their men visiting prostitutes, and many considered sex to be essential to morale: there was no social stigma attached to VD. 'It should be clearly understood by every man', Lees wrote, 'that it is a disgraceful act to endanger his health while on active service, by consorting with any loose women. A high code of personal morality must be followed and all must be taught that complete abstinence from sexual intercourse is not detrimental to health or vigour. Association with public prostitutes is "conduct unbecoming an Officer and Gentleman".'[120] Similar appeals to abstinence were made to other ranks through such media as the *Union Jack*. 'There is only one certain way of avoiding venereal disease,' it stated in January 1944, 'and that is to steer clear of sexual intercourse.'[121]

Although it probably did little to deter officers from visiting prostitutes, propaganda of this kind may have induced a kind of 'VD phobia'. This 'phobia' affected individuals who thought that they had contracted the disease, sometimes even though they had not had sexual intercourse—or at least who refused to admit to it. According to one medical officer who served in Italy: 'They never developed symptoms or signs of disease and could not be persuaded that they were not ill. I am sure that it was a guilt reaction with stress and often involved highly intelligent individuals. There did not seem to be anything one could do for them. There was no element of malingering.'[122] The Adviser in Psychiatry, Lieutenant-Colonel J. D. W. Pearce, claimed that fear of VD had reached epidemic proportions:

> Immediately after the cessation of hostilities the incidence of psychiatric casualties became very slight, but within a matter of only a few weeks there was a sharp and sudden increase and the majority of cases were much more serious in type than had been seen during the period of hostilities. Within Army territory some 30% of cases seen were officers and men with a belief of delusional strength that they were infected with venereal disease. Many of these cases were seriously depressed and called for careful observation to prevent suicide.[123]

Most of these cases were presumably among men who had had sexual intercourse during their time in Italy, which shows that the Army's hygienic propaganda had little effect in actually deterring sexual relations. In many

---

[119] CMAC RAMC 478/6, Diaries of Col. Ernest Scott, 16 Feb. 1943; 4 Mar. 1943.
[120] CMAC RAMC 466/36, Lees to Cowell, 'Recommendations for the Prevention of VD, Dec. 1943.
[121] CMAC RAMC 651/3, *Union Jack*, 26 Jan. 1944.
[122] Communication from L. M. Franks.
[123] CMAC GC/192/18, Papers of Lt.-Col. J. D. W. Pearce, 'Report by Adviser in Psychiatry', 11.

4. 'Just Another Claptrap', poster warning against VD, Italy 1943–4, CMAC RAMC 466/48

cases it succeeded only in creating grave anxiety. The limited success of the Army's strictures on VD was recognized by many of those involved in treating VD patients. One MO reporting on the incidence of VD among British troops in Italy concluded that: 'The only measure likely to produce any substantial lowering of [the] V.D. rate in an expeditionary force is leave to the U.K. at reasonable intervals.' Most VD cases were men who had served overseas for two or more years.[124] Length of service took its toll on all ranks, though not apparently equally:

[124] CMAC RAMC 1849, 'Medical Reports on the Italian Campaign', 149.

The newcomer to any formation which has been serving overseas for a considerable length of time observes a subtle peculiarity of psychology which is difficult to define, but which is reflected in the case of officers in a narrowing of intellectual activity and in the type of conversation and humour which finds favour. Amongst other ranks, with their more limited resources for sublimation through social and intellectual interests, the effect of long continued service overseas is seen in an increase in the V.D. rate.[125]

All the appeals made by the likes of Brigadier Lees, and the measures taken in conjunction with the civilian authorities to discourage prostitution, had no appreciable effect on the rate of venereal infection, which increased with each year. It is probable that the only measure that made much difference was the distribution of condoms, but even these were unpopular with soldiers.[126] In these unfavourable circumstances, VD was all but impossible to control. From twenty-seven admissions to hospital from VD per thousand men in 1943, the rate in the British Army in Italy rose to fifty-one per thousand and sixty-four per thousand in 1944 and 1945, respectively.[127] Lees himself was forced to concede in April 1945 that: 'Reviews of admissions to hospitals show that the majority take little or no precautions to prevent infection, although the facilities are everywhere adequate.'[128]

With such high rates of infection, it was fortunate that facilities for treatment improved markedly during the campaign. During 1944 special VD-treatment teams were established—one for each Army Corps—to relieve the pressure on beds in ordinary hospitals. Thereafter, only the most serious cases proceeded to general hospitals.[129] During 1943 treatment with sulphonamide drugs was gradually phased out and replaced with penicillin, which, by the summer of 1944, had become the norm.[130] Gonorrhoea could now be cured in a matter of days: the *British Medical Journal* reported that in cases treated over twenty-four hours with a series of intramuscular injections, the discharge could be 'turned off like a tap'. The same article also stated that trials with intramuscular injections in cases of syphilis enabled it to be effectively treated in around eight days, instead of the forty to fifty days taken using the old treatment of arsenical drugs and bismuth.[131] This was a very considerable improvement and one which did much to stem the haemorrhage of manpower, especially as up 60 per cent of gonorrhoea cases were

---

[125] CMAC RAMC 1849, 'Medical Reports on the Italian Campaign', 149.
[126] Communication from L. M. Franks.
[127] Franklin Mellor, *Medical Statistics*, 240, 242, 246.
[128] PRO WO 222/1300, Lees, 'Report of the Consulting Venereologist for the First Quarter of 1945', 13 Apr. 1945, p. 1.
[129] PRO WO 222/1300, Brig. Lees, 'Quarterly Report of Consulting Venereologist, July–September 1944', 1.
[130] Ibid., 2.
[131] *British Medical Journal*, 25 Mar. 1944, 428–9.

now of a sulphonamide-resistant type.[132] However, it was not until the end of 1944 that penicillin was produced in sufficient quantities to permit its extensive use in simple cases of VD. Until that time it was used only to prevent the infection of wounds, and in sulphonamide-resistant cases of gonorrhoea.

Casualty Disposal and Treatment

The evacuation and treatment of battlefield casualties in North Africa depended heavily upon inter-Allied co-operation from the moment the landings took place. In the Middle East the medical services had been able to utilize an existing medical organization, including large hospitals in Alexandria and Cairo, but in North Africa virtually everything had to be brought in by sea.[133] The British 1st Army was fortunate in that it was able to land its medical units at the same time as its combat troops, though the Americans were initially without adequate hospital accommodation and had to rely upon the British.[134] This accommodation comprised 9,300 beds in general hospitals established in requisitioned buildings, located in or near the four coastal bases of Algiers, Bougie, Philippeville, and Bone. There were also many smaller units such as CCSs, field surgical teams, and specialist formations for transfusion and maxillo-facial and neuro-surgery. These hospitals were organized by a committee chaired by the consulting surgeon Brigadier J. M. Weddell and a representative from the US Army.[135] Their co-operation continued after the Americans had been able to establish hospitals of their own: the consulting surgeons of both armies toured each other's hospitals, and surgical teams spent time working with their Allied colleagues. During the battle of Tunisia no fewer than sixteen American surgical teams were working with British 1st Army, which, according to Weddell, 'increased the surgical potential very largely'.[136] Although the British and the Americans worked well together, there was some resentment on the part of the French medical staff whose hospitals were taken over, many of whom had Vichy sympathies. Lieutenant-Colonel George Feggetter, RAMC, recalled on arrival at Bougie hospital that:

[132] 'Sulphonamide Resistant Gonorrhoea', editorial, *Journal of the Royal Army Medical Corps*, 82 (1944), 283–5; Maj. Herbert Bell, 'Gonorrhoea in Italy', *Journal of the Royal Army Medical Corps*, 84 (1945), 21–6.

[133] J. M. Weddell, 'Surgery in Tunisia: November, 1942, to May, 1943', *British Medical Journal*, 7 Oct. 1944, pp. 459–62.

[134] CMAC RAMC 466/36, Ernest Cowell, 'Lessons Learned from the Tunisian Campaign'.

[135] CMAC RAMC 466/38, Brig. J. M. Weddell, 'Report on Surgery in North Africa, January–May 1943', 1–2.

[136] CMAC RAMC 466/38, 'Surgery in North Africa', 5.

after much acrimonious discussion with the French we were ordered to take over part of the French civilian hospital and our wounded men were transferred to it. The French surgeon who was operating in his theatre accepted us with great reluctance nor were the nursing sisters (nuns) at all pleased,—we later learned that when they had heard on the radio about the invasion of Algiers . . . they had resolved not to help the British in any way if we reached Bougie. However, we took over some wards and staffed them with our own personnel.[137]

During the early months of the campaign the medical services concentrated on the clearance of casualties from the hills overlooking the Tunisian plain. At the same time CCSs and FSUs were relatively static, becoming fully mobile only with the beginning of the general advance in April 1943. Even in later stages of the campaign the distances between CCSs were comparatively short, allowing them to be grouped together in five distinct corps, which worked closely together, sharing the casualties between them.[138] One CCS would admit one hundred casualties and then close until a hundred casualties had been taken by each of the other two. All low-priority cases were evacuated straight back to the general hospitals. The system of grouping enabled surgery to be carried out continually: in the week ending 2 May 1943 no fewer than 5,671 sick and wounded passed through the hospital group at Thibar and 1,043 surgical operations were performed. These hospitals were light, tented establishments intended for mobile warfare, and the Royal Engineers had to prepare their sites from scratch, providing piped water and concrete floors for the operating theatres.[139] Conditions in the CCSs were therefore rather primitive, and Lieutenant-Colonel Feggetter recalled that 'it was a question of everyone working day and night in pouring rain erecting tents, handling equipment . . . having scratch meals at a convenient time, then trudging in ankle deep mud from ward to ward . . . sleeping hugger-mugger on a veranda without any proper sanitation . . .'[140]

The disposal of casualties in North Africa proved much easier than in the Western Desert. Evacuation from FAs to clearing hospitals proceeded smoothly and the majority of cases were operated on within the recommended twelve-hour period. The medical services made use of ambulance cars and hospital trains improvised from rolling-stock available locally. Much use was also made of aircraft, and here the presence of the Americans made a crucial difference. American aircraft evacuated over 16,000 British and American troops during the battle for Tunisia; the less urgent cases were sent

---

[137] CMAC RAMC 1776, Lt.-Col. George Y. Feggetter, 'Diary of an RAMC Surgeon at War, 1942–1946', 17.
[138] CMAC RAMC 466/38, Weddell, 'Surgery in Tunisia', 460.
[139] Ibid., 'Surgery in North Africa', 5.
[140] CMAC RAMC 1776, Feggetter, 'Surgeon at War', 37–8.

directly to CCSs, and those requiring blood transfusion and resuscitation were dealt with nearer the fighting by FSUs.[141] The FSUs in Tunisia were slightly different from those used in Egypt and Libya, having more equipment, including twenty hospital beds and an electric lighting set—lighting having been a major problem in the Western Desert.[142] These units had been formed prior to embarkation, rather than improvised as before. They provide a clear illustration of the principles outlined by the Hartgill Committee in 1941: flexibility, mobility, and forward treatment. They were also popular with the RAMC. Lieutenant-Colonel Feggetter recalled that:

Field surgical units were happy mobile establishments, because they were small and compact, there was the independence, the freedom from close administrative control that was a feature of C.C.S.'s and general hospitals, the drawing of their own rations, supplies and so forth. There were close personal relationships, when a unit was ordered to another site all members worked together as a team . . . The success depended entirely on the character of the commanding officer . . . A disadvantage of F.S.U.'s lay in the fact that it was not always possible to recognise and deal with the rare case of an officer unsuited to command such a small unit.[143]

On the battlefield itself, first aid was carried out quite effectively and broken limbs were immobilized using the 'Tobruk splint'—a godsend for the transportation of casualties over rough ground. This was especially important since many of the wounds were complex, more often the result of shrapnel lacerations than gunshots.[144] But some MOs later reported that they had been posted too far forward. Being in the thick of things, they often found it impossible to find and treat the wounded, whose first instinct was naturally to flee the area of battle.[145] Some problems were also experienced with blood transfusion, so that in emergencies it was sometimes necessary to call on whatever donors were to hand.[146] Nevertheless, the quality of surgical work performed in forward units was generally good, and surgery was successfully undertaken even for difficult chest wounds. It was also considered safe to perform some potentially hazardous abdominal operations. As in the Western Desert, sterile conditions helped to keep wound infection at manageable levels, as did the widespread use of sulphonamides.[147] The usual practice in the British Army was to apply sulphonamide dressings at RAPs or

---

[141] *British Medical Journal*, 10 July 1943, p. 59.
[142] Weddell, 'Surgery in Tunisia', 460.
[143] CMAC RAMC 1776, Feggetter, 'Surgeon at War', 43.
[144] 40% of all British casualties in the battle of the Mareth Line, for example, were caused by shells as against 25% by bullet wounds. See CMAC RAMC 1476/5, Maj. R. Johnston, RAMC, 'The Battle of the Mareth Line. An Analysis of Casualties by Types and Causes, June 1943', 4.
[145] CMAC GC/96/1, E. Grey Turner, Diary of RAMC Service, 25 Dec. 1942.
[146] IWM 83/51/1, Seabrook, 'Field Ambulance', 33.
[147] CMAC RAMC 1630/5, Papers of Sgt. H. Copely, RAMC.

dressing stations, whereas in the US Army each soldier was equipped with a package of sterile crystalline sulphonamide to be sprinkled into the wound before a field dressing was applied.[148]

Most reports of surgery in Tunisia were full of praise for the medical services, but there were some dissenting voices. One such was Major-General Philip Mitchiner, the DDMS of Northern Command, UK, and formerly DDMS in Norway. 'We hear a great deal of the improvement in the medical services in this war,' Mitchiner declared in an article in the *British Medical Journal*, 'but I cannot help feeling that, in spite of advanced surgical units, more rapid ground and aerial transport, and even congratulatory medical broadcasts, this progress is not so great as one would like to believe, especially in the prevention and control of sepsis; for the number of limbless patients landing from the Middle East and North Africa is by no means negligible.'[149] One correspondent to the *British Medical Journal* described Mitchiner's article as 'provocative',[150] although Ernest Cowell may have taken it in good spirit, as he and Mitchiner had long been associates in the Territorial Army.[151] Mitchiner's comments were hardly representative in any case, and amputations and other 'grotesquely radical operations', as one MO termed them, became less common as surgeons gained experience of treating wounds.[152]

One of those who publicly criticized Mitchiner's depiction of surgery in North Africa was Lieutenant-Colonel F. H. Bentley, RAMC, who had gained direct experience of conditions in North Africa when working as head of the Penicillin Control Team, based in Algiers. The team conducted the first field trial of penicillin under the watchful eye of Professor Howard Florey, who had earlier investigated the anti-bacterial properties of penicillin with Ernst Chain and Norman Heatley.[153] The trial showed that penicillin was preferable to sulphonamide drugs because it was less toxic, and that it was effective against a number of micro-organisms—including streptococci—that the latter could not kill.[154] The results from the trials conducted in Algiers were so good that even well-established wound infections could be eradicated. In

---

[148] CMAC RAMC 1154/3/1, Circular letter No. 1, North African Theatre, Office of Surgeon, 'The Surgical use of Sulphonamides', 2, Papers of P. B. Ashcroft.

[149] Maj.-Gen. Philip H. Mitchiner, 'Thoughts on Four Years of War Surgery—1939 to 1943', *British Medical Journal*, 8 July 1944, p. 37.

[150] F. H. Bentley, letter to *British Medical Journal*, 28 Oct. 1944, p. 573.

[151] Obituary of P. H. Mitchener (1888–1952), *British Medical Journal*, 25 Oct. 1952, pp. 943–4.

[152] CMAC RAMC 1154/3/7, Lt.-Col. J. C. Nicholson, 'Surgical Division—Consolidated Report', 3.

[153] Ibid. 6.

[154] Mild side-effects such as fever, rashes, anaemia, and urinary-tract complications were apparently quite common among surgical cases in North Africa who were treated with sulphonamides. See CMAC RAMC 1154/3/1, 'The Surgical Use of Sulphonamides', 3.

soft-tissue wounds the procedure developed was first to excise the skin edges and damaged tissue bordering the wound, and then to complete the suture, leaving in the wound cavity several narrow tubes through which penicillin solution passed intermittently. In the case of compound fractures more drastic measures were required, involving around five days of intramuscular injections with penicillin.[155] The successful treatment of a variety of wounds led Florey and his team to conclude that 'penicillin can make a substantial contribution to the health of wounded soldiers, with corresponding saving of hospital time'.[156]

The only limiting factor at this time was production: a case of severe sepsis required the brewing and processing of up to 2,000 litres of medium. By 1943, however, large-scale manufacture of penicillin was well under way in the United States, and during the Italian campaign it was routinely used in the treatment of war wounds.[157] The plentiful supply of penicillin to the Allied armies constituted one of the chief differences between medical provisions for Allied and German troops. Whereas German hospitals were found to be full of cases of chronic sepsis,[158] Allied surgeons recorded almost 'miraculous' results using penicillin to prevent wound infection in forward areas.[159] The difference made by penicillin became evident when German patients suffering from severe sepsis were treated with the drug, most of them making a rapid and complete recovery.[160]

Penicillin was also transforming the treatment of burns. The treatment of burns in the field had formerly consisted of covering the burnt area with a sterile dressing and a dusting of sulphonamide powder. This proved to be reasonably effective in preventing infection and permitted further treatment to be conducted quickly, as there was no adherent tan to remove.[161] Investigations conducted by the MRC also revealed that tannic acid—often used in the treatment of burns at the beginning of the war—could cause liver damage, and the procedure was eventually phased out.[162] But tannic acid still had some advocates. Philip Mitchiner, who had been an eminent surgeon

---

[155] 'Penicillin in Tunisia', Editorial, *British Medical Journal*, 20 Nov. 1943, p. 650.
[156] 'The Treatment of War Wounds with Penicillin', ibid., 11 December, p. 756.
[157] Green and Covell, *Medical Research*, 258–74; Peter Neushul, 'Science, Government, and the Mass Production of Penicillin', *Journal of the History of Medicine and Allied Sciences*, 48 (1993), 373–95; id., 'Fighting Research: Army Participation in the Clinical Testing and Mass Production of Penicillin During the Second World War', in R. Cooter, M. Harrison, and S. Sturdy (eds.), *War, Medicine and Modernity* (Stroud: Sutton, 1998), 203–24.
[158] CMAC RAMC 651/3, *Eighth Army News*, 9 June 1945.
[159] IWM 91/16/1, Jones, 'Memoirs of Service in North Africa and Italy', 10 May 1944.
[160] Ibid., 16 Oct. 1944.
[161] Lt.-Col. N. J. Logie, 'Organisation and Treatment of Burns: Experiences at Tobruk, 1942', in H. Letheby Tidy (ed.), *Inter-Allied Conferences on War Medicine 1942–1945* (London: Staples Press, 1947), 123–6.
[162] Green and Covell, *Medical Research*, 75.

at St Thomas's before the war, favoured its use on the grounds that sulphonamides dusted onto burns in the early stages were liable to produce toxic
complications, unless fluids were given intravenously in large doses.[163] These
complications were avoided by the use of penicillin, which was shown to be
effective in the treatment of burns by trials carried out under Leonard Colebrook at the Glasgow Burns Unit in 1942–3 and, simultaneously, at the RAF
hospital at Halton.[164] Further work was conducted in the field at Algiers and
later in Naples.[165] Although penicillin was quite scarce in forward areas until
May 1944, it soon became a common treatment for burns. Solutions of penicillin were applied to burns in the form of a compress, cream, or powder. By
the end of the year it was being used extensively, either by itself or in conjunction with sulphonamides. The most severe cases, which had been evacuated to the larger hospitals, were sometimes treated further with the saline
bath method developed by A. H. McIndoe. In this treatment the patient was
immersed in a bath of continuously flowing saline solution for one hour, at
a constant temperature. The burns were then dusted with sulphonamide or
penicillin, and covered with a light dressing that was floated off in a subsequent bath. Although this method was used with great success in several
centres, it was not suitable for most hospitals on account of the special facilities it required.[166] In most theatres of the war, not least in North Africa and
Italy, early treatment in the field was the key to the recovery of burns cases,
and the medical services aimed to treat all such patients at a general hospital within forty-eight hours. While this was not always possible along
extended lines of communication, an intravenous drip was kept running
throughout the journey to prevent loss of fluids and the onset of shock.[167]

Another notable feature of surgery during the Tunisian campaign was the
development of specialist surgery—such as neurosurgery—in forward areas.
Prior to December 1942, neurosurgical battle casualties in the 8th Army were
operated on in forward areas by general surgeons, or, if possible, evacuated
directly by air to No. 1 Neuro-Surgical Unit at the base. Experience showed
that better results were obtained if operations were conducted in these specialist units than in general hospitals. During the operations at El Alamein
conditions favoured the evacuation of such cases by air, and a substantial

[163] Mitchiner, 'Thoughts on Four Years of War Surgery', 39.
[164] Green and Covell, *Medical Research*, 274; Leonard Colebrook et al., *Studies of Burns and Scalds (Reports of the Burns Unit, Royal Infirmary, Glasgow, 1942–3)* (London: HMSO, 1944).
[165] CMAC RAMC PP/COL/C.1, Colebrook Papers, Letter from Patrick Clarkson to Leonard Colebrook, 2 July 1945.
[166] Zachary Cope, 'General Treatment of Burns', in Z. Cope (ed.), *History of the Second World War United Kingdom Medical Services: Medicine and Pathology* (London: HMSO, 1953), 294.
[167] CMAC RAMC 779, Brig. F. A. R. Stammers, 'Report of the Consulting Surgeon to Allied Armies in Italy, 1 July–30 September, 1944', App. VII, 2.

number (22 per cent) were evacuated straight to specialist and other units at the base. Afterwards, as the lines of communication lengthened during operations in Tripolitania and Tunisia, it was found necessary to send a mobile neurosurgical unit into forward areas. Different methods of transport were tried, but No. 4 Mobile Neuro-Surgical Unit eventually opted for an abandoned Italian diesel coach, which suited its purposes admirably. This unit was equipped to deal with head wounds, spinal injuries, and other complex operations.[168] In 1st Army the development of specialist surgical units seems to have been somewhat slower, and for the first few months it was conducted largely at base hospitals in Algiers, in the case of maxillo-facial surgery at least. Most maxillo-facial cases reached the base within a week of being wounded. It was only in the last month of the campaign that a forward maxillo-facial unit was sent to Tunisia, and then only the dental section.[169]

Surgeons measured the success of medical arrangements by the proliferation of these forward units, and it is this feature of military surgery that captured the imagination of the British press. But the preservation of manpower depended equally upon facilities for convalescence and rehabilitation. In North Africa these were established on a generous scale: each of the four general hospitals provided facilities for massage, remedial mobility exercises, and weight exercises using improvised rope-and-pulley systems. Some sense of the scale of rehabilitation can be derived from the fact that the civilian masseuses attached to these hospitals treated as many as 600–900 patients per week.[170] Occupational therapy was also organized at these hospitals, and a few RAMC NCOs received special training in this area of medicine. Most occupational therapy consisted of handicrafts—the materials for which were supplied by the BRCS—and employment in routine work around the hospital.[171] Similar provisions were made in convalescent depots for the less seriously sick and wounded.[172] But while these facilities were impressive, some MOs involved in rehabilitation felt that better use could have been made of those men who had been downgraded in physical category as a result of sickness or injury. Towards the end of the campaign, however, following the appointment of an Adviser in Physical Medicine, greater attention was paid to finding appropriate postings. All men who had been downgraded were sent to an Army Selection Centre that made a detailed assessment of their capabilities.[173]

168 CMAC RAMC 1154/3/4, 'Report on the Work of No. 4 Mobile Neurosurgical Unit in the 8th Army Campaign in Cyrenaica, Tripolitania, and Tunisia, 19 December 1942–24 May 1943'.
169 Maj. Patrick Clarkson, 'Quarterly Report of No. 4 MFSU, 31 December, App. A—Treatment of 1000 Jaw Fractures', 1, RAMC 1816/4/4/3, CMAC.
170 CMAC RAMC 466/38, Report by Adviser in Physical Medicine, 1943, p. 3.
171 Ibid. 4.   172 Ibid. 6–11.   173 Ibid. 12.

It was generally agreed that the chief lesson of the Tunisian campaign was that medical formations should be landed at the same time as troops. Although this had been achieved in the case of the British 1ˢᵗ Army, American soldiers had found themselves without sufficient medical support.[174] Little appeared to have learned from these experiences, as medical provisions for the force landing in Sicily still left much to be desired. Confusion over whether medical units belonged to corps or divisions meant that many of those sent to Sicily were poorly equipped and lacking transport. The landing of vehicles was said to be 'most irregular', and many were 'not only hours, but days behind the allotted time', imposing a 'great strain on the units affected'.[175]

The evacuation of casualties from the beaches went off without too many problems, but it was clear in retrospect that it could have been smoother. Stretchers and other equipment taken on board hospital ships with casualties were not returned; there were also considerable delays in evacuation due to poor co-ordination between medical staff on the beaches and the Royal Navy. Embarkation was further delayed because no one had arranged for casualties to be hoisted from landing craft onto naval vessels. The medical officers in charge of embarkation had assumed that the Navy would arrange this, but had not bothered to check.[176] This led some senior combatant officers to question the competence of the MOs concerned. 'The SMO has a very important and tricky job to carry out,' wrote Colonel Robert Atkins in his medical report on the Sicily landings:

The man chosen must be known for sound common sense, administrative ability, and a thorough knowledge of his job, which means a good and previous experience as a Major *in the Field* and a period of C.T.C. training. These characteristics were not apparent in those selected and with one exception it was decided 'not to change horses in mid-stream'. These jobs were carried out on the whole satisfactorily but during the concentration period and also after the operation their lack of experience was seen in their foolish requests, their general attitude . . . etc.[177]

After the problems encountered in Sicily it was decided that all senior medical staff involved in future amphibious operations should have prior experience or command and control training, that responsibility be more clearly defined, and that wireless links between medical staff on the beach and the Royal Navy should be worked out in detail. The same applied to communications between field ambulance commanders and airborne medical personnel, as the medical staff of the airborne division had been

174 CMAC RAMC 466/36, 'Lessons learnt from the Tunisian Campaign'.
175 Atkins, 'Operation Husky', 7.
176 Ibid. 4.   177 Ibid. 5–6.

unsure about whom they should contact in order to evacuate their wounded.[178] As in most airborne operations, casualties were relatively high— amounting to some 30 per cent of all troops, or around 450 casualties in each of the two airborne brigades involved. The situation was aggravated by the fact that some of the medical staff who took part in the second of the two airborne landings died when their glider crashed into the sea. This left only the MDS of 16th Battalion, the Parachute Regiment, to deal with as many as 109 British and thirty-eight German casualties on the first day.[179] In future landings, such as those on the Italian mainland and Normandy in June 1944, these mistakes were not repeated and there was fuller co-opera-tion between the different arms. A crucial lesson had been learned: it was imperative that airborne medical units be relieved of their casualties at the earliest opportunity, because they had only limited supplies and equipment. After the invasion of the Italian mainland this was much easier to achieve, because there were excellent arrangements for evacuation by air. Within weeks of the landing the Air Medical Transportation Service—a combined operation involving the RAF and the USAAF—had evacuated 40,000 British casualties from Italy.[180]

For the remainder of the campaign in Italy the greatest problems experi-enced in evacuation were of a technical and military nature: aircraft employed in evacuation became worn out through overuse and hospital ships were vul-nerable to enemy action. It was even claimed that one hospital ship—the *Newfoundland*—had been bombed deliberately, causing the death of sixteen medical staff. Fortunately there were no patients on board. The allegation rested on the fact that the *Newfoundland* carried illuminated signs and was in the company of three other hospital ships, well away from combatant vessels.[181] There were also reports that a German aircraft had deliberately bombed a hospital ship off the east coast of Italy, despite the fact that there were no warships in the area. Such incidents were normally accidents of war, and were certainly untypical of what was generally a chivalrous campaign. Yet there appears to be evidence of clear intent, in this case at least. At the time of the attack the US Navy picked up a wireless message which stated: 'I am now going in to bomb a hospital ship.'[182] No chances were taken during the landing at Anzio in January, when hospital ships remained at least

---

[178] Ibid. 9.
[179] Lt.-Col. Howard N. Cole, *On Wings of Healing: The Story of the Airborne Medical Services 1940–1960* (Edinburgh and London: William Blackwood, 1963), 34–50.
[180] CMAC RAMC 466/36, Ernest Cowell to Lt.-Gen. A. Hood, DGAMS, 27 Sept. 1943, and War Diary, 14 Jan. 1944.
[181] CMAC RAMC 466/36, Ernest Cowell, 'Report on the Bombing of the Hospital Ship *Newfoundland*, on 12 September 1943'.
[182] CMAC RAMC 466/36, Cowell, War Diary, 8 Dec. 1943.

2 miles from the shore because of heavy shelling. The distance between the ships and the shore had to be covered by landing craft, which unfortunately 'rolled in a most disconcerting manner and caused much distress to the patients'.[183]

As the campaign progressed the Allies became increasingly proficient at estimating the amount of medical cover needed for operations, yet the uncertainties of combat, as Clausewitz famously observed, meant that warfare would always be an art rather than a science. While hospital accommodation was set for a casualty rate of 6 per cent, at the end of January 1944 there were beds for only 5 per cent. These hospitals were grouped in Naples, Baria, Taranto, and Barletta, providing beds for 45,000 troops, some way short of the 60,000 that had been projected. Even the latter figure was an underestimate according to Sir Ernest Cowell, since not all the base hospitals were easily accessible from the firing line.[184] Continuing complaints from medical staff led, in January 1944, to a crisis expansion of hospital accommodation of the order of 20 to 30 per cent. This rapid expansion meant that the Allies had to employ a large number of Italian military doctors to compensate for the shortage of suitably qualified Allied personnel. Adam complained constantly that there was a shortage of MOs in the Army, and was often accused of special pleading. Yet this was one of the few occasions on which the Army did face a severe shortage of medical personnel.[185]

As the need for more hospital beds came to be generally recognized, medical officers cast a jealous eye on the substantial amount of accommodation that remained unused. Ernest Cowell told AFHQ that:

It is of extreme importance that there should be no delay in opening up hospitals in Italy. There is already a deficiency of hospital beds in the theatre . . . Here is an instance where valuable accommodation is available and should have been taken into use a considerable time ago. Yet we are content to let the claims of two theological schools take precedence over the urgent needs of the medical services. It is requested that immediate action be taken to remedy this state of affairs.[186]

The Allies were at first wary of treading heavily on the sensibilities of the Italian people, but the requisitioning of public buildings became increasingly common through 1944. Pressure on public buildings was relieved somewhat

---

[183] CMAC RAMC 779, Brig. F. A. R. Stammers, 'Report of the Consultant Surgeon to the Allied Armies in Italy, March 1944–April 1945', 4.

[184] CMAC RAMC 466/36, Ernest Cowell, 'Appreciation of the Factors Governing the Allocation of Hospital Beds to a Force Overseas, with particular Reference to the North African and CMF Forces', Dec. 1943, 3.

[185] CMAC RAMC 466/38, Ernest Cowell, 'Appreciation of the Medical Situation, 29 January 1944', RAMC 466/36; Adam, 'The Health of the Army', 3.

[186] CMAC RAMC 466/36, Cowell to AFHQ, 28 Jan. 1944.

after the Allies finished rebuilding the hospitals they had inadvertently destroyed: a task to which the Allied Military Government attached the highest priority.[187]

In forward areas the main factors affecting medical arrangements were the tactical situation and the terrain, both of which were often difficult. This was especially true of Monte Cassino in the Appenine mountains. The fighting around Monte Cassino, from December 1943 to May 1944, produced a steady stream of casualties, which arrived at CCSs or FSUs in between three and fourteen hours, depending on the severity of the fighting. Cassino village itself presented particular difficulties, being dominated by German positions on Monastery Hill and Monte Cassino. Casualty clearance had to be carried out within full view of the enemy, and in many cases the wounded had to be carried long distances by hand as parts of the hillside were inaccessible to motor vehicles.[188] Elston Grey Turner, a medical officer with the Guards, recalled that: 'We could do nothing more than the simplest first-aid work on the bare mountain, and the unfortunate casualties were exposed to the snow and rain for many hours before they could be transported even as far as the advanced dressing station. And yet, by some miracle, they nearly all survived.'[189] Further insight into the difficulties faced by stretcher-bearers can be gained from the story of Private John Tancred of 187 Co., the Royal Pioneer Corps, which provided bearers for 10th Corps in forward positions at Cassino. On the night of 4 December he came across a wounded officer on Monastery Hill; it was bitterly cold and the going was treacherous because of mud and continual rain. Few details are known of that night, but some sixteen hours after he had left Tancred stumbled into an ADS, handed over the officer, and promptly collapsed and died—seemingly from exhaustion. Although he was never decorated, a silver statuette displayed at the RPC's depot in Northamptonshire later commemorated his effort.[190]

There were considerable dangers, too, in the evacuation of the wounded by ambulance car. Although the Germans in the vicinity of Monte Cassino respected the Red Cross, ambulances would occasionally find themselves hemmed in by military vehicles and subjected to hostile fire. Ambulance cars had to run these risks quite often, as it was too dangerous for the wounded to remain at the ADSs—all of which were within range of German artillery. Since little triage or medical work was possible under such conditions, it was

---

[187] Harris, *Allied Military Administration*, 56.
[188] CMAC RAMC 466/36, Cowell, War Diary, 1 Jan. 1944.
[189] CMAC GC/96/1, Diary of E. Grey Turner, 14 Feb. 1944.
[190] CMAC RAMC 487, 'Account of the Work of the Royal Pioneer Corps at the Battle of Monte Cassino, including the Death from Exhaustion of Pte. John Tancred, having rescued a wounded Officer', 2.

decided to evacuate every case to MDSs north-east of Cassino, near the village of Portello. But Portello, which was known to British soldiers as 'the Inferno', was scarcely less dangerous or distressing to patients. In what amounted to a reversal of the general policy that had developed since the Western Desert, it was decided that too much surgery was being carried out close to the front and that the average belly or chest wound would fare better if sent to hospital two or three hours further back.[191] The static conditions of warfare and the short distances between forward medical units permitted a 'grouping system' of the kind first seen in the battle of Tunisia. In the final, successful offensive at Cassino, which began on 11 May, Nos. 7 and 19 CCSs and their FSUs alternated, admitting one hundred cases at a time. Surgeons worked twelve-hour shifts, with two teams working at any given time. Well co-ordinated teamwork enabled forward units to deal with many of the 3,140 casualties inflicted during the first forty-eight hours, but during the first two days of the offensive the number of wounded was so large that only first-priority cases could be admitted: the rest were evacuated to the control post at Capua and thence to hospitals further down the line. Fortunately transport arrangements were now so efficient that no case took longer than two hours from CCS to Control Post—an average time after wounding of eight to ten hours. Base hospitals also expressed high praise for the quality of surgery and judgement in triage conducted in forward areas.[192]

However, the Second World War offered few opportunities for surgeons to develop new skills, and the age-old maxim that 'He who would be a surgeon should go to war' was no longer appropriate. Apart from specialist work, such as maxillo-facial or neuro-surgery, there were few intellectual challenges but, instead, an endless round of cleaning, shaving, trimming, packing, and plastering. If surgeons faced challenges they were usually of an ethical or organizational nature, as the medical officer 'J. A. R.' recalled in his memoirs. His first duty in Italy was as a surgeon in a CCS in the British medical area at Anzio. The hospital opened on 8 March 1944 and began immediately to receive patients, most suffering multiple wounds from shrapnel and bullets. As the Germans went all out in their efforts to remove the Allies from their beach-head, the CCS became choked with wounded and it was impossible to treat all patients immediately. 'J. A. R.' was now faced with one of the most difficult dilemmas confronting surgeons in forward units: to decide which patients to treat first. Surgeons were well aware that difficult cases, such as abdominals, took three or four times longer to operate on than a man with simple wounds of the extremities, and that the former had only a 50:50 chance of recovery. It did not automatically follow that sur-

---

[191] CMAC RAMC 779, Stammers, 'Report of the Consultant Surgeon', 5.
[192] Ibid. 7.

geons neglected abdominal cases, however. As 'J. A. R.' pointed out: 'It may have seemed a wasteful policy . . . for surgeons to spend valuable time on the more gravely wounded men . . . But the "abdomens", if left, would certainly die. Saving of life is the doctor's aim, and putting an economic viewpoint aside, we regarded the patients in the light of the severity of their wounds and nothing else.'[193] This had not always been the case. In the First World War British and French military surgeons had been urged to concentrate on those most likely to recover. J. Abadie, the French author of a surgical manual commissioned by the DGAMS, Sir Alfred Keogh, took the view that: 'One abdomen, one laparotomy, means a whole hour devoted to an uncertain result . . . An hour given to three other severe wounds means you will save three at least.'[194] In the Second World War such grim logic was less compelling. Sulphonamide drugs and, later, penicillin successfully combated most forms of wound infection, and even abdominal cases had a fair chance of survival.

By early June the Germans had been driven from both Cassino and the Anzio beach-heads and began their rapid retreat beyond Rome. FSUs moved forward with the advancing Allied formations, but there were, at this stage, few casualties to dispose of. During the battle for Rome the majority of cases were evacuated by air from near Anzio, which lies not far to the south-west. Between 23 May and 3 June 4,670 British and American casualties were evacuated in this way to Naples—a journey that took only forty minutes.[195] This marked the beginning of a new era in military surgery, in which early treatment in large and sometimes specialist hospitals became the norm. But air evacuation was far better suited to static than mobile warfare—at least, until the advent of the helicopter ambulance in Korea. These limitations are illustrated by casualty clearance after the fall of Rome, when the tempo of medical work increased greatly with the rapid advance northwards. At this point in time the medical services had to rely almost entirely on roads, since most airfields were not within easy reach. This presented a new series of problems to medical staff, as ambulance cars became trapped in the traffic jams that built up along the narrow roads, hemmed in on both sides by mines. Ambulance cars had often to use side-roads because the bridges on the main roads had been blown, so evacuation took far longer than anticipated. The whole operation was aggravated by weeks of heavy rain, which made minor routes impassable and which washed away embankments and temporary bridges. Fortunately this state of affairs did not last long, and casualty clearance was

---

[193] J. A. R., *Memoirs of An Army Surgeon* (Edinburgh and London: William Blackwood, 1948), 210.

[194] J. Abadie, *Wounds of the Abdomen*, ed. Sir W. Arbuthnot-Lane (London: University of London Press, 1918), 55–6.

[195] CMAC RAMC 779, Stammers, 'Report of the Consultant Surgeon', 9.

aided by the start of air evacuation from Aquino, Frosinone, and later from Rome.

Once the roads were reopened, most cases were brought to surgeons within sixteen hours of collection. Once more, surgical units had to be brought as far forward as possible, with FSUs and FDSs 'leap-frogging' up the lines of communication. By the end of June accommodation for GHs and CCSs had been found in suitable buildings in Rome and Orvieto.[196] Specialist surgical units, which had begun to find their feet in North Africa, were now a familiar feature of medical services at the front. The need for specialist neuro-surgical units in forward areas was always assessed on a case-by-case basis. If casualties could reach general hospitals within twenty-four hours, specialist units were not normally required, for the facilities of larger hospitals more than outweighed any advantage gained by operating a few hours earlier.[197] But this is not to say that forward neurosurgery was second-rate, since well over two-thirds of casualties were returned to their units without the need for further operations.[198] Lieutenant-Colonel Peter Ashcroft, commander of No. 4 Mobile Neuro-Surgical Unit, observed that: 'For the first time in a theatre of war the orthopods and the nutcrackers are working together amicably as regards nerve injuries. This is a golden opportunity . . . to give these patients the care and study of treatment they deserve.'[199]

By the autumn of 1944 the front ran from Cecina on the west coast to a few miles north of Ancona on the east. During the next six weeks the Allies moved steadily northwards, but it became apparent that the Germans were putting up stiffer resistance and were intending to make a stand along the Gothic Line. The unexpectedly large number of casualties seems to have left some forward units overstretched. Brigadier F. A. R. Stammers, the Consultant Surgeon to Allied armies in forward areas, recorded in his diary that: '4 CCS [is] very busy. 340 cases passed through yesterday. I have urged them to work a 3–4 hour programme rather than 6, thus evacuating earlier. C. O. says he could want more ambulance cars . . . Cases now are sometimes waiting 10 hours.' He went on to complain that there was 'too much complacency about', after learning that No. 4 CCS had withheld cases merely on the basis of a rumour that its partner, No. 2 CCS, was too busy to take further patients.[200] Stammers was otherwise complimentary about the working relationship between the different nationalities employed in Allied

[196] CMAC RAMC 779, Stammers, 'Report of the Consultant Surgeon', 10.
[197] CMAC RAMC 1154/4/14, Lt.-Col. Peter B. Ashcroft, No. 4 MNSU, Italy, to Brig. Edwards.
[198] CMAC RAMC 1154/4/28, 'Medical History of the War and Quarterly Report of No. 4 Mobile Neuro-Surgical Unit, July 31st to September 30th 1944'.
[199] CMAC RAMC 1154/4/1, Ashcroft to Brig. Weddell, 12 Jan. 1944.
[200] LHCMA Acc. 361, Diary of Brig. F. A. R. Stammers, 30 July 1944.

medical formations, which included Britons, New Zealanders, South Africans, Indians, Poles, and Greeks. Relations between the staff were 'most cordial' and there was an 'harmonious intermingling of personnel and units and a free interchange of knowledge'.[201]

Having encountered increasing resistance north of Rome, 8th Army moved secretly in mid-August to the east coast to prepare for an offensive, which began on 25 August. Its objective was to drive up the coastal plain to the Po Valley, while the British part of 5th Army traversed the mountains north of Florence en route to Bologna, with US forces on their left. As the line advanced, fifteen general hospitals (of all nationalities) were brought forward, providing around 6,000 beds in addition to those at the base hospitals in Rome, Bari, and Naples. The advance meant once again that there would be a considerable distance—of up to 140 miles—between the nearest general hospitals and advanced surgical centres. General hospitals had therefore to function more as clearing stations, and only the most serious cases could be retained. Fortunately, air evacuation permitted the rapid transportation of the less serious cases from the forward general hospitals to the base. The east coast route was especially good, as planes were able to fly lower than 2,000 feet, ensuring a smooth journey without changes in atmospheric pressure. The central route was almost as comfortable, as the pilots went out to sea, but the third route, east to west across the Apennines, was much more turbulent because the aircraft had to climb to over 7,000 feet. Abdominal, chest, and head injuries fared badly on this route, and it was eventually used for limb and flesh wounds only. The only other major disadvantage of air evacuation was the weather, for the Allies had long since established air superiority in Italy. Bad weather also constrained evacuation by sea, but the Allies were able to fall back on the ambulance trains that ran in the central sector from Assisi to Arezzo. The journey from the front to Rome by rail took, on average, sixteen hours, and to Naples twenty-four hours.[202]

The weather in the last quarter of 1944 was so poor that it put paid to hopes of a further breakthrough. After the fall of Rimini, the 8th Army became literally bogged down on the eastern side of the country; further inland, along Route Nine, 5th Corps advanced laboriously to the River Senio, whilst winter conditions in the Apennines reduced fighting to a standstill. Battle casualties were consequently light, and there was little use of the lines of communication to evacuate the sick and wounded.[203] The spring of 1945

[201] CMAC RAMC 779, Stammers, 'Report of the Consultant Surgeon, 1 July–30 September 1944', 2.
[202] Ibid. 5.
[203] Ibid., Stammers, 'Report of the Consultant Surgeon, 1 October 1944–28 February 1945', 2.

saw 8th Army concentrated in the area west of Faenza, north of Ravenna, with 5th Army on its left. The objective of 8th Army was now to destroy the German army south of the Po and then to advance northwards, taking Trieste as a jumping-off point for a later invasion of Austria. Surgical work and evacuation during this advance was less arduous than during the battle for the Gothic Line: the roads were good, ambulance trains were available to take patients to base hospitals, and air evacuation was impressive, with around 2,000 patients flown to base out of a total of 6,000 wounded in 8th Army.[204]

One notable feature of forward work at this point in the campaign was the number of POWs passing into advanced surgical centres. From the first day of battle around 20 per cent of patients were Germans, Turkomans, Chetniks, Slavs, Croats, and Cossacks. The proportion increased to between 40 and 50 per cent after the crossing of the Po. While treating enemy POWs posed few ethical dilemmas for British doctors, some were distinctly uncomfortable when doing so. The surgeon 'J. A. R.' admitted that he:

was never quite at ease when treating prisoners. It was difficult sometimes, when dressing some burly storm-trooper, to make him realise we were doing this, not to curry favour with the master race but merely carrying out routine. It must be confessed, however, that at the back of one's mind the suggestion intruded itself . . . that if we were overrun, then well-treated wounded, erstwhile prisoners would prove good advocates on our behalf.[205]

The capture of enemy wounded revealed systemic problems in the German medical services. 'One could not fail to realise', wrote Brigadier Stammers in his report for the second quarter of 1945, 'that the German standard of war surgery was very much lower than our own.'[206] L. M. Franks, a medical officer with the 6th Armoured Division, recalled that: 'The medical facilities we found when we overran a base hospital were dirty, short of basic supplies and with more amputees than I had ever seen.'[207] At Abano Terme, for instance, the British captured 1,700 surgical patients, nearly all of whom were suffering from chronic sepsis, spreading osteomyelitis, and septic joints. At least 400 were in need of repeated blood transfusions to combat secondary anaemia.[208] The Germans had previously been very skilful at evacuating their wounded during their retreat, and only one hospital had previously been captured in Italy. But now a large number of German hospitals fell into Allied hands, which was indicative of a general collapse in organization.[209] The prevalence of severe cases of sepsis was due, in part, to the slowness of evac-

---

[204] CMAC RAMC 779, Stammers, 'Report of the Consulting Surgeon, 1 March 1945–31 June 1945', 4–5.
[205] J. A. R., *Memoirs*, 224.   [206] Ibid. 6.
[207] L. M. Franks, Personal communication.   [208] J. A. R, *Memoirs*, 7.
[209] CMAC RAMC 779, Stammers, 'Report of the Consultant Surgeon, 1 March 1945–31 June 1945', 6.

uation in the German army, which, on every front had to rely increasingly on draught animals.[210] At Imola, formerly occupied by the Germans, civilians told the British medical authorities that the Germans were evacuating their wounded using ox-wagons, travelling by night and hiding by day. This led to long delays before primary surgical treatment could be given, and left ample time for wounds to become infected with the many lethal microbes that inhabited Italian soil.[211]

Unlike the relatively sterile environments of North Africa and the Western Desert, much of central and northern Italy was intensely cultivated and the bacteria causing gangrene and other infections were plentiful. It was therefore standard practice in the British Army for surgeons to excise any necrotic material as soon as possible and routinely to administer large doses of penicillin. Typically, 15,000 units of penicillin were given to each surgical patient every three hours for three days, or 30,000 in established cases of gangrene.[212] Interviews with captured patients and medical staff revealed, according to Stammers, that: 'German surgeons had never heard of anything like penicillin, and they had never developed organised primary suture of wounds . . . For blood transfusion they used the direct method through a three-way syringe, a method which even though theoretically more ideal does not permit of large numbers of patients being treated.'[213] It is not clear from Stammers' report why the Germans 'did not like storing blood', as some POWs remarked, but it may well have been due to a lack of facilities for refrigeration. Stammers claimed that a visit to a German hospital was 'like stepping back into 1914–16'.[214] It was also widely believed that there was something inherently defective in German medical care, which, it was assumed, had been given little priority by the Nazi regime. A medical report by 8th Army concluded that: 'Despite the fact we have an advantage in the use of Penicillin, it can only be concluded that German surgery failed to make any real advance during the war. Evidently the Nazis gambled their all on the science of killing, ignoring or under-estimating the value of preserving their own Army in the field.'[215] This verdict may seem rather harsh, but it is in many respects true. Other contemporary accounts also indicate that German surgery was 'patchy',[216] while Michael H. Kater, a leading historian of German medicine under Nazism, has concluded that 'there is sufficient evidence to demonstrate

[210] R. L. Di Nardo and A. Bay, 'Horse-drawn Transport in the German Army', *Journal of Contemporary History*, 23 (1988), 129–42.
[211] CMAC RAMC 779, Stammers, 'Report', 7; Franks, 'A Winter in the Appenines, 1944'.
[212] CMAC RAMC 779, Stammers, 'Report of the Consulting Surgeon, 1 July–30 September 1944', 10, 19.
[213] Ibid., Stammers, 'Report of the Consulting Surgeon, 1 March–31 May 1945', 7.
[214] Ibid.
[215] CMAC RAQMC 651/3, 8th Army Medical Report.
[216] Fegeggetter, 'Diary of an RAMC Surgeon at War', 80.

that the Nazis were lacking in medical concern as early as the Polish campaign in autumn 1939'. According to Kater, the German army's medical system was outmoded even before the war began. Field hospitals were generally less mobile than those of the Allies, and shortages of surgical instruments and sanitary equipment meant that conditions in hospitals were often shocking; in some cases, scissors had to be used as scalpels. Medicines were scarce too, and there was no attempt to develop antibiotics; auxiliary personnel were also in short supply and poorly trained.[217]

But for the Allies the Central Mediterranean theatre was a veritable crucible of military medicine. The campaigns in North Africa and Sicily coincided with the advent of penicillin and new anti-malarial drugs, and what appeared then to be an almost magic solution to insect-borne diseases in the form of DDT. One other area in which change occurred apace was in military psychiatry, albeit in the organization of psychiatric facilities rather than the content of psychiatry itself. In the Western Desert forward psychiatry was still in its infancy. Due to the ebb and flow of battle, it had been impossible to establish psychiatric units west of Alexandria, and most cases had been evacuated to Egyptian bases or even to Palestine. Only a few psychiatric facilities were created in forward areas, in preparation for the battle of El Alamein and, later, at Tripoli. These, however, were of great value, as commanders found that many casualties could be quickly returned to battle if treated near the front.[218] In North Africa and Italy psychiatric provision grew quickly, although after a far-from-promising start. No provisions for forward psychiatric treatment were made for the Allied force that landed in North Africa, and this was seemingly a result of deliberate neglect rather than an administrative oversight. Sir Ernest Cowell, the DMS in North Africa, felt that too much emphasis had been placed on psychiatry in other theatres of the war. Known as 'Two-Gun Pete' on account of his militaristic bearing and long service in the Territorial Army, Cowell was a surgeon of the old school and viewed psychiatrists with suspicion.[219] This prejudice against psychiatry appears to have been the one blot on Cowell's otherwise impressive performance as DMS.

This, at any rate, was the state of affairs in January 1943, when two British psychiatrists—Majors John Wishart and Colman Kenton—arrived in North Africa. Kenton built up a psychiatric centre in the British general hospital in Algiers, treating both British and American patients (the Americans, like the

[217] Michael H. Kater, *Doctors Under Hitler* (Chapel Hill and London: University of North Carolina Press, 1989), 52.

[218] CMAC GC/135, 'An Experimental Forward Psychiatry Unit', Dec. 1943.

[219] Ben Shephard, *War of Nerves: Soldiers and Psychiatrists, 1914–1994* (London: Jonathan Cape, 2000), 210.

5. Major-General Ernest Cowell, DMS Central Mediterranean Force, a.k.a. 'Two-gun Pete', CMAC 466/45

British, had made no special provisions for the treatment of psychiatric casualties).[220] Wishart worked as a psychiatric adviser in forward areas, where he
noticed that there was 'a certain amount of opposition to the advent of a
psychiatrist and it was apparent, too, that anxiety existed in administrative
quarters lest my arrival should provoke a sudden increase in the number of
psychiatric cases, and that these would be dealt with more "leniently" than
heretofore'. 'This anxiety', he continued, 'was evidenced in the excessive
stressing of the disciplinary aspect of cases, and the variations in diagnosis
which were introduced—the term "effects of explosion" being an attempt to
distinguish the "genuine" case from the so-called "N.Y.D. (N)" who was fundamentally regarded as a coward to be disciplined.'[221] This diagnosis was

[220] CMAC RAMC 466/49, Lt.-Col. Roy R. Grinker and Capt. John P. Spiegel, 'War Neuroses in
North Africa: The Tunisian Campaign (January–May 1943)', 7, (Unpublished MS, USAAF, Sept.
1943). See also Nathan G. Hale, Jr., *The Rise and Crisis of Psychoanalysis in the United States: Freud
and the Americans, 1917–1985* (New York and Oxford: Oxford University Press, 1995), 187–204.
[221] CMAC GC/135, Maj. J. W. Wishart, 'Experiences as a Psychiatrist with BNAF and CMF—
January 1943 to June 1944, With Special Reference to Work in the Forward Area', 1.

eventually abandoned, however, as it proved too difficult to prove cowardice in the face of the enemy. The preference, as in the later stages of the Western Desert campaign, was for the diagnosis of 'exhaustion', which conveyed the idea of rapid recovery after rest.[222]

Suspicion of psychiatry was initially widespread in the Army, but once troops and medical officers had gained experience of battle, attitudes to psychiatrists and psychiatric casualties generally became more sympathetic. Heavy psychiatric casualties also forced Cowell to fly to Cairo to seek the advice of the Middle East's psychiatric consultant, Brigadier G. W. B. James.[223] Combatant officers, too, tended to become more open to the demands of psychiatrists, once it became apparent that the presence of psychiatric specialists in forward areas did much to stem the wastage of manpower. In North Africa this point was reached in March, when hospitals at the base became overcrowded with psychiatric patients. It was generally recognized that this overcrowding could only be alleviated if the less severe cases were treated near the front. Wishart was despatched first to No. 70 GH and then, in April, to No. 100 GH, to commence psychiatric work. This coincided with the arrival in North Africa of the recently appointed Adviser in Psychiatry, Lieutenant-Colonel Stephen MacKeith—formerly of the Tavistock Clinic in London—who took over responsibility for this side of medical work from the Consulting Physician with AFHQ, who had taken no obvious interest in psychiatry. The time was now ripe for the establishment of a psychiatric centre that was transferred in July from No. 100 GH to 104 GH at El Arrouch and expanded to 200 beds; specialist psychiatric nurses were also made available.[224]

As in the forward units established in the Western Desert, treatment at this stage consisted of simple restorative and psychotherapeutic measures, such as suggestion and continuous narcosis.[225] But such rudimentary treatments, if given far enough forward, tended to be far more effective than complex psychoanalytical therapies, which succeeded in returning only a small proportion of cases to full duty.[226] The main principles of military psychiatry were now firmly established: immediacy, proximity of treatment, and 'positive expectancy', the latter being enshrined in the reassuring diagnosis of 'exhaustion'.[227]

---

[222] CMAC RAMC GC/135, MacKeith Papers, Consulting Psychiatrist to the Army, 'Report of a Visit to Gibraltar, North Africa and the Middle East, 25 May–29 June, 1943', 6.

[223] Shephard, *War of Nerves*, 211.

[224] CMAC RAMC GC/135, 'Report of a Visit to Gibraltar', 2.

[225] Ibid. 4.

[226] Ibid., Meeting of Allied Psychiatrists, BNAF, 95 GH, 5 May 1943.

[227] Hans Binneveld, *From Shell Shock to Combat Stress: A Comparative History of Military Psychiatry*, trans. John O'Kane (Amsterdam: Amsterdam University Press, 1997), ch. 8.

The creation of facilities for forward psychiatry was timely in view of the near collapse of morale in some units of the British Army. Major John Wishart witnessed at first hand a mass breakdown of troops at the battle of Two Tree Hill on 17 January 1943, in which sixty-six of 450–500 casualties were psychiatric. In the 3rd Battalion of the Grenadier Guards there had been a 'generalised panic',[228] which was attributed to fatigue, inadequate rations, poor selection of personnel, heavy losses, and the fact that many men were inexperienced.[229] There was little that could be done to prevent fatigue on active service, but there was a widespread belief that personnel selection—both during and after training—could do much to weed out those psychologically unfit for battle. 'The Medical Officer, particularly the psychiatrist,' wrote the Adjutant-General in his statement on the health of the Army in 1943, 'can help enormously by detecting at an early stage the man who by reason of emotional instability, or mental backwardness, may be constitutionally unable to resist displaying fear to such a degree that he not only becomes useless as a fighting unit but a menace as a source of infection to others.'[230] As Adjutant-General, Adam was following advice from psychiatrists who claimed that, in the majority of cases of battle exhaustion, there was a previous history of minor neurotic symptoms, if not of nervous breakdown.[231] It was said that those who possessed low intelligence fared badly in Tunisia. After visiting North Africa, the Consulting Psychiatrist for the British Army noted that: 'The Pioneer Corps were doing well but the dullards and some of the men who after transfer have been upgraded at home from Unarmed Sections, have broken down badly. It seems clear that dullards of this war vintage do not shine in the stress of conditions in Africa and certainly not in or near the fighting line.'[232]

There was fairly widespread agreement amongst medical officers—both regimental MOs and psychiatric specialists—when it came to the role of predisposing factors such as education and character. Both psychiatrists and regimental MOs believed that there were essentially two types of men who succumbed to battle exhaustion: good men who had been ground down by arduous service, and those of weak will who sought early release from combat. The former, according to Grey Turner, a medical officer with the Guards, consisted of 'a small group of "old soldiers"—good men whose nerve has at

[228] CMAC RAMC GC/135, Consulting Psychiatrist to the Army, 'Report on a Visit to Gibraltar, North Africa and the Middle East', 5.
[229] Ibid. 6.
[230] CMAC RAMC 466/38, R. F. Adam, 'The Health of the Army', 5.
[231] CMAC GC/135, Maj. H. A. Palmer, 'The Problem of the P & N Casualty—A Study of 12,000 Cases', 4.
[232] Ibid., Consulting Psychiatrist, 'Report on a Visit to Gibraltar, North Africa and the Middle East', 6.

last been worn away by continued subjection to the hardships and danger of battle'. Such cases, he insisted, should be treated with sympathy and evacuated to base for rest and rehabilitation. The other, much larger group consisted of 'soldiers whose characters are simply too weak to stand the strain of battle and who break down early':

If these men are treated with sympathy and evacuated [he warned], the rot spreads like a prairie fire, and the morale of the entire unit is quickly undermined. Hence it is the unpleasant duty of the medical officer to treat this group harshly, to order them back to their posts, under escort if necessary, and at last when all useful service has been extracted from them, but not before, to cast them away, like squeezed sponges, to the psychiatrists.[233]

Psychiatrists also believed that breakdown usually occurred when environmental stimuli compounded some inherent flaw of character or caused a reversion to former patterns of behaviour. They acknowledged, too, that the seriousness of the patient's condition depended on unit morale. As the psychiatrist Major H. A. Palmer put it: 'If it [morale] is very low, and if he [the soldier] possesses what may be thought of as a perverted form of moral courage, he may desert. If he is not possessed of this perverse form of moral courage . . . he throws in the sponge, reports sick and may be evacuated.' Palmer referred to this type of case—which constituted some 30 per cent of psychiatric cases—as the 'Simple Stress Reaction' or 'Simple Loss of Grip'.[234] Individuals of high morale who exhibited symptoms of stress, by contrast, often suffered what Palmer termed a 'False Blackout', commonly known as 'Guardsman's Hysteria', on account of the generally high morale of Guards regiments. 'Such a man', explained Palmer:

will undoubtedly vaguely consider what ways of honourable escape lay open to him. He is finding it almost impossible to tolerate his fear, anxiety or grief, but his good morale prevents him from deserting. It is possibly fair to say that his central nervous system lets him down at this stage, and he may develop a condition of vague dissociation and wander from the field of battle. If the hysterical constitution is marked . . . such a man at this point will often develop conversion symptoms, in the form of gross tremor, stammer or paralysis.[235]

Men of high morale who lacked this 'inborn capacity for dissociation' might, according to Palmer, experience what he termed a 'true battle anxiety reaction'. Such a man typically had a marked startle reflex, a fine tremor, and a tendency to sweat excessively; he found difficulty in sleeping and had a poor appetite. A vicious circle was established in which these individuals declined

[233] CMAC GC/96/1, Diary of E. Grey Turner, 19 Jan. 1943.
[234] CMAC GC/135, Palmer, 'The Problem of the P & N Casualty', 5.
[235] Ibid. 6.

rapidly to the extent that they became a liability; they were what the ordinary soldier called 'bomb happy'. This was a sub-chronic condition which, if improperly handled, could develop symptoms of secondary hysteria. A more serious chronic condition, found among troops of previously high morale, was what Palmer termed a 'Campaign Neurosis'. As Palmer put it: 'Tommy recognises this burnt-out type of man and bears him no ill-will or scorn, and such a man coming into my clinic is usually ushered out by my Corporal with the aside remark to me "He's had it Sir".'[236]

Palmer's elaborate typology of neuroses reflected the conventional wisdom of soldiers themselves. A Mancunian of forthright views, Palmer prided himself on his tough, 'no-nonsense' attitude to psychiatry. Although he relied principally on rest and recuperation to treat around two-thirds of psychiatric cases ('simple stress reactions'), his therapeutic repertoire included some drastic methods of treatment. Men experiencing dissociation were given ether and then abreaction therapy, which aimed to produce an emotional catharsis. As well as combating repression and inhibition, ether made the patient more amenable to suggestion and persuasion.[237] As one MO later put it, Palmer's approach—though effective—'was not for the timid',[238] and did not go down terribly well with some of the psychoanalytically inclined Tavistock men who advised the Adjutant-General. As a result, Palmer's methods never became widespread, though his approach was acceptable to Brigadier James, who had authorized his appointment.[239]

Perhaps the most significant feature of Palmer's report was his acknowledgement that domestic or 'emotional' problems could be as important in precipitating a mental breakdown as the stress of battle.[240] As a later report on psychiatric casualties in the Italian campaign stated: 'Anxiety over alleged or admitted infidelity on the part of a soldier's wife has without doubt the most adverse effect on his morale and is the commonest cause, apart from battle stress, of psychiatric breakdown in the Army.'[241] This was reiterated in a study of morale commissioned for the War Office. The report's author, Lieutenant-Colonel John Sparrow, who was later to become one of the more colourful wardens of All Souls College, Oxford, concluded that:

The psychological effect of prolonged absence from home began to be apparent in most men after two year's absence . . . The effects were most marked in those who

---

[236] Ibid. 7.   [237] Ibid. 16.
[238] Communication from Dr R. S. Morton, MBE.
[239] See Ben Shephard, ' "Pitiless Psychology": The Role of Prevention in British Military Psychiatry in the Second World War', *Journal of the History of Psychiatry*, 10 (1999), 491–524.
[240] CMAC GC/135, Palmer, 'The P & N Casualty', 4.
[241] Ibid., Maj. H. D. Hunter, 'Notes and Recommendations on Issues Affecting Morale, No. 5, Compassionate Postings', Sept. 1944, p. 1.

had left a wife or 'girl' at home . . . it was found that it was usually from two to three years of separation that the woman's fidelity broke down. The number of wives and fiancées who were unfaithful to soldiers serving overseas almost defies belief . . . Nothing did more to lower the morale of troops serving overseas than news of female infidelity . . . and no disease was more infectious than the anxiety and depression arising from bad news or the absence of reassuring news on this topic.[242]

Sparrow's uncompromising reports were political dynamite, and the Secretary of State for War demanded that they be toned down because they revealed too much sensitive information.[243] Nevertheless, the Army was generally willing to consider the impact of 'domestic' factors upon morale, and indeed had deliberately encouraged the soldier to see himself as a citizen with a life beyond the Army.[244] The reports are also refreshingly frank about sexual matters: as in the case of mental illness, a scientific outlook was replacing the traditional emphasis on morality and willpower. In the work of Palmer and other military psychiatrists the two sat uneasily together, hence the ambiguity of a condition that could be termed either a 'simple stress reaction' or a 'simple loss of grip'.

In view of the fact that traditional notions of good character still existed in the writings of some military psychiatrists, it is hardly surprising that they dominated the perspectives of regimental MOs, who were generally of a more traditional cast of mind. 'The main function of military psychiatry seems to me to be selection,' opined Elston Grey Turner, 'because the results of psychiatric treatment of battle-exhaustion cases were, in my experience, very disappointing. This is not a reflection on the army psychiatrists. Character is partly inherited and partly the result of environment and training . . . The psychiatrists could not be expected to remodel their patients' characters in a few days or weeks.'[245] Grey Turner's emphasis upon character and upbringing was very much at odds with the egalitarian spirit of Army propaganda:

The nauseating misery and stark terror of the battlefield are utterly indescribable in

---

[242] J. H. A. Sparrow, *The Second World War 1939–1945 Army: Morale* (London: HMSO, 1949), 9.

[243] Noel Annan, *The Dons: Mentors, Eccentrics and Geniuses* (London: Harper Collins, 1999), 195.

[244] See S. P. MacKenzie, *Politics and Military Morale: Current Affairs and Citizenship Education in the British Army 1914–1950* (Oxford: Oxford University Press, 1992).

[245] CMAC GC/96/1, Diary of E. Grey Turner, 19 January 1943. Elston Grey Turner (1916–84) was the son of a distinguished surgeon and was educated at Winchester and Trinity College, Cambridge. He joined the RAMC on a temporary commission after qualifying in medicine at St Bartholomew's Hospital in 1942. He served first in North Africa and then in Italy, where he received the MC for rescuing wounded under fire at Monte Cassino. He ended the war as a Lieutenant-Colonel on Montgomery's staff in Germany. He continued to serve in the TA after the war. Grey Turner was Secretary of the BMA from 1976 to 1979 and became its Vice-President in 1982. He was awarded the CBE in 1980. Obituary by F. Anderson, in *As You Were: V.E. Day: A Medical Retrospect* (London: BMA, 1984), 178–81.

words—they can only be experienced. When I reflect that young officers, sometimes mere boys, must and do successfully lead and command their men under such conditions: and that I only once knew an officer to break down under the strain . . . I must say that these facts speak volumes for the methods of selection and training of officers, and for the qualities of the officer class . . . [T]he main burden of responsibility and danger, the principal share in winning the battle, is borne by the Warrant Officers (be it noted that I place them first) and the Officers. I state this fact as an impersonal observer, and I know that no honest fighting soldier will deny it. Left-Wing politicians will question it, because they fall into the error of confusing the officer class, which can most conveniently be described as the product of the Public Schools, with the class of persons who inhabit expensive cars and luxury hotels, most of whom are of questionable antecedents and unpleasant manners, and for whom the officer class have a more profound distaste . . . than even the Left-Wing politicians themselves.[246]

It was, no doubt, the prevalence of such sentiments among regimental medical officers that prompted the Adjutant-General to write in his circular letter to all MOs in December 1943 that: 'Fear is a universal emotion. Like jealousy, hatred or love, it is experienced by every normal human being under conditions which are conducive to it . . . The vast majority of men can be trained to deal with fear just as they can be trained to deal with Germans.'[247]

Following the invasion of Sicily and Italy, psychiatry was placed on a firmer footing under the guidance of Lieutenant-Colonel Stephen MacKeith, the recently appointed Adviser in Psychiatry. By December 1943 a definite chain of evacuation and treatment had been established, whereby psychiatric casualties left FAs to be received by the Corps Psychiatrist and committed to the Corps Exhaustion Centre (CEC), if necessary. For most patients a few days at the CEC proved sufficient and many were returned from here directly to their units. Some needed more time to recuperate and were sent to an Advanced Rehabilitation Centre or, if further treatment was required, to an Advanced Base Psychiatric Centre (BPC), where they spent from four to ten days. If the patient had not yet recovered and needed additional treatment, he would be sent to the base and, if recovery was made, to the reallocation centre, where an assessment was made of his suitability for military duties. Psychotics and the most intractable cases of neurosis were evacuated from Italy to the United Kingdom by hospital ship.[248] By contrast with the US Army, which returned maximum numbers of psychiatric casualties straight to battle, the British reallocated a much higher proportion of their casualties

[246] CMAC GC/96/1, 28 Apr. 1943.
[247] CMAC RAMC 466/38, R. F. Adam, 'The Health of the Army', 5.
[248] CMAC GC/135, Minutes of 29th Meeting of Command Psychiatrists, London, 26 January 1945; Lt.-Col. S. A. MacKeith, 'Psychiatric Comments on Some Current Issues Affecting Morale, Italy', 19 Sept. 1944; interview with S. A. MacKeith, OBE.

to non-combatant duties. The Canadians took a rather different approach, and sent most of their psychiatric casualties to Special Employment Companies, which aimed to rehabilitate men by stages.[249]

The basis of all psychiatric treatment in the British Army was the 'psychiatric interview,' which was conducted at each CEC. This was a short examination lasting no longer than fifteen minutes, designed to establish the nature and severity of the patient's condition. The brevity of the examination meant that it lacked the scientific rigour that many psychiatrists would have liked. 'This limitation', admitted the psychiatrists Major F. P. Haldane and Captain J. L. Rowley, 'precludes the employment of entirely rational criteria, forcing us to fall back upon psychiatric intuition as the principal basis of our evaluation.' The aim was to establish a rapport with the patient and a degree of what psychiatrists called 'transference'. Haldane and Rowley were confident that only a quarter of an hour would enable them to estimate the strength of their patient's ego, for it was weakness of the ego, they argued, rather than neurosis, which was the commonest disability of patients seen at this level.[250] 'The function of the ego', they explained:

is the integrated adaptation of the individual's attitudes and behaviour, in accordance with the current and fore-seeable future reality setting, and with the distribution of intra-psychic forces, in such a way as to acquire the maximum . . . advantages to the individual in relation to his environment . . . Its successful functioning, therefore, has two essential aspects: extensive and accurate reality testing . . . competent manipulation and control of conscious and unconscious psychic forces . . .[251]

The extent to which such ideas were shared by other corps psychiatrists is unclear.

Treatment in forward areas followed much the same lines as in North Africa, with sedation (and, in some cases, prolonged narcosis) forming the major part of the psychiatrists' repertoire. Abreactive therapy and electro-convulsive therapy were also employed, though to a lesser extent than in North Africa.[252] But front-line psychiatrists rarely employed insulin sub-coma therapy, which had been found useful in cases of what had become known as 'campaign neurosis', in which 'good men' had broken down after prolonged stress. Though controversial, insulin coma therapy had been used

[249] Terry Copp and Bill McAndrew, *Battle Exhaustion: Soldiers and Psychiatrists in the Canadian Army, 1939–1945* (Montreal, Kingston, London, and Buffalo: McGill-Queens University Press, 1990), 88.

[250] CMAC GC/135, Maj. F. P. Haldane and Capt. J. L. Rowley, 'The Technique of the Psychiatric Interview at the Corps Exhaustion Centre'.

[251] Ibid., F. P. Haldane and J. L. Rowley, 'Psychiatry at the Corps Exhaustion Centre: A Technique of Rapid Psychiatric Assessment', 1 Dec. 1944.

[252] Ibid., Director of Army Psychiatry, 'Report on a Visit to CMF, 1 December–23 December 1944', 7.

in some British mental hospitals since its accidental discovery by the psychiatrist William Sargant in 1933. During the war its use was largely confined to a few hospitals in the United Kingdom, owing partly to the cost of the treatment and the apparent efficacy of simpler measures such as rest and recuperation.[253]

One innovation in front-line psychiatry was the formation of what became known as Corps Psychiatric Teams, in which registered mental nurses worked alongside psychiatrists. Lieutenant-Colonel J. D. W. Pearce, who replaced MacKeith as Adviser on Psychiatry in December 1944, reported that: 'These teams have done first-class work and have succeeded in returning many cases to full fighting duty: and by prompt and early treatment have lessened the severity of the breakdown in those whom they have evacuated.'[254] The vast majority of cases were treated within four days, although teams were allowed to use their initiative and hold cases for several weeks if they thought it appropriate.

The psychiatric cases seen in Italy were much the same as in other theatres, most being different varieties of anxiety state, although generally somewhat milder than in North Africa. MacKeith ascribed this to quicker evacuation and early contact with a psychiatrist at the CEC, which meant that there was less time for symptoms to become fixed.[255] While it is difficult to generalize about such matters, morale amongst British troops was high for most of the campaign, boosted, as MacKeith observed, by the progress of the Allies through Italy and the establishment of air superiority.[256] Good leadership also played its part, and the 8th Army, especially, was well known for its relaxed competence and *esprit de corps*. 'If it were not for the "immunising effect" in the psychiatric field of this well-braced morale structure,' concluded MacKeith, 'half the expeditionary force would become psychiatric casualties, or desert, however harsh the disciplinary regime might be; and the psychiatrist's job would be impossible.'[257] He rated morale as a far more important factor than mental type.[258] However, in the latter part of 1944 there is some indication that morale had begun to deteriorate, despite Allied successes in northern Italy. A secret memorandum on 'The Status of the Infantry', circulated in September 1944, reported that there was much

[253] William Sargant, 'Physical Treatment of Acute War Neuroses', *British Medical Journal*, 14 Nov. and 3 Dec. 1942, pp. 574, 675; id., *The Unquiet Mind* (London: Heinemann, 1967), 119–21; CMAC GC/192/18, Papers of Lt.-Col. J. D. W. Pearce, 'Report by Adviser in Psychiatry', 10. See also Copp and McAndrew, *Battle Exhaustion*, 24–5.
[254] CMAC GC/192/18, 'Report by Adviser in Psychiatry', 10.
[255] S. A. MacKeith, 'Lasting Lessons of Overseas Military Psychiatry', *Journal of Mental Sciences*, 92 (1946), 542–50; interview with S. A. MacKeith, OBE.
[256] CMAC GC/135, Minutes of 29th Meeting of Command Psychiatrists.
[257] MacKeith, 'Lasting Lessons', 543; interview with S. A. MacKeith, OBE.
[258] MacKeith, 'Lasting Lessons', 547–8.

bitterness amongst infantrymen on account of the fact that they were poorly paid by comparison with non-combatants such as RAMC orderlies.[259] Psychiatrists were also spending a good deal of their time dealing with disciplinary cases, which they had to examine for signs of mental disorder. Lieutenant-Colonel Pearce reported that as many as 5,000 such cases had come under review during the final year of the campaign in Italy. A large proportion of these were cases of desertion, and a good many were sentenced by courts martial before psychiatric scrutiny of disciplinary cases began in earnest. According to Pearce, many men were given heavy sentences for desertion despite being sick at the time of the offence; others deserted because of poor leadership.[260]

The most intractable psychiatric cases, which included many of those with VD phobia and other non-battle cases, were treated at the Base Psychiatric Centres, which were fully functioning by December 1943.[261] These centres employed many of the techniques of forward psychiatry but made more extensive use of therapies such as prolonged narcosis and abreactive therapy, which aimed to release previously repressed emotions. These were usually combined with physical training and various forms of entertainment, to prevent the patient dwelling on his illness and to return a feeling of normality. Since abreaction therapy had been used in British military hospitals during the First World War, psychiatrists had little new to offer except a few experiments in Italy with group therapy, which had also been used on occasion in North Africa.[262] Group therapy—which involved free collective association and dynamic analytical methods—emerged from a long chain of developments within the Army.[263] The most notable of these were aptitude testing with leaderless groups,[264] and psychiatric interviews conducted in wards in front of other patients, in order to produce repeated reassurance.[265] Group therapy also had roots in civilian psychiatry, including the use of psychodrama, which was pioneered by J. L. Moreno in 1937.[266] In psychodrama, patients were encouraged to relive their experiences and to show what happened to them, often with help from other members of the

[259] CMAC GC/135, 'The Status of Infantry', Sept. 1944.
[260] CMAC GC/192/18, 'Report by Adviser in Psychiatry', 7.
[261] CMAC GC/135, Minutes of the 29th Meeting of Command Psychiatrists.
[262] Grinker and Spiegel, *War Neuroses in North Africa*, 228.
[263] MacKeith, 'Lasting Lessons', 546.
[264] CMAC PP/SHF/C.3/4, R.T.C. Technical Memo. No. 1, 'Leaderless Group Tests', issued by the Directorate of Selection of Personnel.
[265] Grinker and Spiegel, *War Neuroses*, 153; CMAC PP/SHF/C.3/2, Foulkes Papers, Lt.-Col. G. R. Hargreaves, AMD 11 to S. H. Foulkes, Northfield Hospital, Birmingham, 30 Aug. 1945.
[266] See J. L. Moreno, *Who Shall Survive? Foundations of Sociometry, Group Psychotherapy and Sociodrama* (London: Beacon House, 1953).

group.[267] It was a kind of collective abreactive therapy, which drew on Aristotle's idea that theatre could have a cathartic effect.[268] It often took the form of a discussion about some topic chosen by a member of the group rather than by the psychiatrist. 'In this way', declared one of the major proponents of group therapy, Sigmund ('Michael') Foulkes, 'deep material can be loosened by apparently superficial handling.'[269]

Little is known of the group therapy sessions that took place in Italy, but they may have been similar to those conducted by Foulkes at Northfield Hospital near Birmingham.[270] Perhaps the most interesting aspect of these sessions is that they reflect the egalitarianism of Army propaganda, with group identity being fostered in order to engender a feeling of equality of sacrifice. The themes chosen for discussion at group meetings promoted this idea, and included democratic representation and social reconstruction. The affinity between group psychiatry and contemporary ideas of social citizenship also existed at a more fundamental level. In his address to a US psychiatric mission attending Northfield Hospital, Foulkes placed great emphasis on the individual's relationship to the group. The soldier who entered hospital with a psychiatric disorder, he claimed, had failed in 'his duties as a soldier and a fighting man and as a citizen of a community at war'.[271] Group therapy also entailed thinking about psychiatry in a more democratic way, as one psychiatrist explained: 'I started off with a resistance to the idea of groups. I think the reason was a personal one, encouraged to some extent by other psychiatrists. I was rather suffering from the conception that a psychiatrist must be someone who is omniscient in the psychological field, superior to the patient, who must be a psychological God . . .'[272] This anti-authoritarianism also came out strongly in the choice of psychodrama as a therapeutic technique. Psychodrama was said to open the way for 'a more flexible and systematic process of learning, providing a more reliable foundation for the absorbing of discipline than authoritarian methods'.[273] Such ideas were very much in harmony with contemporary notions of democracy and active citizenship.

Social psychiatry manifested itself, too, in the increasing emphasis upon mental hygiene, or the prevention of psychiatric breakdown in war. Speaking on a film to be shown to all new recruits, entitled *The New Lot*, Brigadier

[267] CMAC PP/SHF/C.3/8, Record of group meeting of Northfield Hospital, 3 May 1945.
[268] CMAC PP/SHF/C.3/23, Foulkes, notes on 'Role Analysis and Audience Structure', by Zerka Toeman.
[269] CMAC PP/SHF/C.3/2, Record of group meeting at Northfield Hospital, 11 Nov. 1944.
[270] For a full account of the work at Northfield see Tom Harrison, *Bion, Rickman, Foulkes and the Northfield Experiments: Advancing on a Different Front* (London: Jessica Kingsley, 2000).
[271] CMAC PP/SHF/C.3/8, S. H. Foulkes, Address to US Psychiatric Mission, 6 June 1945.
[272] Ibid., Contribution by Dr Mead to group meeting, Northfield Hospital, 8 Nov. 1945.
[273] Ibid., Foulkes, notes on 'Role Analysis and Audience Structure'.

G. W. B. James, the British Army's psychiatric specialist in the Central
Mediterranean theatre, declared:

This study of a group is what we are beginning to call social medicine and I
commend the film to you as an example of new work in which the army is showing
the way to a wider conception of medicine . . . We must learn much more of the
way in which great groups live and die, work and play, love and hate; only so shall
we acquire an adequate knowledge of the circumstances in which human material
shows manifestations which may begin as disharmonies and discomforts and end in
gross disorders of various kinds, including the greatest social disgrace of poverty.[274]

Psychiatry had captured the mood of Beveridgian Britain. It was confidently
anticipated that mental hygiene would alleviate a whole range of social dis-
contents, laying bare the unconscious mechanisms that lay behind strikes,
crime, poverty, and even war itself. It promised, in the biblical language of
Brigadier James, nothing less than 'a peace among men that so far has passed
all understanding'.[275] These sentiments were shared by that champion of
Army psychiatry Ronald Adam, who had been the architect not only of personnel selection but also of the Army Bureau of Current Affairs and the Army
Education Corps. Adam was renowned throughout Britain for his progressive views, and was referred to in one newspaper as the 'the Army's No. 1
democrat'. Sir Ronald, it noted, had 'encouraged experiments with democratic citizenship' and had set out to turn the troops into 'well-informed and
democratic citizens'.[276]

For the time being, however, psychiatry was very definitely in the service
of Mars. It was the duty of the psychiatrist to highlight those features of military life—lack of privacy, discomfort, boredom, separation from loved ones,
and so forth—that created stress among new recruits.[277] He was to persuade
medical and combatant officers that the basis of courage was social rather
than individual.[278] He was to advise on training and to ensure that the new
recruit became accustomed to or 'inoculated' against the stresses of battle by
' "debunking" battle noise, the tank, and the morale-destroying aspects of the
dive bomber'.[279]

It is hard to judge whether 'preventive' psychiatry was successful, although
it is clear that many medical officers—let alone combatant officers—still

---

[274] CMAC GC/135, Address by Brig. G. W. B. James introducing the film *The New Lot* to a
medical audience at St Mary's Hospital, p. 1.
[275] CMAC GC/135, Address by James, 3.
[276] LHCMA, Adam Papers, 2/6/1, *Leicester Evening Mail*, 27 Apr. 1946, p. 3.
[277] CMAC GC/135, Address by James, 3; MacKeith, 'Lasting Lessons', 542.
[278] E. Wittkower and J. P. Spillane, 'Neuroses in War', *British Medical Journal*, 10 Feb. 1940,
pp. 223–5.
[279] Brig. J. R. Rees, 'Three Years of Military Psychiatry in the United Kingdom', *British Medical
Journal*, 2 Jan. 1943, p. 6.

believed that individual character was vitally important and had a great bearing on resistance to the stresses of battle. Even if preventive psychiatry did have some impact, it would be almost impossible to disentangle its effects from those of good discipline and leadership, which owed far more to regimental officers than psychiatrists. The psychiatrists' greatest contribution lay, rather, in the field of therapy and returning patients to active service. In these terms some British military psychiatrists were remarkably successful, not least Major Palmer, who returned no less than 98 per cent of the 1,414 patients he received at his hospital in Tripoli to duty in less than three weeks. Though controversial, Palmer's 'no-nonsense' methods were apparently more successful and, perhaps, more humane than the more protracted therapies carried out in hospitals at the base, which may have reinforced the patient's feeling that he was mentally ill. But the success of military psychiatry had as much to do with the decisions of government as with therapeutic techniques. The success of psychiatrists like Palmer can be attributed in part to official policies designed to discourage war neuroses: the replacement of medical terms with that of 'exhaustion', the extreme reluctance of the government to award pensions to those with war neuroses, and the fact that it was impossible for soldiers to use 'neurosis' as grounds for discharge from the Army.[280] All these factors undoubtedly played their part, but just as important—perhaps even more important—was the desire not to fail one's comrades, and the sense that the war was both winnable and just. All these factors contributed to the very real success of British military psychiatry in Italy and North Africa, and in the other theatres in which the Army fought in 1944–5.

Conclusion

The direction in which military psychiatry developed during the North African and Italian campaigns typified more general changes occurring in therapeutic and preventive medicine during the 1930s and 1940s; namely, growing recognition of the social dimensions of health and illness. A number of military psychiatrists believed that mental breakdown in wartime needed to be understood in a broader context, which took into account the patient's history and personal relationships. Psychotherapy had itself begun, in a small way, to change its orientation from the individual to the group, just as the content of group discussions reflected prevailing concerns about civic responsibility and social reconstruction.

The Army, therefore, provided an environment in which exponents of 'social medicine' could put their theories into practice and develop them in

---

[280] Shephard, 'Pitiless Psychology'.

new ways. It was receptive, perhaps, because military medicine encouraged a holistic view of health. It had long taken into account the effects of training and morale upon the health of the soldier, in addition to general environmental conditions. The climate of opinion within the Army—and not only in medical circles—was also in favour of education in health and its relation to the rights and responsibilities of citizenship. As such, the Army provided the model for what could be achieved in civilian life. As P. S. Lelean had put it, in an article in the journal *Health and Empire* in 1929: 'the outstanding need for both present and future is that of education for every individual, so that intelligent cooperation in all hygienic measures may be secured from all good citizens as it has been from all good soldiers.'[281] But the poor record of British soldiers in respect of VD and malaria shows that it is important not to overstate the degree to which compliance was achieved. Despite appeals to comradeship and patriotic duty, the success of military medicine still depended crucially on effective discipline. This was true no less of hygiene and sanitation than of mental health. While discipline was generally good in North Africa, it was often lax in Italy, perhaps because active service was punctuated by periods of relative calm and because of the greater opportunities that existed for fraternization with civilians. Growing weariness among the troops, and greater opportunities to contract infections such as VD, led to a marked deterioration in the health and morale of British soldiers. Admissions to hospital for sickness were approximately seven times greater than admissions from wounds.[282] Appeals for sanitary discipline seem to have made little impact in such circumstances, and had it not been for penicillin and DDT, venereal disease and malaria might have crippled the British Army.

[281] CMAC RAMC 565, P. S. Lelean, 'The Evolution of Public Health', repr. from *Health and Empire*, Dec. 1929, p. 10.
[282] IWM Montgomery Collection, Montgomery to Frank Simpson, 17 Dec. 1943.

5
Burma and North-East India

The campaign in Burma and North-East India was the longest of any fought by British and Imperial forces during the Second World War. Beginning with the Japanese invasion of southern Burma in December 1941, and ending with the Japanese surrender in August 1945, it epitomized the miltary fortunes of the British Empire. An early, ignominious defeat had been transformed, as Field-Marshal Viscount Slim was to put it, into victory.[1] Some of the tactical and logistical innovations made during the campaign were of enduring importance, not least the large-scale use of air transport to supply ground forces. In the densely forested hills of Assam and Arakan the movement of supplies by road and rail was often impossible, and transportation by air was frequently the only means available. This was true not only of the long-range penetration columns formed by Brigadier Orde Wingate and immortalized as the 'Chindits', but also of regular forces involved in operations in such decisive engagements as those around Imphal and Kohima. Air support remained equally important during the pursuit through Burma, owing to 14th Army's rapid movement and the vast distances between bases in India and the front. Air superiority was therefore vital to the success of almost every aspect of operations in the India/Burma theatre, not least the medical.

Medicine itself played an important part in the victory of 14th Army, and the Burma campaign is seen as one of the classic illustrations of the importance of medicine in war. It has often been claimed that the superiority of British medical arrangements, and in particular those designed to prevent malaria, provided the 14th Army with the decisive edge it needed for victory over the Japanese.[2] The official medical historian of the Burma campaign, F. A. E. Crew, went so far as to conclude that 'the marked difference in the degree to which malaria was brought and held under control in the Allied and the Japanese land forces respectively during the course of the years

---

[1] Field-Marshal Viscount Slim, *Defeat into Victory* (London: Macmillan, 1986; first published 1956), 551.
[2] Col. Ronald F. Bellamy and Col. Craig H. Llewellyn, 'Preventable Casualties: Rommel's Flaw, Slim's Edge', *Army* (May 1990), 52–6.

1943–1945 was one of the reasons, and indeed one of the most important reasons, why the Japanese were defeated'.[3]

Crew makes a convincing case for the effectiveness of preventive medicine, and of malaria prophylaxis in particular. Admissions to hospital dropped from a high of 1,850 per thousand troops per annum in 1942 (equivalent to almost two serious bouts of sickness per man per year) to 500 per thousand per annum in 1945.[4] Set against rising rates of malarial infection in the Japanese Army,[5] these figures would seem to support the view that preventive medicine made a crucial difference to the effectiveness of the respective forces. But the official history may have exaggerated the difference that existed between the British and the Japanese: malaria rates in the opposing forces did not differ markedly until after the battle for Meiktila in February–March 1945, by which time the Japanese had already suffered their most decisive defeats. Until that point, as Slim readily acknowledged, the Japanese may actually have suffered fewer casualties from disease than 14th Army.

The official history also attributes the medical success of 14th Army chiefly to preventive medicine. But its main advantage lay, rather, in the rapid *recovery* of those who contracted malaria and other diseases. The key factor here was the development of facilities for forward treatment, including the formation of a number of integrated medical units, or Corps Medical Centres, which were a novel feature of the Burma campaign. These conglomerates consisted of medical units from many Commonwealth countries, from Africa to India, which worked closely alongside those of the British Army.[6] Besides enabling the rapid treatment and return of casualties to active service, forward treatment discouraged those who saw sickness as a ticket back to the relative comfort of India. In both respects, forward treatment did much to maintain morale and cohesion within the 14th Army, as numerous medical and psychiatric reports testify.

Retreat

The events that culminated in the longest retreat in the history of the British Army began on 14 December 1941, when the Japanese captured the airfield at Victoria Point, at the southernmost tip of Burma. Five days later two Japanese divisions—the 33rd and 55th—crossed the border from Thailand to

[3] F. A. E. Crew, *The Army Medical Services: Campaigns: Volume V, Burma* (London: HMSO, 1966), 647.

[4] Ibid. 612.   [5] Ibid. 647.

[6] See e.g. NAM 8206/58, descriptions of 10 Belgian Congo CCS in Burma and the East African General Hospital, Bengal, in 'The K. A. R. in Burma'.

take the area around Moulmein and Kawkareik, and by 8 March the Burmese capital Rangoon had fallen. In the same month British-led forces in Burma were reconstituted into Burcorps and placed under the control of Lieutenant-General William Slim (1891–1970), a veteran of the First World War and of the East African and Syrian campaigns of 1941. Slim led the army back to India in a fighting retreat that ended only in May 1942, during which time he became increasingly concerned about the health and morale of his force.[7]

During the retreat it quickly became apparent that no sick or wounded men could be left to the mercy of the Japanese, who often killed patients and medical staff in cold blood. A number of badly wounded men who were left in ambulances when the 1st Burma Division broke out of Gweygo had their throats cut or were bayoneted to death by the Japanese.[8] Colonel Alfred Craddock of the Indian Medical Service recalled that 'armed medical personnel captured by the Japanese were executed on the spot, usually by bayoneting, and we felt happier for being unarmed'.[9] Medical officers were permitted under the Geneva Convention to carry arms, though only to defend their patients.

Due to the shortage of transport, many sick and wounded men were denied the comforts usually provided during evacuation. Those with light wounds or mild sickness were instructed to proceed by any means available to airfields in the north. The seriously sick and wounded were placed on trains, although lying compartments were few and infectious cases had to travel separately up the Irrawaddy on hospital ships and barges. The journey by train itself was not without difficulties. The wreckage of vehicles destroyed by the Japanese had frequently to be cleared from the line, and Gurkha guards had regularly to keep refugees from rushing the train.[10]

At first it was intended to evacuate the sick and wounded by air from Schwebo—on the railway line just to the north of Mandalay—straight to Dum Dum, the site of the famous barracks near Calcutta. However, the rapidity of the Japanese advance meant that plans to fly casualties directly to Bengal had to be scrapped, and they were flown instead from Myitkina, just across the Indian border, to Dinjan in Assam. This arrangement was far from perfect, as Dinjan had few medical installations and there was little transport available to evacuate patients to other hospitals in India. Immediate steps were therefore taken to reinforce the medical units at Dinjan and to dispatch

[7] For Slim's early career see Ronald Lewin, *Slim: The Standard Bearer* (London: Leo Cooper, 1990).
[8] Slim, *Defeat into Victory*, 73.
[9] CMAC RAMC 1994, Recollections of Col. Alfred L. Craddock, OBE, IMS, 7.
[10] Ibid. 7–9.

a hospital to Tijpur (Tezpur) further west on the Brahmaputra river. Tijpur itself was shortly to be linked by a metre-gauge railway, which would enable the most serious cases to be transported back to larger stations in Bengal.[11]

At Dinjan medical and surgical cases were treated in a small combined military hospital and in the planters' hospital at Paritola, a few miles from the aerodrome. From here casualties were evacuated via two routes: the most serious were sent to Dibrugarh and from there downriver to Tijpur; those who were able to look after themselves were sent by ambulance train to Pandu, ferried across the Brahmaputra, and then carried by ordinary train to Dimapur and ultimately to Lucknow in northern India. Improvisation was the order of the day, and until June proper hospitals, rest camps, and feeding arrangements were practically non-existent. Indeed, the situation became seriously embarrassing when several trainloads of sick and wounded were forced to rely on local civilians for their provisions. Most of the men were exhausted and dirty, and despite being lightly wounded or mildly sick, appeared 'desperately ill to the uninformed onlooker'.[12] But it was not only the 'uninformed onlooker' who was dismayed by the condition of men evacuated from Burma. The British staff of No. 14 General Hospital stationed in Lucknow recalled that: 'We had not seen men in such poor shape since May 1940. They had been many days on the railway, following long and exhausting marches during the evacuation. No arrangements had been made for their medical attention or feeding during the rail journey, the evacuation having apparently taken the authorities by surprise.'[13]

Since most of these men were Indian, the British were vulnerable to the accusation that they cared little for the lives of their imperial subjects—a serious matter, considering that India was moving towards open rebellion, which ultimately erupted in the 'Quit India' protests of August 1942. After hearing about the poor condition of the evacuated men, Eastern Command took steps to improve matters: more money was spent on amenities in way-stations such as Gorakhpur, and additional medical facilities were established at various points along the lines of evacuation, including a CCS at Gauhati and extra staff and ambulance cars for Assam Division.[14] Despite these improvements, medical provisions in eastern India remained inadequate throughout the summer of 1942. Mrs G. E. Portal, a VAD nurse at the hospital at Ranchi, Burma Corp's HQ in Bihar, told her sister-in-law in June

---

[11] OIOC L/WS/1/886, Enclosure with letter from P. N. Coats, Office of the Commander-in-Chief (India) to Gilbert Laithwaite, Private Secretary to the Viceroy, 12 June 1942, p. 1.

[12] Ibid. 1–2.

[13] *The History of the Fourteenth General Hospital R.A.M.C. 1939–1945* (Birmingham: The Birmingham Printers, undated), 23.

[14] OIOC L/WS/1/886, Coats to Laithwaite, 12 June 1942, 2.

that: 'The hospital is heart-breaking . . . This is called a casualty clearing station and has equipment and staff for 250 patients. Our score stood at 788 yesterday and the army at Burma are being admitted at the rate of 70 and 80 a day! They are all medical cases, malaria and dysentery.'[15] This flood of medical cases was partly a consequence of the monsoon, during which malaria-bearing mosquitoes were provided with numerous breeding sites, and rainwater contaminated with faeces found its way easily into drinking water. The hospital at Ranchi was barely able to cope with such large numbers of sick, especially as it had no modern lavatories and only a single water tap. According to Nurse Portal, this desperate state of affairs could easily have been avoided:

It is a shocking crime and may God forever damn the Eastern Command staff, in fact the whole of G.H.Q. They must have known a month ago that the Burma Army was done for . . . and would be back in a state of collapse . . . The medical wards are like 'Gone with the Wind'—patients touching each other, people moaning for water and sicking up and so on everywhere. 150 of my surgicals are now on the floor, as they are in pukka buildings and we've had to give up their beds for the medical tents. The nursing sepoys and the menials are thoroughly overworked and very Bolshy, but one has to drive them like galley slaves, and this I find the worst of all my jobs . . . But I hate worst of all having to refuse all help to patients in great pain because we haven't even got aspirin . . . Ranchi is milked dry of practically everything, but there are all these drugs elsewhere, and may God perish the Medical Directorate for not having laid them on.[16]

Nurse Portal was not without influence: her sister-in-law was Mrs R. A. Butler, wife of the Minister of Education. After receiving Portal's letter, Mrs Butler passed it on to the wife of the Secretary of State for India, L. S. Amery, who brought the matter to the attention of her husband. Amery demanded of the Viceroy, Lord Linlithgow, that the matter be investigated but the Viceroy replied that 'exhaustive enquires' had already been made, and that the situation at Ranchi was merely symptomatic of shortages affecting the whole of India. He warned the Secretary of State that he would soon have to request further staff and medical supplies from Britain, having already 'drained India dry of both doctors and nurses'.[17] But no additional medics were sent from Britain, and as Slim regretted in his memoirs, his army was bottom of the list for medical aid.[18]

The War Office, however, was well aware of the seriousness of the

---

[15] Ibid., letter from Mrs G. E. Portal, Ranchi, to Mrs R. A. Butler, 7 June 1942.
[16] Ibid.
[17] Ibid., telegrams from Secretary of State to Viceroy, 6 July 1942 and from Viceroy to Secretary of State, 13 July 1942.
[18] Slim, *Defeat into Victory*, 177.

situation in India. After completing a tour of India in 1942, the Adjutant-General, Sir Ronald Adam, was 'horrified' by what he saw of medical arrangements there. 'The Indian Medical Service', he reported, 'has broken down. The Indian doctor will not join unless he is an indifferent doctor and cannot make a living otherwise.' 'Unless something can be done to put the situation right,' he warned, 'I am afraid there will be a complete breakdown of medical services.'[19] He noted that the total deficiency of medical officers was 795 and that the shortage had been brought to the attention of the War Office in September 1942 by the DGAMS, Alexander Hood. But the Adjutant-General was adamant that no more doctors could be sent from Britain to make good the deficiency in India. Two hundred and ninety-five doctors had been sent out to the theatre since April and another 160 were on their way; no more could be spared without seriously undermining civilian medical arrangements at home. The solution, according to Adam, was 'to press India to introduce conscription for doctors and put her own house in order'.[20] In view of the political situation, this was easier said than done. Conscription was out of the question, and despite further efforts to recruit more doctors and nurses for the IMS and the Indian Military Nursing Service, they remained in short supply throughout the war. Emoluments and other conditions of service were still insufficiently attractive compared to civilian practice.[21] Medical supplies did improve when General Auchinleck took over from Wavell as GOC India in 1943, but in the meantime hospitals in eastern India were barely able to function.[22] Had it not been for the support of planters and other civilians, who worked in the hospitals as ward assistants, cooks, and administrators, and who opened their homes to convalescents, it is likely that medical arrangements would have collapsed altogether.[23]

As well as managing the evacuation of sick and wounded troops from Burma, medical staff of the British and Indian armies assisted in the care of the many thousands of refugees who fled Burma as the Japanese advanced. This human stream flowed northwards through Burma by road, rail, and river, but communications between Burma and India were poor, especially once the central Burmese plain gave way to the razor-edged hills of the north. Here the refugees converged on two or three bottlenecks, the most important of which was Tamu, on the edge of a range of hills separating the notoriously unhealthy Kabaw Valley (literally, the 'Valley of Death') from the Manipur plain. The passage through the valley and across these hills was

[19] LHCMA, Adam Papers 3/6/1, 'Report by the Adjutant-General on his Tour of the Middle East, India and West Africa, August, 1942', 5.

[20] Ibid. 2.

[21] B. L. Raina (ed.), *Official History of the Indian Armed Forces in the Second World War 1939–45. Medical Services: Administration*, 2 (Kanpur: Combined Inter-Services Historical Section, India and Pakistan, 1953), 82.

[22] Slim, *Defeat into Victory*, 176.   [23] Ibid. 125–6.

extremely difficult, and most refugees had to make the journey on foot. Lieutenant-Colonel Lindsay of the IMS, travelling with the refugees, reckoned they walked around 20 miles, or around ten to thirteen hours per day. Their progress was impeded by having to stick to minor trails in the mountains, in order to avoid attack from the Japanese. Although the refugees were well treated by the tribes living in the hills, they were never allowed to rest in their villages for fear of Japanese reprisals.[24] Many had also to suffer the debilitating and often deadly effects of diseases such as malaria, dysentery, and cholera: the few sources of water available were fouled and host to a multitude of lethal bacteria.[25]

Civilian refugees were not technically the responsibility of the military authorities, and the main task of the retreating army was to get back to India as quickly as possible. Nevertheless, medical staff of the British and Indian armies often worked together to control the spread of disease among the refugees. Their humanitarian intentions were bolstered by the need to prevent disease from spreading to civilian and military personnel in India, but this was easier said than done. There was a shortage of experienced medical personnel, and most of the subordinate staff were not regular army but had been recently recruited from the civilian medical establishment of Assam. These men were comparatively poorly trained and had little or no military experience. Added to these difficulties were those of communication: many Indian refugees were Madrasis, who knew Tamil or Telugu but not the Urdu spoken in the Indian Army. Sepoys recruited mainly in the United Provinces or the Punjab were also unable to understand many local languages, including Assamese and Naga, which were spoken by labour detachments connected to Burcorps.[26] The threat or actuality of epidemic disease also hampered sanitary arrangements. H. E. Shortt, a medical officer with a refugee column approaching Tamu, complained in March 1942 that: 'it was very difficult to keep the whole force working, as there seemed to be a feeling of unrest owing to . . . cases of sickness. I had to keep driving the Nagas hard all the morning to prevent them from thinking about cholera.'[27] British and Indian medical personnel, however, had been vaccinated against cholera and typhoid and were less susceptible to these infections.[28]

Sanitary work on the evacuation lines depended heavily on the labour detachments, which were used to construct and clean refugee camps at

[24] PRO WO 222/84, Lt.-Col. D. Kenneth L. Lindsay, IMS, 'Story of my last Weeks in Burma, April–May 1942', 11.

[25] CMAC WTI/HES/1/5, 'Report on Medical Aspects of the Evacuation of Refugees from Burma (January–June 1942)', 1–2, papers of Henry Edward Shortt.

[26] Ibid. 4.

[27] Ibid. 14.

[28] www.burmastar.org.uk/eason.htm, E. H. Eason, 'Burma 1942 Retreat: A Doctor's Retreat from Burma', 3.

bottlenecks such as Tamu on the Indo-Burmese border. Tamu camp, constructed for around 600 Indians and eighty Europeans, held in excess of
3,000 people, creating a sanitary problem of Augean proportions. The
massive daily toll from disease meant labour was in short supply, and it was
not always easy to supplement the detachments with workers recruited
locally, as the 'coolies' charged exorbitant prices.[29] To cope with this shortage, Shortt was forced to impress 150 coolies from the Tamu area,[30] but the
numbers engaged were still insufficient to keep the camp properly cleansed.[31]

Conditions were no better at the large camp at Korengei, 6 miles to the
north of Imphal. This camp, located in the healthier Manipur plain, was
designed as a reception centre to hold refugees until they could be transported to Dimapur. There they were entrained for Pandu, ferried across the
Brahmaputra, and entrained again for Calcutta. The situation at Korengei
was desperate: the camp was massively overcrowded and sanitary discipline
was lax. The camp's commandant, Mr Carroll, reported that: 'Children and
the sick were dirtying all around the show, and others were polluting the
water by throwing food into it.'[32] The Revd G. Molyneaux, assisting with
sanitation at Korengei, concurred: 'The state of the camp was revolting, filth
and human excretions were everywhere . . . during a preliminary inspection,
I discovered a skeleton in one of the houses, and two or three corpses in the
jungle.'[33] Shortt blamed this desperate situation on the failure of the military authorities to supply enough aircraft to transport refugees from northern Burma before they converged on Assam. He felt that 'only those in close
touch with the evacuation movement had any idea of the gravity of the situation', and requested that Sir Robert Reid, the Governor of Assam, broach
the matter with the Viceroy. Shortt's letter may have spurred the authorities
to arrange for the evacuation of refugees by air from Myitkyina, once
the evacuation of troops had been completed.[34] Those stuck at Imphal, he
warned, were at risk not only from disease but also from air attacks by the
Japanese, who regularly strafed the area. One attack claimed between 200
and 250 refugees, mown down as they staggered along the road to
Korengei.[35]

The other main refugee route was through the Hukawng Valley in northern Burma, and into the Naga Hills on the Indo-Burmese border. One of
those who completed the arduous journey was A. D. Stoker, second-in-

[29] CMAC WTI/HES/1/5, 'Medical Aspects of the Evacuation of Refugees', 20.
[30] Ibid. 21.[31] Ibid. 26.
[32] CMAC WTI/HES/1/7, Mr Carroll, Camp Commandant, to Hon. Justice H. B. L. Brand,
Imphal, 7 June 1942.
[33] Ibid., 'Report of the Revd G. Molyneux on Korengi Evacuation Camp, Imphal', 1.
[34] CMAC WTI/HES/1/5, 'Medical Aspects of the Evacuation of Refugees', 19.
[35] Ibid. 30.

command of the No. 57 Indian Field Ambulance, who had just missed evacuation from air at Myitkina. Stoker and some of the remaining staff of his field ambulance decided to make their way back to India by foot, along with the civilian refugees. There was no transport available for either the sick or the healthy, so the choice, as one MO put it, was 'march or die'.[36] The journey, which entailed a trek across the Kumoni Mountains, was difficult under any conditions, let alone during the monsoon, which had just broken. Stoker and the refugees were often walking thigh-deep in mud, while at the same time labouring under the effects of malaria or dysentery, both of which were widespread.[37] Writing on his sickbed in Meerut, Stoker recalled that:

So heavy a toll was disease, starvation and the country taking that we saw corpses every hundred yards or so and nowhere for the rest of the journey were we to be out of sight or smell of a dead body . . . No single disease was predominating but one saw every state and condition of malaria, cholera and dysentery and all, both human and animal, complicated by exhaustion and starvation.[38]

Casualties along the Hukawng Valley track were afterwards estimated at 20,000 dead, out of a total of 33,000 who began the journey.[39]

Health, Discipline, and Morale

No less than 80 per cent of the force evacuated from Burma in 1942 had contracted some form of disease. The survivors were also thoroughly dispirited, and many of the sick and wounded had lost the will to live.[40] But, despite a severe shortage of medical supplies and manpower, Slim was determined to nurse his army back to health; as he later recorded in his memoirs: 'We had to stop men going sick, or, if they went sick, from staying sick.'[41] Slim's medical plan had four main elements: the application of the latest medical research to the prevention and treatment of disease; the treatment of the sick in forward areas instead of evacuating them to India; the evacuation by air of serious casualties in order to free beds in forward areas; and, last but not least, the lifting of morale.

The 14th Army was fortunate in that it was able to take advantage of valuable research recently conducted into malaria prophylaxis by the Australian Army. At Cairns and Atherton in northern Queensland, Army Medical Research Units had been testing a variety of anti-malarial drugs under the

[36] PRO WO 222/107, Lt.-Col. G. Singh, IMS, 'Evacuation of No. 60 Indian General Hospital from Burma to India', 7.

[37] CMAC RAMC 2006, Dr A. Desmond Stoker, 'Stoker through Hukawng', 28, 33, 35.

[38] Ibid. 36–7.   [39] Ibid. 56.   [40] Slim, *Defeat into Victory*, 113.   [41] Ibid. 178.

direction of Brigadier N. Hamilton Fairley of the Australian Army Medical Corps. At Cairns, volunteers were subjected to bites from mosquitoes infected with malaria and treated with various anti-malaria drugs. At Atherton, a non-malarious area, scientists investigated whether the infected patients had been cured, or whether they still harboured parasites in their blood. Among the drugs tested were sulphamerazine, mepacrine, and a new compound, paluride, which did not come into general use until after the war.[42]

The Australian research, together with work conducted at the Royal Army Medical College, showed that mepacrine was not toxic if taken in small doses,[43] and that side-effects such as dermatitis occurred in only a small number of cases.[44] The great value of this research, together with data collected from the US Army,[45] was that it showed that mepacrine was effective against all forms of malaria. These findings led senior commanders to the embarrassing conclusion that problems hitherto encountered in malaria prophylaxis were not due to any defect in the drugs themselves, but to poor discipline.[46] Malaria control was shown to be a problem of command rather than a purely technical problem—a point quickly grasped by Slim, if not by all his subordinates. Slim's solution to the problem was to put pressure on unit commanders. 'Good doctors are no use without good discipline', he noted: 'More than half the battle against disease is fought not by doctors, but by regimental officers. It is they who see that the daily dose of mepacrine . . . is taken . . . If mepacrine was not taken, I sacked the commander. I had only to sack three; by then the rest had got my meaning.'[47]

On the advice of the Consultant Malariologist, India Command, Major-General Sir Gordon Covell, mepacrine suppression was stepped up throughout the army in north-eastern India and Arakan—the north-western part of Burma, which the Japanese had not succeeded in taking. Malaria casualties in this theatre of the war were still enormous: there were 83,000 admissions to hospital from this disease in Eastern Army during 1942, and there were

[42] CMAC RAMC 1939/6, N. Hamilton Fairley, 'Researches in Malaria Therapy (Secret)'; id., 'Researches on Paluride (M.4888) in Malaria', *Transactions of the Royal Society of Tropical Medicine and Hygiene*, 40 (1946), 105–53.

[43] CMAC RAMC 2065, Maj. J. Reid, 'Studies on the Pharmacology of Mepacrine'.

[44] V. Zachary Cope (ed.), *Medical History of the Second World War: Medicine and Pathology* (London: HMSO, 1953), 200.

[45] CMAC RAMC 1939/7, 'US Army Field Experiment on Suppressive Treatment'.

[46] F. H. K. Green and Sir Gordon Covell (eds.), *Medical Research: Medical History of the Second World War* (London: HMSO, 1953), 158–9; N. Hamilton Fairley, 'Tropical Diseases with Special Reference to Malaria in the Eastern Theatres of War', in Sir Henry Letheby Tidy (ed.), *Inter-Allied Conferences on War Medicine 1942–1945: Convened by the Royal Society of Medicine* (London: Staples Press, 1947), 94–5.

[47] Slim, *Defeat into Victory*, 180.

many more that could not be admitted to hospital. In the last three months of the year no fewer than 18,000 men had to be evacuated from Eastern Army to hospitals further west.[48] Covell, who was formerly Director of the Institute of Malaria in Delhi, urged suppressive treatment after visiting Cairns and New Guinea, where—observing the Australian Army—he had witnessed the benefits of anti-malaria discipline in the field.[49] Like many others, he was convinced that the Australians were leading the way in jungle warfare and that theirs was the example to follow.[50] Lord Mountbatten, who was appointed head of the new South-East Asian Command, also enthusiastically endorsed the anti-malaria campaign. Mountbatten took a personal interest in the medical aspects of the war, and began a vigorous onslaught on the Indian administration to secure better medical provisions.[51] Anti-malarial discipline was consequently tightened, although prevention proved far easier in theory than in practice.

Suppressive treatment was instituted even before Mountbatten's appointment, in time for the operations in Arakan, which lasted from March to June 1943. The precautions taken in 6th Infantry Brigade (part of 2nd British Division) were typical. The administration of mepacrine began early in March, before the brigade entered the theatre, and continued until the beginning of June, when all units had returned to Ahmednagar in India. A dose of 0.1 grams was taken twice daily for three consecutive days each week, the drug being distributed at evening parades.[52] Anti-malaria discipline was generally good, and lectures that aimed to dispel fears concerning mepacrine and sexual impotence led men to place considerable reliance on the drug. It was claimed that soldiers 'would come round to the R.A.P. . . . if they missed it for any reason'. Nor were there many complaints about side-effects, apart from a few cases of nausea, stomach pain, and skin discolouration.[53] Soldiers were also encouraged to take more conventional measures against mosquitoes: mosquito nets and creams were widely used, and long trousers were the rule at night.[54]

Despite these efforts, 6th Infantry Brigade lost around half its total strength from malaria in the space of only eight weeks—three-and-a-half times as many as were wounded by the Japanese. While easy to maintain in quiet

[48] Opening speech by Maj.-Gen. T. O. Thompson, DDMS, *Proceedings of the Conference of Medical Specialists of Eastern Army held in March 1943* (Calcutta: Government of India Press, 1943), 1.
[49] Green and Covell (eds.), *Medical Research*, 159; Crew, *Burma*, 645–6; CMAC RAMC 1939/7, N. Hamilton Fairley, 'Medicine in Jungle Warfare', 198.
[50] G. Covell, 'How They Control Malaria in the Pacific', *Indian Army Review*, 3 (1945), 7–10.
[51] Philip Ziegler, *Mountbatten: The Official Biography* (London: Collins, 1985), 250–1.
[52] PRO WO 222/150, Maj. R. Bevan, 'Malaria in 6th Infantry Brigade, Arakan Operations'.
[53] Ibid. 13.   [54] Ibid. 14–15.

periods, the administration of mepacrine was liable to be forgotten in the heat of battle or when men were on patrol for several days. Most of the cases were fortunately mild, and not the potentially fatal strain of malaria contracted by some of the men evacuated from Burma in 1942.[55] The medical report on the Arakan operation attributed the failure of anti-malarial measures to the arduous nature of the campaign, which entailed sixty-six days of constant fighting and patrolling. It concluded that: 'The psychological effect of the jungle, an unseen enemy and our own casualties on the mind of the British soldier also cannot be ignored. These conditions seemed likely to have their effect on the malaria incidence in the Brigade.'[56] The state of 6th Brigade was such that it was sent in its entirety to the hill station at Mahabaleshwar, in western India, for rest and recuperation.[57]

The experience of 6th Brigade was typical of the army as a whole. For every soldier evacuated with wounds, 120 were evacuated through disease.[58] This placed a tremendous burden on medical units and the lines of evacuation. Little provision was made for the forward treatment of malaria cases, and most were evacuated to avoid overcrowding of forward units. During the greater part of the campaign all cases were evacuated to No. 15 Indian CCS at Maungdaw on the northern coast of Arakan, which entailed an uncomfortable ride by motor ambulance of some 15 to 20 miles. From Maungdaw, the sick and wounded were evacuated by hospital ship directly to Chittagong, until the monsoon made this too dangerous. After the onset of the rains patients had to travel by shallow barge up the Naf River to Tumbru Ghat, 30 miles north, and thence by road to Dohazari or Cox's Bazar on the coast. After this tortuous journey, Chittagong was finally reached by rail or sea. Here surgical cases and patients suffering from malaria could receive proper attention, for the quinine stage of malaria treatment was the only one generally available at the level of the field ambulance.[59] The complete regime of malaria treatment involved the administration of the anti-malaria drugs mepacrine and parmaquine, which killed the malaria parasite at different stages in its life-cycle.[60] But treatment entailed an absence from duty of at least twenty-five days, in addition to time spent in travelling, which left the army in Arakan denuded of men. Many cases were absent for considerably longer, being sent back to large general hospitals in India. During their long evacuation it was common for reinfection to occur.[61] This situation was

[55] PRO WO 222/150, Maj. R. Bevan, 18–19.   [56] Ibid. 8.

[57] CMAC RAMC 1512, 'The Sixth British Field Ambulance', 18.

[58] John A. Baty, *Surgeon in the Jungle War* (London: William Kimber, 1979), 12, 80.

[59] PRO WO 222/150, 'Malaria in 6th Infantry Brigade', 11.

[60] Col. G. F. Taylor, 'Some Medical Aspects of the Eastern Army', *Procs. Conference of Medical Specialists of Eastern Army Held in March 1943* (Calcutta: Government of India, 1943), 7.

[61] Baty, *Surgeon in the Jungle War*, 80.

clearly unsustainable, and medical officers began to urge that more provisions for the treatment of malaria be made at the front.[62]

Slim was impressed by the logic of this argument and sanctioned the organization of Malaria Forward Treatment Units (MFTUs). These were, in effect, field hospitals, housed in tents or bamboo huts, and situated a few miles from the fighting. The units were large enough to deal with 600 men at a time, and provided the full range of anti-malarial treatment within twenty-four hours of an attack, without the necessity for time-consuming evacuation. A malaria patient was now able to rejoin his unit in a matter of weeks rather than months, so the strain on the lines of communication was lightened and an uncomfortable journey avoided.[63] In addition to these benefits, the MFTU improved unit cohesion. When morale was low, as it was in Arakan, some men welcomed malaria and took no precautions against it— it was their ticket back to a comfortable billet in India.[64] A short stay just a few miles behind the fighting line was nowhere near as attractive.

But anti-malaria treatment was not entirely without its hazards: it was only in 1943 that doctors agreed upon a dose that was both effective and safe. Research conducted at the Malaria Treatment Centre at Kasuali, India, and at the Liverpool and Calcutta schools of tropical medicine, showed that treatment in excess of thirty grams of quinine had no effect on the course of the disease and was actually harmful to patients.[65] Serious problems had also arisen with the intramuscular injection of quinine, which had been introduced on an experimental basis in 1942. At least twelve men died in Eastern Army during 1942 as a result of this injection.[66] Covell was uncertain about whether these injections should be allowed to continue. On the one hand, he acknowledged that excessive doses of quinine given by injection could cause tetanus and gangrene, and also chemical abscesses and paralysis, if peripheral nerves were infected. On the other, he was aware that intramuscular injection was the only treatment feasible when a patient was unable to swallow. For this reason it continued to be used under certain conditions throughout the campaign.[67]

Another medical problem giving cause for concern at this time was venereal disease. A large number of men recently sent to the front from India had contracted one or several sexually transmitted diseases. As the surgeon John

[62] PRO WO 222/150, 'Malaria in 6th Infantry Brigade', 27.

[63] Sanjoy Bhattacharya, *Propaganda and Information in Eastern India 1939–45: A Necessary Weapon of War* (London: Curzon Press, 2001), 177.

[64] Slim, *Defeat into Victory*, 178–9.

[65] G. Covell, 'Treatment of Malaria', *Proceedings of the Conference of Medical Specialists of Eastern Army*, 70.

[66] Taylor, 'Medical Aspects of the Eastern Army', 7.

[67] Covell, 'Treatment of Malaria', 70.

Baty put it: 'the venereologist would understand "Full House" not as a poker term but as referring to a patient who had acquired both syphilis and gonorrhoea, lymphogranuloma and soft-chancre all at one session; the simultaneous combination of these four diseases certainly presented diagnostic problems.'[68] Before long, medical officers began to suspect that some troops had attempted deliberately to contract these diseases before leaving Calcutta for the front. After five days of incubation—which was the time taken to reach the front line—the urethral discharge had developed and the infected man could find himself evacuated back to India for treatment almost as soon as he had arrived.[69]

Prostitution was an established feature of life in most military cantonments and large towns, and it was generally assumed that most soldiers would use prostitutes before their tour of India was completed.[70] On arriving in Bombay, in 1942, one British soldier recalled that: 'In the evening four of us . . . mounted a ghari and instructed the driver . . . to show us the sights. A look of comprehension dawned on his unprepossessing countenance and he made straight for what proved to be the brothel quarter.'[71] The same soldier noted that the only real entertainments available in the town of Bareilly were 'undesirable female company and three bottles of indifferent beer a month'.[72] For this reason, and despite a well-established system of medically regulated prostitution, venereal disease had always been common amongst British troops stationed in India. During the Second World War India recorded the highest VD rate, rising to nearly eighty per thousand troops by 1945—higher even than in Italy.[73] During 1942–3 there was also the added problem of low morale: the British Army was dispirited after its humiliating rout by the Japanese and the enemy seemed to be all but invincible. Slim therefore decided that VD cases, like malaria casualties, should be treated as close to the front as possible, not only to avoid burdening the lines of communication, but also to deter those seeking evacuation back to

---

[68] Baty, *Surgeon in the Jungle War*, 80.   [69] Ibid. 80.

[70] On prostitution and the military in British India see: Kenneth Ballhatchet, *Race, Sex, and Class Under the Raj: Imperial Attitudes and their Critics* (London: Weidenfeld & Nicolson, 1980); David Arnold, *Colonising the Body: State Medicine and Epidemic Disease in Nineteenth-Century India* (Berkeley: University of California Press, 1993), 83–7; Mark Harrison, *Public Health in British India: Anglo-Indian Preventive Medicine, 1859–1914* (Cambridge: Cambridge University Press, 1994), 72–6; Philippa Levine, 'Venereal Disease, Prostitution, and the Politics of Empire: The Case of British India', *Journal of the History of Sexuality*, 4 (1994), 579–602; Douglas M. Peers, 'Soldiers, Surgeons and the Campaigns to Combat Sexually Transmitted Diseases in Colonial India, 1805–1860', *Medical History*, 42 (1998), 137–60.

[71] *The History of the Fourteenth General Hospital R.A.M.C. 1939–1945* (Birmingham: The Birmingham Printers, c.1946), 19.

[72] Ibid. 24.

[73] W. Franklin Mellor (ed.), *Medical History of the Second World War: Casualties and Medical Statistics* (London: HMSO, 1972), 119.

India. Following the same principle as for malaria, VD cases were treated in specialized units whenever possible. This had the desired effect, in that it stemmed the wastage of manpower from these diseases, but the concentration of such patients in special units created problems of its own. The surgeon John Baty recalled that: 'Incidents were not infrequent on the routine inspections of the VD section. The British patients tended to be more militant, no doubt resenting their retention in a Forward hospital.'[74]

As Slim recognized, medicine and morale were mutually dependent. Poor morale encouraged men to 'malinger' and catch disease, while good medical arrangements could do much to maintain morale and unit cohesion. Morale had been poor ever since the ignominious retreat from Burma in 1942, and the failure of the Army to retake Akjab in the Arakan had done little to improve it. The inadequacy of medical arrangements did not help either. Although better organization had improved the hospital situation in India,[75] the evacuation of casualties back to these hospitals remained a serious problem, and this had a very depressing effect on morale. It was sometimes many days before a soldier received adequate surgical treatment. To add insult to injury, it became apparent during 1943 that wounded soldiers in other theatres had been evacuated by air. There was no such provision in Burma, where the most a man could hope for was a ride in a returning transport aircraft. Even then the air evacuation of casualties was rare, as most men were wounded far from the nearest supply depot. After visiting India during 1943, the Adjutant-General reported that there was

great ill feeling that no air ambulances are provided on the Burma Front. Under present conditions a badly wounded man is certain to die before he gets back to base. A few light aircraft, some with floats . . . would save this situation. The soldiers have read about the air evacuation from Sicily and ask why they should not get similar aid. They don't know that the evacuation scheme was due to the U.S. Air Force.[76]

The lack of air evacuation was Adam's main concern during 1943. In one report he warned: 'How we have got away without a political scandal I don't know.'[77] Writing of Burma in particular, he noted that: 'There is a general feeling . . . that G.H.Q., India, does not know and does not care about British troops; that England has forgotten them.'[78]

In these circumstances, it is not surprising that psychiatric casualties were

[74] Baty, *Surgeon in the Jungle War*, 156.
[75] LHCMA, Adam Papers 3/4/2, 'Report by the Adjutant-General on his Overseas Tour, April–May, 1943', 3.
[76] LHCMA, Adam Papers 3/6/3, 'Report by the Adjutant-General on his Tour Overseas, November–December, 1943', 3.
[77] Ibid. 3/4/2, 'Report . . . April–May, 1943', 2.
[78] Ibid. 3/6/3, 'Report . . . November–December, 1943', 4.

common in all units. In some there was a complete breakdown; the entire 14th Indian Division, on its return from the Arakan, was effectively a psychiatric casualty.[79] This was hardly surprising, for the Japanese appeared to be unbeatable; they were better equipped, better trained, and seemingly immune to the discomforts of jungle warfare. The jungle, by contrast, was a constant source of complaint amongst British troops. It aroused a deep-seated fear of the unknown and induced feelings of claustrophobia; fears that were compounded by excessive humidity, the persistent annoyance of insects and leeches, and the prospect of contracting potentially lethal diseases such as typhus and malaria.[80]

There was no easy answer to this problem, and the morale of 14th Army, as Slim's force became known from August 1943, improved only very slowly, as a result of better training and experience gained whilst fighting the Japanese. Army psychologists, however, did their best to demystify their opponents. One study, produced at the end of 1942, concluded that while morale in the Japanese army was currently very high, the Japanese were essentially fatalistic; they had also developed a feeling of invincibility that might lead them to overstretch themselves in future engagements. A number of other weaknesses were detected at different levels in the chain of command. Regimental officers, the report asserted, were conscientious but also prone to be conservative and 'rather slow mentally', by contrast with higher commanders who were generally of strong character and high intelligence. Contrary to popular myth, the Japanese soldier was also said to be better at withstanding cold than tropical heat.[81]

Major John Kelnar, RAMC, prepared a more detailed report, in which he reiterated the belief that fatalism and submission to authority were characteristics of the Japanese. 'From the 17th century onwards', he wrote, '. . . Japan remained isolated from external influences and continued to crystallise into a civilisation essentially feudal in nature.'[82] Thus, the whole of Japanese society was controlled from the top down: 'The most humble and implicit obedience was compelled . . . the Japanese as an individual ceased to exist.'[83] According to Kelnar, the Japanese soldier was essentially a sadomasochist. He had given up his independence and individuality, and sought to unite himself

---

[79] B. L. Raina (ed.), *Official History of the Indian Armed Services Medical Services in the Second World War, 1939–45: Medicine, Science and Pathology* (New Delhi: Combined Inter-Services Historical Section, India and Pakistan, 1955), 335–84.

[80] LHCMA II/1, Papers of Col. W. M. McCutcheon, text of a lecture on the role of the RMO in jungle warfare.

[81] CMAC RAMC 1127/1, 'Periodical Notes on the Japanese Army, No. 1—Characteristics, Morale and Tactics, 1942'.

[82] CMAC RAMC 1900/19, Maj. John Kelnar, 'Report to the War Office on the Psychological Effect of Upbringing and Education on Japanese Morale', 8.

[83] Ibid.

with some outside power, 'in order to acquire the strength that he needs as a compensation for his sense of individual insignificance'.[84] The masochistic traits that Kelnar discerned in the Japanese were fatalism and self-abnegation; whereas the desire to make others dependent on oneself, and to hurt and humiliate them, were characteristic of sadism. Both sadism and masochism arose, he concluded, from the same fundamental psychological conflict caused by uncertainty and frustration.[85] It is unlikely that these reports had a general circulation, at least below the level of regimental officers. However, as the war progressed increasing use was made of the supposed contrast between the British 'citizen soldier' and the subservience of the Japanese. Disease prevention, for example, was said to depend not only on the nature of the country but 'on the general and self-discipline of the British soldier as a trained and pre-instructed individual'.[86] This mirrored propaganda in other theatres, which contrasted the supposedly independent-minded and self-disciplined British soldier with his Axis counterparts.

Disease, Medicine, and Special Operations

The biggest boost to the morale of 14th Army during 1943 was provided by Brigadier Orde Wingate's long-range penetration force (popularly known as the 'Chindits'), which, between February and June, engaged in an operation behind Japanese lines. Although operation LONGCLOTH—as the first Chindit operation was known—was of limited strategic value, it proved that British troops were capable of beating the Japanese in jungle warfare. But the operation was costly in terms of manpower, and Wingate lost one-third of his force (around a thousand men), mostly to disease. A subsequent operation involving the Chindits, operation THURSDAY, which lasted from March to December 1944, was more successful but it also ended with much of the force incapacitated by malaria and other infections. These losses, and the limited gains made by way of compensation, have led some to doubt the wisdom of such operations, not to mention the judgement of Wingate. Although his public reputation survived the war intact, the official history of the campaign regretted his 'fanaticism' and 'instability'. A similar appraisal was given by Slim in his autobiography, in which he accused Wingate of a 'single-centredness that verges on fanaticism'.[87] Again, in a letter to his friend Major H. R. K. Gibbs, Slim remarked: 'I doubt if Wingate was altogether a

[84] Ibid. 20.   [85] Ibid. 21–2.
[86] CMAC RAMC 740/2/6, 'The Burma Road Sanitary Strategy', 11–12.
[87] Slim, *Defeat into Victory*, 269.

genius. He had sparks of genius but he had some pretty black spots too.'[88] Arguably, one of these 'black spots' was Wingate's attitude to doctors and the medical preparations for his force.

Having died in March 1944, when his aeroplane crashed into a hillside in Manipur, Wingate was unable to answer his critics, but there have been several attempts to restore his reputation, of which Trevor Royle's biography is one of the most balanced. While accepting Royle's conclusion that any assessment of the campaign should not be purely numerical[89]—that is, balancing the casualties sustained against those inflicted by the Chindits—an analysis of the medical aspects of the campaign is vital to any evaluation of its effectiveness. The medical reports on Chindit operations also provide fresh insights into the morale of the force and its commander.

The high incidence of disease among Wingate's force led some medical officers to doubt his suitability for command. It was alleged that Wingate ignored medical advice and that he was contemptuous of hygiene and sanitation. This attitude is supposed to have rubbed off on the rest of the force, who are said to have reacted to any mention of hygiene with 'amusement intermingled with boredom'. One medical report stated that: 'It is not sufficiently realized, even by the more senior officers, that Hygiene is not only a matter of discipline, but it is one of the basic factors upon which discipline is built. It is personal discipline as opposed to collective discipline, and its absence in the individual merely produces an absence of it in the aggregate, which is the unit.'[90] The report claimed that little attention was paid to sanitation during training and that, in operations, the standard of hygiene was even worse. 'The example set by officers was extremely low,' it was later reported, 'and this is not surprising in view of the policy laid down in regard to this important subject by the late Force Commander in his training pamphlet.' In this pamphlet Wingate had written that: 'It will . . . be a waste of labour to dig latrines unless the bivouac is to be occupied for more than one week. Men should carry out their functions at distances not less than 100 yards from the perimeter.'[91] After the war Wingate's medical critics also made much of the fact that he had contracted a near-fatal bout of typhoid by drinking water from a flower vase; an act of carelessness that delayed the second Chindit operation by several weeks.[92]

But Wingate's apparent indifference to hygiene was not shared by all of his officers. Some column commanders, such as Bernard Fergusson and John

---

[88] IWM 54.824, Slim to Gibbs, 14 July 1952.

[89] Trevor Royle, *Orde Wingate: Irregular Soldier* (London: Weidenfeld & Nicolson, 1995), 319.

[90] CMAC RAMC 816, 'Special Force: Report on Medical Operations for the Period 1943–4', Pt. IV, 1.

[91] Ibid., Pt. IV, 2.   [92] Lewin, *Slim*, 191.

Masters, enjoyed good relations with their medical officers and were attentive to hygiene.[93] Philip Stibbe, a young officer serving in Fergusson's 5 Column during the first Chindit expedition, recalled that water discipline was maintained even under the most difficult conditions. Despite extreme thirst, men waited for their sterilization tablets to purify water before they drank it.[94] High rates of malaria in this column were also due to the failure to supply sufficient quantities of mepacrine, rather than to any reluctance on the part of the men to take the drug.[95] Operating behind enemy lines, the Chindits could be supplied only from the air, and drops were very infrequent at the beginning of the second phase of operations in March. This also prevented the men from obtaining an adequate ration of food. While one drop normally provided enough food for one week, it was sometimes as long as sixteen days between drops. To make matters worse, the daily ration was itself inadequate for a man subjected to the long, arduous marches that characterized Chindit operations. By mid-March the doctor with 5 Column—the highly regarded Bill Aird, who later died in captivity—noted that the men were becoming painfully thin and showing signs of starvation.[96] A few became so weak that they were unable to continue, but most persevered despite declining health. Their frailty probably accounts for the high death rate—some 60 per cent—among Chindits captured by the Japanese.[97]

Most of those who fell into Japanese hands did so because they were too sick or badly wounded to continue active operations. There was usually no option but to leave these men behind with such quantities of food, water, morphine, and dressings as could be spared. Where possible, the sick and wounded were entrusted to the care of Burmese villagers, most of whom were friendly and co-operative, having no love for the Japanese. Wingate reassured his men that the care they would receive from villagers would be superior to that in a field hospital; which was probably true in the domestic, if not in the medical sense. To make sure that there was no misunderstanding, each officer carried several letters written in vernacular languages that gave basic instructions on care and retention of the wounded.[98]

A third of Wingate's force failed to return from operation LONGCLOTH, and many of those who did were in very poor condition—emaciated and usually suffering from malaria and other diseases. The remains of four long-range

[93] Bernard Fergusson, *Beyond the Chindwin* (London: Fontana, 1955; first published 1945), 41, 117; John Masters, *The Road Past Mandalay: A Personal Narrative* (London: Corgi, 1973), 265–7.

[94] P. G. Stibbe, *Via Rangoon: A Young Chindit Survives the Jungle and Japanese Captivity* (London: Leo Cooper, 1994), 101.

[95] Fergusson, *Beyond the Chindwin*, 215.

[96] Stibbe, *Via Rangoon*, 104.

[97] Ibid. 176.

[98] Ibid. 145–6.

patrol groups were sent back to southern India for rehabilitation.[99] According to Wingate's critics, the high incidence of disease made little impression on the commander, who was said to have regarded it as inevitable, given the pathogenic environment in which his men were fighting and the nature of the campaign, which made sanitary arrangements difficult. It was also said that Wingate had made very few provisions for the wounded and that he had done little to effect their evacuation. On taking up his appointment on 10 April 1944, the new DDMS, Colonel William Officer, claimed that:

It soon became apparent from the information which I had received from Fourteenth Army and from my A.D.M.S. that the task before me was by no means an easy one. It was common knowledge that the force in general and the late commander in particular were not particularly medically-minded to say the least of it, and from the story given by the D.A.D.M.S. it was quite evident that my predecessor [Colonel Campbell] had been given no active support and had instead only received active opposition.[100]

Officer went on to state that 'any established Medical Organization was completely lacking' in Wingate's force.[101]

After the war Colonel Officer's remarks were vigorously contested by Wingate's friend and biographer Major-General Derek Tulloch, who had been Chief of Staff during the second Wingate operation. Although he made few comments about the medical aspects of the first Chindit operation, Tulloch insisted that Wingate had deeply regretted having to leave sick and wounded men behind in the jungle, and made strenuous efforts to prevent this occurring in the second Chindit operation:

The arrangements made for the evacuation of casualties were efficient and quick. Having been carried out by light aircraft to the nearest stronghold, they would be transferred to Dakotas for the flight back to air base the same night. Ambulances would then complete their journey to Matron McGeary's hospital at Sylhet. I have mentioned these arrangements in detail to combat the frequently repeated charges that Wingate was callous towards wounded men.[102]

When evaluating the medical arrangements made for the second operation, it should be born in mind that it was conducted with a much larger force than was available for LONGCLOTH, and that its structure was more complex. The men of Special Force, as the Chindits were now called, were formed into brigades, each comprising four columns capable of operating deep behind Japanese lines. Each column consisted of a rifle company of four

99 NAM 8209/14, Calder, 'Sloth Belt to Springboard', 98.
100 CMAC RAMC 816, 'Medical Operations', Pt. IV, 1.
101 Ibid., Pt. IV, 2.
102 Maj.-Gen. Derek Tulloch, *Wingate in Peace and War* (London: Futura, 1972), 193.

platoons, a heavy weapons platoon, a commando platoon skilled in demolition and booby traps, and a reconnaissance platoon, including men drawn from the Burma Rifles who were familiar with the territory.[103] This new formation meant that an entirely new medical establishment had to be devised. For each brigade, a new medical unit—the Brigade Medical Unit (BMU)—was formed, commanded by a major from the RAMC, with one assistant MO and twenty-one other ranks. Each was given six ambulance cars capable of carrying four stretchers. The role of the BMUs was never fully clarified, but it was generally thought that they would establish a thirty-bed hospital in the Brigade Area and supply reinforcements and medical stores to the columns.[104] They were to look after casualties until they could be evacuated by light aircraft.

The medical establishment for the columns was a more controversial matter. The DDMS suggested that each column should possess a medical staff of one MO and eleven other ranks, but Wingate had already refused this on the grounds that it would make the columns too unwieldy. He suggested, instead, that two MOs and two other ranks would be sufficient, especially as use could be made of the column padre. A compromise was eventually reached whereby the medical establishment of each column amounted to one MO, one NCO, and two other ranks in columns with padres, or three in columns without. Although GHQ was happy with this arrangement, the DDMS never agreed to it and complained that 'it proved quite inadequate in that the Medical Officer was severely handicapped when a medical orderly was required for an isolated group'. To compensate, members of the columns had to be instructed thoroughly in first aid.[105] The DDMS later referred to Wingate's 'antipathy to all things medical', and claimed that 'the Medical Branch had to fight at every stage for even the smallest concession to the medical care of the troops'. Wingate told the DDMS on their first meeting that: 'I do not want anything medical with my columns though I suppose I must have one doctor with each for the sake of the morale effect on the families at home.' He further insisted that: 'Every man with my force must be a fighting man', and made it clear that he wanted 'no passengers nor Geneva Convention people'.[106]

The medical problems experienced during operation THURSDAY were not, however, due solely to the lack of personnel, since arrangements for evacuation depended crucially on military success or failure. The original

[103] Shelford Bidwell, *The Chindit War: The Campaign in Burma, 1944* (London: Book Club Associates, 1979), 46–7, 53.
[104] CMAC RAMC 816, 'Special Force, Medical Operations', Pt. I, 2–3.
[105] Ibid., Pt. I, 4.
[106] Ibid., 'Notes on the Report by the former DDMS'.

plan that each BMU would be responsible for the medical supply of its own brigade became impossible, because most were too busy looking after casualties at the airstrips, from where they were taken to the Indian General Hospital in Sylhet. The engagement of most BMUs in these tasks meant that 16th Brigade's unit had to supply the whole force.[107] Although plans were made to evacuate casualties by air wherever possible, uncertainty over whether evacuation could be carried out meant MOs tended to retain the sick and wounded with their columns. This is not what Wingate had intended, as he had ordered that:

In the event of it being found impossible owing to enemy action to evacuate your casualties . . . you should try every means of carrying your casualties with you . . . As a last resort where delay is likely to cost lives or cause the failure of an allotted task, the casualty or casualties must be left in the nearest village under the care of the village headman with money and as much rations, drugs and dressings as can be spared. There is a form which can be given to the headman, with instructions to take good care of the injured, conceal him from the Japanese and hold him, till it is possible to hand him over to a party of British troops.[108]

While some Burmese villagers surrendered their patients to the Japanese, the Nagas were said to be 'one-hundred per cent loyal' and to have carried out instructions as requested.[109] Sick and wounded men who remained with the columns were usually transported using makeshift stretchers cut from bamboo, which were dragged behind a mule. Otherwise Naga tribesmen were employed as bearers to carry the sick and wounded, and as many as eight men were required to carry a stretcher on the rougher trails.[110] Despite what must have been an excruciating journey over rough, densely forested terrain, it was usually possible to keep surgical cases alive for several days by providing fluids through an intravenous drip.[111] Sometimes the sick managed to walk from the area of operations to nearby hospitals. On one occasion, when Special Force was only three days' walk from the nearest outpost of 14th Army, all the sick and wounded who could walk—around 150 in all—made their way to the station on foot.[112] Evacuation by jeep ambulance was also possible when conditions permitted. During the second phase of operation THURSDAY a jeep track from the central Burma plain to Mokochaung was opened once the last

---

[107] CMAC RAMC 816, 'Special Force, Medical Operations', Pt. I, 2.
[108] CMAC RAMC 1789, Instructions to MOs quoted in Capt. H. W. W. Good, 4th Btn. Border Regt., 'Some Medical Aspects of Long-Range Patrols (Chindits)', 1944, p. 8.
[109] CMAC RAMC 1789, Instructions to MOs, 8.
[110] www.burmastar.org.uk/roberts.htm, Pte. J. R. Robert, RAMC, 'A Journey Through World War Two', 4.
[111] CMAC RAMC 1830, Desmond Whyte, 'A Trying Chindit', repr. from *British Medical Journal,* Dec. 1982, pp. 1776–9.
[112] www.burmastar.org.uk/roberts.htm, 'A Journey Through World War Two,' 4.

of the retreating Japanese had passed through, and it became the main line of communication along which casualties were evacuated.[113]

Evacuation to India by air did become possible once strongholds around airstrips at BROADWAY and ABERDEEN, to the north of the Irrawaddy River, had been established, together with air superiority over the area of operations. Sunderland flying boats also took casualties from Lake Indawgi, in the heart of Japanese Burma, to the Brahmaputra river.[114] Wing Commander Sir Robert Thomson, who took part in both Chindit campaigns, later claimed that the majority of wounded men were flown to base hospitals in India in less than twenty-four hours.[115] American support proved to be crucial at this juncture, for nearly all the evacuations were carried out by men of the American Air Commando; the Americans also supplied assault craft to ferry some of the sick and wounded by river. Once the force had gained control of the Myitkyina–Moyaung railway, it was also used for evacuation. As in Arakan, however, Special Force operated a policy of forward treatment of medical— as opposed to surgical—cases. This often included some fairly drastic measures, known to carry considerable risks. Colonel Officer stated that: 'Every means available to get the man back on his feet was adopted, and gradually it became the accepted practice to treat nearly all cases of Malaria with an initial dose of quinine intravenously.'[116] He regretted that, 'so long as an operational task remained and so long as those responsible remained deaf to the Medical Reports of the state of the men's health and their consequent non-effective fighting state, this policy had to be adhered to as strictly as ever'. However, forward treatment was extremely difficult with a medical establishment as limited as that attached to the columns. According to Officer, it was insufficient even to deal with the comparatively low numbers of sick occurring in the pre-monsoon period.[117] Medical work was also hampered by poor communications, as column MOs had little contact with senior doctors, including the DDMS. Much of the fault, according to Officer, lay in the training of MOs who saw themselves as dependent on their brigades, rather than as part of a medical organization directed by the DDMS.[118]

As in the first Chindit operation, there were many casualties from disease, especially malaria. Of the 5,422 patients evacuated because of sickness, 3,108 (57 per cent) were classified as malaria or 'Not Yet Diagnosed

---

[113] www.burmastar.org.uk/joesbury.htm, Thomas Joesbury, '60 and 80 Column Chindits', 2.
[114] www.burmastar.org.uk/admin_troops.htm; 'How Admin Troops backed-up the Fighting Men', 2.
[115] Wing Commander Sir Robert Thomson, Foreword to Peter Mead, *Orde Wingate and the Historians* (Braunton: Merlin Books, 1987), 11.
[116] CMAC RAMC 816, 'Special Force, Medical Operations', Pt. II, 3.
[117] Ibid., Pt. II, 3–4.　　[118] Ibid., Pt. II, 5.

Fever', amounting to some 17 per cent of the total force. These figures compare quite favourably with sickness rates for other forces serving in malarious theatres, like the South-West Pacific, but the true number of casualties is masked by the fact that many were treated in forward areas and not recorded as admissions to hospital.[119] It was generally agreed that the condition of the force after the second operation was poor, but it became even worse after command of Special Force was transferred to the American general 'Vinegar Joe' Stilwell, who used it in an ordinary infantry role alongside his Sino-American force. In the prolonged battle for Mogaung the Chindits sustained hundreds of casualties from wounds, exhaustion, and sickness. Their resistance was so low that the slightest of cuts was often fatal. Concerned at the condition of the Chindits, Mountbatten visited the force and arranged an inspection by an Anglo-American team of doctors. It found that the men were mentally and physically exhausted and that they had been kept fighting despite repeated bouts of disease. It was agreed that 77 and 111 Brigades should be evacuated, although 14 Brigade and the West African contingent did not get out until later.[120]

Although it was his decision to transfer the command of Special Force to Stilwell, Slim later admitted that it had been a mistake in view of their already poor condition:

The Chindits, with the possible exception of 23 Brigade used in Assam, were completely exhausted, terribly reduced in strength and quite incapable of further effort when they were withdrawn. They could not have been kept in the field any longer— in fact they were kept too long. A considerable period of rest, recovery and great deal of reinforcement and re-training would be necessary before they could be fit for active service again—several months at least.[121]

Most of these casualties were attributed to poor anti-malaria discipline and the reluctance of the men to take mepacrine. Rumours that the drug caused sexual impotence and that it sapped strength still circulated widely.[122] In one column the administration of mepacrine was actually suspended before troops went into action because the officers believed it would reduce the fighting efficiency of the unit.[123] Fortunately, other commanders were more enlightened and did their best to dispel the myth surrounding the drug. One MO declared that mepacrine was so popular with the men in his column that they stored it up like ammunition.[124] But even those who took

[119] CMAC RAMC 816, 'Special Force, Medical Operations', Pt. IV, 7–8.
[120] David Rooney, *Burma Victory: Imphal and Kohima March 1944 to May 1945* (London: Cassell, 1992), 139–40.
[121] IWM 54.824, Slim to Lt.-Col. H. R. K. Gibbs, 17 Oct. 1963.
[122] Masters, *Road Past Mandalay*, 134.
[123] Ibid. 205; Whyte, 'A Trying Chindit', 1777; Officer, 'Special Force', Pt. IV, 17.
[124] CMAC RAMC 816, 'Some Observations of a Column MO'.

mepacrine regularly could not be sure that it was totally effective. After prolonged use the drug appeared to lose its potency, possibly because of some change in the soldier's metabolism that led to an increased rate of excretion.[125] As Bernard Fergusson later noted with amusement:

The contention of the doctors that mepacrine was a certain bulwark against malaria lost a good deal of ground when two of my medical officers themselves contracted the disease in the middle of a crash course. By the time we came out four out of nine doctors had caught it. It was most enjoyable to see them trying to persuade their own superiors (who had been loud in their quotations from the Australian statistics) that they had honestly not been dodging their mepacrine.[126]

Other methods of individual protection against malaria, such as mosquito nets, were too unwieldy for operations like those in which the Chindits were engaged.[127]

Bernard Fergusson later admitted that: 'In one respect we had the wrong attitude to malaria: we looked upon it as inevitable; we believed that we were all bound to get it every so often . . . But in one respect we had the right attitude, in that we never treated malaria as a disease meriting evacuation. Unless, of course, it was cerebral, the man would get over it and be fit for work again in a week.'[128] But malaria had a depressing effect on morale. Colonel Officer observed that 'the fighting efficiency and morale of personnel who had suffered from three or four attacks of malaria diminished considerably'. Malaria also weakened the general health of the force and increased their susceptibility to diseases such as dysentery and anaemia.[129] The latter was probably aggravated by the shortage of certain items of fresh food available to long-range patrols. A decent jungle ration had still to be developed, and over thirty cases of vitamin B deficiency were recorded.[130]

The poor quality of the K ration, as it was known, was also held partly responsible for the sickness and diarrhoea suffered by most men while their columns snaked through the Naga Hills. Thomas Joesbury recalled that: 'The mere sight of some of its items—the tin of corned beef loaf, especially, was enough to create feelings of nausea.' Another contributing factor in this outbreak of 'Naga Hills Tummy' may also have been the high altitude at which the columns were operating, and the sheer physical strain of walking up the steep slopes. The mountain springs may also have been contaminated, and were later found to be rich in magnesium sulphate—a powerful aperient.[131]

---

[125] Ibid., 'Medical Operations', Pt. IV, 10.
[126] Bernard Fergusson, *The Wild Green Earth* (London: Fontana, 1956; first published 1946), 176.
[127] CMAC RAMC 1789, Good, 'Medical Aspects of Long-Range Patrols', 4.
[128] Fergusson, *Wild Green Earth*, 176.
[129] CMAC RAMC 816, 'Medical Operations', Pt. IV, 8.
[130] Ibid., Pt. IV, 17.
[131] www.burmastar.org.uk/joesbury.htm, Joesbury, '60 and Column Chindits', 2.

Other medical problems encountered by Special Force included dysentery and typhus, both of which were probably contracted in Naga villages. Dysentery was a persistent complaint, although the outbreak of typhus was quickly brought under control. As soon as typhus was diagnosed, a new clothing drop was ordered for the entire force, as most of the men were already infested with lice. All old clothing was burned and the outbreak quickly subsided, although not before several dozen men had died from the disease.[132]

The various nationalities that constituted Special Force were differently affected by disease and the general strain of jungle warfare. The following table shows that the highest incidence of malaria and most other diseases was found amongst British other ranks (officers were said to have a higher level of anti-malaria discipline), and it was 'appreciably lower' among the Gurkhas (GORs), and lowest of all among the West African troops (WAORs). The lower incidence of malaria and dysentery among non-British troops was attributed not to superior hygiene but to a specific immunity against these diseases. The Africans, in addition, were said to bear the hardships of the campaign more easily on account of their 'great physique'. Their general health, indeed, remained very good, at least until after the onset of the monsoon.[133]

Those who did fall sick during operation THURSDAY faced an uncertain fate. The psychiatrist Captain J. S. Dawson, who compiled a report on the mental health of Special Force, claimed that:

Despite the admirable efforts of the M.O.s (with two exceptions) treatment was described variously as inadequate to ridiculous to call it treatment at all. It was common for sick to be turned away by the M.O. with the apology that he had nothing to give them. On occasion it was impossible to get even a bandage, parachute cloth having ultimately to be torn up to serve the purpose.[134]

In addition, few men had confidence that they would be evacuated if sick or wounded. Dawson claimed that 'the one concern in the mind of each individual was the fear of falling sick with the disturbing prospect of having to endure hardships in the column'.[135] MOs had to make great efforts to keep these dispirited men going, and must sometimes have appeared rather harsh as they did so. As one such officer, Captain H. W. W. Good of the 4th Battalion, the Border Regiment, recalled: 'The maxim I used to lay down in lecturing troops was that as long as a man is conscious, is not in severe pain and has no impediment of locomotion . . . he will keep marching . . . The

---

[132] Ibid.; www.burmastar.org.uk/roberts.htm, Robert, 'A Journey Through World War Two', 4.
[133] CMAC RAMC 816, 'Medical Operations', Pt. VII, 2.
[134] Ibid., Capt. J. S. Dawson, 'Psychiatric Report'.
[135] Ibid.

Table 5.1. Incidence of casualties among Special Force, 1943–1944

	Strength	Admissions		Sickness		Battle casualties	
		Actual	Per 1,000	Actual	Per 1,000	Actual	Per 1,000
Officers	1,050	259	246.7	201	191.4	58	35.2
BORs	10,800	4,770	441.6	3,760	348.2	1,010	93.5
GORs	3,450	1,391	403.2	902	261.5	489	141.7
WAORs	2,700	797	295.1	559	207.0	238	88.1
TOTAL	18,000	7,217	401.0	5,122	301.2	1,795	99.0

Source: CMAC RAMC 816, Col. W. J. Officer, 'Special Force: Report on the Medical Aspects of Operations For the Period 1943–4', Pt. VII, 1.

reason for putting it so strongly is to be able to give the benefit of what transport is available to the more ill men and not to be encumbered with the less ill but weaker willed ones.'[136] But Wingate had never been coy about the dangers his troops would face on long-range patrols. Most accepted these risks willingly, if not lightly, and were under few illusions about the perils that awaited them.[137]

It is difficult to generalize about medical provisions in Special Force. Antimalarial discipline and hygiene appear to have differed considerably from one column to another, while arrangements for treatment and evacuation depended on the proximity of airstrips and other forms of transportation. Allied air superiority meant that Special Force could be supplied directly with medical necessities, but it is clear that these did not always reach columns operating far from strongholds such as BROADWAY and ABERDEEN, and the lack of even basic supplies like wound dressings created a 'Bolshy' attitude among the MOs.[138] Apart from the obvious problem of supplying long-range penetration columns operating in difficult terrain, there was a general distrust of medical involvement, which was seemingly fostered by Wingate himself. As Captain J. S. Dawson put it in his psychiatric report: 'The habit of looking upon the doctor as a Fifth Columnist, likely to blab the merest piece of confidential information which is vouchsafed to him, is still all too prevalent.'[139]

It is too easy, especially with the benefit of hindsight, to portray Wingate as harsh and uncaring: the nature of the Chindit operations was such, as its first PMO, Colonel Campbell realized, that medical comforts would have to be kept to a minimum owing to the difficulty of supplying columns behind

[136] CMAC RAMC 1789, Good, 'Medical Aspects of Long-Range Patrols', 3.
[137] Royle, *Orde Wingate*, 261.
[138] CMAC RAMC 816, 'Some Observations by a Column MO'.
[139] Ibid., Dawson, 'Psychiatric Report'.

Japanese lines. While showing some apprehension about food and medical supplies prior to LONGCLOTH, Campbell had recommended only a few additions to the standard medical kit, including snake-venom and anti-anthrax serum.[140] As far as evacuation was concerned, Wingate acknowledged after LONGCLOTH that having to leave men behind had had a depressing effect on morale, and it was for this reason that he was keen to arrange for evacuation by air for the second and much larger operation.[141] In this, Wingate seems to have been quite successful, within the constraints imposed by terrain and the military operations themselves.

Nevertheless, it seems that Wingate attached a relatively low priority to medicine by contrast with Slim, who placed special emphasis on hygiene and sanitary discipline. Slim was the very model of the new professional soldier: strict yet compassionate, and with a keen awareness of the importance of manpower economy. This was acquired, in part, from his days as a student at the Indian Army's Staff College at Quetta, where he studied attentively at the feet of one of Britain's foremost military theorists, Percy Hobart.[142] Slim also learned much from the Australian Army and the advice given by experts such as Gordon Covell. Wingate, by contrast, refused to listen or defer to anyone.[143] Like an Old Testament prophet, he preached that victory could be gained only with the sacrifice of men committed to the cause. He expected physical hardship and high casualties, and warned his men to expect them too—it was a risk that they evidently accepted.[144] But Wingate's obsession with hardening troops for jungle warfare also stems, perhaps, from his paranoia about anything that smacked of hypochondria and his belief that the mind could control the body to the extent of blocking physical pain.[145] He had himself endured considerable discomfort on active service and had been reluctant to seek medical treatment, as on the occasion when he contracted malaria in Egypt during 1941. Having rejected treatment until the illness had reached a very advanced stage, a fit of depression brought on by the disease induced him to attempt suicide.[146] Wingate appears to have seen illness, or at least succumbing to it, as a kind of moral failure; a product, no doubt, of his rather dour religious upbringing (his parents were Plymouth Brethren) and his enduring commitment to a Christianity of a distinctly Old Testament kind. Wingate was, to all intents and purposes, a Victorian: a muscular Christian who equated disease with dishonour. He was singularly out of step with an army that espoused the principles of social medicine and

[140] Royle, *Orde Wingate*, 261.   [141] Ibid. 261.   [142] Lewin, *Slim*, 47.
[143] Bidwell, *Chindit War*, 39.
[144] Masters, *Road Past Mandalay*, 139.
[145] Sir Robert Thompson, Foreword to Mead, *Orde Wingate and the Historians*, 11.
[146] Royle, *Orde Wingate*, 216, 219.

which saw the prevention of disease as a matter of collective, as well as individual, responsibility.

1944: The Turning-Point

In 1944 the military situation in India and Burma changed markedly in favour of the Allies. Wingate's second operation formed part of a broader offensive in the Northern Combat Area by American and Chinese troops under the command of Stilwell. On the central (Assam) front, the 17th and 20th Indian Divisions of Slim's 4th Corps were to push forward into Burma via Tiddim and Tamu; meanwhile 15th Corps would advance southwards in the Arakan to take Akyab. To counteract this move, the Japanese army conducted two operations that anticipated the Allied advance. The first of these was in the Arakan, where the Japanese attempted to surround and destroy two divisions, preventing reinforcements being sent from there to the central front. The second was a much larger offensive against Imphal, which aimed to capture likely starting-points for a British invasion of Burma. The failure of both these operations amounted to the biggest defeat so far suffered by the Japanese army, which sustained 71,289 casualties including 27,000 fatalities. The Japanese defeat in the Arakan was, as Slim put it: 'the turning point of the Burma campaign',[147] while the battle around Kohima–Imphal was one of the two decisive engagements in the recovery of Burma, the other being Meiktila in February–March 1945.

What role did medicine play at this crucial juncture? Were Slim's attempts to improve hygiene and anti-malaria discipline successful; were other features of his 'medical plan', such as air evacuation and forward treatment, adequately developed? The medical statistics presented in the official history suggest that disease—especially malaria—was being brought under control in 14th Army, even before the attack on Kohima–Imphal. From a high of 1,850 per thousand troops in 1942 (roughly two admissions per man per year), admissions to hospital were reduced to 1,400 in 1943 and 100 per thousand in 1944.[148] Reports from MOs with troops on active service tend to confirm this picture of general improvement, although it is clear that many men were reluctant to undergo suppressive treatment for malaria until they had actually experienced the disease. A medical report on 7th Indian Division in the Arakan recorded that:

All units since arrival in Arakan had undergone mepacrine treatment and malaria cases were very few. The Medical authorities were still not very certain of the effect

---

[147] Slim, *Defeat into Victory*, 246.   [148] Crew, *Burma*, 612.

of prolonged mepacrine dosage, and it was thought advisable to cease taking the drug as soon as possible. By mid-December [1943], the worst mosquito breeding season was believed to have passed, and all troops underwent the blanket treatment intended to kill finally any malaria parasites still lingering in the blood. Within a fortnight to three weeks . . . men began to go down with malaria at an alarming rate. Mepacrine dosage was immediately re-introduced, and after the drug had had time to take effect malaria rates dropped as if by magic. From that day everybody had the utmost confidence in mepacrine and it was no longer necessary to order the taking of these evil tasting yellow tablets.[149]

Anti-malaria precautions were certainly very much in evidence in the Kohima–Imphal area. In addition to suppressive treatment, the Imphal military base was able to provide labour for anti-mosquito brigades. One such was No. 44 Indian Anti-Malaria Unit, commanded by Captain S. Ramaswamy, whose task it was to survey campsites for mosquitoes, spread oil on breeding grounds, and to spray the camp and its environs with the insecticide Paris Green. Detachments of the AMU were also sent out to forward areas to spray inhabited localities liable to harbour mosquitoes. In addition to these duties, the AMU distributed spray-guns and anti-mosquito cream to the troops, and did its best to raise awareness of the malaria problem. But it was already widely known that malaria could cause massive wastage of manpower, not least by the veterans of 6th Infantry Brigade, who had suffered a near 100 per-cent infection rate during the first Arakan operations in 1943.[150]

The standard of hygiene amongst British and Indian troops was also good. Many of the men comprising 14th Army had been trained in jungle warfare at Belgaum, where great emphasis was now placed on hygiene and sanitation. There was also a Field Hygiene Section operating in the Kohima–Imphal area, consisting of a specialist MO and twenty-eight other ranks. But while sanitary conditions in camp were of a high order, it was not always possible to maintain them in the hills around Imphal and Kohima, especially when Allied troops moved into sites recently occupied by the Japanese, who were said to have fouled them indiscriminately. As a result, fly-borne bacillary dysentery was rife in localities such as 'Summerhouse Hill',[151] most of the cases occurring among British rather than Indian troops. The latter may have acquired immunity to infection.[152] Despite these set-

---

[149] CMAC RAMC 1900/17, 'A Brief History of the Seventh Indian Division', 10.
[150] CMAC RAMC 814, 'The Medical Services with 2nd Division During Operations for the Capture of Kohima and the Opening of the Diamapur–Kohima–Imphal Road, April–June 1944', 58.
[151] Ibid. 56
[152] CMAC RAMC 1237/1/1, 'Account of Operations by 33 Indian Corps, Vol. I, From the Start of the Assam Campaign in April 1944 until the Relief of 4 Corps at Imphal on 22 June 1944', App. 13, p. 4.

backs, the ratio of sickness to battle casualties was low: 6,695 sick to 4,038 wounded—a considerable improvement on earlier battles in the theatre.[153] Weakened by disease and malnutrition, the Japanese suffered more casualties from sickness than either the British or the Indian troops. The Japanese had staked everything on a rapid and overwhelming victory, and had not anticipated a drawn-out siege.[154]

The prevention of disease was part of an integrated medical strategy, for previous campaigns, such as first Arakan, had shown how vital it was to provide treatment for medical and surgical cases at the front. Forward treatment was important not only because it reduced manpower wastage, but because it discouraged malingering and the deliberate disregard of sanitary precautions. War-weary soldiers no longer had the option of evacuation back to the relative comfort of hospitals in India. But the first real test of forward treatment facilities, during the second battle of Arakan, was formidably difficult. The Japanese attack on the Allied position at the 'Admin Box' inflicted heavy casualties on the defenders (some 3,506), though at the cost of 5,335 casualties themselves. Many of the wounded were in need of specialist treatment that could not be provided by the local MDS, and owing to the fact that the Box was surrounded, these men could not be evacuated for two weeks, when the siege was finally lifted by British reinforcements.[155] But the availability in the Admin Box of blood transfusion facilities meant that many surgical cases could be operated on quickly, and several patients owed their lives to the fact that surgical work was performed within an hour of their being wounded. Nevertheless, it was difficult to perform surgery under heavy fire and wholly impossible during the hours of darkness, as lights would have provided a target to the Japanese.[156]

All surgical work in the MDS came to an end when it was overrun by the Japanese. Many of the hospital staff and some of the wounded managed to escape and established another dressing station on the other side of the hill on which the original MDS was situated.[157] The capture of the dressing station was the occasion for yet another atrocity. The wounded were bayoneted as they lay in their stretchers and the MOs were lined up against the wall and shot. The Indian orderlies were forced to carry wounded Japanese back to the dressing stations but were themselves killed afterwards. A counter-attack the following morning recaptured the MDS but it was found to be a shambles, the only survivors were a handful of wounded men who

---

[153] CMAC RAMC 814, 'Medical Services with 2nd Division', 61.
[154] See G. Evans and A. Brett James, *Imphal* (London: Macmillan, 1965); Slim, *Defeat into Victory*, 352.
[155] CMAC RAMC 1900/17, 'History of Seventh Indian Division', 19.
[156] IWM 87/48/1, Lt.-Col. B. Lilwall, 12 Mobile Surgical Unit, Burma, 'Clinical Impressions'.
[157] Ibid.

had crawled into the jungle or feigned death. This outrage impaired medical treatment for the remainder of the battle, but as Slim observed in his memoirs, it had steeled the resolve of the defenders.[158]

The intensity of fighting in the Admin Box left its mark on many of the men who had served in the 14th Army, and there was a high incidence of psychiatric casualties. Some units appear to have experienced a complete collapse in morale. Most of the British psychiatric casualties had occurred in one battalion, the 2nd Battalion of the King's Own Scottish Borderers. A psychiatric report on the battalion, some months after the battle, stated that:

August 1944 found the Btn. resting in Kohima. They were much below strength, many of them were absent on leave, and the morale of those remaining at the time was decidedly low. In addition they had lost a great many officers in their previous periods of action. The sickness rate, especially from malaria, was uncomfortably high. Some of the material removed at this time was appallingly bad, and it was a constant source of wonder to me that the Btn. had previously been able to carry such a large number of dull and backward men, and still conduct itself favourably in action.[159]

The report called for more careful attention to personnel selection through intelligence- and character-testing. Many NCOs had apparently been reluctant to accept responsibility and show leadership, while an examination of the officers placed some in the lowest possible category.[160] Training also left much to be desired, according to the report, which concluded that: 'The general feeling appears to be that acceptance of training implies the acceptance of increased aggression and risk, and [the men] are therefore unwilling to make any spontaneous effort to learn.'[161] While there may be some truth in both these explanations, one should be wary of accepting the report too readily. If the quality of NCOs and officers, and consequently the training, was inferior, this was probably due not to any failing of character or intelligence but simply to inexperience, for the 2nd Battalion had recently lost many of its seasoned veterans.

Despite heavy casualties, the medical situation at Kohima and Imphal was somewhat less desperate than during the battle of the Admin Box. Prior to the Japanese advance, Kohima had been a hospital centre on the line of evacuation from Imphal, and it held large numbers of sick in order to reduce the need for evacuation back to eastern Bengal. Although the impending threat

---

[158] Slim, *Defeat into Victory*, 240–1; CMAC RAMC 1900/17, Special Order to 66th Indian FA, by Brigadier E. H. W. Cobb, OC 7th Infantry Division, 20 October 1946.
[159] CMAC RAMC 1900/18/1, 'Psychiatric Report of Divisional Psychiatrist to Commander 7th Indian Division', 1.
[160] Ibid. 2; RAMC 1900/18/2, 'Notes re. Capt. Gottelier'.
[161] CMAC RAMC 1900/18/1, 'Psychiatric Report', 2.

to Kohima led to the withdrawal from the area of most of the larger and least mobile medical units, the arrival of two CCSs and two mobile surgical units (one neurosurgical) at nearby Dimapur meant that sufficient facilities for forward treatment were available.[162] In Kohima itself there were a number of smaller medical units, and a network of dressing stations was established along the ridges to serve outlying emplacements. Evacuation to these units from the front line was usually carried out using jeep ambulance cars, which had often to make the journey under heavy mortar fire. Jeeps were also used for evacuation back to the larger centres, together with five armoured ambulance cars.

The quality of surgical work in forward areas was reportedly excellent, despite the fact that many of the hospital buildings were destroyed during the Japanese attack.[163] Blood transfusion had to be carried out using local donors only, but there were always a sufficient number of volunteers.[164] Resuscitation played a vitally important role in the successful treatment of surgical cases, particularly in the management of chest and abdominal injuries. But there were limits to what could be achieved. A patient whose blood pressure could not be brought above a systolic rate of one hundred was unlikely to survive.[165] Another problem faced by some front-line units was wound infection. One of several officer-patients who later compiled an official report on medical care in the Burma–India theatres complained that: 'A number of individuals died of gas-gangrene to my knowledge at Kohima, and there was no serum for this either at the RAP or ADS. The first place I saw the serum in use was as the CCS at Dimapur. If possible, I would suggest that supplies of the serum should be kept with the RAPs and ADSs for immediate use as casualties occur.'[166] The problem of wound infection was soon rectified with the more general use of penicillin later in 1944, but even allowing for the difficulties experienced at Kohima, conditions for the sick and wounded were markedly better than those after the Arakan campaign. Major C. L. Heanley, commanding an FSU in Bengal, reported that:

In the early summer of 1943, we were busy again with casualties from the Arakan campaign. These casualties were of poor morale and had a feeling that they had been let down. In the campaign of 1944 . . . it was noticeable that we had a much higher proportion of severe injuries: this indicated that the evacuation and medical treatment in the Arakan campaign of 1943 was not up to that of 1944 from the Imphal and Kohima campaigns.[167]

---

[162] CMAC RAMC 1237/1/1, 'Operations by 33 Indian Corps', App.13, p. 1.
[163] Ibid. pp. 2–3.   [164] CMAC RAMC 1512, 'Sixth British Field Ambulance', 35.
[165] Baty, *Surgeon in the Jungle War*, 125.
[166] OIOC L/WS/1/892, DGMS India to ADMS, War Staff, India Office, 31 July 1945, enclosing report from officers evacuated from India on conditions in hospitals in India and Burma.
[167] CMAC RAMC 1816/4/4/2, Maj. C. L. Heanley, 'The Trend of Field Surgery'.

Successful facilities for forward treatment meant that medical units at the rear received only the most severe cases from Imphal and Kohima. Even so, many hospitals within easy reach of Burma were overcrowded with casualties from the fighting there.[168] Some difficulties were also encountered during evacuation, as transport for the evacuation of casualties was not quite ready for their reception. There were numerous complaints from patients about evacuation by boat and by rail, although these were mostly about relatively minor things such as the quality of food. The most serious complaints concerned the insanitary condition of some of the steamers employed to take casualties down the Brahmaputra, delays in rail transport, and the condition of some of the rolling stock, which was unsuitable for carriage of the sick and wounded. It appears that these problems were soon rectified, however.[169]

Forward treatment developed further after the Japanese offensive had been repelled and when Slim's forces began their pursuit to the Chindwin river, during June–December 1944. One of the main features of this phase of the campaign was the increasing use of air evacuation, made possible by the Japanese retreat, Allied air superiority, and the provision of air ambulances by the USAAF. Although as many as 17,000 casualties had been flown out of Imphal during the siege in returning supply planes, aeroplanes did not become the chief means of evacuation until the push further south, when American air ambulances became available. [170] By November Yazagyo, in the heart of the Kabaw Valley, had been developed into a fully sized airstrip, which became the HQ of a squadron of light aircraft.[171] The establishment of this air base was vital, as formerly the only means of evacuation had been along the precipitous Ukhrul track, which at points was passable only to stretcher-bearers. Being manpower-intensive, evacuation left surgical teams stretched to their limit, despite the extensive employment of Naga porters.[172]

Evacuation by air was a vast improvement, but it was reserved for only the most serious casualties, and for the great majority evacuation ended at the new Corps Medical Centre on the Tamu–Kalewa road. It was the first unit of its kind—an integrated medical and surgical centre capable of accommodating 1,600 patients, and fed by its own airstrip. The Medical Centre proved to be an outstanding success and continued to support the advance a long time after the Chindwin bridgehead was established.[173] Now that the Japanese were in retreat, forward medical staff—right down to MDS level—

---

[168] AMSM M/12 ADMS 2000: 39, 'An Indian Odyssey: War Memoirs of Sgt. J. Titchener, RAMC', 36.
[169] OIOC L/WS/1/892, DGMS, India to ADMS, War Staff, India Office, 31 July 1945.
[170] CMAC RAMC 1237/1/2, 'Operations 22 June–16 December 1944', App. L, p. 134.
[171] Ibid. 137.   [172] Ibid. 136.
[173] Ibid. 137.

could also be supplemented by the employment of female nurses. Despite some misgivings on the part of the male orderlies, the women helped to improve efficiency and boosted the morale of the patients.[174] Another key factor in the success of forward treatment was rigorous selection of personnel. By this stage in the campaign medical units were thoroughly integrated in all respects, with Indian and British personnel serving alongside each other, all selected purely on the basis of competence. The importance of racial integration was constantly reiterated in the remaining months of the campaign in Burma, although it was often found that the best personnel, at all levels, were usually trained in Britain. This meant that hospital facilities near the front tended to have a higher proportion of British doctors, orderlies, and nurses than those at the rear.[175] The difference was often remarked on by British commanders and the patients who passed through the hospitals. It was said that the largely Indian staff at hospitals in the rear were often poorly motivated and disciplined, whereas staff of all races serving in front-line medical units, almost without exception, received great praise. As one patient remarked: 'From my own experiences in India, it struck me that the nearer one got to the front, the better the medical attention.'[176]

But at this point in time facilities for forward treatment were not tested severely; battle casualties were few, and despite cases of scrub typhus and malaria, the health of the force was 'exceedingly satisfactory'.[177] Apart from improved hygiene and anti-malaria discipline, the fall in sickness may have been due to the use of the insecticide DDT. Anti-malaria units in India and Burma had previously attempted to control the disease by oiling mosquito breeding pools and draining marshes, or by spraying mosquito-ridden areas with Paris Green. Such measures were moderately successful in preventing malaria around permanent encampments, but they were of little use in forward areas. By the time 14th Army had moved into the Kabaw Valley the spraying of DDT from the air was an essential feature of anti-malaria work, and specially adapted Hurricane fighters dusted DDT over large tracts of land prior to the Allied advance. Although 14th Army moved into the valley at the most unhealthy time of the year—immediately after the monsoon—casualties from disease were surprisingly light.[178] But while the 'Valley of Death' failed to live up to its reputation, the 14th Army did not escape unscathed. From 26 June to 16 December admissions from malaria and

[174] Ibid. 136.
[175] OIOC L/WS/1/881, Minutes of a Meeting held at the India Office, 15 Feb. 1945; Report by DGAMS on a visit to India and SEAC, 21 January 1945; L/WS/I/892, DGMS, India, to ADMS, War Staff, India Office.
[176] OIOC L/WS/1/892, DGMS, India to ADMS, War Staff, India Office, 31 July 1945.
[177] CMAC RAMC 1237/1/2, 'Operations 22 June–16 December', 140.
[178] CMAC RAMC 1237/2, Photo journal of 33rd Indian Corps.

typhus numbered 20,430 and 6,849, respectively. This was equivalent to the absence of nearly 1,200 men per week, out of an average weekly strength of 88,578.[179]

The incidence of malaria and other diseases during the pursuit over the Chindwin serves as a qualification to the somewhat exaggerated accounts given of preventive medicine in 14th Army at this time. A myth soon developed to the effect that Slim and Mountbatten had chosen deliberately to advance through the monsoon, such was their confidence in DDT and the anti-malarial discipline of their force. Nearly twenty years after the war this myth was still very much alive. In his foreword to the official medical history of the Burma campaign, the Director-General of the Indian Army Medical Service stated that 'the highly malarious and unhealthy areas in Burma were deliberately selected by the Supreme Commander . . . to give battle to the Japanese, relying on the efficiency of our medical services, the superiority of our health measures and the training and health discipline of our forces as compared to that of the enemy'.[180] Or as another general put it, when commenting on the first draft of the British official history: 'For the first time in war, *malaria* was used as a weapon by the Allies, whose troops protected against malaria by chemoprophylaxis fought the Japanese in highly malarious areas and defeated them.'[181]

Slim was under no such illusions, and in this crucial passage in his memoirs he made it clear that there was little difference between the health of his army and that of the Japanese, despite the fact that the latter were in retreat:

I have heard it said that in Burma we often selected particularly disease-ridden spots in which to fight the Japanese because our scientific safeguards against malaria, scrub typhus, and other jungle ills were so much better than theirs. I certainly never deliberately did this. When we were retreating in 1942, and our men were dispirited, undernourished, and exhausted, our sickness rate was vastly higher than the enemy's; when they in turn retreated in 1944 and their men were in that state, the position was reversed. But at most periods of the campaign, even after our anti-malaria discipline had improved and our superior remedies were available, I do not think our casualties from sickness were any lower than theirs. I always believed—and this I confirmed later by the observation of large bodies of Japanese prisoners—that both British and Indian troops were more susceptible to these diseases than were the enemy.[182]

179 CMAC RAMC 1237/1/2, 'Operations 22 June–16 December 1944', 141.
180 Foreword by Lt.-Gen. C. C. Kapila to B. L. Raina (ed.), *Official History of the Indian Armed Forces in the Second World War 1939–45: Medical Services: Campaigns in the Eastern Theatre* (Delhi: Combined Inter-Services Historical Section, India and Pakistan, 1964).
181 CMAC RAMC 1000, Comments of Maj.-Gen. A. N. T. Mences on Vol. V of the official medical history of the war, p. 1.
182 Slim, *Defeat into Victory*, 354.

During the monsoon campaign and pursuit Slim reckoned that 'we probably had a rather higher total [of sick] than the Japanese'.[183] Despite marked improvements in anti-malaria discipline, he decided that the first troops to move into the Kabaw Valley should be the newly arrived East African Division, because he assumed they were more resistant to malaria than either Indian or British troops. While their casualties were not light, Slim doubted whether any other troops would have kept them so low.[184] This can be the only explanation for his decision to put the East Africans at the head of the advance, for Slim apparently had 'scarcely a good word to say' about either West or East African troops.[185] However, the crucial difference between the effectiveness of Allied and Japanese medical arrangements at this stage in the campaign lay in the treatment of the sick rather than in the prevention of disease. The vast majority of Allied casualties recovered and were returned to duty quickly thanks to forward treatment, but the Japanese, whose medical services had fallen into disarray, died from 'lack of medical care, exposure and exhaustion'.[186]

Another notable feature of medical work in the wake of the Kohima and Imphal campaigns was the treatment of psychiatric casualties. There were many such casualties, owing to the savage hand-to-hand fighting that occurred there, but it was difficult to administer proper treatment because of a shortage of trained personnel and suitable accommodation. In the first weeks of the attack the only specialist personnel were the two psychiatric orderlies attached to each of the field ambulances.[187] A good many cases had had to be evacuated back to India, and the psychiatric wards of hospitals there were at times full to overflowing.[188] By 24 April, however, it had been possible to establish a forward psychiatric centre at Priphema, some 18 miles from Kohima. Here Captain P. J. R. Davis, a psychiatrist with 2nd Division, did valuable work treating 181 (mostly British) patients, 117 of whom were returned to duty within five days.[189] He was one of the few British psychiatrists ever to be decorated for his work.[190]

---

[183] Ibid. 378.   [184] Ibid. 355.

[185] LHCMA, Adam Papers 3/6/4, 'Report by the Adjutant-General on his Overseas Tour, January–February, 1945', 3.

[186] Slim, *Defeat into Victory*, 378.

[187] CMAC RAMC 814, 'The Medical Services with 2nd Division', 11. There were three classes of mental nursing orderlies; each class received a six-month course of instruction at the Royal Victoria Hospital, Netley. See *Standing Orders for the Royal Army Medical Corps, Royal Army Medical Corps (T.A.) and the Army Dental Corps—1937* (London: HMSO, 1938), 112–16.

[188] AMSM M/37, 'History of 18th General Hospital', 33.

[189] CMAC RAMC 1237/1/1, 'Operations by 33 Indian Corps', 3–4.

[190] Ben Shephard, *War of Nerves: Soldiers and Psychiatrists, 1914–1994* (London: Jonathan Cape, 2000), 222.

As in North Africa and Italy, the most effective methods of psychiatric treatment were often the simplest. In his report on medical services with 2nd Division, Davis noted that:

There seems to me to be no point in a case of acute anxiety, agitation, or depression, taking him back over his experiences and making him re-live them in all their intensity . . . [I]t was remarkable how well the simpler methods worked, i.e. sedation and later a discussion on common sense lines of the causes of the breakdown, and the possible means of avoiding another one.[191]

The vast majority of the 218 psychiatric casualties at Imphal and Kohima (amounting to some 10 per cent of battle casualties) were, indeed, cases of acute anxiety reaction, complicated by physical exhaustion.[192] The relatively low number of such casualties—which might well have been higher, given the particularly bloody and exhausting nature of the battle—was attributed to three factors: the careful attention given to the selection of personnel; the high standard of officers and leadership in the Division; and the exceptionally high morale of the Division as a whole. It was precisely the absence of these factors that had led to the collapse of some British units during the battle of the Admin Box. The high morale of 2nd Division, by contrast, is demonstrated by the fact that many psychiatric patients felt shame at letting their comrades down, despite being told that 'any man may break down after great stress, and particularly when they are exhausted and short of sleep and food'.[193]

Despite these reassurances, it was still believed that different 'personality types' were prone to certain mental disorders. MOs confirmed observations made in North Africa that 'the active, agitated type of reaction seemed more commonly to affect men of good personality, whilst the passive or stupose type with violent tremors, seemed to affect men of less good personality or of rather timid, non-aggressive temperaments'.[194] This recalls the distinction made between repressive and passive neuroses during the First World War, in which officers were said to be more likely to repress their feelings, leading to complex anxiety states, whereas stupose and tremulous reactions (indicative of passivity and poor self-control) were supposedly common amongst the rank and file.[195] Still, the question remained of why psychiatric casualties at Kohima and Imphal were confined to British troops. The author of

---

[191] CMAC RAMC 814, 'The Medical Services with 2nd Division', 54. See also P. J. R. Davis, 'Psychiatry in a Division on the Burma Front', *Journal of the Royal Army Medical Corps*, 84 (1945), 66–7.
[192] CAMC RAMC 814, 'Medical Services with 2nd Division', 51.
[193] Ibid. 55. [194] Ibid. 51.
[195] See Shephard, *War of Nerves*, 57–8; Elaine Showalter, 'Male Hysteria', in her *The Female Malady: Women, Madness and English Culture* (New York, 1985).

one psychiatric report on Indian soldiers—Major J. Matas of the Canadian Army Medical Corps—concluded that Indians were accustomed to a lower standard of living in civilian life and found the hardships of war less onerous than their British counterparts. Moreover, as a volunteer soldier and a member of a 'martial race', the Indian soldier or the Gurkha did not need to alter fundamentally his outlook on killing, as did the vast majority of British troops, who were conscripts.[196]

Central Burma and Beyond

Forward treatment continued as a vital element of medical work during the pursuit into central Burma. The campaign was characterized by rapid movement, and it was considered unwise to bring in general hospitals in view of the time required to move and install such heavily equipped units. In the time it would have taken to erect them, the battle would have moved far ahead, leaving the hospital approachable only by air. The maintenance of such units would have also imposed a heavy burden on road and railway transport. It was therefore decided to evacuate all serious cases by air, and to carry CCSs and MFTUs as the only hospital units with the army. This formed a general principle out of the practice that had developed around Kohima and Imphal during 1944.[197] It was again found that these units could be usefully combined into a Corps Medical Centre. The general idea was for two CCSs and two MFTUs to be allotted to each corps, the remaining units being held in reserve. If the tide of battle swept forward more quickly than anticipated, a CCS or MFTU from the reserve could be leapfrogged forward to be joined by its opposite number from an existing medical centre. Flexibility was the order of the day, with medical centres being continually reconstituted. This was the practice during the advance through central Burma and the crossing of the Irrawaddy, and on the whole it worked very well. A report on the medical aspects of operations in Burma between December 1944 and May 1945 stated that: 'The whole hearted acceptance of the principle of the 'Corps Medical Centre' made possible by the first rate air evacuation facilities provided by the USAAF has proved its value continually.'[198] But the limiting factor was, at all times, the shortage of transport, both road and air; the lack of vehicles in the three-ton class

---

[196] J. Matas, 'A Note on Psychiatry in Indian Troops', *Journal of the Royal Army Medical Corps*, 84 (1945), 69.
[197] CMAC RAMC 1117, 'Fourteenth Army: Medical History of the Burma Campaign November 1944–May 1945', 20.
[198] Ibid. 84.

being a particular problem. Replacement vehicles became available towards the end of the campaign, but initial shortages were never completely made up.[199]

The chief centre of medical work during the initial phase of the advance into Burma was the medical centre at Schwebo, the foundational units of which were No. 10 MFTU and No. 8 CCS, both of which were flown in from Imphal.[200] From these two units developed what one report described as the 'most ambitious medical organization that had been attempted' in Burma,[201] or probably, for that matter, in any forward area during the war. The Schwebo centre was ideally suited to such an establishment, since it had easy access to both light and main airstrips, and was relatively close to the area of operations. Easy road access existed with the 19th Division at Kyaukmaung, and it was also in reach of the bridgehead at Thabbikyin, once a light airstrip had been conducted there; 2nd Division operations were within twenty minutes flight and 20th Division within fifty minutes. The massive hospital complex that developed at Schwebo eventually comprised two CCSs, one MFTU, a psychiatric centre, a field transfusion unit, three dental units, and a neurosurgical unit.[202] Despite these facilities, by early February the pressure on Schwebo had become so great that a subsidiary centre had to be opened at Sadaung to relieve the main corps centre. These two centres successfully covered operations involving 33rd Corps during their crossing of the Irrawaddy and the subsequent advance of 19th Division to Mandalay.[203]

At this stage in the campaign the emphasis was very much upon mobility. It would be tedious to relate the movements of various medical units for the remainder of the campaign, but the execution of 14th Army's medical plan can be illustrated by showing how the medical organization of 33rd Corps was reconstituted immediately after crossing the Irrawaddy. As the fighting moved south and east, the Schwebo medical centre began to break up, as its constituent units were sent to different points. No. 8 CCS moved to Tad-U to cover 19th Division's operations south of Mandalay; No. 16 CCS was moved forward to Toungoo in preparation for the subsequent advance to Meiktila, leaving No. 10 MFTU as the only unit remaining at Schwebo. These units joined two forward centres already in place near Meiktila and at Myitche, but as 7th and 20th Divisions of 33rd Corps advanced down the Irrawaddy axis, the latter was moved forward to cover them, joining the centre at Meiktila and a new base at Allanmayo.[204]

[199] CMAC RAMC 1117, 21.   [200] Ibid. 23–4.
[201] CMAC RAMC 1237/1/3, 'Operations 16 December–20 March 1945', 81.
[202] Ibid.; RAMC 1117, 'Medical History . . . November 1944–May 1945', 24.
[203] CMAC RAMC 1117, 'Medical History . . . November 1944–May 1945', 24.
[204] Ibid. 25.

These movements occurred during some of the bitterest fighting of the central Burma campaign, particularly the decisive battle at Meiktila from February to March 1945. How did the new medical services cope? At this point the main medical centre was still at Myitche, on account of the heavy artillery and mortar bombardment of the area around Meiktila. Myitche had both heavy and light airstrips and was able to take large numbers of casualties flown in directly from the vicinity of Meiktila. The fly-in began on 14 March and was completed within a week. This was an impressive achievement, considering the delays in the evacuation of the wounded that had dogged early phases of the Burma campaign, but patients were not entirely free from danger; the use of Dakota aircraft had to be discontinued as the heavy airstrip was within range of the Japanese artillery. Until 30 March, when the Japanese were pushed back from the vicinity of the airstrip, the heavy strain of evacuation from Meiktila was placed solely on light aircraft such as C64s and L5s. While the evacuation was taking place further medical units were being flown into both Myitche and Meiktila. There were now two theatres and three surgical teams operating at the latter, and four theatres and four teams at Myitche.[205] The importance of air transport for medical work at this stage in the campaign—both for supply and evacuation—cannot be stressed too much. As one commentator put it after the war: 'The superb efforts made by the RAF and USAAF in 1944 and 1945 to produce combat and logistical support, revolutionised the evacuation of battle casualties. Journeys that had previously taken one week to ten days by surface were accomplished by air in *three hours*. This had immense surgical value and saved many lives.' It was estimated that as many as 200,000 casualties were evacuated by air during the campaign as a whole,[206] which had a wonderful effect on morale. Ronald Adam, who had long insisted on the importance of air evacuation, reported in 1945 that the provision of light aircraft solely for medical purposes had been 'invaluable'. 'The morale of the troops in Burma wants to be seen to be believed,' he added: 'I have never seen anything better.'[207] From now on, air evacuation was to become the norm in all major conflicts, although, as early as the Korean War, winged aircraft had largely been replaced by helicopters which could get even closer to casualties at the point of wounding.

Despite the relief provided by air evacuation, the forward medical centres found themselves overwhelmed by casualties. During the first half of April the rate of admissions to the Meiktila Medical Centre was between 200 and

[205] Ibid. 25–6.
[206] CMAC RAMC 1000, Comments of Maj.-Gen. A. N. T. Mences on Vol. V of the official history, p. 1.
[207] LHCMA, Adam Papers 3/6/4, 'Report by the Adjutant-General on his Overseas Tour, January–February, 1945', 3.

300 per day, making it impossible for the two CCSs to hold cases for more than forty-eight hours unless they were too ill to move. Inevitably, a number of patients had to be evacuated by air directly to hospitals at Comilla and Argtala in Bengal, contrary to the principle of forward treatment established at the end of 1944.[208] As the army moved south, however, evacuation by air was hampered considerably by the onset of the monsoon. At the beginning of May torrential rain brought all air evacuation to a standstill, and towards the end of the month the rain was so heavy that the airfield at Pegu had to be abandoned. Until the monsoon had passed most evacuation had to take place by road, but fortunately casualties were light.[209] Many casualties were taken to ports on the Burmese coast, from where they were dispatched by hospital ship to India. Medical facilities in India were now organized into three distinct zones: a reception zone based around Madras on the south-east coast; a holding and treatment area, inland at Bangalore and Secunderabad; and a transit area at Poona, which was close to the major port of Bombay, the main port of evacuation to the United Kingdom. The policy was to treat all cases likely to be fit for duty within three months in Burma, and to send the remainder to India. In India, if a man was likely to be returned to some kind of duty within four months he was retained; if not, he was invalided home. It is a testament to the success of forward medical provisions that the scale of hospital provision in India was reduced by 2.5 per cent from the initial estimates. According to the DGAMS, Alexander Hood, this was due to 'the success in dealing with malaria and other preventable diseases, and the establishment of MFTUs for malaria'. [210]

On those occasions when evacuation back to India was required, it needed to be as swift as possible, not only to relieve the lines of communication, but also because it contributed greatly to surgical success. The employment of light aircraft forward of the CCS enabled the rapid transfer of wounded men virtually from the firing line, except at night, and in high-priority cases, such as chest wounds and abdominals, which were always sent to mobile surgical units. The most serious cases could also be evacuated to Bengal within thirty-six to forty-eight hours of wounding, making it possible to give practically every evacuable casualty the advantage of delayed primary suture.[211] Surgical practice was initially based on the experiences of surgeons in the Western Desert, whose achievements had been well publicized. Following their example, surgeons in all theatres proceeded as if formal excision of the wound

---

[208] CMAC RAMC 1117, 'Medical History . . . November 1944–May 1945', 30.
[209] Ibid. 31.
[210] OIOC L/WS/1/881, Report by DGAMS on a Visit to India and SEAC, 2 January 1945, pp. 1–4.
[211] CMAC RAMC 1117, 'Medical History . . . November 1944–May 1945', 37.

was unnecessary, or even dangerous. Infection was countered instead by early and thorough cleansing of the wound and a limited amount of 'trimming', together with the introduction locally of sulphonamide drugs. Such procedures worked well in relatively sterile environments, but the wound infections that developed in a large number of cases early in the Burma campaign made it clear that surgery in SEAC was a different proposition from that in the Western Desert. Shrapnel tended to carry not only clothing and equipment into the wound, but also jungle debris and dirt.[212] In addition to the usual gunshot and shrapnel wounds, there were also several injuries peculiar to jungle warfare, which were very liable to become infected. As two surgeons of No. 18 General Hospital recollected:

There were . . . a number of penetrating wounds caused by the bamboo spikes planted in the ground by the Japanese and intended to maim the Indian or African soldier, who was often inclined to dispense with his boots in battle. Ghastly wounds were caused by the Japanese torture, and a young Ishwka soldier came in with both his hands missing. These cases give some idea of the barbarity and cruelty of jungle warfare. The climate and general insanitary conditions caused much wound infection, and many of those surgical cases were in a dreadful state.[213]

Surgeons working in the Arakan campaigns began to develop alternative methods, more suited to jungle conditions. The procedure was that limb wounds were left open to relieve tension, and damaged muscle or bone was removed. No attempt was made to stitch the wound. The excised area was sprayed with sulphonamide powder and a protective layer of lint covered with vaseline was laid upon the raw surface before the appropriate splint or plaster was applied. Even abdominal wounds were left partially open, as infections developed if wounds were completely closed. As with limb wounds, the procedure was to clean the wound and leave it open for around ten days, after which it would be sutured. These procedures were very effective but few surgeons new to the theatre knew of them, and tended to plug such wounds with vaseline gauze, which invariably led to complications.[214]

The most pressing task of the Consultant Surgeon, John Bruce, was therefore to reverse the policy of conservative surgery and to emphasize the need for scrupulous primary attention to the wound, as well as the danger of relying solely on local sulphonamide and occlusive dressings. This was accomplished only slowly, but by the close of the Imphal campaign most forward surgeons were convinced that excision was both necessary and practicable. A surgical

[212] Ibid. 34–5.
[213] CMAC RAMC 877, T. D. Pratt and G. A. Bramley, 'The Story of the 18th General Hospital, 1939–45', 33.
[214] Baty, *Surgeon in the Jungle War*, 109.

conference held at Secunderabad in India, in September 1944, provided a further stimulus to primary excision, and after that there was sustained progress.[215] The whole process mirrored almost exactly the gradual realization amongst surgeons on the Western Front during the First World War that methods of surgery perfected in the drier climate of South Africa in 1899–1902 were quite unsuitable for the microbial fields of France and Flanders.

Radical excision of wounds, improved evacuation (enabling delayed primary suture), and the use, in limited quantities, of penicillin from November 1944 meant that survival rates for those wounded during the Burma campaign were good. During the first three months of 1945 there were 394 deaths out of 8,178 battle casualties, representing a survival rate of 95 per cent. This compared favourably with results in other theatres; for example, among British troops in the five months following the Normandy landings, the survival rate was 93 per cent, and in the Central Mediterranean Force it was 96 per cent.[216] But penicillin was by no means a panacea. The Penicillin Research Unit attached to 14th Army found that nearly 50 per cent of infecting bacteria were insensitive to penicillin.[217] Surgeons still faced some agonizing dilemmas, too. As Lieutenant-Colonel B. Lilwall explained, the policy adopted in the case of patients with penetrating head wounds was 'to allow natural selection to weed out those who were not worth wasting time on'. Those who survived, as in the case of other complex wounds like abdominal and chest wounds, fared very well due to the combined used of resuscitation and antibiotics.[218]

In view of the poor medical arrangements that existed in 14th Army at the beginning of 1942, the successful outcome of so many surgical operations was a considerable achievement, and one that conferred a great advantage on the Allied force. Surgical and medical treatment in 14th Army reached peak efficiency just as the Japanese medical organization collapsed. In the final stages of the campaign Japanese troops received scant medical attention, and many of the sick were left to die.[219] In other cases, the sick and wounded were killed by the Japanese to prevent the dishonour of falling into enemy hands.[220] It was very rare for the British to take control of a Japanese hospital with any patients left alive.[221] The one area in which the Japanese appear to have an advantage was first aid. As one British patient complained:

[215] CMAC RAMC 1117, 'Medical History . . . November 1944–May 1945', 36.
[216] Ibid. 38.[217] Baty, *Surgeon in the Jungle War*, 109.
[218] IWM 87/48/1, Lilwall, 'Clinical Impressions'.
[219] Slim, *Defeat into Victory*, 524.
[220] CMAC RAMC 814, 'Medical Services with 2nd Division', 61.
[221] Slim, *Defeat into Victory*, 473.

The Jap carried a small personal Medicine Chest, containing those medicines etc. likely to be needed during field operations. Whereas we only carried the first-field-dressing, and depended on the RAP for everything else. The advantage of the Jap method is that the man is able to cure himself in the earliest stage of jungle sores etc whereas our men usually carried on until they got really bad, and then had to be evacuated to hospital.[222]

Nevertheless, by the monsoon season of 1945 there was a marked difference between sickness rates in the Japanese army and 14th Army. In March 1945 Slim ordered that every Japanese POW was to be questioned about the incidence of malaria and supplies of quinine, and that blood slides should be taken wherever possible to show the level of malarial infection. Between the battle of Meiktila and the fall of Rangoon in August over 200 such slides were taken, showing the incidence of parasitic infection rising steadily from about 30 per cent to 49 per cent in the last weeks of the campaign.[223] Malaria was still the largest single cause of sickness in 14th Army, and there were 13,952 cases (24 per cent of all admissions to hospital) between November 1944 and May 1945. But the rate of infection was falling at a time when that of the Japanese was increasing. The total army rate fell from just over one per thousand per day in the middle of November 1944 to 0.23 per thousand in March 1945. Malaria increased again during the monsoon, but the infection rate was never higher than 0.6 per thousand per day. This fortunate outcome was attributed to the rigid enforcement of mepacrine prophylaxis.[224] By the middle of 1945 it was generally assumed that any soldier who had fallen victim to malaria had failed to take his mepacrine—a military offence. George MacDonald Fraser recalled one such incident in his personal account of the war in Burma, *Quartered Safe Out Here*. On reporting sick, the MO had accused him of not taking his mepacrine tablets: 'but when I pointed out that, like everybody else, I was a rich yellow in colour from swallowing the bloody things, he admitted grudgingly that they were not an infallible prophylactic. Half the section was feverish to some degree . . . '[225]

Other common ailments, such as dysentery and diarrhoea, were also kept at manageable levels. These conditions accounted for a large number of admissions—4,398 cases, or nearly 8 per cent of total admissions to hospital—but not as many as might have been expected given the nature of the campaign and the toll these diseases had taken at Kohima and Imphal. The

---

[222] OIOC L/WS/1/892 DGMS, India, to ADMS, War Staff, India Office, 31 July 1945.
[223] Crew, *Campaigns*, v. 647.
[224] CMAC RAMC 1117, 'Medical History . . . November 1944–May 1945', 48–9; RAMC 816, Col. W. J. Officer, 'Report on the Medical Aspects of the Operations of the 2nd Division for the Period November 1944 to April 1945', 25.
[225] George MacDonald Fraser, *Quartered Safe Out Here: A Recollection of the War in Burma* (London: Harvill, 1993), 164.

reduced dysentery rate was probably due to the high standard of hygiene that now existed in 14th Army.[226] The Director of Hygiene, on tour in the theatre, noted that 'British troops were so afraid of getting dysentery after one or two sharp reminders, that they prefer to taste the chlorine and so be sure the water has been treated'. He also observed that 'the sanitation was surprisingly good in view of the fact that the methods employed were mainly improvisations'.[227] It was, of course, much easier to maintain hygienic standards in static formations, and troops in the Army Areas therefore had the lowest rates of disease. The incidence of dysentery also varied among front-line troops, with the 11th East African Division and 19th Division suffering unusually high rates of infection, apparently on account of their poor standard of hygiene. However, the low level of dysentery and diarrhoea in forward areas was also due to the use of sulphaguanidine in bacillary cases. As with malaria, rapid and effective treatment proved to be just as important as prevention.[228]

The incidence of most other diseases during the campaign was similarly low. Compared with the situation in 1942–3, the amount of VD in the force at this stage of the campaign was negligible. The war in Burma was characterized by rapid movement and, unlike the Italian campaign, the troops had few opportunities to dally with civilians. For the same reason, Army Area troops in Burma suffered higher rates of venereal infection than troops at the front, sexual opportunity being the crucial variable.[229] Of the other diseases, the most important was typhus. Although there were only 768 cases of typhus between November 1944 and May 1945, the disease caused great alarm as it had a comparatively high fatality rate.[230] As Major-General D. T. Richardson, Director of Hygiene, explained: 'The disease has got hold of the soldier more than any other. He is genuinely afraid of it to such an extent that in battle he is tempted to avoid suspicious areas and not to lie down. This fear is engendered by the severity of the illness and to the high death date. The result is that he willingly adopts any measures which will reduce the risk.'[231] This was true at least of British soldiers, who seldom contracted the disease by comparison with African and Indian troops who often walked bare-footed, in spite of the risk of being bitten by lice.[232] The Chindits appear to have been an exception, and there were reports of several deaths from typhus occurring among British members of the columns in 1944.[233] The condi-

---

[226] See e.g. *The History of the Fourteenth General Hospital*, 43.
[227] CMAC RAMC 648, 'D. of H. Tour of Far East 1944–1945', 7.
[228] CMAC RAMC 1117, 'Medical History . . . November 1944–May 1945', 52.
[229] Ibid. 53.[230] Ibid. 71.
[231] CMAC RAMC 648, 'D. of H., Tour of Far East 1944–1945', 23.
[232] Ibid. 54–5.
[233] OIOC L/WS/1/892, DGMS, India to ADMS, War Staff, India Office, 31 July 1945.

tions endured by this force would have made it far harder to control lice and hence to prevent the disease.

Conclusion

'When for the first time in history a combatant officer was considered unfit to command a unit on the grounds that he had allowed his men to become ineffective through disease', wrote the DGAMS, Lieutenant-General Sir Neil Cantlie, in 1950, 'a new day dawned. The clouds of forgetfulness must not be allowed to overshadow the brightness of the day.'[234] Cantlie was referring to the determined effort made by William Slim in restoring his army to health. By any standards it was a great achievement, and one that illustrates the overriding importance in military medicine of good relations between combatant and medical officers. During the Second World War a new generation of commanders like Slim began to attach much greater importance to medical provisions for troops, in the belief that they would improve manpower economy and bolster morale. This new ethos was in keeping with both contemporary ideals of social citizenship—of the provision of a 'social wage' in return for service to the state—and the principles of man-management developed in such fields as hygiene and industrial psychology between the wars. The prevalence of these attitudes in SEAC ensured that new technologies such as mepacrine were exploited to the full.

Yet we must be wary of accepting uncritically the triumphalist rhetoric that emerged during and after the Burma campaign. Even if one accepts that different rates of sickness in the British and Japanese armies were 'one of the most important reasons why the Japanese were defeated',[235] it is quite another thing to claim that Slim and Mountbatten deliberately exploited their medical superiority by choosing to fight in the most malarious areas. There is no evidence for this, and Slim stated as much in his memoirs; indeed, there was probably no significant difference in the health of the opposing armies until 1945, after the 14th Army had completed its advance through the malarious 'Valley of Death'. Another point often overlooked is that 14th Army owed as much, if not more, to facilities for the treatment of malaria and other casualties in forward areas as to preventative measures such as DDT and prophylactic doses of mepacrine. The medical services of 14th Army reached their peak just as those of the Japanese began to collapse.

[234] Lt.-Gen. Sir Neil Cantlie, 'Health Discipline', *US Armed Forces Medical Journal,* 1 (1950), 237.
[235] Crew, *Campaigns,* v. 647.

6

Medicine Victorious: North-West Europe, 1944–1945

The Normandy landings presented some formidable difficulties to the medical services of the Allied armies. The evacuation of numerous casualties from the beaches, under heavy fire, and the care of soldiers injured or wounded in airborne landings were problems that taxed the best medical planners. But medical arrangements were in the hands of men who possessed a wealth of experience and who had learnt valuable lessons from the mistakes made in earlier campaigns. The medical services were also better equipped than before, possessing a full complement of medical staff, and generous stores of medical and surgical supplies. Aware of the need to maintain a continuous flow of men and supplies between Britain and mainland Europe, the Allies threw the full weight of their industrial and technological resources behind the campaign. This meant that medical personnel were generously supplied and normally able to rely on the rapid evacuation of casualties. This vital chain of support had sometimes been missing or difficult to maintain in other theatres of the war.

Of all the modes of transportation serving the front, by far the most important in medical terms was the aeroplane; over 100,000 wounded men were evacuated from front-line units to base hospitals within just a few hours of being injured, dramatically improving their chances of recovery. Deaths from wounds, the average time spent in hospital, and levels of sickness among Allied troops were all lower than in previous campaigns. Field-Marshal Montgomery (GOC 21st Army Group) acknowledged this when he wrote of the 'truly remarkable success of the medical organisation'.[1] But, as in other theatres of the war, the success of medical arrangements depended heavily on the military situation, and while this generally favoured medical work in north-west Europe, stubborn opposition from highly trained and desperate German troops meant that conditions were often far from ideal. On the Normandy beaches, and later at Caen and Arnhem, medical personnel

[1] Montgomery's dispatch in *London Gazette*, 3 Sept. 1946, quoted in F. A. E. Crew, *The Army Medical Services: Campaigns, Volume IV: North-West Europe* (London: HMSO, 1962), 560.

worked in circumstances of exceptional hardship and danger. Nowhere in northern Europe were the Allies given a free hand, and as Montgomery and his fellow Allied commanders acknowledged, the quality of German forces was such that they could be defeated in only the 'most overwhelmingly favourable conditions'.[2]

The Normandy Landings

The Allied landings in Normandy in June 1944 was one of the most daring and complex operations in military history, as well as one of the largest. Though approved, in principle, at the Casablanca Conference in January 1943, there was no definite plan of action for the landing and subsequent campaign (together known as operation OVERLORD) until the Quebec Conference in August. Final permission for the expanded force desired by Churchill was given in January 1944, leading quickly to the activation of the Supreme Headquarters of the Allied Expeditionary Force under General Eisenhower. In the four months preceding the landings the land, air, and sea commanders (Montgomery, Leigh-Mallory, and Ramsay, respectively) drew up plans for NEPTUNE, the amphibious landing, which was to take place between Cherbourg and Le Havre in the Baie de la Seine.[3] Medical cover for the landings was the responsibility of Sir Percy Tomlinson, the DMS of 21st Army Group, a combined Allied force consisting of the 1st US Army under Bradley and the 2nd British Army under Dempsey, together with British and American airborne divisions.

Tomlinson had been appointed to 21st Army Group in 1943, after a long career in the RAMC spanning both world wars. Immediately prior to this appointment he had been DMS at the HQ of the Middle East Force, where he had earned the praise of all who served under him. Recently knighted and an honorary physician to the king, Tomlinson was a medical administrator of almost unparalleled experience. Yet, at nearly 60 years of age, some felt that he lacked the vigour and flexibility for protracted negotiations with American and Canadian colleagues. At a meeting in April 1944 General Kenner of the US Army protested to Tomlinson about the 'inadequacy of the medical support in the initial stages and the late phasing in of evacuation hospitals by the American 1st Army'; Tomlinson was strongly reminded

---

[2] Max Hastings, *Overlord: D-Day and the Battle for Normandy 1944* (London: Macmillan, 1984), 14.

[3] For the Normandy landings, see John Keegan, *Six Armies in Normandy: From D-Day to the Liberation of Paris* (London: Pimlico, 1982); Carlo D'Este, *Decision in Normandy* (London: William Collins, 1983); Hastings, *Overlord*.

of 'his responsibility for *all* of the forces of General Montgomery'.[4] In his reply, Tomlinson admitted that he had had little to do, personally, with the medical planning of 1st Army, and explained that he had delegated the matter to Colonel Gorby of the US Army Medical Corps, whom he assumed had taken the matter in hand.[5]

Some looked upon this as evidence that Tomlinson was not up to the job, but such misunderstandings were common during the planning of OVERLORD, owing to the long hours worked and the absence of formal memoranda. In such circumstances it was easy for disparities to emerge and go unnoticed. By June, however, differences between the American and British medical services appear to have been resolved, perhaps due to the involvement of the DGAMS, Alexander Hood. The prospect of a repeat of the Gallipoli landings—when the seaborne evacuation had been completely disorganized—haunted him. He later recorded that he had 'made this problem my own very personal responsibility and wrote many papers on different facets of it'.[6] He was determined that there should be close co-operation between all the services and between the different nations involved. Thus, before the landing British and American MOs changed places in order to familiarize themselves with each other's procedures, and close relations were maintained throughout the campaign. The frequent exchange of information made mutual arrangements possible and brought about what one report termed 'the most happy, effective and friendly co-operation'. According to the report, these contacts more than compensated for any deficiencies that had formerly existed in medical support for US soldiers.[7] Canadian units fighting with British 2nd Army had their own medical units, but these were even more closely integrated with those of the British: half of 2nd Army—1st British Corps—was a combined force of Britons and Canadians, and these formations often used the same medical units.

But NEPTUNE was also a combined operation in the sense that it involved all the armed services. The success of the operation largely depended on the Sea Evacuation HQ under the ADMS Evacuation, who worked in conjunction with the Navy, the EMS, and the Movement Control Branch of the Army. Particular attention was given to the provision of light medical equipment, specially designed for use in an amphibious assault. This equipment had to be plentiful enough to allow medical units to function fully on landing, yet compact enough not to take up too much room on board ships

[4] CMAC RAMC 408/2/3, Tomlinson Papers, minute of a meeting between Gen. Kenner and Maj.-Gen. Tomlinson, 8 Apr. 1944.

[5] Ibid.

[6] CMAC RAMC 1338, Autobiography of Alexander Hood, p. 25.

[7] CMAC RAMC 1184/1, '21 Army Group, the Medical Services, June 1944 to May 1945', 3.

and landing craft. As most of the evacuation would be by sea, until air bases could be established in Normandy, it was necessary to train staff of LSTs (Landing Ship Tanks) how to load and unload casualties from DUKWs and other amphibious craft; this training was completed in the months running up to D-Day on beaches in southern England and the Isle of White.[8] When it came to D-Day, 21st Army Group was supported by seventy LSTs specially adapted for medical work, thirty-eight of which were staffed by the Navy and thirty-two by the Army.[9] In addition, one company of DUKWs was specifically allotted for medical work—one platoon for each of the three British beaches.[10] However, Alexander Hood expressed great unease about the fact that the bulk of troops would be evacuated in craft not specifically assigned for medical work; that is, in landing and other craft returning from the beaches. Hood managed to ensure that each landing craft was equipped with at least one man trained in first aid, and that each would be met in England by consulting surgeons who would evaluate immediately the gravity of cases.[11] It was anticipated that this would be enough to transport the estimated number of casualties: a total of 50,493 up to D + 14, or 25,296 American and 25,197 British and Canadian.[12] In the event the number was considerably less, among the British and Canadians at least, though Hood later concluded that the arrangements for medical evacuation had been left much to chance. If casualties had been higher, the weather less favourable, or if there had been more enemy interference, a medical disaster might have ensued.[13]

Medical provisions on the beaches themselves were inevitably quite basic, as there was no scope for the erection of large field hospitals until a secure beach-head had been established. The medical units that landed on each beach during the first day consisted of two FDSs, two FSUs, one Field Hygiene Section, two Field Transfusion Units, one company of Pioneers (for stretcher-bearing), and half a Corps Field Dressing Station to serve as a casualty embarkation point. It was also intended that a CCS would be landed on each beach on D-Day, but bad weather prevented their arrival until the following day.[14] To compensate for the lack of medical facilities on the beaches, there were four field ambulances sited across the Channel—one on the Isle of Wight and the rest along the south coast. These units acted as advanced dressing stations for resuscitation, while hospitals at the Channel ports func-

---

[8] Communication from Dr R. S. Morton, MBE.
[9] CMAC RAMC 1184/1, '21 Army Group, the Medical Services', 1–2.
[10] Ibid. 2.
[11] CMAC RAMC 1338, 'Autobiography of Alexander Hood', 26–7.
[12] CMAC RAMC 408/2/6, 'Provisional Estimate of Casualties requiring Evacuation'.
[13] CMAC RAMC 1338, 'Autobiography of Alexander Hood', 27.
[14] CMAC RAMC 408/2/6, 'Provisional Estimate of Casualties', 3.

tioned as surgical centres for wounds requiring immediate operation. This arrangement continued until general hospitals could be established on the other side of the Channel.[15] Up to this time all casualties were evacuated to Britain, except for those few cases whose survival would have been prejudiced by transportation.[16]

Cover for airborne operations on D-Day evolved separately, on account of the special problems that the medical staff of airborne brigades had encountered on previous operations. Airborne units landing in North Africa had been hampered by the lack of light ground transport and by the absence of medical equipment suitable for dropping,[17] although both of these problems were solved by the time of the landing on Sicily. Earlier that year, in May 1943, an Airborne Force Development Centre was established with a separate medical section. Its senior officer, Major R. West, took an active role in designing airborne medical equipment, such as folding stretchers and trestle operating tables, and reinforced plasma containers—all of which were standard issue by D-Day.[18] Glider transport was also arranged for Sicily to provide medical staff with specially modified jeeps capable of carrying stretchers and heavy medical stores, and similar measures were taken in all subsequent operations, including OVERLORD.[19] The main principle underlying airborne medical provisions was that airborne forces were the 'cavalry of the air', so their organization was modelled on that of the cavalry field ambulance, with two surgical teams plus nursing orderlies attached to each battalion. The method adopted following Sicily was that a lightly equipped medical section was dropped or landed with each battalion, and that the HQ of the field ambulance, along with two of its surgical teams, formed an MDS.[20]

On 6 June the 6th British Airborne Division was dropped on the eastern flank of the main seaborne invasion force, while the American 82nd and 101st Airborne Divisions were dropped to the west. The two brigades of British paratroops landed 9 miles apart in order to destroy gun batteries and bridges, and generally to 'infest' the area between the rivers Orne and Dives. An airlanding brigade of gliders came in on the evening of D-Day to consolidate the position.[21] The medical service attached to the British airborne division comprised three field ambulances, each of twenty men, including an MO

[15] CMAC RAMC 542/7/3, R. E. Barnsley, DDMS Southern Command, Lecture notes on 'Air and Sea Evacuation', given to Shaftesbury Military Hospital Medical Society, 1 Nov. 1944, p. 3.

[16] CMAC RAMC 471/7, Col. R. G. Atkins, 'Basic Principles in the Organisation and Handling of Medical Units in a Combimed Operation', 3.

[17] PRO WO 222/23, Brig. A. A. Eagger, DDMS 1 British Airborne Corps, 5 July 1945, 'The Development of Airborne Medical Services, November 1941–July 1945', 1.

[18] Ibid. 2, 7.   [19] Ibid. 5, 9.   [20] Ibid. 5.

[21] AMSM M/37, 'The Capture of the Orne River and Caen Canal Bridges: The Coup de Main Special Force'.

and a driver who were detached, if necessary, to form an ADS. Each of these, together with its corresponding RAP, had to look after patients until they could be evacuated to the MDS, set up by the main body of the field ambulance. Here there were two surgical teams whose task it was to give blood transfusions and perform operations until patients could be sent to general hospitals at the beach-heads or back in England. Each battalion also possessed its own medical officer and orderlies who performed medical work in the field.[22] More than a third of the medical staff attached to the airborne division consisted of conscientious objectors. While these individuals were unarmed, the rest of the medical staff had the option of carrying a revolver if they wished.[23] Fortunately these were rarely needed, as the Germans generally respected the status of medical personnel.

'Never before in history has a British Expeditionary Force left the country so well equipped medically', claimed one senior MO quoted in the *Evening News* on the eve of the landings.[24] These claims were justified in the main, but not everything went according to plan. The formidable difficulty of dislodging the Germans from their defensive positions on the beaches, and later from cities such as Caen, hindered the evacuation and treatment of casualties. As the general editor of the official medical history acknowledged, medical priorities had sometimes to be sacrificed, or at least compromised, in view of military necessities.[25] The landings and the subsequent campaign in Normandy also revealed a number of oversights in the medical plan, not least the lack of proper facilities for the treatment of psychiatric cases, which occurred in unexpectedly large numbers. But these problems were quickly rectified, and medics were generally under few illusions about the arduous tasks that awaited them. Most would have been aware of the appalling injuries inflicted upon the predominantly Canadian force during the Dieppe raid of August 1942. Having taken part in a frontal assault on highly developed defences, the landing force had been subjected to concentrated artillery and gunfire, which left few men 'injured by less than several jagged, explosively destructive, high velocity projectiles, affecting various regions and various systems'.[26] According to the consultant surgeon attached to Canadian Military HQ, it was possible that such horrific wounds could be avoided

[22] CMAC RAMC 695, '"The Red Devils": The Story of the 224 Field Ambulance in Normandy', 1.

[23] Ibid. 8.

[24] CMAC RAMC 408/3/2, A 'distinguished medical man' (probably Sir Percy Tomlinson), quoted in Elsie Ridell, 'If your man is wounded. This is how they care for him', cutting from *Evening News*.

[25] Arthur S. MacNalty, quoted in Crew, *Campaigns*, iv. p. x.

[26] PRO WO 222/120, Col. J. A. MacFarlane, Consultant Surgeon Canadian Military HQ, 'Report on Surgery in the Dieppe Raid', 3.

under conditions of greater surprise and dispersal than those at Dieppe. Otherwise, he warned, the medical services in any future amphibious operation could anticipate radial nerve paralysis in as many as 40 per cent of fractured humeri, and joint involvement in an almost equal percentage of compound fractures.[27]

Fortunately, the invasion force in June 1944 was better equipped and better informed than that at Dieppe; it also had the benefit of surprise and of tactical air support. Crucially, German resistance was less than in 1942, thanks to skilful deception on the part of the Allies which had led the Germans to anticipate an invasion further north. With the exception of Omaha beach, where a German division had recently moved for training exercises, Allied troops had relatively little difficulty in establishing beachheads. Of the 75,215 British and Canadian troops and 57,500 American troops landed on D-Day, the former sustained 4,300 casualties and the latter 6,000. In the case of the British and Canadians the number of casualties was rather lower than expected: an estimated 6.5 per cent of the invasion force, or 4,889 casualties. The American casualty rate, however, was considerably higher than the 3,737 expected.[28]

The first field ambulances landed one hour after the leading assault troops, whose medical care in the interim was entrusted to regimental personnel. At the same time as the ambulances came ashore, the light sections of the beach group FDSs were landed, and within minutes were receiving casualties. On D-Day, 1st British Corps (a British and Canadian formation) embarked no fewer than 1,700 casualties from Sword and Juno beaches, while 30th Corps, on Gold beach, where the fighting had been less severe but evacuation more difficult, embarked 200.[29] The wounded were conveyed back to England in specially converted amphibious vehicles and landing ships, most arriving in twenty-six to thirty hours, in spite of rough seas.[30] The speedy evacuation of wounded Allied troops contrasted sharply with the situation faced by the Germans, who found themselves unable to evacuate many of their wounded owing to the intense Allied bombardment.[31]

An impressive average of 80 per cent of Allied surgical cases treated during June 1944 survived, including 68 per cent of abdominal wounds with vis-

[27] PRO WO 222/120, Col. J. A. MacFarlane, Consultant Surgeon Canadian Military HQ, 'Report on Surgery in the Dieppe Raid', 3.

[28] These figures are calculated from the casualty ratios estimated by planners in the spring of 1944. The figures given here differ slightly from the original estimates owing to the fact that the force that landed on 6 June was larger than that originally anticipated. See CMAC RAMC 408/2/6, 'Comparison of British and US Casualties requiring Evacuation'.

[29] CMAC RAMC 1184/1, '21 Army Group, the Medical Services', 5.

[30] CMAC RAMC 1218/2/6, Brig. H. Glyn Hughes, RAMC, diary, entry of 10 June: 'Shipping still very difficult.'

[31] Hubert Fischer, *Der deutsche Sanitätsdienst 1921–1945* (Osnabrück: Biblio Verlag, 1984), 1664.

ceral injuries—notoriously one of the most difficult injuries to treat. In the coming months the figure was to improve even more dramatically.[32] Surgical success was due not only to efficient evacuation but also to the generous amounts of refrigerated whole blood available to medics on the beaches. During D-Day alone, five field transfusion units were landed, and five more the following day, together with 1,150 bottles of blood. Thereafter, blood reached the Normandy beaches by naval dispatch boat at the rate of 400 bottles per day. Wound shock was therefore much less of a problem than it might have been, as was wound infection, since penicillin was routinely administered from the beginning of the campaign.[33]

These figures convey nothing of the trials faced by medical personnel during the first decisive days of the Normandy campaign. Medical officers, many of whom had not seen active service before, were apprehensive about how they would discharge themselves in battle. As E. H. Lessen, commander of No. 21 FDS, of 5 Beach Group, recalled: 'An untried medical unit has difficulties peculiar to itself; individual and unit training has been long and as thorough as possible, but there remains a world of difference between handling and caring for an exercise casualty labelled G.S.W. [gunshot wound] Abdomen and a wounded man with his intestines protruding from a gaping wound in his stomach.'[34] When they landed on the beaches medics had mostly to work under heavy fire, using what little shelter was available. The beach dressing stations were overwhelmed with casualties. Lessen remembered that:

on the first night, some time towards midnight, I counted 60 priority II casualties awaiting or receiving plasma transfusion both inside the department set aside for this purpose and also outside lying stretcher to stretcher around the main medical centre vehicle circuit and in not inconsiderable danger of being run over by the DUKW amphibious vehicles collecting casualties. These numbers of course were dwarfed by the far larger numbers of walking wounded and less seriously injured.[35]

The main problem faced by medical staff was tiredness, as medical personnel worked for many hours without relief. Lieutenant Mitting, a young British surgeon, was typical in that he worked from 6.30 a.m., when he and his team established an RAP in the back of a lorry, until late at night. Although he should have been relieved that day, the expected field surgical unit had been unable to land due to rough seas. As one of his colleagues recalled: 'We got up in England at 0500 on Monday morning and stayed awake and working

[32] CMAC RAMC 408/3/2, 'Summary of Surgical Results—June 1944 (major lesions only)'.
[33] CMAC RAMC 408/3/2, Capt. H. K. Lucas, RAMC, to DDMS 2nd Army, 21 June 1944, memo. on 'Blood Transfusion Service, June 6–17', 1–2.
[34] Brig. E. H. Lessen, 'D-Day 6 June 1944', *Army Medical Services Magazine*, 38 (Oct. 1984), 83.
[35] Ibid. 85.

under arduous conditions until order came that No. 20 FDS could stand down . . . at 2400 on Thursday. We were then holding forty or fifty wounded awaiting evacuation so not everyone was able to get his head down.'[36] Some doctors found that the only way to keep going was to take Benzedrine tablets or 'pep pills', which had first been used in the Middle East to overcome extreme tiredness.[37] The initial dose was one-and-a-half tablets two hours before the maximum benefit was required, with a further tablet for another six hours.[38] In Normandy these tablets were issued to troops as a special ration, following tests that showed there were no serious after-effects.[39]

It was not simply tiredness that affected medical personnel; most were mentally unprepared for the hideous injuries inflicted by high-explosive shells. This was especially true of unseasoned stretcher-bearers, who were less accustomed than doctors to the sight of blood and gore. Aitken recalled that: 'The fellows in the echelon are helping and looking rather apathetic at their first sight of real injuries. They hesitate to lift a stretcher unless they can turn their backs on the injured.'[40] As for his own feelings at the end of D-Day, Aitken recorded that he was: 'Not very happy. Apprehensive and a bit shaken in spite of being accustomed to blood and all. That no doubt will improve, but I would much rather be in charge of a killing machine, than playing about with the wounded as a non-combatant.'[41] Forbidden all but imaginative retribution, military doctors sometimes felt what Aitken called 'a sense of impotency' at being unable to revenge the deaths of their comrades.[42] This must have been especially true of those, like Aitken, who were conscripted into the RAMC on temporary commissions, as opposed to those who had chosen military medicine as a career. But Aitken later came to appreciate the calm of medical work in the general hospitals that were landed once the beach-head had been firmly established, and he expressed surprise that some of their MOs 'would give anything to change for a job like mine!'[43]

Meanwhile, on the eastern flank, the medics of 5th and 3rd Parachute Brigades were attempting to cope with casualties sustained in the landings, and afterwards as a result of hostile fire. Three field ambulances dropped with the two brigades. No. 224 FA, commanded by Lieutenant-Colonel D. H. Thompson, was dropped with 3rd Brigade and established its MDS in a farmhouse near Le Mesnil. Here casualties were collected and treated until they could be evacuated to 3rd British Division. No. 225 FA, commanded by

---

[36] CMAC RAMC 1525, Lt. A. C. Halliday, 'Some Reminiscences of Operation Overlord—the D-Day Landings', 1, 3.

[37] CMAC RAMC 1668, Diary of Dr Aitken, RMO 24th Lancers, June–July 1944, p. 19.

[38] Q. V. B. Wallace, 'The Battle of Alamein and the Campaign in Libya', in H. Letheby-Tidy (ed.), *Inter-Allied Conferences on War Medicine* (London: Staples Press, 1947), 316.

[39] CMAC RAMC 408/4/3, 'Precis of Report on Results of Special Tablet Issued to Troops'.

[40] CMAC RAMC 1668, Diary of Dr Aitken, 15.

[41] Ibid. 13.   [42] Ibid. 32.   [43] Ibid. 34–5.

Lieutenant-Colonel E. I. B. Harvey, was dropped with 5th Brigade and established its dressing station near Le Bras de Ranville. No. 195 FA, under Lieutenant-Colonel W. M. E. Anderson, opened another MDS nearby.[44]

No. 225 FA worked under constant sniping and mortar fire throughout the day, but by 9 p.m. Major MacDonald of 3rd British Division had established contact and began to evacuate casualties back to the beach area. Some sixty wounded were evacuated from No. 225 FA during the first twenty-four hours. The MDS closed at 5 a.m. the next day, having admitted 380 casualties, but thereafter the situation became quieter, with only occasional shell and mortar fire.[45] No. 195 FA also encountered determined opposition. Its dressing station, which was situated in a large building at Le Mariquet, began receiving casualties almost as soon as it opened. The surgeons unpacked their equipment as quickly as possible and converted the cellar into an operating theatre, which was fully functioning by the next morning. By the end of the day there were 154 admissions, and twenty-three surgical operations had been performed. Luckily, the MDS was relieved of its wounded by the evening of 8 June, although hundreds of casualties continued to pour in over the next couple of days.[46]

Surgery at the dressing stations was primitive but effective: instruments were sterilized by holding them over a primus stove; the wounds were then excised to remove any damaged tissue, and dressed once bleeding had been controlled. Wounded limbs were placed in plaster and immobilized as far as possible. This not only reduced the pain, but also minimized shock and assisted in the control of infection. Amputation was carried out only when absolutely necessary, and then in as conservative a way as possible. The blast effect of high explosive coupled with the basic conditions of field surgery meant that infection was quite likely, and further amputation was sometimes necessary.[47]

Doctors new to combat learned fast, as J. C. Watts, commander of No. 195 FA recalled:

These men were learning war surgery the hard way, under terrific pressure, whereas I had been gradually initiated, with five years' experience before the Mareth Line battles, at which I had first met more cases than I could deal with. I was now astounded to see the rapidity with which a green team could settle down and almost become veterans in an afternoon. I do not recall that I have ever had to show them a procedure twice . . .[48]

[44] Howard N. Cole, *On Wings of Healing: The Story of the Airborne Medical Services 1940–1960* (Edinburgh and London: William Blackwood, 1963), 80–1.
[45] Ibid. 85–6.
[46] Ibid. 86–7.
[47] J. C. Watts, *Surgeon at War* (London: George Allen & Unwin, 1955), 88–9.
[48] Ibid. 90.

Watts believed that the keenness and ability of the young surgeons he commanded could be attributed in large part to the training they had received, in many cases for up to a year before the invasion. This was the general impression of those who served with the new men.[49] Yet the abiding impression left on those who took part in the airborne landings was one of confusion, at least in the first few hours, with indiscriminate shooting, the frantic search for wounded men, and the capture of some medical staff by the Germans.[50] This was especially true of No. 224 FA, which was dropped wide of its destination: 'No one knew what was going on,' its historian recorded, 'and once casualties began to pour in the situation hardly seemed to concern us.'[51] The medics at its MDS lived in a world of their own, 'quite cut off from the fighting which brought the wounded to the operating table, and detached from the process of evacuation which removed their patients in a matter of hours'.[52] Medical personnel were fortunate that contact with ground troops was made at a very early stage—as early as 9 p.m. on D-Day. Evacuation of casualties could therefore begin immediately, although the lack of ambulance cars initially caused some anxiety.[53]

Surgical work at the MDS proceeded satisfactorily, despite the constant explosion of mortar shells around it. All but a few casualties were operated on within twenty-four hours of being wounded, and this was later reduced to only ten hours when another MO was added.[54] Nevertheless, some serious cases died during the first few days because medical staff had to rely almost exclusively on plasma, which lacked the oxygen-carrying capacity of whole blood. Fresh blood could be kept for only one hour without refrigeration— a facility that airborne forces lacked. During the first week whole blood was used only in a few desperate cases, when it was obtained from volunteers among the orderlies.[55] However, wound infection, which had been a major problem in France during the First World War, was countered very effectively with local applications of sulpha drugs and penicillin, which were sometimes given in conjunction with anti-gas-gangrene serum in the comparatively few cases where gangrene was present or suspected.[56] The efficacy of these procedures is shown by the fact that, out of a total of 822 casualties treated by No. 224 FA between 6 and 19 June, only twenty-two died.[57]

---

[49] J. C. Watts, 84, 90; AMSM M/37 2001, Diary of Maj. E. H. McLaren, 1 July 1944.

[50] CMAC RAMC 695, '224 Field Ambulance in Normandy', 4–5.

[51] Ibid. 17.   [52] Ibid. 25.

[53] Lt.-Col. T. B. H. Otway, *The Second World War 1939–1945: Army Airborne Forces* (London: Imperial War Museum, 1990), 197.

[54] CMAC RAMC 695, '224 Field Ambulance in Normandy', 25.

[55] Ibid. 26.   [56] Ibid. 33.

[57] Ibid. 41.

The atmosphere in the dressing stations was one of relative calm by comparison with the conditions faced by medical officers in the thick of the fighting. The RAP of 9th Battalion was located in a stone villa on a slope facing the River Orne. Casualties were brought into a small yard at the back and dressed in a tool shed; at times, after a bloody engagement, the yard looked like 'the threshold of a slaughter house . . . blood-stained clothing and boots lay about in grim disorder'. The country around the RAP was known as 'Bomb Alley', and the bitterness of the fighting certainly justified its reputation. MOs received fulsome praise for their work under fire, and as the history of No. 224 FA put it: 'Those who had been conscious that the RAMC did not cut a very glamorous figure beside the fighting parachutists felt that they had come into their own; the changed attitude towards them was a matter of satisfaction, apart from the profounder satisfaction of working to save life when everyone else had the duty of destroying it.'[58] Brigadier A. A. Eagger, DDMS of 1st British Airborne Corps, also commented that 'one of the most striking features of British Airborne Divisions is the high esteem in which their Medical Services are held by the fighting troops and the active cooperation with them which is always present'.[59] The close bonds that existed between the medical and combatant personnel of airborne units developed as a result of working in isolation, and in close proximity with one another. In such circumstances, mutual trust and respect were essential.

Another interesting feature of medical work in the airborne brigades was the presence of German prisoners on the staff of British dressing stations. British doctors and orderlies formed a very favourable impression of these men, who were probably drawn from Salmuth's 15th Army rather than from the SS units located further to the east. They proved very useful in dealing with German patients, and according to the history of No. 224 FA: 'Their punctilious behaviour towards our officers disprove[d] the Intelligence maxim that to treat a prisoner like a human being is to make him disrespectful.'[60] The Germans, at the same time, impressed the British with their reception of enemy wounded, who were treated equally with their own.[61] Some mention should also be made of medical staff serving with the SAS, who were dropped behind enemy lines shortly after D-Day, well to the south of the beach-head, and who remained there for many weeks in medical charge of casualties among their own men and those of the Maquis. SAS medics moved from place to place, setting up temporary dressing stations as they went, always with the Germans in hot pursuit. They depended heavily on

[58] Ibid. 45.
[59] PRO WO 222/23, 'Airborne Medical Services', 12.
[60] CMAC RAMC 695, '224 Field Ambulance in Normandy', 27.
[61] Ibid. 108.

aircraft for supply and evacuation, with aircraft picking up casualties from areas still under German control.[62]

The overall performance of the airborne medical services during the landings exceeded expectations. Medical and combatant personnel had worked in harmony and, crucially, the dressing stations had been relieved of their burden of casualties at an early stage. The surgical establishment of the field ambulances was also found to be adequate, although in future it was decided to attach a trained anaesthetist to each surgeon, as many cases presented technical difficulties beyond the scope of a dental officer or regimental MO. Medical officers involved in the landings also suggested that surgical personnel and equipment should be detached from field ambulances to form FSUs, in order that surgical centres could be established closer to the fighting.[63]

By the end of D-Day 2nd British Army had established a firm foothold in Normandy and contact had been made between 50th British Division, which had landed on Gold beach, and 3rd Canadian Division to the east. Despite heavy mortar and artillery fire on the beaches, the Canadians had moved out from Juno some considerable distance, while 3rd British Division on the eastern flank captured Ouistrehem and made contact with 6th Airborne Division near Benouville. But the scene on the beaches was still chaotic: they were congested with troops and equipment still coming ashore and casualties being assembled for evacuation. The routes inland were filled with endless columns that moved with excruciating slowness, and the roads themselves often amounted to little more than dirt tracks. The constant traffic filled the air with dust when the weather was dry, and churned the ground into a quagmire when it rained. As the report on the medical services of 21st Army Group put it: 'Happy was the man who owned a jeep . . . the ambulance car often took an hour or more to travel ten miles.'[64] 'Had the DADsMS and clerks in formation Headquarters had time to think about it,' the report concluded, 'they would have imagined themselves in a nightmare of everlasting new problems and instructions.'[65] But no plan, however thorough, could have prepared the medical services for the difficulties they encountered; moreover, morale was high and 'No matter what the problem, or how difficult, there was someone to tackle it cheerfully and tirelessly. Experience was being bought but it was paid for readily and without grumble.'[66]

On 11 June the responsibility for medical services in the bridgehead fell on the DDMS of 2nd Army, who remained in charge until 13 July, when the HQ Lines of Communication took over responsibility for all areas in the

[62] PRO WO 222/23, 'Airborne Medical Services', 3–4.
[63] Cole, *Wings of Healing*, 107.
[64] CMAC RAMC 1184/1, '21 Army Group, the Medical Services', 4.
[65] Ibid. 4.   [66] Ibid. 4.

rear. It was not until 22 July that Tomlinson, as DMS 21st Army Group, appeared in the theatre to take overall control. These first few weeks saw the establishment in France not only of CCSs but also of general hospitals, one of which, at Bayeux, formed the nucleus of what became the main medical centre in Normandy. This hospital was open and receiving patients by 20 June. Five other 1,200-bed hospitals arrived at around the same time to take the place of the CCSs, which moved forward as the Allies advanced.[67] These large general hospitals formed what later became known as 'Harley Street'. But, despite the expansion of surgical beds in Normandy, many of the wounded were still evacuated straight to the United Kingdom, chiefly from Courseulles-sur-Mer at the centre of the beach-head. Until 13 June all evacuation was still by sea, with DUKWs and other small craft loading hospital ships anchored one or two miles off the coast. Thereafter an increasing number of casualties were carried from Normandy to England by air, and by 26 July some 7,719 cases had been evacuated in this way.[68]

Once they had arrived at ports on the south coast of England, all the wounded stretcher cases were examined by a surgeon before being allocated to various hospitals depending on the nature and severity of their wounds. This system of sorting casualties was increasingly known as 'triage', although some medical officers objected to the use of a 'foreign term'.[69] Men requiring urgent surgical treatment and unable to travel further were sent to hospitals at ports such as Southampton; the rest were taken to road or rail transit hospitals for evacuation to different parts of the United Kingdom.[70] To begin with, few patients received any surgical treatment before arriving in England and most still wore their original dressings. Around 20 per cent of these men had to be sent to the port hospitals, but the condition of the wounded gradually improved, and by the end of June it was exceptional to find serious cases arriving in Britain without prior treatment.[71] Conditions in British hospitals also gave reason for reassurance. Shortly after D-Day Churchill (who did not like visiting hospitals) asked his Deputy Prime Minister, Clement Atlee, to inspect arrangements at Portsmouth. Atlee was taken by Alexander Hood to see the arrival of landing craft and to various hospitals in the vicinity, and was apparently very pleased with everything he saw.[72]

[67] Ibid. 5–6.

[68] CMAC RAMC 524/7/3, 'Air and Sea Evacuation', 4; RAMC 1184/1, '21 Army Group, the Medical Services', 8–9.

[69] W. H. Ogilvie, *Forward Surgery in Modern War* (London: Butterworth, 1944), 6.

[70] L.t-Col. R. K. Debenham and Lt.-Col. A. B. Kerr, 'The Triage of Battle Casualties', *Journal of the Royal Army Medical Corps*, 84 (1945), 125–9.

[71] CMAC RAMC 471/8, Col. R. G. Atkins, 'Report on the Surgical Aspects of Casualties Disembarked at Southampton from France between 7 June 1944 and 6 July 1944', 1–2. During this period some 12,327 casualties were landed at Southampton.

[72] CMAC RAMC 1338, 'Autobiography of Alexander Hood', 27.

As 2nd Army moved out from the beaches, British and Canadian soldiers met fierce resistance from German troops who maximized the defensive potential of the *bocage*. The thick hedgerows of Normandy were ideal defensive terrain, and even tanks were unable to traverse them until American-built Shermans were specially adapted to do so. Unlike the heavily armoured German Panthers and Tigers, Allied tanks were also vulnerable to light, hand-held, infantry anti-tank weapons such as the German *Panzerfaust*, while German tanks and 88 mm artillery pieces proved even more formidable. Consequently, many Allied casualties during this phase of operations in Normandy were sustained in or near armoured fighting vehicles (AFVs), and some suffered burns in addition to wounds caused by shrapnel and high explosives. Such cases made a profound impression on the men who had to treat them: Aitken of the 24th Lancers recalled one such casualty, the sergeant-commander of a tank, who 'was badly burned on his right side, and the skin of his whole right arm was loose and well fried. There was nothing I could do for him except morphia, antibiotics, and wrap the arm in acriflavine gauze.'[73] However, as many MOs had found in the Western Desert, early intervention was often effective in the treatment of burns, and this was fortunately true of Aitken's patient, despite the severity of his wounds. MOs were greatly assisted by the fact that crews of AFVs were issued with first-aid kits which they used to treat burns and splint the lightly wounded, leaving doctors to attend to the more serious cases. Captain G. P. Mitchell, a medical officer with a Guards division, remembered: 'How often in the dull periods of teaching "First Aid" to tank crews at home I used to think "Is it doing any good?"' Fortunately he was 'amply rewarded on many occasions'.[74]

As the campaign progressed, the large number of AFV casualties prompted several studies of their causes and treatment. These showed that the Sherman tanks, which predominated in Normandy, were marginally more vulnerable than others such as the British-built Cromwell. In tanks hit by artillery, in which some of the crew were injured, an average of 55 per cent of the crew in Cromwells escaped unhurt as opposed to 35 per cent in Shermans; a greater number of Sherman casualties (46 per cent) also died from their injuries, as opposed to 33 per cent in Cromwells.[75] Yet there was apparently 'a lot of anxiety amongst drivers and co-drivers of Cromwells', who had 'difficulty in getting out of their rather small hatches';[76] Cromwell tanks were

---

[73] CMAC RAMC 1668, Diary of Dr Aitken, 14.

[74] CMAC RAMC 1449, Capt. G. P. Mitchell, 'A Regimental Medical Officer in Armour'.

[75] CMAC RAMC 1783, Capt. H. B. Wright and Capt. R. D. Harkness, RAMC, 'The Distribution of Casualties Amongst the Crews of Cromwells and Shermans', in *Reports of the Military Personnel Research Committee of the MRC (Sub-Committee on AFVs)*, 6.

[76] Ibid. 6.

also more vulnerable to mines on account of their floor plate being half the thickness of that in Shermans.[77] An examination of AFV cases treated in EMS hospitals in the United Kingdom revealed that 90 per cent had been injured by armour-piercing shells and that 25 per cent had received burns; a number of cases suffered both. Some of these injuries were regarded as preventable, however: 10 per cent were caused by commanders carelessly raising their head above their hatch, while many burns could have been lessened or prevented if crews had worn protective clothing.[78]

One particularly bloody engagement in this phase of the Normandy campaign was at Caen, where the Germans fought the British 2nd Army to a standstill. The city of Caen was central to Montgomery's battle plan, occupying a commanding position over the Caen–Falaise plain—the intended route of the Allied advance towards Paris. It was anticipated that the city would be taken shortly after the seaborne invasion, but the presence of 2nd SS Panzer Corps and other armoured units meant that the Germans could not easily be dislodged. This is not the place to enter into the controversy over Caen and the question of Montgomery's true intentions (he later claimed that he had always anticipated a protracted struggle to provide cover for the American breakout, rather than a rapid victory),[79] but it is clear from the medical situation that arrangements were hastily improvised and that they fell far short of what might have been expected for a heavy engagement with the enemy.

Soon after D-Day British and Canadian troops were deployed in a semicircle around Caen, but found they were unable to enter. The first concerted attempt to envelop the city—operation EPSOM—was launched on 25 June, utilizing the forces of 30th Corps and the newly arrived 8th Corps. To all intents and purposes the operation was a failure, since only limited gains were made in the form of a bridgehead over the River Odon and the capture of Hill 112, which soon had to be relinquished. Most of the Caen area was captured after an attack by heavy bombers on 7 July, forcing the Germans out of the northern part of the city and onto the other side of the River Orne, where they re-established defensive positions. Another offensive—GOODWOOD—was launched on 18 July after a heavy preparatory bombardment to the east of the city. The offensive was spearheaded by the three armoured

---

[77] Ibid. 7.

[78] CMAC RAMC 1783, R. Mangon White, 'Casualties in Armoured Fighting Vehicles: A Survey of Patients in Emergency Medical Service Hospitals', *Reports of the Military Personnel Research Committee*, 1.

[79] On the controversy over Montgomery's actions at Caen, see Alexander McKee, *Caen: Anvil of Victory* (London: Pan Books, 1964); Henry Maule, *Caen: The Brutal Battle and Breakout from Normandy* (London: David & Charles, 1976); Nigel Hamilton, *Monty: Master of the Battlefield* (London: Hamish Hamilton, 1983); D'Este, *Decision in Normandy*; Hastings, *Overlord.*

6. Jeep ambulance crossing the Caen Canal, June 1944, CMAC RAMC 1637/6

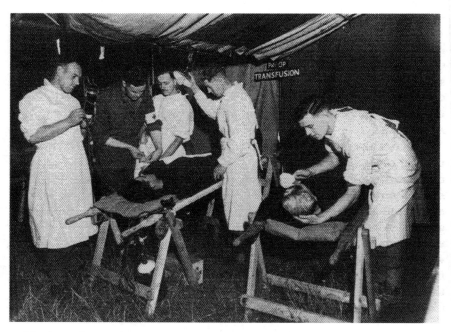

7. Blood transfusion at No. 13 FDS, Normandy, 1944, AMSM 2001: 62

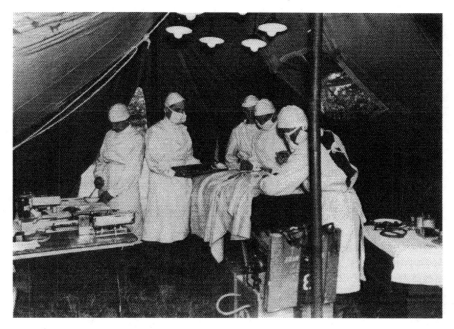

8. Surgery in No. 13 FDS, Normandy, 1944, AMSM 2001: 62

brigades of 8th Corps plus three others. After three days of heavy fighting the Germans managed to halt the offensive, establishing a formidable anti-tank screen east of the Orne. By the time Montgomery had called off the attack, on 20 July, the British had lost 4,000 men and 500 tanks; yet German forces had been contained, leaving the way free for the sweeping advance of the Allied armies.

The narrowness of the front during the EPSOM offensive meant that medical cover was organized on a corps rather than a divisional basis, the main principle being to open as few medical units as possible. Thus, the medical services at Caen had to rely heavily on the evacuation of casualties to larger units well away from the fighting, such as 30th Corps's CCS and the general hospital at Bayeux. In the early stages of the operation evacuation was confined to a single route with one MAC control point, but as the front widened additional routes were opened.[80] The constraints upon evacuation meant that it was extremely difficult for front-line medical units to relieve themselves of the large number of casualties inflicted among British and Canadian troops: 3,500 among British 1st Corps and 4,000 among 51st

[80] Crew, *Campaigns*, iv. 176.

Infantry Division.[81] Hill 112, captured at great cost to the Allies as well as the enemy, was literally covered with twisted corpses and burnt-out vehicles.[82] Those cases that did make it back to the base hospitals were often in very poor shape due to the severity of their wounds (most caused by high-explosive shells) and delays in evacuation; amputations were common.[83]

The fighting around Caen also threw up a large number of psychiatric casualties. The commanding officer of the 1st Gordon Highlanders was very worried about the morale of his battalion, continual shelling having made a number of men 'bomb happy'.[84] The number of 'exhaustion' cases had been growing steadily since D-Day, and this had led to the creation of a forward exhaustion centre for the men of 30th Corps, who would otherwise have been sent to the handful of special units in the rear. Lieutenant-Colonel T. F. Main, the Adviser in Psychiatry to 21st Army Group, reported in October that: 'All psychiatrists on the bridgehead deplored the lack of accommodation and personnel, which made it impossible to hold cases for longer than 48 hours.'[85] Compared with other aspects of medicine, psychiatry was comparatively neglected in the first phase of the campaign in Normandy. There were only four psychiatrists attached to the invasion force, with more to follow as and when required. The lack of specialists meant that many psychiatric cases received scant attention, and some were treated quite harshly by ordinary MOs. Mrs Mary Morris, with No. 101 British GH at Bayeux, recalled one such encounter between a young officer evacuated from Caen and the chief MO of the hospital, Colonel Cardwell:

Lt. Martin seems to be a little less withdrawn this morning. He smiled at me as I held his hand and talked to him. He looks so bronzed and fit, but he is a very sick boy. Col. Cardwell disagrees with me and thinks that he is 'swinging the lead'. John Cardwell is kind and competent in dealing with the physically injured. Why can he not see that the mind of this sensitive man has been shattered by the horrors he has seen here in Normandy. I wish we could get him back to England for psychiatric treatment.[86]

Though Main later complained about the shortage of psychiatric specialists in Normandy, this initial shortage was due, in part, to his own underesti-

---

[81] Maule, *Caen*, 63.

[82] CMAC RAMC 801/13, 'The Story of 34 Armoured Brigade (23 Light Field Ambulance)', 5.

[83] IWM 80/38/1, Mrs Mary Morris, 'Diary of a Wartime Nurse', I, 107, 101 British GH, Bayeux, 23 June 1944.

[84] Martin Lindsay, *So Few Got Through: The Personal Diary of Lieut.-Col. Martin Lindsay, D.S.O., M.P., who served with the Gordon Highlanders in the 51st Highland Division from July 1944, to May, 1945* (London: Collins, 1946), 13.

[85] CMAC GC 135/B.1, Lt.-Col. T. F. Main, Adviser in Psychiatry, 21 Army Group, 'Quarterly Report, October 1944', 2.

[86] IWM 80/38/1, Morris, 'Diary of a Wartime Nurse', 116, entry of 28 June 1944.

mate of the number of breakdowns that would occur. He believed that high morale and personnel selection would result in fewer breakdowns than in previous campaigns. Yet this has to be set against the fact that some felt Main's estimates were actually too high and that he had effectively accused British soldiers of cowardice.[87] He had to strike a very delicate balance between his professional judgement and military realities, and probably achieved the best that he could under the circumstances.

As in North Africa and Italy, psychiatric casualties were sedated and then interviewed by a psychiatrist, the only 'therapy' then available at the front being a break from the fighting. It was frankly acknowledged that this was inadequate, and as many as 85 per cent of cases had to be evacuated back to the United Kingdom, constituting a considerable drain on manpower.[88] By the time of the first major offensive against Caen admissions were still very numerous, according to Major Donald Watterson, a psychiatrist attached to 2nd Army.[89] Although they never amounted to more than 10 per cent of battle casualties, this was enough to overwhelm the limited provisions made for psychiatric cases in Normandy, and the majority of cases had to be evacuated back to Britain. By the end of June, after the first Caen offensive, it was clear that mass evacuation of casualties was having a disastrous effect upon manpower, and consequently upon the morale of units which had been denuded of men. On their own initiative, psychiatrists in Normandy began to establish forward treatment centres. This was welcomed by Watterson, the most senior psychiatrist on the ground, who seems to have eclipsed Main as the guiding light of British military psychiatry in the theatre.[90] However, Main did respond constructively to these initiatives by confirming the policy of holding and treating all recoverable casualties at the front. He also appears to have been instrumental in the creation of a Rest Centre for 2nd Army, which was opened during the first week of July, and in the dispatch of a personnel selection team which graded the fitness of casualties and gauged their readiness for return to duty. These measures, combined with forward treatment at divisional level, led to a dramatic improvement in the return-to-duty rate, from 15 per cent in June to 45 per cent in July.[91] The high recovery rate of many psychiatric casualties inflicted in Normandy, by comparison with those in some previous campaigns, was also attributed to the fact that

---

[87] Ben Shephard, *War of Nerves: Soldiers and Psychiatrists, 1914–1994* (London: Jonathan Cape, 2000), 248–9.

[88] CMAC RAMC 408/3/2, Maj. J. W. Wishart, Psychiatrist, 30 Corps Exhaustion Centre, 'Psychiatric Summary, Week Ending Sunday 18 June 1944'.

[89] CMAC RAMC 408/3/2, Maj. D. J. Waterson, 'Weekly Report by Psychiatrist attached to 2nd Army for Week Ending 24 June'.

[90] Shephard, *War of Nerves*, 255.

[91] CMAC GC 135/B.1, Main, 'Quarterly Report, October 1944', 2.

morale was high, and that the men were less inclined to dwell upon discomfort and were willing to return to the fray.[92]

With this in mind, it is interesting to note that that there were supposedly few cases of 'exhaustion' amongst the Germans, notwithstanding the severity of the Allied bombardment. Brigadier Glyn Hughes, RAMC, was puzzled by this, especially in view of the fact that 'our shelling and aerial attacks were much more intense than anything they produced'. 'We were certainly up against the flower of their troops,' he acknowledged; '. . . there is no doubt that they made their troops psychologically prepared for war; desertion whatever the cause was punished by death . . . Interrogation of captured German doctors, and direct observation of POW immediately after capture, showed that it ['exhaustion'] was practically unknown in both Panzer, SS and Wehrmacht troops alike.'[93] However, this statement contrasts markedly with reports that German POWs showed signs of severe nervous fatigue.[94] It appears that some cases of what would have been labelled 'exhaustion' in the British Army were diagnosed as organic complaints in the Wehrmacht. In the Wehrmacht, and still more in the SS, MOs may have been reluctant to report psychological cases, as such a diagnosis cast doubt on the bravery and patriotism of the soldier. Although the Wehrmacht seems to have dealt sympathetically with the few psychiatric cases that occurred early in the war, an increasingly harsh attitude became evident towards its end, as the morale of the army began to collapse. In the final phase of the war it was not uncommon for psychiatric patients to be threatened with execution or the concentration camps.[95] Some MOs may have therefore recorded only the symptoms of psychiatric conditions, such as 'heart disease' and 'gastric complaints', to protect soldiers.[96] It was also common practice for German psychiatrists to tell soldiers that they were suffering from physical complaints rather than mental ones, in the belief that this would encourage recovery, and this may also explain why so many apparently 'nervous' cases were recorded as having organic diseases. Treatment—often in the form of electric-shock therapy— also tended to focus on removing the physical symptoms of mental disorders.[97] It is important to note, too, that the mental state of the German army deteriorated sharply during the Normandy campaign, and so much depends on when reports were made. Hughes was commenting on an early phase of

[92] Charles Anderson, 'Psychiatric Casualties from the Normandy Beach-Head', *Lancet*, 12 Aug. 1944, pp. 218–20.

[93] CMAC RAMC 1218/2/11, Brig. Glyn Hughes, 'Normandy to the Baltic from a Medical Angle', 7–8.

[94] Terry Copp and Bill McAndrew, *Battle Exhaustion: Soldiers and Psychiatrists in the Canadian Army, 1939–1945* (Montreal: Queens/McGill University Press, 1990), 127.

[95] Hans Binneveld, *From Shellshock to Combat Stress: A Comparative History of Military Psychiatry* (Amsterdam: Amsterdam University Press, 1997), 129.

[96] PRO WO 177/316, Medical War Diary, DMS 21ˢᵗ Army Group, 1 July 1944 to 30 Sept. 1944.

[97] Binneveld, *Shellshock to Combat Stress*, 127–9.

the operations in Normandy, and not the period from the late summer when the German army collapsed beneath the weight of the Allied offensive. By the end of July psychiatric breakdown had become a serious problem, even amongst elite regiments such as the SS Panzergrenadiers. By this time few German troops in Normandy had the stomach for more fighting, and most could think of nothing but returning home.[98]

At the start of operation GOODWOOD, in mid-July, facilities for the care of psychiatric casualties had improved markedly, but the medical services still faced the enormous problem of having to operate in a narrow area. Because of the concentration of British forces in the congested bridgehead east of the Orne, all evacuation had to take place against a heavy stream of fighting troops and across two waterways—the River Orne and the Caen Canal. It was imperative that nothing impeded the forward movement of British forces, and so it was decided that no ambulance traffic should pass back over the bridges unless special permission was granted. The only alternative was to strengthen one of the footbridges so that casualties could be carried across it, before being transferred to ambulance cars waiting on an island between the Orne and the canal. Patients could then be driven to the hospital area surrounding Bayeux.[99] This was achieved, but only with some difficulty because of the heavy casualties inflicted by the Germans. Many of these casualties were due not to hostile fire, but to wounds caused by the mines planted as part of the deep German defences. A number of men had such mangled limbs that surgeons had no choice but to amputate.[100] Battle casualties were also accompanied by a much higher incidence of sickness than had hitherto characterized the campaign. Dysentery and diarrhoeal diseases were quite prevalent amongst Allied troops owing to the large number of flies that covered the battlefield.[101]

For some doctors there was also the unusual and unpleasant task of performing post-mortem examinations on some of the victims of alleged war crimes. Dr Donald Isaacs recalled that one SS officer, Kurt Meyer, had shot twenty-five Canadians and one Durham Light Infantry officer in a chateau outside Caen because they 'would not talk'. He performed the post-mortem examinations with a Canadian pathologist, and both seem to have been satisfied that Meyer had executed the men.[102] As the Allies encountered more committed Nazis in the form of SS soldiers, attitudes towards the Germans became increasingly hostile. One nursing sister recorded her feelings about

[98] Hastings, *Overlord,* 325–6.
[99] Crew, *Campaigns,* iv. 176.
[100] Watts, *Surgeon at War,* 108.
[101] Maule, *Caen,* 13; AMSM M/37, Capt. G. P. Mitchell, 'A Regimental Medical Officer in Armour During the Break Out South of Caumont', 3.
[102] Maule, *Caen,* 18.

a German patient admitted with gunshot wounds of the shoulder and forearm, who 'lost no opportunity of telling us that he suffered *schmerzen* (pain). My limited German fortunately precluded my telling him that the thousands of others who were in real agony and far worse *schmerzen* than he was had uttered no word of complaint. I suppose I was prejudiced but it was difficult to be patient with this man.'[103] Major R. R. Hughes, attached to one of the general hospitals on the Bayeux–Cherbourg road, also recorded an incident in which a British MO by the name of Braun, who was presumably of German extraction, refused to have anything to do with the German sick and wounded and denied all knowledge of the language.[104]

Breakout and Pursuit

The problem of how to deal with German POWs—of whom half were sick or wounded[105]—became acute as the Allies began their breakout from the Normandy bridgehead on 26 July. Operations from this time to the end of September can be divided into four stages: the combined Allied operations in the Falaise area, culminating in the crossing of the Seine; the pursuit of the German army through France and Belgium by 2nd Army; the advance of 1st Canadian Army up the coast of France and Belgium; and the Allied advance eastwards and northwards in Belgium and Holland, culminating in US and British airborne landings at Nijmegen and Arnhem.

The medical problems that characterized the first two operational phases were those caused by rapid movement, as the sudden extension of the lines of communication made road evacuation impracticable without staging arrangements and a greater number of ambulance cars than were available. Brigadier A. E. Porritt, the Consultant Surgeon with 21st Army Group, reported to Tomlinson on 4 September that: 'The phenomenal rapidity of the advance has rapidly lengthened the lines of evacuation. In miles, these are not yet dangerously long from a surgical viewpoint, but transport and traffic difficulties and enemy demolitions have made the time of evacuation to Bayeux longer than one would have liked.'[106] Specifically, he complained of poor weather, which had rendered the airstrip in the Canadian sector too muddy to permit aircraft to land and take off. The destruction of the

103 IWM 89/19/1, Mrs Ann Radloff, 'Going in to Gooseberry Beach: Travels and Adventures of a Nursing Sister', 5.
104 CMAC RAMC 1771/1, Maj. R. R. Hughes, 'Diary of Experiences in a Tented Hospital in France after D-Day', entry of 21 Aug.
105 Lindsay, *So Few Got Through*, 109.
106 CMAC RAMC 406/3/7, Brig. E. A. Porritt to Tomlinson, 4 Sept.

Mezidon rail-bridge over the Seine and the bombing of strategically important towns had also caused diversions and roadblocks.[107] Problems were also encountered when armoured vehicles moved off road. When armoured units moved into the *bocage*, medical half-tracks and dingo scout cars found it hard to keep up.[108]

Fortunately any cases of wound infection, which might have occurred as a result of delayed evacuation, were countered by penicillin, supplies of which were 'very adequate'.[109] This contrasted sharply with the situation in the German army, whose casualties often suffered from gangrene and tetanus owing to shortages of prophylactic serum and antibiotics.[110] Rapid retreat had also led to a deterioration in hygiene at German hospitals, most of which were crawling with lice and other vermin by the time they were captured by the Allies.[111]

The organizational problems experienced by the British medical services at this time were compounded by the inefficiency of some personnel. Major E. H. McLaren, serving with a field ambulance, recorded in his diary: 'Internal friction is increasing and I feel I must act. One MO who refuses to fit in—both regimentally and medically—upsets all our work. One MO here is inefficient both as an officer and a doctor—how do these people qualify?'[112] It was inevitable that a few bad apples would find their way into the barrel, but there was also said to be a more general problem with the officers commanding general hospitals. Referring to elderly regular officers and reservists called back to the colours, Brigadier R. H. Lucas, the DDMS of the Lines of Communication, informed Tomlinson that: 'From their arrival in this country, it has been obvious that many of them are not suitable to command a General Hospital and they compare very unfavourably with many younger Commanding Officers . . . For the most part their failures are due to lack of drive and initiative and to their inability to get the best out of the Officers and Men under their Command.'[113] Many of these men had served previously in tropical or sub-tropical commands and had retired early on the grounds that climate had impaired their health. As soon as the problem was brought to his attention, Tomlinson agreed to the removal of all inefficient officers.[114] But such men were the exception rather than the rule. The

[107] CMAC RAMC 408/3/13, 'Description of Medical Arrangements for Rapid Advance of British Forces North of Seine', 1.
[108] Mitchell, 'A Regimental Medical Officer in Armour', 2.
[109] CAMC RAMC 406/3/7, Porritt to Tomlinson, 15 Aug. 1944.
[110] Ibid., Porritt to Tomlinson, 4 Sept. 1944.
[111] Ibid., Porritt to Tomlinson, 23 Aug. 1944.
[112] Diary of Maj. E. H. McLaren, 12 July 1944.
[113] CMAC RAMC 408/3/13, Brig. R. H. Lucas to Tomlinson, 6 Oct. 1944.
[114] Ibid., Tomlinson to Lucas, 9 Oct. 1944.

medical officer R. S. Morton recalled that the commanding officer of No. 6 General Hospital, an 'old Regular', was quietly capable and ran his hospital well.[115] Lieutenant Robert Barer, temporarily commissioned as a MO with the Guards, also told his wife that: 'I think there's no doubt the RAMC is doing a magnificent job in the forward areas, under very difficult conditions. Despite everything there must be many thousands of people who owe their lives to their initial treatment. It's quite pathetic how grateful they are too. Time and time again they make remarks like "Thank God we've got such a medical service".'[116]

The most obvious solution to the problems faced by surgeons during the advance was to increase the number of hospital beds available in forward areas by the movement of hospitals up the lines of communication. But transport was at a premium, and the needs of the medical services were subordinated to those of the combatant branches of the Army, which were desperate for supplies and ammunition to be brought forward. The situation was not helped by the fact that general hospitals were cumbersome and difficult to transport. Reflecting some months later on the difficulties encountered during the advance, Tomlinson was convinced that:

The present 1,200-bed and 600-bed hospitals are quite unsuited for the necessary ease of movement now required in order to be able to be available early behind the rapid forward move of the present excessively mobile forces forming the British Armies both in the Western Desert of the Middle East and in North West Europe; nor are they suitable for combined operations such as occurred in Crete, Greece, Sicily or Normandy.[117]

Such hospitals were too unwieldy for mechanized warfare, and the shortage of transport meant that the quartermaster's branch tried wherever possible to 'veto the move forward of the bulky equipment and tentage of general hospitals'. As a result there was a 'great delay in the transference of hospital beds required for casualties requiring major hospital treatment' causing great hardship to casualties.[118] To alleviate the situation, Tomlinson recommended that the basic general hospital should consist of a composite HQ and four 100-bed sections, or a 600-bed hospital of three sections, permitting greater flexibility and mobility.[119] His willingness to rethink hospital organization in the light of the challenges posed by mechanized warfare shows that he was a forward-looking and innovative administrator, not the careless manager he was made out to be by some critics in the run-up to D-Day.

Tomlinson was also the guiding light behind the massive expansion of air

[115] Communication from Dr R. S. Morton, MBE.
[116] Capt. Robert Barer, *One Young Man and Total War—From Normandy to Concentration Camp: A Doctor's Letters Home*, ed. G. Barer (Edinburgh: Pentland Press, 1998), 118.
[117] CMAC RAMC 408/3/13, Tomlinson to Under-Secretary of State for War, 23 Feb. 1945, p. 1.
[118] Ibid.   [119] Ibid. 2.

evacuation, which occurred as the Allies secured airfields in Belgium and Holland. In view of the difficulties involved in transporting patients by road and rail, air evacuation was vital if front-line medical units were to be relieved of their casualties. Given the lack of surgical facilities in forward areas, and lengthening seaborne lines of communication, air evacuation was the only solution to the medical problems faced by 21st Army Group. Tomlinson therefore decided to return to the initial procedure of evacuating all but the slightest casualties directly to the United Kingdom.[120] It was necessary to ensure a steady lift of 500–700 cases per day in view of the shortage of beds in forward areas and potential casualties from forthcoming airborne operations. This objective was eventually achieved, but only after 'continued and urgent representations to very high quarters'.[121]

One of the main airfields for the evacuation of the wounded was at Brussels. It made quite an impression on those who visited it, as R. E. Barnsley, the DDMS of Britain's Southern Command, recalled: 'The Brussels airfield was seething with activity. Dakotas were arriving every few seconds and forming up a long line which stretched almost as far as the eye could reach. The ground staff were working all-out and were in great spirits.'[122] Back in the United Kingdom the wounded arrived in a regular stream, and there was not the same frenzied activity as in the ports immediately after D-Day, when 300 or more casualties had to be quickly unloaded from the hospital carriers before their return to France.[123] By the time Barnsley witnessed air evacuation from Brussels, a definite plan had been agreed and air evacuation had progressed from its initial 'hitch-hike' stage to one in which medical priority was established for the use of certain aircraft.[124]

Air transport also proved vital in alleviating the shortage of supplies and medical equipment in forward areas. These shortages were so severe at one point that they 'threatened disaster to Second Army'.[125] Army holdings were fast diminishing and Sparrow aircraft did their best to fill the gap by flying up loads from the rear. But representations were made sufficiently early to allocate enough aircraft for medical purposes, and while the demands of the medical services in forward areas could never be met in full, they were met sufficiently to forestall disaster.[126] Moreover, the medical lessons of the advance were well learned, and never again in the campaign in north-west Europe did evacuation or supply cause real anxiety.[127]

---

[120] CMAC RAMC 408/3/7, 'Evacuation Policy, 2nd Army Sector'.
[121] CMAC RAMC 1184/1, '21 Army Group, the Medical Services', 17.
[122] CMAC RAMC 524/7/3, 'Air and Sea Evacuation', 5.
[123] Ibid. 4.   [124] Ibid. 9.
[125] CMAC RAMC 1184/1, '21 Army Group, the Medical Services', 18.
[126] Ibid. 14–15.
[127] Ibid.

The general difficulties encountered by 2nd Army were the price of success, but those encountered by the airborne medical services at Arnhem were the cost of failure. The Arnhem landing was part of operation MARKET GARDEN, conceived by Montgomery with the object of outflanking the German defensive line known as the 'West Wall'. The operation comprised two parts. The first, MARKET, consisted of the airborne landing of British and American troops at Arnhem and Nijmegen in order to secure bridges over the Rhine; the second, GARDEN, consisted of the advance of Horrocks's 30th Corps across them. The British airborne landing at Arnhem was a model of accuracy, but from then on the fortunes of the 16,500 paratroopers and 3,500 infantry rapidly deteriorated. The remains of two SS Panzer divisions were refitting in the area and had just completed an exercise on how to counteract an airborne landing. As at Caen, intelligence reports of the proximity of these formations were ignored. It took British troops four hours to reach the bridge at Arnhem, by which time the Germans had been able to prepare their defences. Bad weather also prevented the landing of reinforcements from the Polish Parachute Brigade, while German forces succeeded in hindering the progress of 30th Corps. Although 30th Corps arrived in time to assist the American airborne divisions, which had succeeded in capturing the bridges leading to Nijmegen, it arrived too late to prevent British airborne forces at Arnhem from being driven back from the bridge. On 25 September the British withdrew, leaving most of the force—some 6,000 men, of whom nearly half were wounded—in the hands of the Germans.

The medical organization of the British airborne contingent consisted of two parachute field ambulances (Nos. 16 and 133) and an air-landing field ambulance (No. 181). As in Normandy, each possessed two surgical teams. The total medical establishment amounted to forty-seven MOs and 545 other ranks. The plan was, again, to hold casualties in divisional areas until they could be relieved by 30th Corps—relief which never arrived. Early evacuation of casualties was vital, since each medical unit was equipped with only enough stores to deal with the estimated number of casualties for forty-eight hours.[128]

The drop took place between 1–2 p.m. on 17 September. By 4 p.m. No. 181 FA had established itself according to plan in the Wolfhezen area, a few miles to the north of Oosterbeek; a dressing station was also opened in four small houses near the Arnhem–Utrecht railway line, and by the evening sixty casualties had been admitted.[129] No. 16 FA dropped intact near Heebum, north west of Arnhem, and moved straight to the outskirts of Arnhem, taking

---

[128] Cole, *On Wings of Healing*, 108–9.
[129] Ibid. 111; CMAC RAMC 696, 'Reports by Medical Officers of 1 A/B Division on Operation "Market" and their Subsequent Experiences', 4.

over the St Elizabeth Hospital. The latter was a well-equipped modern establishment with a normal capacity of about 300 beds, and the Dutch medical
staff willingly assisted the British.[130]

So far everything had gone according to plan, and there had been virtually no opposition from the Germans. But the calm was deceptive. Casualties mounted rapidly over the next twenty-four hours, and by 8 p.m. there
were 180 patients at the dressing station at Wolfhezen, forcing it to move to
larger accommodation in a former mental hospital. Throughout the day the
RAPs were working flat out under heavy fire, but evacuation by jeep to the
dressing station at Wolfhezen was going well.[131] Later that day orders were
given to concentrate all troops near Arnhem, leading to the relocation of No.
181 FA to the Hotel Schoonhord at Oosterbeek, which subsequently became
the main hospital for the area.[132]

On 19 September casualties continued to flood into RAPs and dressing
stations, but the medical team was coping admirably: the hospital at the
Hotel Schoonhord alone had facilities for as many as 300 casualties. The
wounded, too, were in good spirits, though frustrated at being forced out of
the battle so early.[133] At this point both surgical teams of No. 16 FA were
working at the St Elizabeth Hospital, despite several personnel having been
captured; No. 133 FA was running the annex to the MDS at Oosterbeek,
but half the unit was lost as a result of the drop and vigorous German opposition. No. 181 FA was still complete and running the MDS in the hotel.[134]
On the following day the situation deteriorated rapidly, with mounting casualties and many medical staff being taken prisoner. At this point the ADMS
of 1st Airborne Division, Graeme Warrack, realized that:

the medical situation was deteriorating: the 16th (Parachute) Field Ambulance were
in enemy hands in St Elizabeth Hospital . . . but very much reduced in strength; I
was out of touch with the 133rd Field Ambulance . . . the 181st were still functioning and had taken over no fewer than six houses, though unhappily most of them
were in the hands of the enemy; the RAPs were still doing magnificent work; and
the water supply had been cut off.[135]

The medical situation at this time was extraordinary. While Warrack was
working at St Elizabeth's: 'A German officer called to inquire about the
German wounded being treated there, one of whom a young Nazi, refused
treatment for a shattered knee for four hours until the pain became too great

130 IWM P. 7, 'Report of Work at St. Elizabeth's Hospital, Arnhem, September 17–27 1944', 2–6.
131 CMAC RAMC 696, 'Reports by Medical Officers', 5.
132 Cole, *Wings of Healing*, 112.
133 CMAC RAMC 696, 'Reports by Medical Officers', 9.
134 Ibid. 10.
135 Graeme Warrack, *Travel by Dark: After Arnhem* (London: Harvill Press, 1963), 32.

and he consented to the British tending him.'[136] Conversely, British paratroopers who had just been wounded fighting the Germans were taken in
some instances straight to a dressing station guarded by Germans, and then
returned to their own lines to continue the fight. This strange state of affairs
persisted for several days until the British withdrew.[137]

Over the next few days medical care for the airborne landing force became
increasingly untenable. On 21 September the Germans captured the MDS
at Schoonford and evacuation to the hospital area was no longer possible.
Buildings still in the possession of the British were under mortar fire almost
the entire time. As the medical report on operation MARKET recorded: 'It was
one of the most tragic experiences to see these men who had been wounded
in the battle coming to the medical services for help and protection and
finding themselves still in the firing line and even more exposed than in their
slit trenches.'[138] By the 22nd surgery in the remaining medical units had
become virtually impossible: there was little warmth or protection from the
elements, and fluids and morphia were in short supply. Many wounded men
were simply lying on the floor with only a single blanket to share between
two.[139] Private James Sims, admitted to a dressing station run by a Scottish
MO, Captain Logan, recalled that:

The scene was a grim one. The floors were carpeted with dead and badly wounded
airborne soldiers, more and more of whom were brought in every minute. Many of
the Royal Army Medical Corps orderlies had already been killed attempting to rescue
the wounded; consequently the survivors of this brave band of men were out on
their feet with exhaustion . . . The wound was cleaned and I was given an injection
while an orderly scribbled details of my treatment on a tie-on label, which he
attached to a camouflage jacket.[140]

This injection may well have been for tetanus or a prophylactic dose of penicillin; if not, these would soon have been administered. A. V. Tennuci, the
commanding officer of the MDS at St Elizabeth's, insisted that: 'Penicillin
undoubtedly saved the lives of a number of men hit in the abdomen who
had been left lying for days in houses because of the difficulties of casualty
collecting in the street fighting that was going on.'[141]

By 23 September Warrack felt that the best option for his wounded men

[136] Mag.-Gen. R. E. Urquhart, *Arnhem* (London: Cassell, 1958), 112.
[137] Ibid. 113.
[138] CMAC RAMC 696, 'Reports by Medical Officers', 16.
[139] Ibid. 17.
[140] James Sims, *Arnhem Spearhead: A Private Soldier's Story* (London: Imperial War Museum, 1978),
77.
[141] CMAC RAMC 1787, 'Memoirs of Col. A. V. Tennuci, through the Battle of Arnhem, POW
Camp and the Journey Home', 5.

was to hand them over to the Germans, who would place them in the hands of captured medical staff. He admitted to having 'qualms of conscience' about his actions, but felt that 'on the battlefield they could receive no proper care and even if relief were to come up soon their treatment would be delayed for a further forty-eight hours, during which time many would inevitably die'.[142] The Germans, however, were courteous and helpful:

The German G.O.C. appeared and stated 'he was very sorry indeed that there should be this fight between our two countries', he agreed to help over the matter of wounded of both sides. The ADMS and interpreter were given sandwiches, allowed to help themselves to stocks of captured morphia in the HQ, given a bottle of brandy to take away and finally sent off in the Red Cross jeep this time with an armed guard in attendance.[143]

The report goes on to confirm that British POWs were well looked after in the captured hospitals, as were the wounded left behind when the remnants of the airborne force withdrew behind the Rhine.[144] From 26 September German Red Cross personnel were also tending British wounded, the attitude of the Germans throughout being one of respect.[145] The author of the medical report (presumably Warrack) concluded that:

In the writer's opinion a great deal of help was given to the Airborne Medical Services because the Germans were so impressed with the splendid fighting qualities of the men who had been wounded, and awed by their great gallantry in the recent battle. It is also felt that many of the considerations were in the nature of a second string so that when the collapse which appeared imminent took place the victorious British Armies would find that the 'nice, kind Germans' had treated our wounded very correctly, and in the hope that this might off-set their other crimes. When the imminence of collapse passed, their attitude became, generally, much tougher.[146]

The report appears to be an accurate account of the treatment of British wounded by the Germans; indeed, some patients at dressing stations overrun by the Germans were given champagne on their arrival in German military hospitals.[147] However, their treatment seems to have varied considerably. When St Elizabeth's was captured by the Germans it was first placed under the command of the SS Division's dental officer—a man who was 'ridiculously Prussian in appearance and attitude: short and pompous, shaven skull, angry stoat's eyes in a contemptuous face'.[148] Under his command there was a great deal of interference in the running of the hospital, and little attempt

---

[142] Warrack, *Travel By Dark*, 72.
[143] CMAC RAMC 696, 'Reports by Medical Officers', 17.
[144] Ibid. 21–3.   [145] Ibid. 24.   [146] Ibid. 28.
[147] CMAC RAMC 1787, 'Memoirs of A. V. Tennuci', 5.
[148] Daniel Paul, with John St John, *Surgeon at Arms* (London: Heinemann, 1958), 16.

to improve the lot of the wounded. Tennuci recalled that: 'Our guards were young, arrogant SS men. They held us up as we tried to prepare meals and carry out urgent jobs, fanatically waiting on details from their NCOs. Our privileges as protected personnel, under the Geneva Convention, were completely ignored, as were the needs of the sick men we attended.'[149] Captain A. W. Lipmann-Kessel of 16 Parachute FA soon found a solution, however: 'Two particularly unpleasant SS soldiers were posted at my theatre door, but I managed to get rid of them by the simple expedient of performing an amputation right under their noses.'[150] After the battle at Arnhem had finished, the command of St Elizabeth's was transferred to another SS doctor, Divisionarzt Skalka, who proved to be far more accommodating—quite suspiciously so. Daniel Paul, a surgeon at St Elizabeth's, suspected that 'despite their having won the battle, he [Skalka] thought he would be wise to insure himself by a show of humanity'.[151]

Once they reached POW camps, British casualties could expect little in the way of medical treatment. Despite the Geneva Convention, the medical needs of POWs were a low priority for the Germans, who were now finding it difficult to provide adequate care for their own troops. The paratrooper James Sims recalled of Fallingbostel camp that: 'Medical attention of any sort was virtually unobtainable and anyone taken really ill just died. Indeed, the funerals each day became a sort of relief in the monotony of Stalag life.'[152] Major P. Smith, of 133 Parachute FA, later reported of the lazaret at Stalag XI B that:

The German supplies were utterly inadequate. This was largely due to the attitude of the chemist and dispenser. The latter was quite corrupt and the British had insufficient Red Cross material to bid high enough on his black market. At times we received only 100 paper bandages per barrack per week. We ceased dressing wounds at regular intervals when we had nothing with which to do them. Remedies for dysentery were almost non-existent and consisted of charcoal and tannic acid in very limited supply.[153]

Under such conditions it was impossible to do much for the patients, and the aim was merely to keep them alive until they were liberated. 'Making every allowance for the conditions in Germany,' Smith concluded, 'there was nothing to excuse the way in which they administered this hospital.' He closed his report with the last sentence of his diary of life in Stalag XI B: 'It

---

[149] CMAC RAMC 1787, 'Memoirs of A. V. Tennuci', 7.
[150] IWM P.7, Capt. A. W. Lipmann-Kessel, 'Report on Operation Market'.
[151] Paul, *Surgeon at Arms*, 15–16.
[152] Sims, *Arnhem Spearhead*, 106.
[153] IWM P.7, Maj. P. Smith, 'Report on the Lazaret at Stalag XI B', 2.

is hard, even in the hour of our liberation, to see anything good or pardonable in our sadistic detainers.'[154]

Into Germany

Preparations for the crossing of the Rhine began in mid-January 1945, with moves to clear the Germans from the area east of Nijmegen. A larger operation—VERITABLE—opened on 8 February with the heaviest artillery barrage of the campaign, enabling the Canadians and British 30th Corps to break through the German defensive formation known as the Siegfried Line. These forces reached the Rhine by 13 February, but clearance of the area to the north proved difficult due to stubborn German resistance and poor weather. The Germans did not withdraw across the river until 9 March, following a thrust by US 9th Army from the south. Operation VERITABLE cost the Germans 70,000 men and their foothold in the Netherlands, but the British also sustained 15,000 casualties. Many of these were 'exhaustion' cases: the consequence of a bitter and protracted struggle against the 1st German Parachute Army. The 53rd Welsh Division, for example, sustained 485 exhaustion casualties during VERITABLE, the largest single cause of casualties after wounds inflicted by high-explosive shells (1,047) and sickness (952)—mostly cases of VD contracted in Holland.[155] In this division two FDSs had to be set aside for exhaustion cases alone, some 52 per cent of which were returned to duty with their units without recourse to evacuation.[156]

It needs to be stressed that 'exhaustion' was, in many cases, a diagnosis of convenience; as the psychiatrist Charles Anderson admitted: 'Of the various terms used to describe the acute psychiatric casualties of the current war, exhaustion is probably the least true clinically. It was probably intended to convey to the man an impression of a temporary and recoverable state, and so to prevent neurotic prolongation of his emotional disturbance and his use of this as a weapon of escape.'[157] The factors that most commonly precipitated psychiatric breakdown, according to Anderson, were several days of

---

[154] Ibid. 7.
[155] VD cases were now dealt with in special treatment centres attached to each corps. Using penicillin, this produced 'revolutionary results': a man suffering from gonorrhoea was now likely to be away from his unit for no more than twenty-four hours, and from seven to ten days for syphilis. See CMAC RAMC 1218/2/11, Hughes, 'Normandy to the Baltic', 13. In addition, one condom was issued to each man as a matter of course, while brothels were placed out of bounds. See CMAC RAMC 1454, 'Standing Orders, Medical', by ADMS 1st Airborne Division, 1 Apr. 1945.
[156] Maj. A. D. Bolland, *Team Spirit: The Administration of an Infantry Division during 'Operation Overlord'* (Aldershot: Gale & Polden, 1948), 56.
[157] Anderson, 'Psychiatric Casualties', 218.

endurance followed by 'blasting by mortar and shell fire and the loss of comrades'.[158] The term 'exhaustion' was used indiscriminately to cover all psychiatric casualties in forward areas,[159] despite instructions that it was to be used only for breakdowns due to 'the gross fatigue which unrelieved tension engenders'. Technically, according to 21st Army Group's instructions in field psychiatry to medical officers, most of the cases described by Anderson—and which occurred during operation VERITABLE—were cases of 'free anxiety': anxiety states of apparently shorter duration, brought on by fear and the stresses of battle.[160] Robert Barer, serving with No. 128 FA, believed that witnessing the death of close friends often brought on such anxiety. He recalled one case where the man was 'so terrified that he tried to climb up the chimney of a farm house—like a hysterical dog'.[161]

The large number of acute psychiatric cases may have led some MOs to question the appropriateness of the term 'exhaustion', but by this stage of the campaign there was no denying the weariness amongst British soldiers. The infantryman R. M. Wingfield remembered one man who sustained a 'nice clean wound which would take him out of this hell for a while. As he made his way back to the Regimental Aid Post, the column chaffed him, envious of his luck.'[162] When admitted to hospital following his burial under a mountain of earth, Wingfield also encountered many patients in the RAP who were less than keen to return to the front:

Carefully they initiated me into the mysteries of the toothpaste, cordite and cotton wool 'rackets'. 'It's like this, mate. You feels fed up, so you goes sick. They're temperature happy here. They'd take the temperature of a bloody stiff before they'd accept it as genuine—You ain't got a temperature. You want one. Easy! As soon as you comes in 'ere, you take your toothbrush, squeezes a nice dose on the 'andle and you shoves the paste as far back under your tongue as you can. . . . Well, this little lot under your tongue froths like hell. When the thermometer goes under your tongue, Bob's your uncle! . . . The medics know what's going on, but they can't prove a damned thing. It ain't an offence in the Army to clean your teeth. The M.O.'s doing his nut.[163]

Wingfield was himself evacuated to Britain in February 1945, after sustaining a bullet wound to the hip and thigh.

[158] Anderson, 'Psychiatric Casualties', 219–20.
[159] F. S. Fiddes, 'Work of a Field Ambulance in the Battle of Normandy', *British Medical Journal*, 31 Mar. 1945, p. 450.
[160] CMAC RAMC GC 135/B.2, Psychiatric Technical Memo. No.1, 'Field Psychiatry for Medical Officers', 21 Army Group, Apr. 1944, pp. 3–4.
[161] Barer, *One Young Man and Total War*, 123.
[162] R. M. Wingfield, *The Only Way Out: An Infantryman's Autobiography of the North-West Europe Campaign August 1944–February 1945* (London: Hutchinson, 1955), 98.
[163] Ibid. 114.

Up until the crossing of the Rhine at the end of March 1945, arrangements for the evacuation of sick and wounded remained much as they had over the preceding months. But with lines of communication about to be stretched again, in the event of a successful crossing of the Rhine, many of the hospitals in Normandy were moved up into Belgium, together with advanced depots of medical stores. Convalescent facilities were by now also fully developed, and casualty evacuation appears to have proceeded smoothly, despite the obvious problem of having to ferry casualties back across the Rhine, which was achieved using amphibious craft such as DUKWs and Buffaloes.[164] The airborne landing, which occurred just after the crossing of the Rhine, also went smoothly from a medical point of view. Airborne units maintained close contact with ground troops to ensure an early link up, and the first airborne casualties were ferried back across the river to the CCSs within eight hours of wounding.[165] Yet evacuation was not without its hazards, as the surgeon J. C. Watts pointed out: 'Driving a jeep-load of casualties, one was between Scylla and Charybdis. The roads were abominably bumpy, but the intense fire directed at the buildings made it inadvisable to dawdle. The courage and phlegm of the wounded were wonderful as they gritted their teeth and suffered the trip without a murmur.'[166]

From the end of March, when 2nd Army broke out of its bridgehead on the east bank of the Rhine, the picture was reminiscent of September 1944, but with two important differences: casualties, though light, were heavier than before, and the army was now advancing on a much broader front. Yet the precarious balancing act performed by the medical services in the autumn of 1944 was not repeated. Although the distances were greater, it was possible to move sufficient medical units and stores forward to keep pace with the advance. The medical services had been allotted their own transport company, while air and rail could also move many units. By the end of April several general hospitals had been transported from Belgium into Germany, where they soon became fully operational.[167]

The maintenance of medical support during such a rapid advance was a great achievement, especially as the medical services in Germany were still under tremendous strain. As well as dealing with British casualties, they had to cope with thousands of POWs liberated from German camps, large numbers of displaced persons, and thousands of sick and wounded abandoned by the German army. All POWs and displaced persons hoping to return to their country of origin were medically inspected and dusted with

[164] CMAC RAMC 1184/1, '21 Army Group, the Medical Services', 34.
[165] CMAC RAMC 1218/2/11, Hughes, 'Normandy to the Baltic', 14–15.
[166] Watts, *Surgeon at War*, 123.
[167] CMAC RAMC 1184/1, '21 Army Group, the Medical Services', 34–5.

DDT powder, in order to prevent the spread of infectious diseases such as typhus down the lines of communication. The responsibility for displaced persons was technically that of the Military Government, but the military medical services provided invaluable assistance in the organization of sanitation and hygiene. A sanitary cordon was placed around Belgium and southern Holland, later extending along the Rhine–Isjell rivers, in order to prevent the movement of displaced persons—and hence of epidemics—into Western Europe. Unlike some of the pre-war cordons designed to prevent typhus in Eastern Europe, this was remarkably successful and there were very few cases of disease traced to those repatriated from Germany.[168]

The relief of German concentration and POW camps presented an equally difficult problem for the medical services. Belsen was the biggest of these, but other camps, including Sandbostel, Fallingbostel, Neuengame, and camps for Russian, Polish, and other Eastern European nationalities, had to be taken over and reorganized. In most of these camps sanitary conditions were appalling and the number of sick requiring attention was out of all proportion to the facilities available. The situation at Belsen was described vividly by D. T. Prescott, a medical officer with No. 32 CCS:

It was a scene of utter chaos with dead and dying everywhere and an estimated 6–10 thousand people dead on site. The fitter ones seemed to be wandering about—a lot of them aimlessly—in the blue and white prison pyjamas, which offered very little protection from the elements. Some of these could hardly shuffle and the odd one or two collapsed and died just as they lay on the ground.[169]

Huts designed to accommodate one hundred people housed as many as a thousand; there was no hygiene at all and no food or water had been issued for over a week.[170] During that time there had been a curious local truce with the British, whereby both sides made 'every effort to avoid a battle in the area'. The truce was made ostensibly to allow the Germans and the British to make arrangements to prevent the spread of typhus, the Germans having reported 1,500 cases at the camp. The agreement, concluded on 12 April, also permitted the Germans to leave the area, save a skeleton staff of German and Hungarian guards.[171]

When the British entered the camp three days after making the agreement they found that the German figure of 1,500 cases was a serious understatement. They found piles of dead and dying people, many suffering from star-

[168] CMAC RAMC 1184/1, '21 Army Group, the Medical Services', 38.
[169] CMAC RAMC 1790, D. T. Prescott, 'Reflections of 40 Years ago—Belsen 1945', 4.
[170] Col. E. E. Vella, 'Belsen: Medical Aspects of a World War II Concentration Camp', *Journal of the Royal Army Medical Corps*, 130 (1984), 36.
[171] CMAC RAMC 1218/12, 'Agreement with regard to Belsen Concentration Camp made Chief of Staff, 1 Parachute Army, Military Commandant, Belsen, and BGS8 Corps', clause 3.

vation in addition to infectious diseases. The dreadful scenes gave rise to reports that Belsen was an extermination camp like Auschwitz, especially as most of its inmates were Jews from Eastern Europe or political prisoners. However, it was an internment and labour camp rather than a death camp, and most of the deaths were said to have been the result of gross neglect rather than deliberate extermination, up to the last days at least.[172] The same was true of Sandbostel prisoner-of-war camp, liberated by the Allies in May 1945, not that this diminished in any way the horror and indignation of those who liberated the camps. H. C. McLaren, who was attached to No.10 CCS, recorded in his journal that:

I am writing this down in case I forget it. This is my second attempt and I have no doubt that once again it will be a poor result. To tell you about this horror camp I want a six hour talking picture. I want colour photography. I want it to be shown in the depths of an old foul sewer. The surroundings and effects would be realistic but still . . . you would never have touched the broken, shrunken men who had one day been ordinary people like ourselves.[173]

The day before the camp had been visited by an ADMS, Colonel J. A. Bearer, and 'although a World War I veteran and a pretty tough egg (CBE, DSO, MC and bars, etc) he had broken down and wept at what he had seen'.[174]

But those who liberated Sandbostel and other camps were aware that conditions there were not quite so bad as those encountered at Belsen. Lieutenant-Colonel F. S. Fiddes, the chief MO at Sandbostel, pointed out in his report on the camp that:

There are two main considerations which prevent one from describing Sandbostel as a 'Second Belsen'. In the first place, the numbers involved at Sandbostel did not approach the gigantic proportions of Belsen, the figures being approximately 8,000 as compared with 40,000. Secondly, the political prisoners at Sandbostel were all adult males, whereas about half of the inmates of Belsen were women, girls and young children, whose degradation added peculiarly to the horror of that vast abomination. Moreover, owing to the relatively short time during which the prisoners had been at Sandbostel, the corpses had not yet accumulated to form the appalling rows and even piles which so horrified the liberators of Belsen.[175]

Unlike Belsen, Sandbostel was essentially a POW camp. Some weeks before the liberation many of the ordinary prisoners were cleared out and political prisoners—mainly Russians and Poles—had been brought in. They were

---

[172] CMAC RAMC 1218/18, Letter to *The Times* from Glyn Hughes, 2 Dec. 1945; Russell Barton, 'Belsen'.
[173] IWM P 435, Papers of Prof. H. C. McLaren, 'Sandbostel Concentration Camp, May 1945'.
[174] Ibid., Letter from L. J. H. Horner, CBE, to McLaren, 2 Aug. 1961.
[175] Ibid., Report by Lt.-Col. F. S. Fiddes, No.10 CCS.

already in poor physical shape after a journey of six to eight days in which they were given practically nothing to eat or drink. Some 7,000–8,000 political prisoners were crammed into one section of the camp and another 15,000 POWs inhabited the other. Conditions were much worse in the political prisoners' section, where the men were crowded into huts designed to hold a total of 2,000 men. By the time they were liberated, several weeks later, most of the inmates were severely malnourished and gravely ill, riddled with typhus, dysentery, and other diseases.[176]

The task of cleaning the camps seemed impossible at first, and so for the first few nights the medical services concentrated on the distribution of food and water. Feeding the former inmates called for great care. The experience of British MOs during the recent Bengal Famine suggested that intake of food and fluids should be initially restricted in cases of starvation and increased only gradually. A maximum of two litres of fluid daily was deemed sufficient for the first few days. The ideal feeding regimen, according to Dr Janet Vaughan, a consultant haematologist who led an MRC team working at the camp, was 100 cc every fifteen minutes of a skimmed milk, glucose, and vitamin solution, given either orally or intravenously.[177] Some military doctors later claimed that this mixture was less than successful, and were critical of what they saw as insensitive experimentation on the survivors.[178]

Medical treatment of the survivors posed other agonizing dilemmas, as Brigadier Glyn Hughes explained:

Under the conditions which existed it was obvious that thorough diagnosis and elaborate treatment of individual patients . . . would take up so much time that only a small fraction of them could be dealt with and that to the exclusion of the elementary care of the remainder. The principle adopted was that the greatest number of lives would be saved by placing those who had a reasonable chance of survival under conditions in which their own tendency to recover could be aided by simple nursing and suitable feeding, and in which further infection could be prevented.[179]

M. F. Beardwell, a Red Cross relief worker at Belsen, put it more starkly:

A CCS doctor, who, in my estimation, had the most gruesome and difficult job of all, was to be responsible for deciding which patients were to come to the hospital. This was almost an impossible proposition—those whom he knew had only a few hours to live he had to leave . . . They crawled to him in hundreds and begged and prayed him to let them out; the stronger ones pushed and screamed their way over

[176] IWM P 435 Report by Lt.-Col. Fiddes.
[177] CMAC RAMC 792/3/4, Dr Janet Vaughan, 'Treatment of Prisoners Suffering from Starvation', report to War Office and MRC, 24 May 1945; IWM 91/6/1, Papers of J. McLuskie.
[178] CMAC RAMC 1790, Prescott, 'Reflections', 5; Paul Weindling, *Epidemics and Genocide in Eastern Europe, 1890–1945* (Oxford: Oxford University Press, 2000), 315–16.
[179] CMAC RAMC 1218/2/13, Brig. Glyn Hughes, 'Report on Medical Aspects of Belsen', 10.

the dead and dying and struggled to get on the stretchers . . . The clamouring masses were so great that they had to have decoy stretchers at one door of the hut whilst the doctor went in at the other and quickly grabbed a sick person.[180]

Within a few weeks treatment of the survivors was placed on firmer foundations when the medical staff at Belsen began to use a large German military hospital located nearby, together with the buildings of a Panzer School. This provided accommodation for around 10,000 patients.[181] In addition to this complex, there was a very efficient smaller hospital named the 'Glyn Hughes Hospital', after the RAMC officer in charge of medical relief for the camp. The hospitals were run by the RAMC in conjunction with the Red Cross, nurses from the Irish Army, and a team of British Quakers who helped with transportation.[182] Many patients did not survive the first few weeks, but the death rate dropped rapidly from 600 per day in early May to sixty per day by the end of the month.[183]

At Sandbostel camp a hospital was improvised in some huts about half-a-mile from the camp. It was under the overall charge of Lieutenant-Colonel Fiddes, who was aided by his colleagues in No. 10 CCS and around thirty doctors of other nationalities. German women were also impressed to act as nurses and assistants at the hospital, and were described as 'easy to work with and obliging'. But their willingness to offer aid gave rise to some uneasiness amongst the British MOs. H. C. McLaren recalled that the German workers bore little resemblance to the SS guards who had turned their guns on the prisoners before leaving the camp, but when he visited their quarters 'when one or other was sick those same black uniforms of the SS featured on their bedsides in photographs of their brothers or lovers'.[184]

As in Belsen, those working in the hospital at Sandbostel were unable to do much for the weakest patients. McLaren recollected that: 'In war surgery when a man comes in wounded 95 times out of 100 we can save him . . . In Sandbostel this was not the case. Our seriously ill cases died. We transfused with plasma and saline. We even let our continental colleagues loose with their beloved camphor but we were too late . . . It seems certain that many died of starvation 10 and even 16 days after our arrival.'[185] Apart from the weakness of the patients, the hospital at Sandbostel suffered from lack of lighting and sanitary facilities, and an intermittent water supply.[186] However, in just over a week the medical situation was under control. McLaren

---

[180] M. F. Beardwell, *Aftermath* (Ilfracombe: A. H. Stockwell, 1945), 39.
[181] IWM 91/6/1, Papers of Dr J. McLuskie.
[182] Beardwell, *Aftermath*, 44.
[183] CMAC RAMC 1218/18, Anny Pfirter, 'Memoirs of a Red Cross Mission', 11.
[184] IWM P 435, McLaren, 'Sandbostel Concentration Camp'.
[185] Ibid.   [186] Ibid., Report by Lt.-Col. Fiddes, 9.

recorded that that 'The Eighth day saw us with no crying on the ward, no shrieks of "Essen! Essen". Those who were doomed had died or were sunk into the typical apathetic state that preceded death from starvation.' The medical teams, including blood transfusion teams, were operating well, and the structural defects of the hospital had been corrected.[187]

The other major medical problem at the newly liberated camps was how to control infectious disease. Typhus was rampant in one of the two encampments at Belsen, known as the 'horror camp' (though not at Camp II),[188] and diarrhoea was almost universal, as were skin diseases. Pulmonary tuberculosis was also present among 6 per cent of those who survived long enough to be admitted to hospital, but may have been more widespread hitherto. Typhus was the most feared of these diseases but fortunately the easiest to prevent, as had been shown by the mass delousing in Naples in the winter of 1943–4. As in Naples, measures for the control of typhus in Belsen, and elsewhere in occupied Germany, were under the direction of a representative of the US Typhus Control Commission. He ordered that the entire population of the camp be deloused by 20 April, allowing the quarantine that had been imposed around the camp to be lifted by 21 May. Ten RAMC men at Belsen contracted the disease, but having been inoculated, their fever was mild and short-lived.[189] At Sandbostel camp No. 168 Light FA and No. 31 Field Hygiene Section constructed what they termed a 'human laundry'. The inmates entered at the 'dirty end', where they were divested of their clothing and had their body hair shaved; they were then washed and dusted with DDT powder before being placed in clean blankets and taken to the hospital. Around 300 patients passed through the 'laundry' every day during the first week of May; a similar system was established at Belsen and the other liberated camps.[190] The prevalence of typhus amongst the survivors provided further evidence, if any were needed, of the barbarism of Nazi Germany, as the disease had become synonymous with bad or tyrannical government. The Western democracies, by contrast, had shown themselves to be remarkably successful in controlling typhus wherever their armies had been stationed. Apart from a few minor outbreaks among POWs and displaced persons further to the West, the same was true in Allied-occupied Germany. Measures instituted at the camps and the sanitary cordon established around Western Europe helped to prevent the disease from spreading west of the Rhine. Mass delousing with DDT even managed to bring typhus quickly under control in Eastern Europe, once Germany had been defeated.[191]

The British Army's role in the relief of Belsen and the other concentration

---

[187] IWM P 435, McLaren, 'Sandbostel Camp'.
[188] CMAC RAMC 792/3/9, Brig. F. M. Lipscombe, 'Medical Aspects of Belsen Concentration Camp'.
[189] Vella, 'Belsen', 39.   [190] IWM P 435, Report by Lt.-Col. Fiddes, 6.
[191] Weindling, *Epidemics and Genocide*, 399–400.

camps, however, continues to arouse controversy. The largely experimental work of Vaughan and her MRC team lies beyond the scope of this book, though it does seem appropriate to make some preliminary comments on the conduct of the RAMC, in the hope that a more detailed assessment will be made in future. The RAMC carries the stigma of the implication that its response to the medical crisis in the camps was tardy and ineffectual, and that the agreement concluded between the Allies and Germans allowed the latter to escape and regroup.[192] This undoubtedly occurred, but the alternative—to delay the relief of Belsen until the Germans had been defeated—would surely have caused more deaths in the camps. On the matter of the medical response, the lapse of three days from the conclusion of the agreement to the arrival of the first medical teams does not seem unreasonable in view of the fact that the Germans were supposed first to complete their movements and then to demarcate the area at risk from typhus. The immediate deployment thereafter of a CCS and a light FA, and, within a few days, a general hospital, field hygiene section, and a mobile laboratory might also be seen as generous, given the likelihood of further engagements against the Germans. With the aid of voluntary relief organizations and captive labour, this small team managed to bring the typhus epidemic quickly under control, and within three weeks had provided hospital beds for 9,000 survivors. Their work in Belsen continued for several more months, during which the number of survivors treated in hospital amounted to 14,000.[193]

One curious way in which medicine contributed to the latter stages of the war in Europe was in the form of psychiatric assessments. British medical officers made a number of psychiatric assessments of the survivors of concentration camps, but their reports appear to do little more than state the obvious: that inmates had long since abandoned conventional moral norms and that their trust was gained only slowly in many cases.[194] Psychiatrists and psychologists also assisted in assessments of German POWs and civilians, with the aim of identifying those likely to cause problems for the Allied authorities. A study conducted in the autumn of 1944, on the basis of interviews with German POWs, predicted that 10 per cent of the German population would be active anti-Nazis; 15 per cent less marked anti-Nazis; 25 per cent modified Nazis; and 10 per cent fanatical Nazis ('idealists' and 'toughs'); the remaining 40 per cent being 'unpolitical'—people who would accept whichever rule gave them security.[195] The key was to learn how to

[192] Ibid. 394–6.
[193] CMAC RAMC 1184, '21 Army Group Medical Services', 38.
[194] Vella, 'Belsen'; CMAC RAMC 1218/2/13, 'Report by Maj. R.J. Philips to Brig. Hughes, 31 May 1945'.
[195] CMAC GC/135/B.1, Lt.-Col. H. V. Dicks, 'German Political Attitudes', Director of Army Psychiatry Research Memo., October 1944, p. iii.

recognize the typical Nazi, and to this end British psychiatrists built up a psychological profile. He or she was likely to be under 35 years of age; drawn from the lower middle class (clerks, tradesmen, students, schoolteachers, policemen, lawyers, provincial doctors, 'unsuccessful intellectuals'); show no positive evidence of religious belief; and possess a peculiar outward bearing. As Lieutenant-Colonel H. V. Dicks put it: 'There is something in the standard description of Hitler's "blond beasts", "the look of a bird of prey"— sharp featured, with thin compressed lips. Young Nazis can not infrequently be diagnosed on their arrogant, hard, cynical expression and bearing, their rather steely, unpleasant, fanatical, "reptilian" eyes, often very pale blue or grey.' Among older men, typically 'Prussian' features, that is, 'Thin, hard-faced, lined features, wiriness, an incisive biting type of speech', were thought to be more suggestive of Nazi sympathies that 'the fatter, merry, convivial sort of German'.[196]

However, the psychological studies of the day tended to see Nazism as merely the most recent incarnation of a primordial cultural type. In their 'Neuropsychiatric View of German Culture', the psychologists R. M. Brickner and L. Vosburgh Lyons declared that:

A dominant German Cultural Attitude has existed for more than one hundred years. The Nazis are merely its current expression. It resembles and behaves like the paranoid constellation in individuals, viz.: Systematized megalomania, sense of mission, suspiciousness, sense of persecution, retrospective falsification, projection, mysticism, lack of critical judgement, lack of humour, extreme use of rationalization, impeccably logical elaboration of original premises. The logical, and often the actual, conclusion is murder.[197]

Such statements were typical of the cultural stereotyping found in the numerous 'national character studies' produced in both Britain and America during the Second World War.[198] These studies probably did little more than reinforce existing prejudices about other nations, and for all their pretensions to scientific accuracy, they appear to have made little difference to the conduct of Allied servicemen in occupied Germany. Most were considered incapable of discriminating between Germans of different stripes and were asked to refrain from all but necessary contact with them. The Commander-in-Chief sent a letter to all troops serving in Germany that stated: 'It is too soon for you to distinguish between "good" and "bad" Germans . . . In streets, cafes, cinemas, etc, you must keep clear of Germans, man, woman and child, unless

[196] CMAC GC/135/B.1, 11–12.
[197] R. M. Brickner and L. Vosburgh Lyons, 'A Neuropsychiatric View of German Culture and the Treatment of Germany', *Journal of Nervous and Mental Diseases*, 98 (1943), 282.
[198] See John W. Dower, *War Without Mercy: Race and Power in the Pacific War* (New York: Pantheon Books, 1986).

you meet them in the course of duty. You will have to remember that these are the same Germans who, a short while ago, were drunk with victory, who were boasting what they as the Master Race would do to you as their slaves.'[199]

Before concluding this medical history of the campaign in north-west Europe, some mention should be made of the continuing role of the medical services in Germany and other territories that fell under Allied military government in 1944–5. For some years after the war the British medical services, along with their Allied counterparts, were involved in the task of 'health reconstruction'. In this, the military medical services worked alongside voluntary bodies such as the Red Cross, national health and medical services, and the United Nations Relief and Rehabilitation Administration (UNRRA). Planning for medical relief and administration following the liberation of occupied countries began in 1941 when, at an inter-Allied conference in London, it was accepted that in the event of victory these tasks should be the joint responsibility of the Allies. This led to the establishment of an Allied Post-War Requirements Committee, whose task was to estimate the immediate post-war needs of the Axis countries and countries under occupation. The work of the committee paved the way for UNRRA, which was formed in November 1943. In practice, however, responsibility for health administration fell most heavily on the Civil Affairs Administrations of the liberating armies. In Germany the British Army continued to have responsibility for some 700 camps containing more than 750,000 displaced persons, many of whom had contracted typhus, typhoid, diphtheria, poliomyelitis, and other diseases.[200] The work of the military governments and of international relief agencies has received very little attention to date, and regrettably falls beyond the scope of this volume. But the importance of this work, and of the political and ethical issues relating to the health of displaced persons, means that it is ripe for reappraisal.[201]

Conclusion

OVERLORD was the first campaign in which the British medical services were organized on the scale recommended by the Hartgill Committee. In broad terms, these new arrangements stood the test: thousands of men received

---

[199] AMSM M/37 2001: 62, 'Letter by the Commander-in-Chief on Non-Fraternisation'.
[200] Crew, *Campaigns*, iv. 92–104; A. S. MacNalty and W. Franklin Mellor, *Health Recovery in Europe* (London: Frederick Muller, 1946).
[201] One of the few recent studies to examine post-war medical work is Paul Weindling's *Epidemics and Genocide*; see ch. 13.

closure of their wounds within three to five days of wounding, as opposed to an average of ten to fourteen days in previous campaigns, and with a success rate of nearly 95 per cent after the bridgehead had been successfully established. This meant that a man with a flesh wound was normally returned to duty within six weeks. Such an achievement would not have been possible but for meticulous planning and the willingness of commanders to supply the medical services with the equipment, transportation, and personnel they required. Although problems were experienced with forward medical care during the rapid advance in the autumn of 1944, these were largely unavoidable and were overcome thanks to the co-operative spirit that prevailed among both medics and combatants. Moreover, the Allies were quick to learn from their mistakes and the serious deficiencies in medical supplies experienced by forward units in September never again occurred, despite rapid movement in later stages of the campaign.

Generous supplies of fresh blood and medicines, especially penicillin, materially assisted the recovery of the wounded. Indeed, the official medical history states that 'the most striking contrast between this and previous campaigns was in respect of the degree of control over the three great hazards to which the wounded man was exposed—haemorrhage, shock and sepsis, the greatest of these being sepsis'.[202] The medical services also deserve enormous credit for their part in the prevention of epidemic diseases in Western Europe, once they became involved in the management of displaced persons and those interned by the Germans. The prospect of a wave of disease—including the potentially fatal disease, typhus—spreading westwards was a very real one, and it is unlikely that the civilian authorities would have been able to prevent it had it not been for military assistance.

[202] Crew, *Campaigns*, iv. 583.

7

Conclusion

Reviewing the development of military medicine during the Second World War, the medical officer Anthony Cotterell noted that: 'The picture has not just been improved; it has been transformed. In some battles the badly wounded man's chances of recovery have been something like twenty-five times as good as in France during the last war.'[1] This was no exaggeration: by 1944 most casualties were receiving treatment within hours of wounding, due to the increased mobility of field hospitals and the extensive use of aeroplanes as ambulances. The care of the sick and wounded had also been revolutionized by new medical technologies, such as active immunization against tetanus, sulphonamide drugs, and penicillin. The importance of penicillin, in particular, is illustrated by contrast with the German army in 1944–5: lacking antibiotics, many German wounded were found to be suffering from severe sepsis, which was very rare in Allied hospitals where penicillin was administered routinely. As well as combating wound infections, penicillin radically improved the treatment of diseases such as syphilis and gonorrhoea, which had traditionally been amongst the chief causes of sickness in wartime. Following the introduction of penicillin, treatment times for syphilis were reduced from an average of forty or fifty days to less than ten.

Although the survival of British casualties depended to a great extent on immunization and the administration of new drugs, it owed as much, if not more, to efficient organization. This was especially true of arrangements for blood transfusion and resuscitation, without which forward surgery on a large scale would have been impossible. The establishment of the Army Blood Transfusion Service in 1938 meant that the British Army was the only army to enter the war with an organization devoted entirely to transfusion. The fact that transfusion became one of the focal points of patriotic sentiment during the war also ensured that it was given a high priority in the field, and that sufficient resources were directed to it. Other nations took far longer to develop the expertise and facilities that were necessary to provide transfusion facilities at the front. For example, whole blood was in short supply in the US Army during operations in North Africa in 1942 and the US medical

---

[1] Anthony Cotterell, *RAMC* (London: Hutchinson, 1943), 7–8.

Table 7.1. Admissions to hospital from disease and injuries in the British Army (per 1,000 strength)

(a) *South-East Asia*

	1942	1943	1944	1945
Disease	702	657	538	418
Injuries	49	38	42	32

(b) *The Middle East*

	1939	1940	1941	1942	1943	1944	1945
Disease	427	552	677	579	428	395	380
Injuries	50	42	92	92	75	38	41

(c) *The Central Mediterranean*

	1943	1944	1945
Disease	564	552	468
Injuries	133	173	94

(d) *North-West Europe*

	1944	1945
Disease	129	163
Injuries	92	64

Source: W. Franklin Mellor (ed.), *Casualties and Medical Statistics: History of the Second World War: United Kingdom Medical Services* (London: HMSO, 1972), 226, 239, 241, 244, 282, 432.

services were forced to rely too heavily on plasma, which was of little use in cases of severe blood loss. The contrast between the British and German medical services is far starker. Although blood transfusion was carried out in the German army from the beginning of the war, heavy bombing disrupted the German blood programme and little thought was given to the collection and storage of blood in forward areas. The deathly complexion of many wounded men captured by the Allies in Italy and after the Normandy landings shows that both whole blood and blood substitutes were in short supply.

There were significant developments, too, in the prevention of disease. Much had already been achieved in preventive medicine during the First World War, which was the first major conflict in which the number of deaths from wounds exceeded those from disease.[2] As Table 7.1 shows, this improvement continued throughout the Second World War, despite the fact that the British Army was fighting in some notoriously unhealthy areas, such as Burma and north-eastern India. Although hygienic and anti-malaria discipline was fairly lax at the beginning of the war, it was gradually tightened and ultimately gave the British Army a crucial edge over its opponents. The incidence of disease was high in some theatres, but rates of sickness were considerably lower than those in the German, Italian, and Japanese armies. The prevention of disease was aided materially by the widespread use of more effective anti-malaria drugs such as mepacrine, which were developed during the war, and by the insecticide DDT, which proved invaluable in Burma and Italy in the prevention of both malaria and typhus. These innovations, together with more effective treatments made possible by sulphonamide drugs and penicillin, meant that the ratio of deaths from disease to deaths to wounds in the British Army was as low as 0.09 : 1.[3] In other words, fewer than one in ten deaths in the British Army between 1939 and 1945 were attributable to disease; a quite remarkable achievement considering the heavy casualties of previous wars.

The military benefits of these scientific and technological advances are obvious, and there was good reason for the optimistic outlook of many medical practitioners during and immediately after the war. The successful application of DDT, for example, led many to anticipate not only the control, but also the eradication of malaria and other vector-borne diseases. Similarly penicillin, which cured a far wider range of infections than any previous drug, was the nearest the medical profession had ever come to possessing a 'magic bullet'. But the medical war was not won with bullets alone; even the most effective drugs counted for little if military and organizational factors hindered their distribution and administration. The Second World War shows that an army in disarray, or undergoing rapid retreat, finds it extremely difficult to implement effective measures for the prevention of disease and treatment of the sick and wounded. Yet such difficulties were never insurmountable. The British Army experienced all the problems normally associated with a defeated and dispirited army during 1940–2, but it never suffered the complete collapse in medical arrangements that occurred in the German and Japanese armies at the end of the war. It came close to collapse in the India–Burma theatre in 1942, but shortages of medical personnel were gradually overcome by efficient organization and strict sanitary discipline.

[2] Roger Cooter, 'War and Modern Medicine', in W. F. Bynum and R. Porter (eds.), *Companion Encyclopedia of the History of Medicine* (London: Routledge, 1994), 1542–3.
[3] *Ibid.*

The success of medical arrangements in wartime depended very largely on the attitudes of commanders: on whether or not they were prepared to give medicine the high priority it deserved. It was this 'culture of command', rather than simply advances in science and technology, which was *the* crucial variable in the success of medical arrangements. One could cite many examples to reinforce this point, not least the differing degrees of success with which Wingate and Slim tackled the problem of disease in Burma and northeastern India. But perhaps the clearest example is that of the British and Axis armies that fought the second battle of El Alamein in October 1942. In the twelve months preceding the battle the German army had a sickness rate nearly three times as high as the British, and during the battle itself nearly one in five Germans were listed as sick. As the opposing forces were otherwise evenly balanced, this was undoubtedly a significant advantage for the British. Moreover, this disparity developed despite the fact that the British and the Germans possessed much the same technologies of disease prevention. Although the British anti-typhoid vaccine was probably more effective than that of the Germans and the Italians, the diseases responsible for most of the sickness in the Western Desert were not typhoid fevers but dysentery and diarrhoea. The latter were diseases for which no vaccine or inoculation was available and which could only be prevented by good personal hygiene and sanitation. This depended, in turn, on strong leadership and a high level of sanitary awareness among soldiers. Despite their legendary prowess in battle, Rommel and the Afrika Korps showed little interest in sanitation and paid the price.

One cannot be certain why Rommel paid so little attention to hygiene and sanitation, but it may have been due to his style of leadership and his relative neglect of organizational matters by comparison with tactics. There also appears to have been an attitude—pervasive among Rommel's junior officers—which treated sanitary matters as beneath the dignity of fighting troops. But such attitudes were the exception rather than the rule during the Second World War. The majority of officers in all armies seem to have taken medical matters seriously, for the armed forces, like sections of industry and public administration, had come to view medicine as a resource that could maximize the potential of manpower. This interest in medicine was dictated, to some extent, by the logic of modern warfare; or more specifically, of 'total war', which required the mobilization of the entire population—military and civilian—in the war effort. With manpower at a premium, commanders came to see that military success depended on keeping their soldiers fit for service. Yet German doctors seem generally to have worked in a less favourable environment than their British counterparts. The medical services ranked lower on the Wehrmacht's list of priorities, and they were comparatively poorly equipped. Although a good air evacuation system compensated for some of these shortcomings in the first years of the war, the indequacies of German front-line medical provisions became increasingly apparent as the war drew to a close.

Forward treatment facilities were, in many respects, the touchstone of military medical efficiency. Forward treatment had been pioneered in the First World War by the consultant surgeon Sir Anthony Bowlby, who was instrumental in ensuring that the majority of casualties were treated in casualty clearing stations near the front, rather than at hospitals at the base or in the United Kingdom. In the coming years these provisions became increasingly specialized, after it became clear that certain kinds of casualty—such as psychiatric and gas casualties—could be treated more effectively in units staffed by experts. The same was true of the Second World War, during which the development of new forms of forward surgery, such as maxillo-facial and neurosurgery, enabled complex operations to be conducted as far forward as field ambulances. As in the First World War, most of these developments were overseen by specialists—in the form of consultants and advisors—who saw in war an opportunity to advance their professional interests. It would be too simplistic to conclude that the Second World War was 'good for medicine',[4] yet some medical specialties undoubtedly improved their status and secured more resources as a result of their relevance to combat; albeit, in some cases, only for the duration of the war. One such was psychiatry, which, despite the high incidence of 'war neuroses' in 1914–18, was relatively neglected in military circles at the beginning of the Second World War. After the campaigns of 1940–1 it became clear that provisions for psychiatric casualties in forward areas were negligible and unable to cope with the 10–15 per cent of battle casualties that were generally of this type. Many of these cases were not treated effectively and had to be discharged from the Army; indeed, 40 per cent of medical discharges during the war were for psychiatric reasons.[5] The turning-point came in North Africa, following the breakdown of entire units; this paved the way for the appointment of psychiatrists in forward areas, a move that was initially resented by many regimental officers, medical as well as combatant. Despite widespread scepticism, the psychiatrists succeeded in returning the majority of their 'exhaustion' cases to duty, often within days of their evacuation from the front. This was a great achievement, although, as psychiatrists acknowledged at the time, their success owed much to the fact that soldiers regarded the war as both winnable and just, as well as to the remote prospect of any material reward in the form of pensions in the event of invalidity.

---

[4] For a fuller discussion of war and medical innovation, see Roger Cooter, 'Medicine and the Goodness of War', *Canadian Bulletin of Medical History*, 12 (1990), 147–59.

[5] John Ellis, *The Sharp End of War: The Fighting Man in World War II* (London: David & Charles, 1980), 246.

Psychiatrists lost many of the professional gains they had made in the armed services once the war had ended, but at least one aspect of their work—the selection of personnel though intelligence, aptitude, and psychological testing—had a lasting effect upon military and civilian life. Personnel selection came to the fore during the Second World War because it was generally recognized that modern warfare required that infantrymen, quite apart from technical specialists, be capable of operating sophisticated weapons and, to some degree, of acting on their own initiative. As Major-General Sir Ernest Cowell memorably remarked in 1943: 'The modern soldier is not a body; he is a highly trained specialist, a man taught to think for himself.'[6] Although many—not least, Churchill—were sceptical of the grandiose claims made for testing by some psychiatrists, aptitude and intelligence testing remained important elements of military recruitment during and after the war, and were later to form the basis of entrance examinations for the Civil Service and other civilian organizations. Incidentally, this is very much what Ronald Adam had hoped when he argued for the introduction of personnel selection in 1941–2.

But the most important change in military medicine during 1939–45 was not so much the growth of medical specialties like psychiatry, as the creation of more mobile and flexible medical units. Mechanized warfare required that medical units become more mobile than those used in the First World War, so cumbersome general hospitals and CCSs were phased out or broken into smaller and more mobile units. This was a problem that faced all armies, but the British appear to have tackled it as, if not more effectively, than the Germans, for example. In some theatres, like the Western Desert, GHs and CCSs became practically obsolete, as the majority of work was done at the level of the field ambulance. Field surgical and malaria treatment units were also fully motorized and able to keep pace with armoured divisions; the same was true of regimental MOs, who were given their own motorized transport. When it came to organizing forward treatment, flexibility was just as important as mobility; medical units were of most use if they could be separated or added to formations, as the occasion required. This trend culminated in the Corps Medical Centre, which came into being during the Burma campaign. These centres were composed of many specialist units, which could be detached if necessary when the army moved forward. Medical units moved forward in stages to form new centres, leaving a skeleton staff further back. However, such units treated the lightly wounded and the least serious medical cases only; those requiring urgent or complex operations were flown immediately to hospitals at the base. This became the pattern in all theatres during

---

[6] CMAC RAMC 466/36, Cowell, memo. on health to combatants, 16 Dec. 1943.

1944–5, as the number of transport aircraft increased and once air superiority had been established.

The main driving force behind medical provisions in the British, as in all other armies, was the conservation of manpower. But this was not the only consideration. During the First World War it was recognized that medicine was a vital factor in morale on the battlefield, and that good medical provisions for soldiers also contributed to 'the happiness and confidence of our population in their homes'.[7] The relationship between medicine and morale was even more apparent during the Second World War, because the provision of medical care for British soldiers was inseparable from wartime propaganda that emphasized equality of sacrifice and collective endeavour against the enemy.[8] In democratic countries like Britain, health care was an important unifying force; as Richard Titmuss commented in his *Essays on 'The Welfare State'* (1958): 'The aims and content of social policy, both in peace and war, are . . . determined—at least to a substantial extent—by how far the co-operation of the masses is essential to the prosecution of war.'[9] Titmuss may, perhaps, have neglected other imperatives behind social policy but it is true that military medicine formed part of a broader strategy that aimed to unite British society; health care was seen as a kind of 'social wage' that could be earned by participation in the war effort.

These ideas had been expressed often in the years since the First World War, and had some impact upon a new generation of officers that came to occupy senior positions during 1939–45. Slim and Montgomery, for instance, were keenly aware of the contribution that good medical provisions could make to morale and unit cohesion; a view shared by the Adjutant-General, Sir Ronald Adam, who did much to improve the welfare of soldiers.[10] But citizenship cut both ways: with rights came responsibilities, including the responsibility to keep 'fighting fit'. Thus, through the films, lectures, and leaflets of the Army Education Corps and the Central Council for Health Education, the British soldier was encouraged to take responsibility for his own health and was informed about disease prevention to a far greater extent than before. In this as in so many other respects, developments within the Army mirrored those in the civilian sphere, especially the growing emphasis upon the social causes of ill health. It is noteworthy that the

[7] CMAC RAMC 466/13, Sir Alfred Fripp, Sir Alexander Ogston, Sir Cooper Perry, and Dr T. J. Horder, memo. containing criticisms of the medical services.

[8] Jeremy A. Crang, *The British Army and the People's War 1939–1945* (Manchester University Press, 2000), 138.

[9] Richard Titmuss, 'War and Social Policy', in his *Essays on 'The Welfare State'* (London: George Allen & Unwin, 1958), 86.

[10] S. P. MacKenzie, *Politics and Military Morale: Current Affairs and Citizenship Education in the British Army 1914–1950* (Oxford: Clarendon Press, 1992), 156.

concluding volume of the official history of the Army Medical Services during the war contained a section entitled 'The Enlargement of the Concept of the Nature of Health', in which F. A. E. Crew observed:

With the growth of the social sciences man came increasingly to be looked upon as a social being living in a social mileu and being affected by the attitudes and actions of other members of the group and by social institutions, aims and values. It came to be recognised that disharmony between the individual and the conditions and circumstances that obtained within the community was the cause of much ill-health and so the search for causation became extended from the physical to the social environment of individuals and groups.[11]

For enthusiasts of social medicine, like Crew, the war had been a victory in more than just the military sense. It had provided a great impetus to the expansion—both of the content and scope—of preventive medicine, the utility of which had been proven time and time again on the battlefield.

But in this respect at least, the victory was a partial one. The scope of preventive medicine had broadened in the ways that Crew suggested, and the welfare of the individual was generally regarded as inseparable from that of society as a whole. The formation of the National Health Service in 1948 and the establishment of a Department of Social Medicine at the University of Oxford exemplified this trend. But the confidence placed in health education, even within such a regulated environment as the Army, was to some extent misplaced. The level of sanitary awareness among British soldiers during the Second World War was probably much higher than in previous conflicts, but it took some time for the message to sink in. The mere mention of hygiene was often met with indifference or mild amusement, and some specific methods of preventing disease were distinctly unpopular, not least chemical prophylaxis against malaria. Medical officers had to labour hard against rumours that anti-malaria drugs caused physical and sexual impotence, and played down lurid stories about their side-effects, even though these were usually minor. Deeply ingrained traditions of masculine behaviour, together with ample opportunity, also served to undermine measures against venereal disease. Ultimately, two things counted far more than education, which in medical as in other areas of military life failed to deliver the anticipated results.[12] These two factors were discipline and experience. Sanitary propaganda was only truly effective if accompanied by a disciplinary regime of the kind instituted by Slim in the 14th Army in Burma. Similarly, many soldiers had personally to experience a dose of malaria or dysentery

---

[11] F. A. E. Crew, 'The Army Medical Services', in A. S. MacNalty and W. Franklin Mellor (eds.), *Medical Services in War: Medical History of the Second World War* (London: HMSO, 1968), 61.
[12] MacKenzie, *Politics and Morale*, 221–4.

before they took precautions against them seriously. Hence, hygiene and sanitation tended to improve the longer a campaign progressed (unless the army was in retreat), and was markedly better in experienced units than amongst newcomers. The inherited wisdom of colonial campaigns may also have given the British Army an edge over the Germans in the Western Desert, as the latter had comparatively little recent experience of sanitation in hot climates.

The experiences of the British Army between 1939 and 1945 thus demonstrate the vital importance of close links between the medical and combatant branches of an army. It was the existence of this 'medical consciousness' among commanders that gave the British Army its crucial edge over the Germans and Italians in the Western Desert, and ultimately, over the Japanese in Burma. As Slim was well aware, the success of medical arrangements depended as much, if not more, on combatant than on medical officers. Indeed, the history of British military medicine during the Second World War shows that medical failures were generally a failure of command, and that their success depended on the intelligent co-operation of the Army as a whole.

APPENDIX

The Organization of Medical Services in the Field

The organization of medical services for the BEF in 1939 differed little from that at the end of the First World War. Medical units formed a chain of evacuation from the Regimental Aid Post on the front line to large hospitals in the United Kingdom. As the sick or wounded soldier was evacuated from the RAP along the lines of communication, he might pass successively through the following units: the Field Ambulance, the Motor Ambulance Convoy, the Casualty Clearing Station, the General Hospital, the Convalescent Depot, and the Hospital Ship or Carrier. Following the report of the Hartgill Committee in December 1941, some of these units were reconstituted and some new ones, like the Field Dressing Station and the Field Surgical Unit, were created. The composition and functions of the chief medical units was as follows:

1. The Regimental Aid Post

This unit existed at battalion level to receive the walking wounded and casualties collected by stretcher-bearers belonging to the battalion. It normally comprised the battalion medical officer and some medical orderlies provided by the unit, and who were trained by the medical officer himself.

2. The Field Ambulance

This was the nearest RAMC medical unit to the front line. It consisted of a headquarters and two companies, each providing stretcher squads for the clearance of casualties from the RAP. Each squad was also equipped to establish an Advanced Dressing Station capable of providing urgent basic treatment, such as the treatment of shock and the immobilization of fractures. The HQ of the FA had somewhat more advanced equipment, which was used in the formation of a Main Dressing Station, located a few miles behind the ADS. Casualties were normally taken to the MDS from the ADS by ambulance vehicles belonging to the FA. At the MDS, all casualties were inspected and their documentation completed; urgent treatment was given if necessary. Thereafter, all surgical cases and serious medical cases were sent to Casualty Clearing Stations. The disposal of less serious cases varied according to circumstances. When the front was relatively static, some patients could be retained at the MDS until ready to return to their units; otherwise, all cases were sent further back to complete their treatment. As a divisional unit, the FA was under the operational control of the ADMS of the division; in expeditionary forces additional FAs were placed under the control of the DDMS Corps, and at least one was held in reserve at Army GHQ.

After the report of the Hartgill Committee, FAs were given a much greater role than before, in order to improve the mobility of medical facilities. The FAs were reconstituted as fully mobile units, comprising an HQ company and two bearer companies, each with more generous motor transport than previously. Although nominally capable of accommodating 150 patients, FAs were no longer supposed to hold casualties if at all possible; their main function was now more than ever to be evacuation.

3. The Field Dressing Station

The FDS was created following the report of the Hartgill Committee, and had very different functions depending on whether it was situated in a corps or a divisional area. In a division, FDSs were provided on the scale of one for an armoured division and two for an infantry division; they were intended primarily as resuscitation centres for casualties who had been evacuated from FAs with severe shock. These units were under the control of the ADMS with each division. In corps areas, FDSs were allocated on a scale of one per corps, with an additional one for each division in that corps. Here they were employed chiefly in surgical centres (the Advanced Surgical Centre) by combining with one or more Field Surgical Units. They also functioned as rest centres or performed other specialist functions as required.

4. The Field Surgical Unit

These were mobile surgical teams that had been detached from 1,200-bed General Hospitals. Following recommendations by the Hartgill Committee, they were used in forward areas to provide surgical assistance in any place it was required. However, in practice the FSUs proved less mobile than anticipated, as they lacked transport of their own.

5. The Field Transfusion Unit

The FTU was another unit formed following the recommendation of the Hartgill Committee. It comprised one medical officer and three other ranks, all specially trained in blood transfusion. FTUs were under the control of the DMS and were allocated to parent units as required, normally to a corps FDS or to a FSU to form an Advanced Surgical Centre.

6. The Motor Ambulance Convoy

The MAC was a medical transport unit commanded by an officer of the RAMC. It consisted of a medical wing and a transport wing and included, in addition to its HQ, three sections of twenty-five motor ambulances each. The chief function of the MAC was to convey casualties from the MDS to the CCS. One MAC was allocated to each corps included in an expeditionary force, and was under the control of the DDMS of the corps to which it was attached.

After 1942 the MAC was reorganized as a unit of the RASC, as experience had shown that these units—which were primarily transport units—could be best commanded by an officer well versed in the technicalities of transportation and vehicle maintenance. However, the MAC still contained a platoon of RAMC other ranks to attend casualties.

7. The Casualty Clearing Station

The CCS was the first unit on the line of evacuation placed properly behind the firing line, and the first at which full medical and surgical facilities were available. Its staff included specialists in medicine, surgery, radiology, and anaesthetics, and also sisters of the QAIMNS. At busy periods the staff of CCSs were often reinforced by staff drawn temporarily from General Hospitals. They initially were provided in the proportion of one for each division, and as GHQ troops, were under the control of the DMS. However, they were usually allotted to the DDMS of each corps for routine administrative and operational control.

Although a wide range of medical and surgical facilities were present at CCSs, their main function was not to hold casualties but to sort and evacuate them as quickly as possible. For this reason, CCSs were located where possible on main roads or railways. Evacuation from the CCS to General Hospitals at the base thus often relied on special ambulance trains, staffed by RAMC personnel and the QAIMNS. The trains were under the administrative control of the DDMS Lines of Communication, although their movement was controlled by the transport branch of the Staff.

Following the report of the Hartgill Committee, CCSs were reconstituted as mobile units with the addition of a second surgical team. It was intended that these units should function much nearer to the fighting than previously, and consequently, their complement of nursing sisters was withdrawn. From 1942 the scale of CCSs was fixed at two per corps, with the addition of one per army. Accommodation for each was placed at 120 patients, but in practice was often larger. The control of these reconstituted units remained under the DDMS.

8. General Hospitals

GHs were initially of two types: a 600-bed hospital and a 1,200-bed hospital. They were established in sufficient numbers to provide hospital beds in the ratio of 6 per cent of the strength of the force. Normally GHs were located at the base and on the Lines of Communication, and often grouped together in a special medical base sub-area accessible to a port of embarkation. They were fully equipped hospitals with complete facilities for the diagnosis and treatment of every kind of disease and injury, each hospital having a medical and surgical division. However, hospitals of GH size were sometimes formed as specialist hospitals, treating psychiatric casualties or certain types of disease. The GH was the unit to which all casualties, except for the most trivial cases, were ultimately admitted for treatment; only cases requiring prolonged treatment were evacuated back to the United Kingdom.

After the report of the Hartgill Committee, the number of large GHs was reduced, as they were found to be too cumbersome for mechanized warfare. New 200-bed hospitals were instead created on the scale of one per corps, at the disposal of the DMS. They operated as intermediary hospitals, situated between CCSs and base hospitals; they also served as holding hospitals for casualties pending evacuation.

9. *The Convalescent Depot*

These units normally held up to a maximum of 1,000 men and were used for the reception and accommodation of sick and wounded men no longer in need of hospital treatment, but not yet sufficiently recovered to return to their units. The chief function of the depots was to prepare men for return to duty, and convalescents received regular physical and military training under medical supervision. The establishment of such depots in most theatres obviated the need to send large numbers of men back to the United Kingdom, and thus played a large part in reducing the wastage of manpower.

10. *Hospital Carriers and Hospital Ships*

These were specially adapted vessels designed to carry casualties from overseas bases to ports in the United Kingdom, or occasionally from the theatre of operations to large hospitals in foreign ports. The hospital carrier differed in function from the hospital ship in that the former operated only over short distances, and had limited facilities for treatment; it was thus comparable in function to an ambulance train. The hospital ship was a much larger vessel intended to serve distant theatres of the war, and contained complete hospital facilities and specialist staff. It was a kind of floating general hospital.

Bibliography

I. Unpublished Official Sources

Army Medical Services Museum, Keogh Barracks, Mychett, Hampshire

Papers of the following:
  A. Adamson
  Dr Attenborough
  Brig. M. Formby
  Pvt. P. Pickard
  Maj. E. H. McLaren
  Capt. G. P. Mitchell
  R. H. Montague
  Sgt. J. Tichener
  T. Toughill
  Various anonymous documents

Contemporary Medical Archives Collection, Wellcome Institute for the History of Medicine Library, London

Papers of the following:
  British Social Hygiene Council
  Leonard Colebrook
  S. H. Foulkes
  E. Grey Turner
  Lt.-Col. S. A. MacKeith
  Medical Women's Federation
  Royal Army Medical Corps Muniment Collection (hundreds of official and private
    papers relating to the Second World War, cited individually in notes)
  H. E. Shortt
  J. Vaughan
  Lt.-Col. J. D. W. Pearce

Gloucestershire County Record Office, Gloucester

Documents deposited by Royal Gloucestershire Hussars

Imperial War Museum, London

Papers of the following:
  Mrs D. Boys
  Lt.-Gen. Sir R. Drew
  P. G. Heath
  Capt. H. M. Jones
  L. E. Le Souef

Lt.-Col. B. Lilwall
E. H. A. Luker
Maj. J. C. McKillop
H. C. McLaren
J. McLuskie
W. L. McWilliam
Field-Marshal Viscount Montgomery
M. Morris
Mrs. A. Radloff
Field-Marshal Viscount Slim
W. M. Stewart

Liddell Hart Centre for Military Archives, Kings College, London
Papers of the following:
Mc Cutcheon
Lt.-Gen. Sir R. F. Adam

Liddle Collection, University of Leeds
Papers of A. G. B. Duncan

National Army Museum, London
Papers of the following:
Lt.-Col. R. S. M. Calder
The King's African Rifles
E. Sims

Oriental and India Office Collections, British Library, London
Government of India (Military)

Public Record Office, London
Cabinet
War Office

Library of the Royal College of Surgeons of England, London
Papers of Sir A. Bowlby

II. Newspapers and Periodicals

British Medical Journal
Bulletin of War Medicine
Crusader
Evening News
Health and Empire
Journal of Nervous and Mental Diseases
Journal of the Royal Army Medical Corps

The Lancet
The News and Gazette of the Royal Army Medical Corps, the Army Dental Corps and Q.A.I.M.N.S.
Proceedings of the Royal Society of Medicine
The Sphere
The Times
Transactions of the Royal Society of Tropical Medicine and Hygiene
Union Jack

III. Personal Recollections and Published Primary Sources

ABADIE, J., *Wounds of the Abdomen*, ed. Sir William Arbuthnot-Lane (London: University of London Press, 1918).

ANDERSON, J. A., 'The Recent Trend in Military Hygiene', *Journal of the Royal Army Medical Corps*, 43 (1924), 81–94.

ARMY ADVISORY STANDING COMMITTEE ON MAXILLO-FACIAL INJURIES, *Report to the Army Council of the Army Advisory Standing Committee on Maxillo-Facial Injuries* (London: HMSO, 1940 [1935]).

ARMY DIRECTORATE OF PATHOLOGY, 'Memorandum Concerning the Use of Sulphonamide Derivatives for Prophylaxis and Treatment of Wound Infections, 11 October 1939', *Journal of the Royal Army Medical Corps*, 73 (1939), 298–300.

—— 'Supplementary Memorandum No. 1 Concerning the Use of Sulphonamide Derivatives for Prophylaxis and Treatment of Wound Infections, 1 November 1939', *Journal of the Royal Army Medical Corps*, 73 (1939), 301.

BARER, ROBERT, *One Young Man and Total War—From Normandy to Concentration Camp: A Doctor's Letters Home*, ed. G. Barer (Edinburgh: Pentland Press, 1988).

BARRETT, JAMES W., *A Vision of the Possible: What the R.A.M.C. Might Become. An Account of Some of the Medical Work in Egypt; Together With a Constructive Criticism of the R.A.M.C.* (London: H. K. Lewis, 1919).

BARTLETT, BASIL, *My First War—An Army Officer's Journal for May 1940* (London: Chatto & Windus, 1940).

BATY, JOHN, *Surgeon in the Jungle War* (London: William Kimber, 1979).

BEAMISH, D. W. and CLARKE, L. B., 'Treatment of Gonorrhoea and Soft Chancre in Egypt by Sulphonamide', *Journal of the Royal Army Medical Corps*, 73 (1939), 96–105.

BEARDWELL, M. F., *Aftermath* (Ilfracombe: A. H. Stockwell, 1945).

BELL, HERBERT, 'Gonorrhoea in Italy', *Journal of the Royal Army Medical Corps*, 84 (1945), 21–6.

BOLLAND, A. D., *Team Spirit: The Administration of an Infantry Division During 'Operation Overlord'* (Aldershot: Gale & Polden, 1948).

BORIE, JOHN, *Despite Captivity: A Doctor's Life as Prisoner of War* (London: William Kimber, 1975).

BOWLBY, ANTHONY A. and WALLACE, CUTHBERT, 'The Development of British Surgery at the Front', *British Medical Journal*, 2 June 1917, pp. 705–21.

BOYD, J. S. K., 'Active Immunization Against Tetanus', *Journal of the Royal Army Medical Corps*, 70 (1938), 289–307.

—— 'Enteric Group Fevers in Prisoners of War from the Western Desert, With Special Reference to Prophylactic Inoculation, Jan. 1941, to Feb. 1943', *British Medical Journal,* 12 June 1943, pp. 719–21.

BRADLEY, W. H., LOLOT, J. F., and MAUNSELL, K., 'An Episode of Homologous Serum Jaundice', *British Medical Journal,* 26 Aug. 1944, p. 268.

BRERETON, F. S., *The Great War and the R.A.M.C.* (London: Constable, 1919).

BRICKNER, R. M. and VOSBURGH LYONS, L., 'A Neuropsychiatric View of German Culture and the Treatment of Germany', *Journal of Nervous and Mental Diseases,* 98 (1943), 282–93.

BULMER, ERNEST, 'Military Medicine in the Middle East: An Experience of 13,542 Cases', *British Medical Journal,* 27 Mar. 1942, pp. 374–7.

BURDETT-COUTTS, WILLIAM, *The Sick and Wounded in South Africa: What I Saw and Said of Them and of the Army Medical Service* (London: Cassell, 1900).

BURMA STAR ASSOCIATION, 'How Admin Troops Backed–up the Fighting Men', http://www.burmastar.org.uk/admin_troops.htm.

CANNON, W. B., 'A Consideration of the Nature of Wound Shock', in Medical Research Committee, *Reports of the Special Investigation on Surgical Shock and Allied Conditions, No. 2* (London: HMSO, 1917), 67–83.

CANTLIE, NEIL, 'Health Discipline', *US Armed Forces Medical Journal,* 1 (1950), 232–7.

Central Council for Health Education, *Proceedings of the Central Council for Health Education Conference on Health Education and the Venereal Diseases, 26 February, 1943* (London: CCHE, 1943).

COHEN, S. M., 'Experience in the Treatment of War Burns', *British Medical Journal* (24 August 1940), 251–4.

COLEBROOK, LEONARD et al., *Studies of Burns and Scalds (Reports of the Burns Unit, Royal Infirmary, Glasgow, 1942–3)* (London: HMSO, 1944).

Committee on the Medical Branches of the Defence Services, *Committee on the Medical Branches of the Defence Services—Report* (London: HMSO, 1933).

COTTERELL, ANTHONY, *R.A.M.C.* (London: Hutchinson, 1944).

COUTTS, G., 'The Japanese Military Medical Service', *Journal of the Royal Army Medical Corps,* 6 (1906), 106–10.

COVELL, GORDON, *Anti-Mosquito Measures With Special Reference to India* (Calcutta: Government of India Central Publications Branch, 1931).

—— 'Treatment of Malaria', *Proceedings of the Conference of Medical Specialists of Eastern Army* (Calcutta: Government of India, 1943), 69–70.

COWELL, E. M., 'The Initiation of Wound Shock', in Medical Research Committee, *Reports of the Special Investigation on Surgical Shock and Allied Conditions, No. 2* (London: HMSO, 1917), 58–66.

CRAIGIE, H. B., 'Neurosis on Active Service: Experiences in the M.E.F.', in H. Letheby Tidy (ed.), *Inter-Allied Conferences on War Medicine 1942–1945* (London: Staples Press, 1947), 228–30.

CRIMP, R. L., *The Diary of a Desert Rat,* ed. A. Bowlby (London: Leo Cooper, 1971).

DAVIS, P. J. R., 'Psychiatry in a Division on the Burma Front', *Journal of the Royal Army Medical Corps,* 84 (1945), 66–7.

DARDANELLES COMMISSION, *First Report of the Dardanelles Commission* (London: HMSO, 1918).

—— *Final Report of the Dardenelles Commission* (London: HMSO, 1919).

DEBENHAM, R. K. and KERR, A. B., 'The Triage of Battle Casualties', *Journal of the Royal Army Medical Corps*, 84 (1945), 125–9.

DILLON, FREDERICK, 'Treatment of Neuroses in the Field: The Advanced Psychiatric Centre', in E. Miller (ed.), *The Neuroses in War* (London: Macmillan, 1940).

DOLL, RICHARD, 'Dunkirk Diary: Experiences of a Battalion Medical Officer in the Retreat to Dunkirk', *British Medical Journal*, Pt. I, 5 May 1990, pp. 1183–5; Pt. II, 12 May 1990, 1256–9; Pt. III, 19 May 1990, 1324–8; Pt. IV, 26 May 1990, 1385–7; Pt. V, 2 June 1990, 1449–52.

DOWSE, J. C. A., 'Mechanization and the Modern Field Ambulance', *Journal of the Royal Army Medical Corps*, 72 (1939), 374–83.

DUNLOP, E. E., *The War Diaries of Weary Dunlop: Java and the Burma–Thailand Railway 1942–1945* (Harmondsworth: Penguin, 1990).

EASON, E. H., 'Burma 1942 Retreat: A Doctor's Retreat from Burma', http://www.burmastar.org.uk/eason.htm.

EDINGTON, G. H., *With the 1/1st Lowland Field Ambulance in Gallipoli* (Glasgow: Alex MacDougall, 1920).

ELLIOT, G. S. McD., 'Notes On Preserving Health of Soldiers in the Field', *Journal of the Royal Army Medical Corps*, 6 (1906), 676–84.

EMERGENCY MEDICAL SERVICE, 'The Local Treatment of War Burns', *British Medical Journal*, 29 Mar. 1940, p. 489.

ESEBECK, HANNS GERT VON, *Afrikanische Schicksalsjahre: Geschichte des Deutschen Afrika Korps unter Rommel* (Weisbaden: Limes Verlag, 1949).

EVATT, GEORGE J. H., 'Army Medical Organization in War, With Suggestions as to Militia and Volunteer Aid', *Journal of the Royal Army Medical Corps*, 22 (1914), 91.

FERGUSSON, BERNARD, *Beyond the Chindwin* (London: Fontana, 1955 [1945]).

—— *The Wild Green Earth* (London: Fontana, 1956 [1946]).

FIDDES, F. S., 'Work of a Field Ambulance in the Battle of Normandy', *British Medical Journal*, 31 Mar. 1945, pp. 448–50.

FOTHERINGHAM, BRYAN J., 'Training a (Mechanized) Cavalry Field Ambulance—Egypt, 1936', *Journal of the Royal Army Medical Corps*, 72 (1939), 151–63.

FOURTEENTH GENERAL HOSPITAL, *The History of Fourteenth General Hospital R.A.M.C. 1939–1945* (Birmingham: The Birmingham Printers, undated).

FRANKS, L. M., Correspondence from Dr L. M. Franks to the author, 19 Apr. 1995.

FRASER, FORBES, 'Primary and Delayed Suture of Gunshot Wounds. A Report of Research at a CCS, Dec. 27 1917–March 1918', *British Journal of Surgery*, 6 (1918–19), 92–124.

FRASER, J. and COWELL, E. M., 'A Clinical Study of the Blood Pressure in Wound Shock', in Medical Research Committee, *Reports of the Special Investigation on Surgical Shock and Allied Conditions, No. 2* (London: HMSO, 1917), 1–26.

—— 'The Preventive Treatment of Wound Shock', in Medical Research Committee, *Reports of the Special Investigation on Surgical Shock and Allied Conditions, No. 2* (London: HMSO, 1917), 84–93.

GEAR, H. S., 'Hygiene Aspects of the El Alamein Victory', *British Medical Journal*, 18 Mar. 1944, pp. 383–7.

GOODWIN, W. R. P., 'The Casualty Clearing Station as a Working Unit in the Field', *Journal of the Royal Army Medical Corps*, 33 (1919), 42–57.

GOVERNMENT OF INDIA, *Field Service Notes—India, 1945* (Calcutta: Government of India Press, 1945).

GRAY, H. M. W., 'Treatment of Gunshot Wounds by Excision and Primary Suture', *Journal of the Royal Army Medical Corps*, 24 (1915), 551–4.

'GUN BUSTER' [pseud.], *Return via Dunkirk* (London: White Lion, 1975 [1940]).

HADFIELD, J. A., 'War Neuroses. A Year in a Neuropathic Hospital', *British Medical Journal*, 28 Feb. 1942, pp. 281–5.

HAMILTON-FAIRLEY, N., 'Researches on Paluride (M.4888) in Malaria', *Transactions of the Royal Society of Tropical Medicine and Hygiene*, 40 (1946), 105–53.

—— 'Tropical Diseases With Special Reference to Malaria in the Eastern Theatres of War', in H. Letheby Tidy (ed.), *Inter-Allied Conferences on War Medicine 1942–1945. Convened by the Royal Society of Medicine* (London: Staples Press, 1947), 88–97.

HARDIE, ROBERT, *The Burma–Siam Railway: The Secret Diary of Dr Robert Hardie 1942–45* (London: Imperial War Museum, 1984).

HARRISON, L. W., 'Venereal Disease: Its Prevention and Treatment on Active Service', *Bulletin of War Medicine*, 1 (Sept. 1940), 41.

HARTIGAN, J. A., 'Training of the R.A.M.C. Officer in Medical Duties in the Field', *Journal of the Royal Army Medical Corps*, 42 (1934), 1–5.

HEWTON, F. S., 'Motor Traction Behind the Fining Line', *Journal of the Royal Army Medical Corps*, 12 (1909), 499–501.

HOOD, ALEXANDER, 'Army Medical Services in Action', *Journal of the Royal Army Medical Corps*, 38 (1943), 287–90.

HOWARD, F., 'The Medical Service in the Field of the German Army', *Journal of the Royal Army Medical Corps*, 2 (1904), 1–11.

J. A. R., *Memoirs of an Army Surgeon* (Edinburgh and London: William Blackwood, 1948).

JEFFREY, J. S., 'Treatment of War Wounds in France, May–June 1940', *Journal of the Royal Army Medical Corps*, 74 (1940), 345–57.

JOESBURY, THOMAS, '60 and 80 Column Chindits 1944', http://www.burmastar. org. uk/joesbury.htm.

JOHNSTON, R., 'The Divisional Field Ambulance in Mobile Warfare', *Journal of the Royal Army Medical Corps*, 82 (1944), 168–76.

KÄFER, HANS, *Feldchirurgie für den Sanitätsoffizer der Wehrmacht* (Dresden and Leipzig: Verlag von Theodor Steinkopf, 1944).

LELEAN, P. S., *How to Feed the Family* (Edinburgh: William Hodge & Co., 1927).

LESLIE, R. W. D., 'R.A.M.C. Field Training—The Casualty Card Scheme', *Journal of the Royal Army Medical Corps*, 72 (1939), 145–50.

LESSEN, E. H., 'D-Day 6 June 1944', *The Army Medical Services Magazine*, 38 (Oct. 1984), 83–6.

LETHEBY TIDY, H. (ed.), *Inter-Allied Conferences on War Medicine 1942–1945* (London: Staples Press, 1947).

LIDDELL HART, B. H. (ed.), *The Rommel Papers*, trans. P. Finlay (London: Collins, 1953).

LINDSAY, MARTIN, *So Few Got Through: The Personal Diary of Lieut.-Col. Martin Lindsay, D.S.O., M.P., Who Served With the Gordon Highlanders in the 51st Highland Division from July 1944, to May, 1945* (London: Collins, 1946).

LOGIE, N. J., 'Organisation and Treatment of Burns: Experiences at Tobruk, 1942', in H. Letheby Tidy (ed.), *Inter-Allied Conferences on War Medicine 1942–1945* (London: Staples Press, 1947), 123–6.

LOW, A. M., *Benefits of War* (London: The Scientific Book Club, 1945).

MACDONALD FRASER, GEORGE, *Quartered Safe Out Here: A Recollection of the War in Burma* (London: Harvill, 1993).

MACKEITH, S. A., 'Lasting Lessons of Overseas Military Psychiatry', *Journal of Mental Sciences*, 92 (1946), 542–50.

—— 'Interview with the author, Oxford, 27 Aug. 1992.

McMILLAN, A., 'Surgical Experiences at a Base Hospital in Egypt', *Journal of the Royal Army Medical Corps*, 78 (1942), 300–6.

MACNALTY, A. S. and FRANKLIN MELLOR, W., *Health Recovery in Europe* (London: Frederick Muller, 1946).

MACPHERSON, W. G., 'The Medical Organisation of the Japanese Army', *Journal of the Royal Army Medical Corps*, 6 (1906), 219–50.

—— 'The Removal of the Sick and Wounded from the Battlefield', *Journal of the Royal Army Medical Corps*, 12 (1909), 78–100.

MAKINS, GEORGE H., *Surgical Experiences in South Africa 1899–1900: Being a Clinical Study of the Nature and Effects and Injuries produced by Bullets of a Small Calibre* (London: Hodder & Stoughton, 1913).

MASTERS, JOHN, *The Road Past Mandalay: A Personal Narrative* (London: Corgi, 1973).

MARSHALL, JAMES, 'Prevention of Venereal Disease in the British Army', in H. Letheby Tidy (ed.), *Inter-Allied Conferences on War Medicine 1942–1945* (London: Staples Press, 1947), 260–2.

MATAS, J., 'A Note on Psychiatry in Indian Troops', *Journal of the Royal Army Medical Corps*, 84 (1945), 69.

Medical Research Committee, *Reports of the Special Investigation on Surgical Shock and Allied Conditions, No. 2* (London: HMSO, 1917).

—— *Reports of the Committee upon Anaerobic Bacteria and Infections. Report on the Anaerobic Infections of Wounds and the Bacteriological and Serological Problems Arising Therefrom* (London: MRC, c.1919).

Medical Research Council, *The Treatment of Wound Shock* (London: HMSO, 1940).

—— *Reports of the Military Personnel Research Committee of the MRC (Sub-Committee on AFVs)* (London: HMSO, c.1944).

MELLING, LEONARD, *With the Eighth in Italy* (Manchester: Torch, 1955).

MELVILLE, C. H., 'The Place of Sanitation as a Factor in Strategy', *Journal of the Royal Army Medical Corps*, 12 (1908), 64–9.

MESOPOTAMIA COMMISSION, *Mesopotamia Commission—Report and Minority Report* (London: HMSO, 1917).

MILLER, E. (ed.), *The Neuroses in War* (London: Macmillan, 1940).

MITCHELL, T. J. and SMITH, G. M., *History of the Great War Based on Official Documents. Medical Services—Casualties and Medical Statistics of the Great War* (London: HMSO, 1931).

MITCHINER, PHILIP H., 'Thoughts on Four Years of War Surgery—1939 to 1943', *British Medical Journal*, 8 July 1944, pp. 37–40.

MORENO, J. L., *Who Shall Survive? Foundations of Sociometry, Group Psychotherapy and Sociodrama* (London: Beacon House, 1953).

MORTON, R. S., MBE, Personal communication to the author, 26 Mar. 2000.

MYERS, C. S. (ed.), *Industrial Psychology* (London: Thornton Butterworth, 1929).

—— *Shell Shock in France 1914–18* (Cambridge: Cambridge University Press, 1940).

NICHOLLS, T. B., *Organization, Strategy and Tactics of the Army Medical Services in War* (London: Ballière, Tindall & Cox, 1937).

—— 'Heat Stroke and Allied Conditions', *Journal of the Royal Army Medical Corps*, 73 (1939), 73–84.

OGILVIE, W. H., *Forward Surgery in Modern War* (London: Butterworth, 1944).

OGSTON, ALEXANDER, *Reminiscences of Three Campaigns* (London: Hodder & Stoughton, 1917).

OLDFIELD, M. C., 'Burns in Wartime', *Journal of the Royal Army Medical Corps*, 77 (1941), 1–13.

PAUL, DANIEL and ST JOHN, JOHN, *Surgeon at Arms* (London: Heinemann, 1958).

PORTER, CHARLES, 'Citizenship and Health Questions in War-Time', *Journal of State Medicine*, 25 (1917), 300–6.

REES, J. R., 'Three Years of Military Psychiatry in the United Kingdom', *British Medical Journal* (2 Jan. 1943), 1–6.

ROBERT, J. R., 'A Journey Through World War Two', http://www.burmastar.org.uk/roberts.htm.

SARGANT, WILLIAM, 'Physical Treatment of Acute War Neuroses', *British Medical Journal* (14 Nov. and 3 Dec. 1942), 574, 675.

—— *The Unquiet Mind* (London: Heinemann, 1967).

SHIRLAW, G. B. and TROKE, C., *Medicine versus Invasion: The Home Guard Medical Service in Action* (London: Secker & Warburg, 1941).

ROYAL COMMISSION ON . . . THE SICK AND WOUNDED DURING THE SOUTH AFRICAN CAMPAIGN, *Report of the Royal Commission Appointed To Consider and Report Upon the Care and Treatment of the Sick and Wounded During the South African Campaign* (London: HMSO, 1901).

SIMS, JAMES, *Arnhem Spearhead: A Private Soldier's Story* (London: Imperial War Museum, 1978).

SLIM, Field-Marshal Viscount, *Defeat into Victory* (London: Macmillan, 1986 [1956]).

SPARROW, J. H. A., *The Second World War 1939–1945 Army: Morale* (London: HMSO, 1949).

STIBBE, P. G., *Via Rangoon: A Young Chindit Survives the Jungle and Japanese Captivity* (London: Leo Cooper, 1994).

TAKAKI, BARON, 'The Preservation of Health Amongst the Personnel of the Japanese Army', *Journal of the Royal Army Medical Corps*, 7 (1906), 54–62.

TAYLOR, G. F., 'Some Medical Aspects of the Eastern Army', *Proceedings of the Conference of Medical Specialists of Eastern Army Held in March 1943* (Calcutta: Government of India, 1943), 7–10.

THISTLETON MONK, H., *Efficiency Ideals: A Short Study of the Principles of 'Scientific Management'* (London: T. Werner Laurie, 1919).

TURNER, R. H. et al., 'Some Clinical Studies of Acute Hepatitis Occurring in Soldiers After Inoculation with Yellow Fever Vaccine: With Special Consideration of Severe Attacks', *Annals of International Medicine*, 20 (1944), 193.

URQUHART, R. E., *Arnhem* (London: Cassell, 1958).

URWICK, L., *The Meaning of Rationalisation* (London: Nisbet & Co., 1929).

VIVIAN, CHARLES E., *With the Royal Army Medical Corps at the Front* (London: Hodder & Stoughton, 1914).

WALLACE, CUTHBERT, *Surgery at a Casualty Clearing Station* (London: A. & C. Black, 1918).

WALLACE, Q. V. B., 'The Battle of Alamein and the Campaign in Libya', in H. Letheby Tidy (ed.), *Inter-Allied Conferences on War Medicine* (London: Staples Press, 1947), 312–19.

WAR OFFICE, *Army Manual of Hygiene and Sanitation—1934* (London: HMSO, 1935).

—— *Royal Army Medical Corps Training—1935* (London: HMSO, 1935).

—— *Memorandum on Venereal Diseases—1936* (London: HMSO, 1936).

—— *Standing Orders for the Royal Army Medical Corps, Royal Army Medical Corps (T.A.) and the Army Dental Corps, 1937* (London: HMSO, 1938).

—— *Handbook of Military Hygiene* (London: HMSO, 1943).

—— *Statistical Report on the Health of the Army 1943–1945* (London: HMSO, 1948).

WARRACK, GRAEME, *Travel by Dark: After Arnhem* (London: Harvill Press, 1963).

WATTS, J. C., *Surgeon at War* (London: George Allen & Unwin, 1955).

WESTMAN, STEPHEN, *Surgeon With the Kaiser's Army* (London: William Kimber, 1968).

WHITBY, LIONEL, 'Blood Transfusion in the Field: Organisation of Supplies', in H. Letheby Tidy (ed.), *Inter-Allied Conferences on War Medicine 1942–1945* (London: Staples Press, 1947), 123–6.

WEDDELL, J. M., 'Surgery in Tunisia: November, 1942, to May, 1943', *British Medical Journal*, 7 Oct. 1944, pp. 449–62.

WINGFIELD, R. M., *The Only Way Out: An Infantryman's Autobiography of the North-West Europe Campaign August 1944–February 1945* (London: Hutchinson, 1955).

WITTKOWER, E. and SPILLANE, J. P., 'Neuroses in Wartime', *British Medical Journal*, 10 Feb. 1940, pp. 223–5.

IV. Secondary Sources

ABEL-SMITH, BRIAN, *The Hospitals, 1800–1948* (London: Heinemann, 1964).

ADAMS, J., *The Doomed Expedition: The Campaign in Norway 1940* (London: Mandarin, 1989).

AHRENFELDT, R. H., *Psychiatry in the British Army in the Second World War* (London: Routledge, 1958).

ALLEN, LOUIS, *Singapore 1941–42* (London: Frank Cass, 1993).

—— *Burma: The Longest War 1941–1945* (London: J. M. Dent & Sons, 1984).

—— 'The Campaigns in Asia and the Pacific', in J. Gooch (ed.), *Decisive Campaigns of the Second World War* (London: Frank Cass, 1990), 162–92.

ALTER, PETER, *The Reluctant Patron: Science and the State in Britain, 1850–1920* (Oxford: Berg, 1987).

ARMFIELD, BLANCHE B., *Medical Department, United States Army: Organization and Administration in World War II* (Washington DC: Office of the Surgeon-General Department of the Army, 1963).

ARMSTRONG, DAVID, *The Political Anatomy of the Body: Medical Knowledge in Britain in the Twentieth Century* (Cambridge: Cambridge University Press, 1993).

—— *A New History of Identity: A Sociology of Medical Knowledge* (Basingstoke: Palgrave, 2002).

AUSTROKER, J. and BRYDER, L. (eds.), *Historical Perspectives on the Role of the MRC: Essays in the History of the Medical Research Council of the United Kingdom and its Predecessor, the Medical Research Committee, 1913–1953* (Oxford: Clarendon Press, 1989).

BAILEY, RONALD H., *Prisoners of War* (Chicago: Time-Life Books, 1981).

BAMJI, ANDREW, 'Facial Surgery: The Patient's Experience', in H. Cecil and P. Liddle (eds.), *Facing Armageddon: The First World War Experienced* (Barnsley: Leo Cooper, 1996), 490–501.

BARGER, A. C., BENISON, S., and WOLFE, E. L., 'Walter B. Cannon and the Mystery of Shock: A Study of Anglo-American Co-operation in World War I', *Medical History*, 35 (1991), 217–49.

BARTOV, OMER, *Hitler's Army: Soldiers, Nazis, and War in the Third Reich* (Oxford: Oxford University Press, 1992).

BEARDSLEY, E. H., 'Allied Against Sin: American and British Responses to Venereal Disease in World War I', *Medical History*, 20 (1976), 189–202.

BECKETT, I. F. W., *The Amateur Military Tradition* (Manchester: Manchester University Press, 1991).

BEEVOR, ANTONY, *Crete: The Battle and the Resistance* (Harmondsworth: Penguin, 1992).

BELLAMY, R. F. and LLEWELLYN, C. H., 'Preventable Casualties: Rommel's Flaw, Slim's Edge', *Army* (May 1990), 52–6.

BEST, GEOFFREY, *Humanity in Warfare: The Modern History of the International Law of Armed Conflicts* (London: Methuen, 1983).

BIDWELL, SHELFORD, *The Chindit War: The Campaign in Burma, 1944* (London: Book Club Associates, 1979).

——and GRAHAM, DOMINICK, *Fire-Power: British Army Weapons and Theories of War 1904–1945* (London: George Allen & Unwin, 1982).

BHATTACHARYA, SANJOY, *Propaganda and Information in Eastern India 1939–45: A Necessary Weapon of War* (London: Curzon Press, 2001).

BINNEVELD, HANS, *From Shell Shock to Combat Stress: A Comparative History of Military Psychiatry*, trans. John O' Kane (Amsterdam: University Press, 1997).

BLAIR, J. S. G., *Centenary History of the RAMC 1898–1998* (Edinburgh: Scottish Academic Press, 1998).

BOGACZ, TED, 'War Neuroses and Social-Cultural Change in England, 1914–22: The Work of the War Office Committee into "Shell Shock"', *Journal of Contemporary History*, 24 (1989), 227–56.

BOND, BRIAN, *British Military Policy Between the Two World Wars* (Oxford: Oxford University Press, 1980).

BOURKE, JOANNA, 'Disciplining the Emotions: Fear, Psychiatry and the Second World War', in R. Cooter, M. Harrison, and S. Sturdy (eds.), *War, Medicine and Modernity* (Stroud: Sutton, 1998), 225–38.

——*An Intimate History of Killing: Face-to-Face Killing in Twentieth-Century Warfare* (London: Granta Books, 1999).

BRANDT, ALLAN M., *No Magic Bullet: A Social History of Venereal Disease in the United States Since 1880* (New York and Oxford: Oxford University Press, 1985).

BRITISH MEDICAL ASSOCIATION, *As You Were, V.E. Day: A Medical Retrospect* (London: BMA, 1984).

BUCHAN, ALASTAIR, *War in Modern Society* (London: Fontana, 1966).

BUCKLEY, SUZANN, 'The Failure to Resolve the Problem of Venereal Disease Among the Troops in Britain During World War I', in B. Bond and I. Roy (eds.), *War and Society: A Yearbook of Military History*, 2 (London: Croom Helm, 1977), 65–85.

BURK, K. (ed.), *War and the State: The Transformation of British Government, 1914–1919* (London: Allen & Unwin, 1982).

BURNHAM, JOHN C., 'The New Psychology: From Narcissism to Social Control', in J. Braeman, R. H. Brencher, and D. Brody (eds.), *Change and Continuity in Twentieth Century America: The 1920s* (New York, 1968), 351–98.

BRINGMANN, JOHANNES, *Problemkreis Schussbruch bei der deutschen Wehrmacht im Zweiten Weltkrieg* (Düsseldorf: Droste Verlag, 1981).

CALDER, ANGUS, *The People's War: Britain 1939–1945* (London: Pimlico, 1992).

CALVOCORESSI, PETER, WINT, GUY, and PRITCHARD, JOHN, *Total War: The Causes and Courses of the Second World War*, 2 vols. (Harmondsworth: Penguin, 1989).

CANTLIE, Sir NEIL, *A History of the Army Medical Department*, 2 vols. (Edinburgh: Churchill Livingstone, 1974).

CECIL, HUGH and LIDDLE, PETER (eds.), *Facing Armageddon: The First World War Experienced* (Barnsley: Leo Cooper, 1996).

CHANDLER, D. and BECKETT, I. F. W. (eds.), *The Oxford Illustrated History of the British Army* (Oxford: Oxford University Press, 1994).

COLE, HOWARD N., *On Wings of Healing: The Story of the Airborne Medical Services 1940–1960* (Edinburgh and London: William Blackwood, 1963).

COOTER, ROGER, 'Medicine and the Goodness of War', *Canadian Bulletin of Medical History*, 12 (1990), 147–59.

—— *Surgery and Society in Peace and War: Orthopaedics and the Organization of Modern Medicine, 1880–1948* (London: Macmillan, 1993).

—— 'War and Modern Medicine', in W. F. Bynum and R. Porter (eds.), *Companion Encyclopedia of the History of Medicine* (London: Routledge, 1994), 1536–73.

——HARRISON, MARK, and STURDY, STEVE (eds.), *War, Medicine and Modernity* (Stroud: Sutton, 1998).

—— (eds.), *Medicine and Modern Warfare* (Amsterdam and Atlanta: Rodopi Press, 1999).

——and PICKSTONE, JOHN (eds.), *Medicine in the Twentieth Century* (London: Harwood, 2000).

COPE, ZACHARY (ed.), *History of the Second World War, United Kingdom Medical Services: Medicine and Pathology* (London: HMSO, 1953).

—— *History of the Second World War, United Kingdom Medical Services: Surgery* (London: HMSO, 1953).

COPP, TERRY and MCANDREW, BILL, *Battle Exhaustion: Soldiers and Psychiatrists in the Canadian Army, 1939–1945* (Montreal: McGill/Queens University Press, 1990).

COULTER, J. L. S., *The Royal Naval Medical Service, Volume I: Administration* (London: HMSO, 1954).

—— *The Royal Naval Medical Service, Volume II: Operations* (London: HMSO, 1956).

COWDREY, ALBERT E., *Fighting for Life: American Military Medicine in World War II* (New York: The Free Press, 1994).

CRANG, JEREMY, A., *The British Army and the People's War 1939–1945* (Manchester: Manchester University Press, 2000).

CREW, F. A. E. 'The Army Medical Services', in Sir A. S. MacNalty and W. F. Mellor (eds.), *Medical Services in the War: The Principal Medical Lessons of the Second World War* (London: HMSO, 1968).

—— (ed.), *The Army Medical Services: Administration*, 2 vols. (London: HMSO, 1953).

—— *The Army Medical Services. Campaigns, Volume I: France and Belgium, 1939–1940, Norway, Battle of Britain, Libya, 1940–1942, East Africa, Greece, 1941, Crete, Iraq, Syria, Persia, Madagascar, Malta* (London: HMSO, 1956).

—— *The Army Medical Services. Campaigns, Volume II: Hong Kong, Malaya, Iceland and the Faroes, Libya, 1942–1943, North-West Africa* (London: HMSO, 1957).

—— *The Army Medical Services. Campaigns, Volume III: Sicily, Italy, Greece (1944–45)* (London: HMSO, 1959).

—— *The Army Medical Services. Campaigns, Volume IV: North-West Europe* (London: HMSO, 1962).

—— *The Army Medical Services. Campaigns, Volume V: Burma* (London: HMSO, 1966).

DAVIS, PAUL K., *Ends and Means: The British Mesopotamia Campaign and Commission* (Rutherford, NJ: Associated University Presses, 1994).

CURTIN, PHILIP D., *Death By Migration: Europe's Encounter with the Tropical World in the Nineteenth Century* (Cambridge: Cambridge University Press, 1989).

—— *Disease and Empire: The Health of European Troops in the Conquest of Africa* (Cambridge and New York: Cambridge University Press, 1998).

DEAR, I. C. B. and FOOT, M. R. D. (eds.), *The Oxford Companion to the Second World War* (Oxford: Oxford University Press, 1995).

DE SWAAN, ABRAM, *In Care of the State: Health Care, Education and Welfare in Europe and the U.S.A. in the Modern Era* (Cambridge: Polity, 1988).

D'ESTE, CARLO, *Decision in Normandy* (London: William Collins, 1983).

DI NARDO, R. L. and BAY, A., 'Horse-drawn Transport in the German Army', *Journal of Contemporary History*, 23 (1988), 129–42.

DREW, Sir ROBERT, *Commissioned Officers in the Medical Services of the British Army 1660–1960*, 2 vols. (London: Wellcome Historical Library, 1968).

DOWER, JOHN, *War Without Mercy: Race and Power in the Pacific War* (New York: Pantheon, 1986).

DUNN, C. L. (ed.), *The Emergency Medical Services*, 2 vols. (London: HMSO, 1952).

ECKART, W. U. and GRADMANN, C. (eds.), *Medizin und der Erste Weltkrieg* (Pfaffenweiler: Centaurus, 1996).

EDGERTON, DAVID, 'Liberal Militarism and the British State', *New Left Review*, 185 (1991), 138–96.

—— *England and the Aeroplane: A Essay on a Militant and Technological Nation* (London: Macmillan, 1991).

—— 'British Scientific Intellectuals and the Relations of Science, Technology and War', in P. Forman and J. M. Sanchez-Rons (eds.), *National Military Establishments and the Advancement of Science and Technology* (Amsterdam: Kluwer, 1996).

ELLIS, JOHN, *The Sharp End of War: The Fighting Man in World War II* (London: David & Charles, 1980).

ELLIS, L. F., *History of the Second World War: The War in France and Flanders 1939–40* (London: HMSO, 1953).

ENGELMAN, R. C. and JOY, R. T. J., *Two Hundred Years of Military Medicine* (Fort Detrick, Md., 1975).

EVANS, G. and BRETT JAMES, A., *Imphal: A Flower on Lofty Heights* (London: Macmillan, 1965).

FARLEY, JOHN, *Bilharzia: A History of Tropical Medicine* (Cambridge: Cambridge University Press, 1991).

FINLAYSON, GEOFFREY, *Citizen, State and Social Welfare in Britain, 1830–1990* (Oxford: Clarendon Press, 1994).

FISHER, H., *Der deutsche Sanitätsdienst 1921–1945*, 2 vols. (Osnabrück: Biblio Verlag, 1984).

FRANKLIN MELLOR, W. (ed.), *Medical History of the Second World War: Casualties and Medical Statistics* (London: HMSO, 1972).

FRASER, DAVID, *Knight's Cross: A Life of Field Marshal Erwin Rommel* (London: Harper-Collins, 1993).

FRENCH, DAVID, *Raising Churchill's Army: The British Army and the War Against Germany 1919–1945* (Oxford: Oxford University Press, 2000).

—— 'Officer Education and Training in the British Regular Army, 1919–39', in G. C. Kennedy and K. Neilson (eds.), *Military Education: Past, Present and Future* (Westport, Conn.: Praeger, 2002), 105–28.

GABRIEL, RICHARD A., and METZ, KAREN S., *A History of Military Medicine*, 2 vols. (New York, Westport, and London: Greenwood Press, 1992).

GEYER, MICHAEL, 'German Strategy in the Age of Machine Warfare', in P. Paret (ed.), *Makers of Modern Strategy from Machiavelli to the Nuclear Age* (Oxford and New York: Oxford University Press, 1986), 527–97.

GODDEN, L. J. (ed.), *History of the Army Dental Corps* (Aldershot: Royal Army Dental Corps, 1971).

GOOCH, JOHN (ed.), *Decisive Campaigns of the Second World War* (London: Frank Cass, 1990).

GRADMANN, CHRISTOPH, ' "Vornehmlich beängstigend"—Medizin, Gesundheit und chemische Kriegführung im deutschen Heer 1914–1918', in W. Eckart and C. Gradmann (eds.), *Die Medizin und der Erste Weltkrieg* (Pfaffenweiler: Centaurus, 1996), 131–45.

GREEN, F. H. K. and COVELL, GORDON (eds.), *Medical Research: Medical History of the Second World War* (London: HMSO, 1953).

GUHA, SUMIT, 'Nutrition, Sanitation, Hygiene, and the Likelihood of Death: The British Army in India *c*.1870–1920', in *Health and Population in South Asia: From Earliest Times to the Present* (London: Hurst & Co., 2001), 110–39.

GUTH, E., 'Der Sanitätsdienst der Wehrmacht im Zweiten Weltkrieg. Ein Überblick', in E. Guth (ed.), *Vorträge zur Militärgeschichte, Band II. Sanitätswesen im Zweiten Weltkrieg* (Bonn: E. S. Mittler & Sohn, 1990), 11–24.

HABER, S., *Efficiency and Uplift: Scientific Management in the Progressive Era, 1890–1920* (Chicago: Chicago University Press, 1964).

HALE, NATHAN G. Jr., *The Rise and Crisis of Psychoanalysis in the Unites States: Freud and the Americans, 1917–1985* (New York and Oxford: Oxford University Press, 1995).

HALES, M., 'Management Science and the "Second Industrial Revolution" ', in L. Levidov (ed.), *Radical Science Essays* (London: Free Association Books, 1986), 62–87.

HALL, LESLEY A., *Hidden Anxieties: Male Sexuality, 1900–1950* (Cambridge: Polity Press, 1991).

HALLER, JOHN S. Jr., *Farmcarts to Fords: A History of the Military Ambulance 1790–1925* (Carbondale and Edwardsville: Southern Illinois University Press, 1992).

HAMILTON, NIGEL, *Monty: Master of the Battlefield* (London: Hamish Hamilton, 1983).

HARMAN, N., *Dunkirk: The Necessary Myth* (London: Hodder & Stoughton, 1980).

HARRIS, C. R. S., *History of the Second World War: Allied Administration of Italy 1943–1945* (London: HMSO, 1957).

HARRIS, JOSE, 'Enterprise and Welfare States: A Comparative Perspective', *Transactions of the Royal Historical Society*, 5th ser., 40 (1991), 175–95.

HARRISON, MARK, 'The British Army and the Problem of Venereal Disease in France and Egypt during the First World War', *Medical History*, 39 (1995), 133–58.

—— 'The Fight against Disease in the Mesopotamia Campaign', in P. Liddle and H. Cecil (eds.), *Facing Armageddon: The First World War Experienced* (Barnsley: Leo Cooper, 1996), 475–89.

—— 'The Medicalization of War—The Militarization of Medicine', *Social History of Medicine*, 9 (1996), 267–76.

—— 'Medicine and the Culture of Command: The Case of Malaria Control in the British Army During the Two World Wars', *Medical History*, 40 (1996), 437–52.

—— 'Medicine and the Management of Modern Warfare', *History of Science*, 34 (1996), 379–410.

—— *Climates and Constitutions: Health, Race, Environment and British Imperialism in India* (New Delhi: Oxford University Press, 1999).

—— 'Sex and the Citizen Soldier: Health, Morals and Discipline in the British Army During the Second World War', in R. Cooter, M. Harrison, and S. Sturdy (eds.), *Medicine and Modern Warfare* (Amsterdam and Atlanta: Rodopi Press, 1999), 225–50.

—— COOTER, ROGER, and STURDY, STEVE (eds.), *War, Medicine and Modernity* (Stroud: Sutton, 1998).

—— —— —— (eds.), *Medicine and Modern Warfare* (Amsterdam and Atlanta: Rodopi Press, 1999).

HARRISON, TOM, *Bion, Rickman, Foulkes and the Northfield Experiments: Advancing on a Different Front* (London: Jessica Kingsley, 2000).

HASTINGS, MAX, *Overlord: D-Day and the Battle for Normandy 1944* (London: MacMillan, 1984).

HAY, IAN, *One Hundred Years of Army Nursing: The Story of the British Army Nursing Services From the Time of Florence Nightingale To the Present Day* (London: Cassell & Co, 1953).

HEATON, L. D. (ed.), *Medical Department, US Army: Preventive Medicine in World War II, Volume V: Communicable Disease* (Washington DC, Office of the Surgeon-General Department of the Army, 1960).

—— *Medical Department, US Army: Internal Medicine in World War II, Volume II: Infectious Diseases* (Washington DC: Office of the Surgeon-General Department of the Army, 1963).

HERRICK, C. E. J., 'Of War and Wounds: The Propaganda, Politics and Experience of Medicine in World War I', Ph.D. thesis, Manchester University (1996).

—— '"The Conquest of the Silent Foe": British and American Military Reform Rhetoric and the Japanese War', in R. Cooter, M. Harrison, and S. Sturdy (eds.), *Medicine and Modern Warfare* (Amsterdam and Atlanta: Rodopi Press, 1999), 99–130.

HOLMES, RICHARD, *Firing Line* (London: Pimlico, 1994).

HONIGSBAUM, FRANK, *The Division in British Medicine: A History of the Separation of General Practice From Hospital Care 1911–1968* (London: Kegan Page, 1979).

HOWELL, JOEL D., '"Soldier's Heart: The Redefinition of Heart Disease and Speciality Formation in Early Twentieth-Century Great Britain', *Medical History*, suppl. no. 5 (1985), 34–52.

—— *Technology in the Hospital: Transforming Patient Care in the Early Twentieth Century* (Baltimore and London: Johns Hopkins, 1995).

HOYT, EDWIN P., *Japan's War: The Great Pacific Conflict 1853–1952* (London: Hutchinson, 1986).

HUTCHINSON, JOHN, *Champions of Charity: War and the Rise of the Red Cross* (Oxford: Westpoint Press, 1995).

HYAM, RONALD, *Empire and Sexuality: The British Experience* (Manchester: Manchester University Press, 1991).

KATER, MICHAEL, *Doctors Under Hitler* (Chapel Hill and London: University of North Carolina Press, 1989).

KEEGAN, JOHN, *Six Armies in Normandy: From D-Day to the Liberation of Paris* (London: Pimlico, 1982).

—— *The Battle for History: Re-Fighting World War II* (London: Pimlico, 1997).

KENDRICK, DOUGLAS B., *Medical Department, United States Army Blood Program in World War II* (Washington DC: Office on the Surgeon-General Department of the Army, 1964).

KOVEN, SETH, 'Remembering and Dismemberment: Crippled Children, Wounded Soldiers, and the Great War in Great Britain', *American Historical Review*, 44 (1994), 1167–202.

LAWRENCE, CHRISTOPHER, 'Incommunicable Knowledge: Science, Technology and the Clinical Art in Britain, 1859–1914', *Journal of Contemporary History*, 20 (1985), 503–20.

—— 'Democratic, Divine and Heroic: The History and Historiography of Surgery', in C. Lawrence (ed.), *Medical Theory, Surgical Practice* (London: Routledge, 1992), 1–47.

—— *Medicine and the Making of Modern Britain* (London: Macmillan, 1994).

—— 'Disciplining Diseases: Scurvy, the Navy and Imperial Expansion', in D. Miller and P. Reill (eds.), *Visions of Empire* (Cambridge: Cambridge University Press, 1994).

LEED, ERIC, *No Man's Land: Combat and Identity in World War I* (Cambridge: Cambridge University Press, 1979).

LEWIN, RONALD, *Slim: The Standard Bearer* (London: Leo Cooper, 1990).

LEVEN, KARL-HEINZ, 'Fleckfieber beim deutschen Heer während des Krieges gegen die Sowetunion (1941–45)', in E. Guth (ed.), *Sanitätswesen im Zweiten Weltkrieg* (Bonn: E. S. Mittler, 1990), 127–66.

LEWIS, JANE, *What Price Community Medicine? The Philosophy, Practice and Politics of Public Health Since 1919* (Brighton: Wheatsheaf, 1986).

LITTLER, CRAIG, *The Development of the Labour Process in Capitalist Societies: A Comparative Study of the Transformation of Work Organization in Britain, Japan and the USA* (London: Heinemann, 1982).

LOVEGROVE, PETER, *Not Least in the Crusade: A Short History of the Royal Army Medical Corps* (Aldershot: Gale & Polden, 1951).

McKEE, ALEXANDER, *Caen: Anvil of Victory* (London: Pan Books, 1964).

MacKENZIE, S. P., *Politics and Military Morale: Current Affairs and Citizenship Education in the British Army 1914–1950* (Oxford: Clarendon Press, 1992).

McLaughlin, R., *The Royal Army Medical Corps* (London: Leo Cooper, 1972).

MacNalty, A. S. (ed.), *The Civilian Health Service and Medical Services*, vol. 1 (London: HMSO, 1953).

—— and Mellor, W. F. (eds.), *Medical Services in War: The Principal Medical Lessons of the Second World War* (London: HMSO, 1968).

MacPherson, W. G., *History of the Great War Based on Official Documents: Medical Services, General History*, 2 vols. (London: HMSO, 1921).

Maier, Charles S., 'Between Taylorism and Technocracy: European Ideologies and the Vision of Industrial Productivity in the 1920s', *Journal of Contemporary History*, 5 (1970), 27–61.

Marx, Leo and Roe Smith, Merrit (eds.), *Does Technology Drive History? The Dilemma of Technological Determinism* (London and Cambridge, Mass., 1995).

Maule, Henry, *Caen: The Brutal Battle and Breakout from Normandy* (London: David & Charles, 1976).

Mead, Peter, *Orde Wingate and the Historians* (Braunton: Merlin Books, 1987).

Mellor, W. Franklin (ed.), *Casualties and Medical Statistics: History of the Second World War: United Kingdom Medical Services* (London: HMSO, 1972).

Merksey, Harold, 'Shell shock', in G. E. Berrios and H. Freeman (eds.), *150 Years of British Psychiatry, 1841–1991* (London: Gaskell, 1991), 245–67.

Milward, Alan S., *War, Economy and Society 1939–1945* (London: Allen Lane, 1987).

Mitchell, T. J. and Smith, G. M., *History of the Great War Based on Official Documents: Medical Services: Casualties and Medical Statistics of the War* (London: HMSO, 1931).

Morehead, Alan, *Montgomery* (London: Hamish Hamilton, 1946).

Murrary, W. and Millet, A. R. (eds.), *Military Innovation in the Interwar Period* (Cambridge: Cambridge University Press, 1996).

Neillands, Robin, *The Desert Rats: 7th Armoured Division 1940–1945* (London: Weidenfeld & Nicolson, 1991).

Neushul, Peter, 'Science, Government, and the Mass Production of Penicillin', *Journal of the History of Medicine and Allied Sciences*, 48 (1993), 373–95.

—— 'Fighting Research: Army Participation in the Clinical Testing and Mass Production of Penicillin During the Second World War', in R. Cooter, M. Harrison, and S. Sturdy (eds.), *War, Medicine and Modernity* (Stroud: Sutton, 1998), 203–24.

Overy, Richard, *Why the Allies Won* (London: Pimlico, 1995).

Otway, T. B. H., *The Second World War 1939–1945: Army Airborne Forces* (London: Imperial War Museum, 1990).

Parker, R. A. C., *The Second World War: A Short History* (Oxford: Oxford University Press, 1997).

Paul, Christa, *Zwangs Prostitution: Staatlich Errichte Bordelle im Nationalsozialismus* (Berlin: Hertrich, 1994).

Perkin, Harold, *The Rise of Professional Society: England Since 1880* (London, 1989).

Peterson, Jeane M., 'Gentlemen and Medical Men: The Problem of Professional Recruitment', *Bulletin of the History of Medicine*, 58 (1984), 457–73.

PICKSTONE, JOHN, 'Production, Community and Consumption: The Political Economy of Twentieth-Century Medicine', in R. Cooter and J. Pickstone (eds.), *Medicine in the Twentieth Century* (London: Harwood, 2000), 1–19.

—— (ed.), *Medical Innovations in Historical Perspective* (London: Macmillan, 1992).

PITT, B., *The Crucible of War*, 2 vols. (London: Jonathan Cape, 1980–2).

PORTER, DOROTHY (ed.), *The History of Public Health and the Modern State* (Amsterdam and Atlanta: Rodopi, 1994).

RAINA, B. L. (ed.), *Official History of the Indian Armed Forces in the Second World War 1939–45. Medical Services: Administration, Volume I* (Kanpur: Combined Inter-Services Historical Section India and Pakistan, 1953).

RAMSEY, L. J., 'Bullet Wounds and X-rays in Britain's Little Wars', *Journal of the Society for Army Historical Research*, 60 (1982), 91–102.

REVERBY, SUSAN, 'Stealing the Golden Eggs: Ernest Amory Cochman and the Science of Management', *Bulletin of the History of Medicine*, 55 (1981), 156–71.

REXFORD-WELCH, S. C. (ed.), *The Royal Air Force Medical Services, Volume I: Administration* (London: HMSO, 1954).

ROLAND, CHARLES G., *Long Night's Journey into Day: Prisoners of War in Hong Kong and Japan, 1941–1945* (Waterloo, Ont.: Wilfred Laurier University Press, 2001).

—— and SHANNON, HENRY S., 'Patterns of Disease Among World War II Prisoners of the Japanese: Hunger, Weight Loss, and Deficiency Diseases in Two Camps', *Journal of the History of Medicine*, 46 (1991), 65–85.

—— 'Massacre and Rape in Hong Kong: Two Case Studies Involving Medical Personnel and Patients', *Journal of Contemporary History*, 32 (1997), 43–61.

ROSE, NIKOLAS, *The Psychological Complex: Psychology, Politics and Society in England 1869–1939* (London: Routledge & Kegan Paul, 1985).

ROSEN, GEORGE, *The Specialization of Medicine with Particular Reference to Ophthalmology* (New York: Froben Press, 1944).

—— 'The Efficiency Criterion in Medical Care, 1900–1920: An Early Approach to an Evaluation of Health Service', *Bulletin of the History of Medicine*, 50 (1976), 28–44.

ROSENBERG, C. E., 'Inward Vision and Outward Glance: The Shaping of the American Hospital, 1880–1914', *Bulletin of the History of Medicine*, 53 (1976), 346–91.

ROYLE, TREVOR, *Orde Wingate: Irregular Soldier* (London: Weidenfeld & Nicolson, 1995).

SAUERTEIG, LUTZ, 'Militär, Medizin und Moral: Sexualität im Ersten Weltkrieg', in W. U. Eckart and C. Gradmann (eds.), *Medizin und der Erste Weltkrieg* (Pfaffenweiter: Centaurus, 1996), 197–226.

—— 'Sex, Medicine and Morality During the First World War', in R. Cooter, M. Harrison, and S. Sturdy (eds.), *War, Medicine and Modernity* (Stroud: Sutton, 1998), 167–88.

SEARLE, G. R., *The Quest for National Efficiency* (Oxford: Oxford University Press, 1971).

SEIDLER, FRANZ, *Prostitution, Homosexualität, Selbstverstümmelung. Problem der deutschen Sanitätsführung 1939–1945* (Neckargemünd: Kurt Vowinkel, 1977).

SHEPHARD, BEN, '"The Early Treatment of Mental Disorders": R. G. Rows and Maghull 1914–1918', in G. Berrios and H. Freeman (eds.), *150 Years of British Psychiatry, Volume 2: The Aftermath* (London: Gaskell, 1996), 434–64.

—— '"Pitiless Psychology": The Role of Prevention in British Military in the Second World War', *Journal of the History of Psychiatry*, 10 (1999), 491–524.

—— *War of Nerves: Soldiers and Psychiatrists 1914–1994* (London: Jonathan Cape, 2000).

SHEPHERD, JOHN, *The Crimean Doctors: A History of the British Medical Services in the Crimean War*, 2 vols. (Liverpool: Liverpool University Press, 1991).

SHOWALTER, ELAINE, *The Female Malady: Women, Madness and English Culture, 1830–1980* (New York: Virago, 1985).

SIMPSON, KEITH, 'Dr James Dunn and Shell-Shock', in H. Cecil and P. Liddle (eds.), *Facing Armageddon: The First World War Experienced* (Barnsley: Leo Cooper, 1996), 502–22.

SMITH, E. D., *Battle For Burma* (London: B. T. Batsford, 1979).

STARNS, PENNY, 'Fighting Militarism? British Nursing During the Second World War', in R. Cooter, M. Harrison, and S. Sturdy (eds.), *War, Medicine and Modernity* (Stroud: Sutton, 1998), 189–202.

STERNBERG, T. H. et al., 'Venereal Diseases', in L. D. Heaton (ed.), *Medical Department, US Army: Preventive Medicine in World War II, Volume V: Communicable Disease* (Washington DC: Office of the Surgeon-General Department of the Army, 1960), 139–331.

STONE, J. and SCHMIDT, E. A., *The Boer War and Military Reforms* (New York: University of America Press, 1988).

STONE, MARTIN, 'Shellshock and the Psychologists', in W. F. Bynum, R. Porter, and M. Shepherd (eds.), *The Anatomy of Madness: Essays in the History of Psychiatry, Volume II—Institutions and Society* (London and New York: Routledge, 1985), 242–71.

STONE, MITCHELL, 'The Victorian Army: Health, Hospitals and Social Conditions as Encountered by British Troops During the South African War, 1899–1902', Ph.D. thesis, University of London (1992).

STURDY, S., 'From the Trenches to the Hospitals at Home: Physiologists, Clinicians and Oxygen Therapy, 1914–30', in J. V. Pickstone (ed.), *Medical Innovations in Historical Perspective* (London: Macmillan, 1992), 104–23.

—— 'The Political Economy of Scientific Medicine: Science, Education and the Transformation of Medical Practice in Sheffield, 1890–1922', *Medical History*, 36 (1992), 125–59.

—— 'Hippocrates and State Medicine: George Newman Outlines the Founding Policy of the Ministry of Health', in C. Lawrence and G. Weisz (eds.), *Greater than the Parts: Holism in Biomedicine 1920–1950* (New York and Oxford: Oxford University Press, 1998), 112–34.

SUMMERS, ANNE, *Angels and Citizens: British Women as Military Nurses 1854–1914* (London: Routledge, 1988).

TEICH, M., 'Science and Food During the Great War: Britain and Germany', in H.

Kamminga and A. Cunningham (eds.), *The Science and Culture of Nutrition, 1840–1940* (Amsterdam and Atlanta: Rodopi Press, 1995), 213–34.

THOMSON, MATHEW, 'Status, Manpower and Mental Fitness: Mental Deficiency in the First World War', in R. Cooter, M. Harrison, and S. Sturdy (eds.), *War, Medicine and Modernity* (Stroud: Sutton, 1998), 149–66.

TITMUSS, R. M., *Problems of Social Policy* (London: HMSO, 1950).

—— *Essays on 'The Welfare State'* (London: George Allen & Unwin, 1958).

TOMKINS, S. M., 'Palminate or Permanganate: The Venereal Prophylaxis Debate in Britain, 1916–1926', *Medical History*, 37 (1993), 382–98.

TOWERS, BRIDGET A., 'Health Education Policy 1916–1926: Venereal Disease and the Prophylaxis Dilemma', *Medical History*, 24 (1980), 70–87.

TRAVERS, T. H. E., 'Command and Leaderships Styles in the British Army: The 1915 Gallipoli Model', *Journal of Contemporary History*, 26 (1994), 403–42.

TULLOCH, DEREK, *Wingate in Peace and War* (London: Futura, 1972).

TURNBULL, P., *Dunkirk: Anatomy of Disaster* (London: Batsford, 1978).

TURNER, BRYAN S., *For Weber: Essays on the Sociology of Fate* (London, Routledge 1981).

TYQUIN, MICHAEL, *Gallipoli: The Medical War. The Australian Army Medical Services in the Dardanelles Campaign of 1915* (Kensington, NSW: New South Wales University Press, 1993).

VALENTIN, ROLF, *Die Krankenbataillone Sonderformation der deutschen Wehrmacht im Zweiten Weltkrieg* (Düsseldorf: Droste, 1981).

VAN CREVELD, MARTIN, *Supplying War: Logistics from Wallenstein to Patton* (Cambridge: Cambridge University Press, 1977).

VATIKIOTIS, P. J., *The History of Modern Egypt: From Muhammed Ali to Mubrarak* (London: Weidenfeld & Nicolson, 1991).

VONDRA, H., 'Die Malaria—ihre Problematik und Erforschung in Heer und Luftwaffe', in E. Guth (ed.), *Sanitätswesen im Zweiten Weltkrieg* (Bonn: E. S. Mittler, 1990), 109–25.

WARD FAY, PETER, *The Forgotten Army: India's Armed Struggle for Independence 1942–1945* (Ann Arbor: University of Michigan Press, 1993).

WEBER, MAX, 'The Technological Advantages of Bureaucratic Organisation', in *From Max Weber: Essays in Sociology*, ed. and trans. H. Gerth and C. W. Mills (New York: Routledge & Kegan Paul, 1972).

WEINBERG, GERHARD L., *A World at Arms: Global History of World War II* (Cambridge: Cambridge University Press, 1994).

WEINDLING, PAUL, *Health, Race and German Politics Between National Unification and Nazism 1870–1945* (Cambridge: Cambridge University Press, 1989).

—— *Epidemics and Genocide in Eastern Europe, 1890–1945* (Oxford: Oxford University Press, 2000).

WHITEHEAD, IAN, *Doctors in the Great War* (Barnsley: Leo Cooper, 1999).

ZIEGLER, PHILIP, *Mountbatten: The Official Biography* (London: Collins, 1985).

Index